Database Internals
A Deep Dive into How
Distributed Data Systems Work

Alex Petrov

Beijing · Boston · Farnham · Sebastopol · Tokyo

Database Internals

by Alex Petrov

Published by O'Reilly Media, Inc., 1005 Gravenstein Highway North, Sebastopol, CA 95472.

O'Reilly books may be purchased for educational, business, or sales promotional use. Online editions are also available for most titles (*http://oreilly.com*). For more information, contact our corporate/institutional sales department: 800-998-9938 or *corporate@oreilly.com*.

Acquisitions Editor: Mike Loukides
Development Editor: Michele Cronin
Production Editor: Christopher Faucher
Copyeditor: Kim Cofer
Proofreader: Sonia Saruba

Indexer: Judith McConville
Interior Designer: David Futato
Cover Designer: Karen Montgomery
Illustrator: Rebecca Demarest

October 2019:   First Edition

Revision History for the First Edition
2019-09-12:   First Release
2019-10-25:   Second Release
2020-01-31:   Third Release
2020-09-04:   Fourth Release

See *http://oreilly.com/catalog/errata.csp?isbn=9781492040347* for release details.

978-1-492-04034-7

[LSI]

*To Pieter Hintjens, from whom I got my first ever signed book:
an inspiring distributed systems programmer, author, philosopher, and friend.*

Table of Contents

Part I.   Storage Engines

Part II.   Distributed Systems

Preface

Distributed database systems are an integral part of most businesses and the vast majority of software applications. These applications provide logic and a user interface, while database systems take care of data integrity, consistency, and redundancy.

Back in 2000, if you were to choose a database, you would have just a few options, and most of them would be within the realm of relational databases, so differences between them would be relatively small. Of course, this does not mean that all databases were completely the same, but their functionality and use cases were very similar.

Some of these databases have focused on *horizontal scaling* (scaling *out*)—improving performance and increasing capacity by running multiple database instances acting as a single logical unit: Gamma Database Machine Project, Teradata, Greenplum, Parallel DB2, and many others. Today, horizontal scaling remains one of the most important properties that customers expect from databases. This can be explained by the rising popularity of cloud-based services. It is often easier to spin up a new instance and add it to the cluster than scaling vertically (scaling *up*) by moving the database to a larger, more powerful machine. Migrations can be long and painful, potentially incurring downtime.

Around 2010, a new class of *eventually consistent* databases started appearing, and terms such as *NoSQL*, and later, *big data* grew in popularity. Over the last 15 years, the open source community, large internet companies, and database vendors have created so many databases and tools that it's easy to get lost trying to understand use cases, details, and specifics.

The Dynamo paper [DECANDIA07], published by the team at Amazon in 2007, had so much impact on the database community that within a short period it inspired many variants and implementations. The most prominent of them were Apache Cassandra, created at Facebook; Project Voldemort, created at LinkedIn; and Riak, created by former Akamai engineers.

Today, the field is changing again: after the time of key-value stores, NoSQL, and eventual consistency, we have started seeing more scalable and performant databases, able to execute complex queries with stronger consistency guarantees.

Audience of This Book

In conversations at technical conferences, I often hear the same question: "How can I learn more about database internals? I don't even know where to start." Most of the books on database systems do not go into details of storage engine implementation, and cover the access methods, such as B-Trees, on a rather high level. There are very few books that cover more recent concepts, such as different B-Tree variants and log-structured storage, so I usually recommend reading papers.

Everyone who reads papers knows that it's not that easy: you often lack context, the wording might be ambiguous, there's little or no connection between papers, and they're hard to find. This book contains concise summaries of important database systems concepts and can serve as a guide for those who'd like to dig in deeper, or as a cheat sheet for those already familiar with these concepts.

Not everyone wants to become a database developer, but this book will help people who build software that uses database systems: software developers, reliability engineers, architects, and engineering managers.

If your company depends on any infrastructure component, be it a database, a messaging queue, a container platform, or a task scheduler, you have to read the project change-logs and mailing lists to stay in touch with the community and be up-to-date with the most recent happenings in the project. Understanding terminology and knowing what's inside will enable you to yield more information from these sources and use your tools more productively to troubleshoot, identify, and avoid potential risks and bottlenecks. Having an overview and a general understanding of how database systems work will help in case something goes wrong. Using this knowledge, you'll be able to form a hypothesis, validate it, find the root cause, and present it to other project maintainers.

This book is also for curious minds: for the people who like learning things without immediate necessity, those who spend their free time hacking on something fun, creating compilers, writing homegrown operating systems, text editors, computer games, learning programming languages, and absorbing new information.

The reader is assumed to have some experience with developing backend systems and working with database systems as a *user*. Having some prior knowledge of different data structures will help to digest material faster.

Why Should I Read This Book?

We often hear people describing database systems in terms of the concepts and algorithms they implement: "This database uses gossip for membership propagation" (see Chapter 12), "They have implemented Dynamo," or "This is just like what they've described in the Spanner paper" (see Chapter 13). Or, if you're discussing the algorithms and data structures, you can hear something like "ZAB and Raft have a lot in common" (see Chapter 14), "Bw-Trees are like the B-Trees implemented on top of log structured storage" (see Chapter 6), or "They are using sibling pointers like in B^{link}-Trees" (see Chapter 5).

We need abstractions to discuss complex concepts, and we can't have a discussion about terminology every time we start a conversation. Having shortcuts in the form of common language helps us to move our attention to other, higher-level problems.

One of the advantages of learning the fundamental concepts, proofs, and algorithms is that they never grow old. Of course, there will always be new ones, but new algorithms are often created after finding a flaw or room for improvement in a classical one. Knowing the history helps to understand differences and motivation better.

Learning about these things is inspiring. You see the variety of algorithms, see how our industry was solving one problem after the other, and get to appreciate that work. At the same time, learning is rewarding: you can almost feel how multiple puzzle pieces move together in your mind to form a full picture that you will always be able to share with others.

Scope of This Book

This is neither a book about relational database management systems nor about NoSQL ones, but about the algorithms and concepts used in all kinds of database systems, with a focus on a *storage engine* and the components responsible for *distribution*.

Some concepts, such as query planning, query optimization, scheduling, the relational model, and a few others, are already covered in several great textbooks on database systems. Some of these concepts are usually described from the user's perspective, but this book concentrates on the internals. You can find some pointers to useful literature in the Part II Conclusion and in the chapter summaries. In these books you're likely to find answers to many database-related questions you might have.

Query languages aren't discussed, since there's no single common language among the database systems mentioned in this book.

To collect material for this book, I studied over 15 books, more than 300 papers, countless blog posts, source code, and the documentation for several open source databases. The rule of thumb for whether or not to include a particular concept in the book was the question: "Do the people in the database industry and research circles talk about this concept?" If the answer was "yes," I added the concept to the long list of things to discuss.

Structure of This Book

There are some examples of extensible databases with pluggable components (such as [SCHWARZ86]), but they are rather rare. At the same time, there are plenty of examples where databases use pluggable storage. Similarly, we rarely hear database vendors talking about query execution, while they are very eager to discuss the ways their databases preserve consistency.

The most significant distinctions between database systems are concentrated around two aspects: how they *store* and how they *distribute* the data. (Other subsystems can at times also be of importance, but are not covered here.) The book is arranged into parts that discuss the subsystems and components responsible for *storage* (Part I) and *distribution* (Part II).

Part I discusses node-local processes and focuses on the storage engine, the central component of the database system and one of the most significant distinctive factors. First, we start with the architecture of a database management system and present several ways to classify database systems based on the primary storage medium and layout.

We continue with storage structures and try to understand how disk-based structures are different from in-memory ones, introduce B-Trees, and cover algorithms for efficiently maintaining B-Tree structures on disk, including serialization, page layout, and on-disk representations. Later, we discuss multiple variants to illustrate the power of this concept and the diversity of data structures influenced and inspired by B-Trees.

Last, we discuss several variants of log-structured storage, commonly used for implementing file and storage systems, motivation, and reasons to use them.

Part II is about how to organize multiple nodes into a database cluster. We start with the importance of understanding the theoretical concepts for building fault-tolerant distributed systems, how distributed systems are different from single-node applications, and which problems, constraints, and complications we face in a distributed environment.

After that, we dive deep into distributed algorithms. Here, we start with algorithms for failure detection, helping to improve performance and stability by noticing and reporting failures and avoiding the failed nodes. Since many algorithms discussed later in the book rely on understanding the concept of leadership, we introduce several algorithms for leader election and discuss their suitability.

As one of the most difficult things in distributed systems is achieving data consistency, we discuss concepts of replication, followed by consistency models, possible divergence between replicas, and eventual consistency. Since eventually consistent systems sometimes rely on anti-entropy for convergence and gossip for data dissemination, we discuss several anti-entropy and gossip approaches. Finally, we discuss logical consistency in the context of database transactions, and finish with consensus algorithms.

It would've been impossible to write this book without all the research and publications. You will find many references to papers and publications in the text, in square brackets with monospace font; for example, [DECANDIA07]. You can use these references to learn more about related concepts in more detail.

After each chapter, you will find a summary section that contains material for further study, related to the content of the chapter.

Conventions Used in This Book

The following typographical conventions are used in this book:

Italic
> Indicates new terms, URLs, email addresses, filenames, and file extensions.

`Constant width`
> Used for program listings, as well as within paragraphs to refer to program elements such as variable or function names, databases, data types, environment variables, statements, and keywords.

This element signifies a tip or suggestion.

This element signifies a general note.

This element indicates a warning or caution.

Using Code Examples

This book is here to help you get your job done. In general, if example code is offered with this book, you may use it in your programs and documentation. You do not need to contact us for permission unless you're reproducing a significant portion of the code. For example, writing a program that uses several chunks of code from this book does not require permission. Selling or distributing a CD-ROM of examples from O'Reilly books does require permission. Answering a question by citing this book and quoting example code does not require permission. Incorporating a significant amount of example code from this book into your product's documentation does require permission.

We appreciate, but do not require, attribution. An attribution usually includes the title, author, publisher, and ISBN. For example: "*Database Internals* by Alex Petrov (O'Reilly). Copyright 2019 Oleksandr Petrov, 978-1-492-04034-7."

If you feel your use of code examples falls outside fair use or the permission given above, feel free to contact us at *permissions@oreilly.com*.

O'Reilly Online Learning

 For almost 40 years, *O'Reilly Media* has provided technology and business training, knowledge, and insight to help companies succeed.

Our unique network of experts and innovators share their knowledge and expertise through books, articles, and our online learning platform. O'Reilly's online learning platform gives you on-demand access to live training courses, in-depth learning paths, interactive coding environments, and a vast collection of text and video from O'Reilly and 200+ other publishers. For more information, please visit *http://oreilly.com*.

How to Contact Us

Please address comments and questions concerning this book to the publisher:

O'Reilly Media, Inc.
1005 Gravenstein Highway North
Sebastopol, CA 95472
800-998-9938 (in the United States or Canada)
707-829-0515 (international or local)
707-829-0104 (fax)

We have a web page for this book, where we list errata, examples, and any additional information. You can access this page at *http://bit.ly/database-internals*.

To comment or ask technical questions about this book, please send an email to *bookquestions@oreilly.com*.

For news and more information about our books and courses, see our website at *http://www.oreilly.com*.

Find us on Facebook: *http://facebook.com/oreilly*

Follow us on Twitter: *http://twitter.com/oreillymedia*

Watch us on YouTube: *http://www.youtube.com/oreillymedia*

Acknowledgments

This book wouldn't have been possible without the hundreds of people who have worked hard on research papers and books, which have been a source of ideas, inspiration, and served as references for this book.

I'd like to say thank you to all the people who reviewed manuscripts and provided feedback, making sure that the material in this book is correct and the wording is precise: Dmitry Alimov, Peter Alvaro, Carlos Baquero, Jason Brown, Blake Eggleston, Marcus Eriksson, Francisco Fernández Castaño, Heidi Howard, Vaidehi Joshi, Maximilian Karasz, Stas Kelvich, Michael Klishin, Predrag Knežević, Joel Knighton, Eugene Lazin, Nate McCall, Christopher Meiklejohn, Tyler Neely, Maxim Neverov, Marina Petrova, Stefan Podkowinski, Edward Ribeiro, Denis Rystsov, Kir Shatrov, Alex Sorokoumov, Massimiliano Tomassi, and Ariel Weisberg.

Of course, this book wouldn't have been possible without support from my family: my wife Marina and my daughter Alexandra, who have supported me on every step on the way.

Storage Engines

The primary job of any database management system is reliably storing data and making it available for users. We use databases as a primary source of data, helping us to share it between the different parts of our applications. Instead of finding a way to store and retrieve information and inventing a new way to organize data every time we create a new app, we use databases. This way we can concentrate on application logic instead of infrastructure.

Since the term *database management system* (DBMS) is quite bulky, throughout this book we use more compact terms, *database system* and *database*, to refer to the same concept.

Databases are modular systems and consist of multiple parts: a transport layer accepting requests, a query processor determining the most efficient way to run queries, an execution engine carrying out the operations, and a storage engine (see "DBMS Architecture" on page 8).

The *storage engine* (or database engine) is a software component of a database management system responsible for storing, retrieving, and managing data in memory and on disk, designed to capture a persistent, long-term memory of each node [REED78]. While databases can respond to complex queries, storage engines look at the data more granularly and offer a simple data manipulation API, allowing users to create, update, delete, and retrieve records. One way to look at this is that database management systems are applications built on top of storage engines, offering a schema, a query language, indexing, transactions, and many other useful features.

For flexibility, both keys and values can be arbitrary sequences of bytes with no pre-scribed form. Their sorting and representation semantics are defined in higher-level subsystems. For example, you can use int32 (32-bit integer) as a key in one of the tables, and ascii (ASCII string) in the other; from the storage engine perspective both keys are just serialized entries.

Storage engines such as BerkeleyDB (*https://databass.dev/links/92*), LevelDB (*https://databass.dev/links/93*) and its descendant RocksDB (*https://databass.dev/links/94*), LMDB (*https://databass.dev/links/95*) and its descendant libmdbx (*https://data bass.dev/links/96*), Sophia (*https://databass.dev/links/97*), HaloDB (*https://data bass.dev/links/98*), and many others were developed independently from the database management systems they're now embedded into. Using pluggable storage engines has enabled database developers to bootstrap database systems using existing storage engines, and concentrate on the other subsystems.

At the same time, clear separation between database system components opens up an opportunity to switch between different engines, potentially better suited for particu-lar use cases. For example, MySQL, a popular database management system, has sev-eral storage engines (*https://databass.dev/links/99*), including InnoDB, MyISAM, and RocksDB (*https://databass.dev/links/100*) (in the MyRocks (*https://databass.dev/links/101*) distribution). MongoDB allows switching between WiredTiger (*https://data bass.dev/links/102*), In-Memory, and the (now-deprecated) MMAPv1 (*https://data bass.dev/links/103*) storage engines.

Comparing Databases

Your choice of database system may have long-term consequences. If there's a chance that a database is not a good fit because of performance problems, consistency issues, or operational challenges, it is better to find out about it earlier in the development cycle, since it can be nontrivial to migrate to a different system. In some cases, it may require substantial changes in the application code.

Every database system has strengths and weaknesses. To reduce the risk of an expen-sive migration, you can invest some time before you decide on a specific database to build confidence in its ability to meet your application's needs.

Trying to compare databases based on their components (e.g., which storage engine they use, how the data is shared, replicated, and distributed, etc.), their rank (an arbi-trary popularity value assigned by consultancy agencies such as ThoughtWorks (*https://www.thoughtworks.com/de/radar*) or database comparison websites such as DB-Engines (*https://db-engines.com/de/ranking*) or Database of Databases (*https://dbdb.io*)), or implementation language (C++, Java, or Go, etc.) can lead to invalid and premature conclusions. These methods can be used only for a high-level comparison and can be as coarse as choosing between HBase and SQLite, so even a superficial understanding of how each database works and what's inside it can help you land a more weighted conclusion.

Every comparison should start by clearly defining the goal, because even the slightest bias may completely invalidate the entire investigation. If you're searching for a database that would be a good fit for the workloads you have (or are planning to facilitate), the best thing you can do is to simulate these workloads against different database systems, measure the performance metrics that are important for you, and compare results. Some issues, especially when it comes to performance and scalability, start showing only after some time or as the capacity grows. To detect potential problems, it is best to have long-running tests in an environment that simulates the real-world production setup as closely as possible.

Simulating real-world workloads not only helps you understand how the database performs, but also helps you learn how to operate, debug, and find out how friendly and helpful its community is. Database choice is always a combination of these factors, and performance often turns out *not* to be the most important aspect: it's usually much better to use a database that slowly saves the data than one that quickly loses it.

To compare databases, it's helpful to understand the use case in great detail and define the current and anticipated variables, such as:

- Schema and record sizes
- Number of clients
- Types of queries and access patterns
- Rates of the read and write queries
- Expected changes in any of these variables

Knowing these variables can help to answer the following questions:

- Does the database support the required queries?
- Is this database able to handle the amount of data we're planning to store?
- How many read and write operations can a single node handle?
- How many nodes should the system have?
- How do we expand the cluster given the expected growth rate?
- What is the maintenance process?

Having these questions answered, you can construct a test cluster and simulate your workloads. Most databases already have stress tools that can be used to reconstruct specific use cases. If there's no standard stress tool to generate realistic randomized workloads in the database ecosystem, it might be a red flag. If something prevents you from using default tools, you can try one of the existing general-purpose tools, or implement one from scratch.

If the tests show positive results, it may be helpful to familiarize yourself with the database code. Looking at the code, it is often useful to first understand the parts of the database, how to find the code for different components, and then navigate through those. Having even a rough idea about the database codebase helps you better understand the log records it produces, its configuration parameters, and helps you find issues in the application that uses it and even in the database code itself.

It'd be great if we could use databases as black boxes and never have to take a look inside them, but the practice shows that sooner or later a bug, an outage, a performance regression, or some other problem pops up, and it's better to be prepared for it. If you know and understand database internals, you can reduce business risks and improve chances for a quick recovery.

One of the popular tools used for benchmarking, performance evaluation, and comparison is Yahoo! Cloud Serving Benchmark (*https://databass.dev/links/104*) (YCSB). YCSB offers a framework and a common set of workloads that can be applied to different data stores. Just like anything generic, this tool should be used with caution, since it's easy to make wrong conclusions. To make a fair comparison and make an educated decision, it is necessary to invest enough time to understand the real-world conditions under which the database has to perform, and tailor benchmarks accordingly.

TPC-C Benchmark

The Transaction Processing Performance Council (TPC) has a set of benchmarks that database vendors use for comparing and advertising performance of their products. TPC-C is an online transaction processing (OLTP) benchmark, a mixture of read-only and update transactions that simulate common application workloads.

This benchmark concerns itself with the performance and correctness of executed concurrent transactions. The main performance indicator is *throughput*: the number of transactions the database system is able to process per minute. Executed transactions are required to preserve ACID properties and conform to the set of properties defined by the benchmark itself.

This benchmark does not concentrate on any particular business segment, but provides an abstract set of actions important for most of the applications for which OLTP databases are suitable. It includes several tables and entities such as warehouses, stock (inventory), customers and orders, specifying table layouts, details of transactions that can be performed against these tables, the minimum number of rows per table, and data durability constraints.

This doesn't mean that benchmarks can be used *only* to compare databases. Benchmarks can be useful to define and test details of the service-level agreement,[1] understanding system requirements, capacity planning, and more. The more knowledge you have about the database before using it, the more time you'll save when running it in production.

Choosing a database is a long-term decision, and it's best to keep track of newly released versions, understand what exactly has changed and why, and have an upgrade strategy. New releases usually contain improvements and fixes for bugs and security issues, but may introduce new bugs, performance regressions, or unexpected behavior, so testing new versions before rolling them out is also critical. Checking how database implementers were handling upgrades previously might give you a good idea about what to expect in the future. Past smooth upgrades do not guarantee that future ones will be as smooth, but complicated upgrades in the past might be a sign that future ones won't be easy, either.

Understanding Trade-Offs

As users, we can see how databases behave under different conditions, but when working on databases, we have to make choices that influence this behavior directly.

Designing a storage engine is definitely more complicated than just implementing a textbook data structure: there are many details and edge cases that are hard to get right from the start. We need to design the physical data layout and organize pointers, decide on the serialization format, understand how data is going to be garbage-collected, how the storage engine fits into the semantics of the database system as a whole, figure out how to make it work in a concurrent environment, and, finally, make sure we never lose any data, under any circumstances.

Not only there are many things to decide upon, but most of these decisions involve trade-offs. For example, if we save records in the order they were inserted into the database, we can store them quicker, but if we retrieve them in their lexicographical order, we have to re-sort them before returning results to the client. As you will see throughout this book, there are many different approaches to storage engine design, and every implementation has its own upsides and downsides.

When looking at different storage engines, we discuss their benefits and shortcomings. If there was an absolutely optimal storage engine for every conceivable use case, everyone would just use it. But since it does not exist, we need to choose wisely, based on the workloads and use cases we're trying to facilitate.

---

1 The service-level agreement (or SLA) is a commitment by the service provider about the quality of provided services. Among other things, the SLA can include information about latency, throughput, jitter, and the number and frequency of failures.

There are many storage engines, using all sorts of data structures, implemented in different languages, ranging from low-level ones, such as C, to high-level ones, such as Java. All storage engines face the same challenges and constraints. To draw a parallel with city planning, it is possible to build a city for a specific population and choose to build *up* or build *out*. In both cases, the same number of people will fit into the city, but these approaches lead to radically different lifestyles. When building the city up, people live in apartments and population density is likely to lead to more traffic in a smaller area; in a more spread-out city, people are more likely to live in houses, but commuting will require covering larger distances.

Similarly, design decisions made by storage engine developers make them better suited for different things: some are optimized for low read or write latency, some try to maximize density (the amount of stored data per node), and some concentrate on operational simplicity.

You can find complete algorithms that can be used for the implementation and other additional references in the chapter summaries. Reading this book should make you well equipped to work productively with these sources and give you a solid understanding of the existing alternatives to concepts described there.

CHAPTER 1

Introduction and Overview

Database management systems can serve different purposes: some are used primarily for temporary *hot* data, some serve as a long-lived *cold* storage, some allow complex analytical queries, some only allow accessing values by the key, some are optimized to store time-series data, and some store large blobs efficiently. To understand differences and draw distinctions, we start with a short classification and overview, as this helps us to understand the scope of further discussions.

Terminology can sometimes be ambiguous and hard to understand without a complete context. For example, distinctions between *column* and *wide column* stores that have little or nothing to do with each other, or how *clustered* and *nonclustered indexes* relate to *index-organized tables*. This chapter aims to disambiguate these terms and find their precise definitions.

We start with an overview of database management system architecture (see "DBMS Architecture" on page 8), and discuss system components and their responsibilities. After that, we discuss the distinctions among the database management systems in terms of a storage medium (see "Memory- Versus Disk-Based DBMS" on page 10), and layout (see "Column- Versus Row-Oriented DBMS" on page 12).

These two groups do not present a full taxonomy of database management systems and there are many other ways they're classified. For example, some sources group DBMSs into three major categories:

Online transaction processing (OLTP) databases
> These handle a large number of user-facing requests and transactions. Queries are often predefined and short-lived.

Online analytical processing (OLAP) databases
> These handle complex aggregations. OLAP databases are often used for analytics and data warehousing, and are capable of handling complex, long-running ad hoc queries.

Hybrid transactional and analytical processing (HTAP)
> These databases combine properties of both OLTP and OLAP stores.

There are many other terms and classifications: key-value stores, relational databases, document-oriented stores, and graph databases. These concepts are not defined here, since the reader is assumed to have a high-level knowledge and understanding of their functionality. Because the concepts we discuss here are widely applicable and are used in most of the mentioned types of stores in some capacity, complete taxonomy is not necessary or important for further discussion.

Since Part I of this book focuses on the storage and indexing structures, we need to understand the high-level data organization approaches, and the relationship between the data and index files (see "Data Files and Index Files" on page 17).

Finally, in "Buffering, Immutability, and Ordering" on page 21, we discuss three techniques widely used to develop efficient storage structures and how applying these techniques influences their design and implementation.

DBMS Architecture

There's no common blueprint for database management system design. Every database is built slightly differently, and component boundaries are somewhat hard to see and define. Even if these boundaries exist on paper (e.g., in project documentation), in code seemingly independent components may be coupled because of performance optimizations, handling edge cases, or architectural decisions.

Sources that describe database management system architecture (for example, [HELLERSTEIN07], [WEIKUM01], [ELMASRI11], and [GARCIAMOLINA08]), define components and relationships between them differently. The architecture presented in Figure 1-1 demonstrates some of the common themes in these representations.

Database management systems use a *client/server model*, where database system instances (*nodes*) take the role of servers, and application instances take the role of clients.

Client requests arrive through the *transport* subsystem. Requests come in the form of queries, most often expressed in some query language. The transport subsystem is also responsible for communication with other nodes in the database cluster.

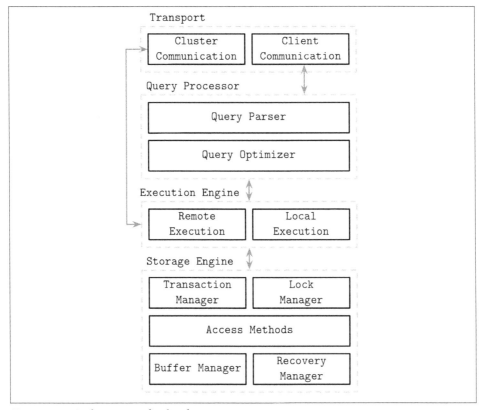

Figure 1-1. Architecture of a database management system

Upon receipt, the transport subsystem hands the query over to a *query processor*, which parses, interprets, and validates it. Later, access control checks are performed, as they can be done fully only after the query is interpreted.

The parsed query is passed to the *query optimizer*, which first eliminates impossible and redundant parts of the query, and then attempts to find the most efficient way to execute it based on internal statistics (index cardinality, approximate intersection size, etc.) and data placement (which nodes in the cluster hold the data and the costs associated with its transfer). The optimizer handles both relational operations required for query resolution, usually presented as a dependency tree, and optimizations, such as index ordering, cardinality estimation, and choosing access methods.

The query is usually presented in the form of an *execution plan* (or *query plan*): a sequence of operations that have to be carried out for its results to be considered complete. Since the same query can be satisfied using different execution plans that can vary in efficiency, the optimizer picks the best available plan.

The execution plan is carried out by the *execution engine*, which aggregates the results of local and remote operations. *Remote execution* can involve writing and reading data to and from other nodes in the cluster, and replication.

Local queries (coming directly from clients or from other nodes) are executed by the *storage engine*. The storage engine has several components with dedicated responsibilities:

Transaction manager
> This manager schedules transactions and ensures they cannot leave the database in a logically inconsistent state.

Lock manager
> This manager locks on the database objects for the running transactions, ensuring that concurrent operations do not violate physical data integrity.

Access methods (storage structures)
> These manage access and organizing data on disk. Access methods include heap files and storage structures such as B-Trees (see "Ubiquitous B-Trees" on page 33) or LSM Trees (see "LSM Trees" on page 130).

Buffer manager
> This manager caches data pages in memory (see "Buffer Management" on page 81).

Recovery manager
> This manager maintains the operation log and restoring the system state in case of a failure (see "Recovery" on page 88).

Together, transaction and lock managers are responsible for concurrency control (see "Concurrency Control" on page 93): they guarantee logical and physical data integrity while ensuring that concurrent operations are executed as efficiently as possible.

Memory- Versus Disk-Based DBMS

Database systems store data in memory and on disk. *In-memory database management systems* (sometimes called *main memory DBMS*) store data *primarily* in memory and use the disk for recovery and logging. *Disk-based* DBMS hold *most* of the data on disk and use memory for caching disk contents or as a temporary storage. Both types of systems use the disk to a certain extent, but main memory databases store their contents almost exclusively in RAM.

Accessing memory has been and remains several orders of magnitude faster than accessing disk,[1] so it is compelling to use memory as the primary storage, and it becomes more economically feasible to do so as memory prices go down. However, RAM prices still remain high compared to persistent storage devices such as SSDs and HDDs.

Main memory database systems are different from their disk-based counterparts not only in terms of a primary storage medium, but also in which data structures, organization, and optimization techniques they use.

Databases using memory as a primary data store do this mainly because of performance, comparatively low access costs, and access granularity. Programming for main memory is also significantly simpler than doing so for the disk. Operating systems abstract memory management and allow us to think in terms of allocating and freeing arbitrarily sized memory chunks. On disk, we have to manage data references, serialization formats, freed memory, and fragmentation manually.

The main limiting factors on the growth of in-memory databases are RAM volatility (in other words, lack of durability) and costs. Since RAM contents are not persistent, software errors, crashes, hardware failures, and power outages can result in data loss. There are ways to ensure durability, such as uninterrupted power supplies and battery-backed RAM, but they require additional hardware resources and operational expertise. In practice, it all comes down to the fact that disks are easier to maintain and have significantly lower prices.

The situation is likely to change as the availability and popularity of Non-Volatile Memory (NVM) [ARULRAJ17] technologies grow. NVM storage reduces or completely eliminates (depending on the exact technology) asymmetry between read and write latencies, further improves read and write performance, and allows byte-addressable access.

Durability in Memory-Based Stores

In-memory database systems maintain backups on disk to provide durability and prevent loss of the volatile data. Some databases store data exclusively in memory, without any durability guarantees, but we do not discuss them in the scope of this book.

Before the operation can be considered complete, its results have to be written to a sequential log file. We discuss write-ahead logs in more detail in "Recovery" on page 88. To avoid replaying complete log contents during startup or after a crash, in-memory stores maintain a *backup copy*. The backup copy is maintained as a sorted

---

1 You can find a visualization and comparison of disk, memory access latencies, and many other relevant numbers over the years at *https://people.eecs.berkeley.edu/~rcs/research/interactive_latency.html*.

disk-based structure, and modifications to this structure are often asynchronous (decoupled from client requests) and applied in batches to reduce the number of I/O operations. During recovery, database contents can be restored from the backup and logs.

Log records are usually applied to backup in batches. After the batch of log records is processed, backup holds a database *snapshot* for a specific point in time, and log contents up to this point can be discarded. This process is called *checkpointing*. It reduces recovery times by keeping the disk-resident database most up-to-date with log entries without requiring clients to block until the backup is updated.

 It is unfair to say that the in-memory database is the equivalent of an on-disk database with a huge page cache (see "Buffer Management" on page 81). Even though pages are *cached* in memory, serialization format and data layout incur additional overhead and do not permit the same degree of optimization that in-memory stores can achieve.

Disk-based databases use specialized storage structures, optimized for disk access. In memory, pointers can be followed comparatively quickly, and random memory access is significantly faster than the random disk access. Disk-based storage structures often have a form of wide and short trees (see "Trees for Disk-Based Storage" on page 28), while memory-based implementations can choose from a larger pool of data structures and perform optimizations that would otherwise be impossible or difficult to implement on disk [GARCIAMOLINA92]. Similarly, handling variable-size data on disk requires special attention, while in memory it's often a matter of referencing the value with a pointer.

For some use cases, it is reasonable to assume that an entire dataset is going to fit in memory. Some datasets are bounded by their real-world representations, such as student records for schools, customer records for corporations, or inventory in an online store. Each record takes up not more than a few Kb, and their number is limited.

Column- Versus Row-Oriented DBMS

Most database systems store a set of *data records*, consisting of *columns* and *rows* in *tables*. *Field* is an intersection of a column and a row: a single value of some type. Fields belonging to the same column usually have the same data type. For example, if we define a table holding user records, all names would be of the same type and belong to the same column. A collection of values that belong logically to the same record (usually identified by the key) constitutes a row.

One of the ways to classify databases is by how the data is stored on disk: row- or column-wise. Tables can be partitioned either horizontally (storing values belonging to the same row together), or vertically (storing values belonging to the same column together). Figure 1-2 depicts this distinction: (a) shows the values partitioned column-wise, and (b) shows the values partitioned row-wise.

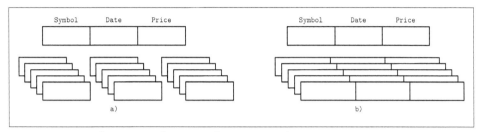

Figure 1-2. Data layout in column- and row-oriented stores

Examples of row-oriented database management systems are abundant: MySQL (*https://dev.mysql.com*), PostgreSQL (*https://www.postgresql.org*), and most of the traditional relational databases. The two pioneer open source column-oriented stores are MonetDB (*https://databass.dev/links/109*) and C-Store (*https://databass.dev/links/110*) (C-Store is an open source predecessor to Vertica (*https://databass.dev/links/111*)).

Row-Oriented Data Layout

Row-oriented database management systems store data in records or *rows*. Their layout is quite close to the tabular data representation, where every row has the same set of fields. For example, a row-oriented database can efficiently store user entries, holding names, birth dates, and phone numbers:

```
| ID | Name  | Birth Date  | Phone Number  |
| 10 | John  | 01 Aug 1981 | +1 111 222 333 |
| 20 | Sam   | 14 Sep 1988 | +1 555 888 999 |
| 30 | Keith | 07 Jan 1984 | +1 333 444 555 |
```

This approach works well for cases where several fields constitute the record (name, birth date, and a phone number) uniquely identified by the key (in this example, a monotonically incremented number). All fields representing a single user record are often read together. When creating records (for example, when the user fills out a registration form), we write them together as well. At the same time, each field can be modified individually.

Since row-oriented stores are most useful in scenarios when we have to access data by row, storing entire rows together improves spatial locality[2] [DENNING68].

---

2 Spatial locality is one of the Principles of Locality, stating that if a memory location is accessed, its nearby memory locations will be accessed in the near future.

Because data on a persistent medium such as a disk is typically accessed block-wise (in other words, a minimal unit of disk access is a block), a single block will contain data for all columns. This is great for cases when we'd like to access an entire user record, but makes queries accessing individual fields of multiple user records (for example, queries fetching only the phone numbers) more expensive, since data for the other fields will be paged in as well.

Column-Oriented Data Layout

Column-oriented database management systems partition data *vertically* (i.e., by column) instead of storing it in rows. Here, values for the same column are stored contiguously on disk (as opposed to storing rows contiguously as in the previous example). For example, if we store historical stock market prices, price quotes are stored together. Storing values for different columns in separate files or file segments allows efficient queries by column, since they can be read in one pass rather than consuming entire rows and discarding data for columns that weren't queried.

Column-oriented stores are a good fit for analytical workloads that compute aggregates, such as finding trends, computing average values, etc. Processing complex aggregates can be used in cases when logical records have multiple fields, but some of them (in this case, price quotes) have different importance and are often consumed together.

From a logical perspective, the data representing stock market price quotes can still be expressed as a table:

```
| ID | Symbol | Date        | Price     |
| 1  | DOW    | 08 Aug 2018 | 24,314.65 |
| 2  | DOW    | 09 Aug 2018 | 24,136.16 |
| 3  | S&P    | 08 Aug 2018 | 2,414.45  |
| 4  | S&P    | 09 Aug 2018 | 2,232.32  |
```

However, the physical column-based database layout looks entirely different. Values belonging to the same column are stored closely together:

```
Symbol: 1:DOW; 2:DOW; 3:S&P; 4:S&P
Date:   1:08 Aug 2018; 2:09 Aug 2018; 3:08 Aug 2018; 4:09 Aug 2018
Price:  1:24,314.65; 2:24,136.16; 3:2,414.45; 4:2,232.32
```

To reconstruct data tuples, which might be useful for joins, filtering, and multirow aggregates, we need to preserve some metadata on the column level to identify which data points from other columns it is associated with. If you do this explicitly, each value will have to hold a key, which introduces duplication and increases the amount of stored data. Some column stores use implicit identifiers (*virtual IDs*) instead and use the position of the value (in other words, its offset) to map it back to the related values [ABADI13].

During the last several years, likely due to a rising demand to run complex analytical queries over growing datasets, we've seen many new column-oriented file formats such as Apache Parquet (*https://databass.dev/links/112*), Apache ORC (*https://data bass.dev/links/113*), RCFile (*https://databass.dev/links/114*), as well as column-oriented stores, such as Apache Kudu (*https://databass.dev/links/115*), ClickHouse (*https://databass.dev/links/116*), and many others [ROY12].

Distinctions and Optimizations

It is not sufficient to say that distinctions between row and column stores are only in the way the data is stored. Choosing the data layout is just one of the steps in a series of possible optimizations that columnar stores are targeting.

Reading multiple values for the same column in one run significantly improves cache utilization and computational efficiency. On modern CPUs, vectorized instructions can be used to process multiple data points with a single CPU instruction[3] [DREP-PER07].

Storing values that have the same data type together (e.g., numbers with other numbers, strings with other strings) offers a better compression ratio. We can use different compression algorithms depending on the data type and pick the most effective compression method for each case.

To decide whether to use a column- or a row-oriented store, you need to understand your *access patterns*. If the read data is consumed in records (i.e., most or all of the columns are requested) and the workload consists mostly of point queries and range scans, the row-oriented approach is likely to yield better results. If scans span many rows, or compute aggregate over a subset of columns, it is worth considering a column-oriented approach.

Wide Column Stores

Column-oriented databases should not be mixed up with *wide column stores*, such as BigTable (*https://databass.dev/links/117*) or HBase (*https://databass.dev/links/118*), where data is represented as a multidimensional map, columns are grouped into *column families* (usually storing data of the same type), and inside each column family, data is stored row-wise. This layout is best for storing data retrieved by a key or a sequence of keys.

A canonical example from the Bigtable paper [CHANG06] is a Webtable. A Webtable stores snapshots of web page contents, their attributes, and the relations among them

---

3 Vectorized instructions, or Single Instruction Multiple Data (SIMD), describes a class of CPU instructions that perform the same operation on multiple data points.

at a specific timestamp. Pages are identified by the reversed URL, and all attributes (such as page *content* and *anchors*, representing links between pages) are identified by the timestamps at which these snapshots were taken. In a simplified way, it can be represented as a nested map, as Figure 1-3 shows.

```
{
    "com.cnn.www": {
        contents: {
            t6: html: "<html>..."
            t5: html: "<html>..."
            t3: html: "<html>..."
        }
        anchor: {
            t9: cnnsi.com: "CNN"
            t8: my.look.ca: "CNN.com"
        }
    }
    "com.example.www": {
        contents: {
            t5: html: "<html>..."
        }
        anchor: {}
    }
}
```

Figure 1-3. Conceptual structure of a Webtable

Data is stored in a multidimensional sorted map with hierarchical indexes: we can locate the data related to a specific web page by its reversed URL and its contents or anchors by the timestamp. Each row is indexed by its *row key*. Related columns are grouped together in *column families*—contents and anchor in this example—which are stored on disk separately. Each column inside a column family is identified by the *column key*, which is a combination of the column family name and a qualifier (html, cnnsi.com, my.look.ca in this example). Column families store multiple versions of data by timestamp. This layout allows us to quickly locate the higher-level entries (web pages, in this case) and their parameters (versions of content and links to the other pages).

While it is useful to understand the conceptual representation of wide column stores, their physical layout is somewhat different. A schematic representation of the data layout in column families is shown in Figure 1-4: column families are stored separately, but in each column family, the data belonging to the same key is stored together.

Column Family: contents			
Row Key	Timestamp	Qualifier	Value
com.cnn.www	t3	html	"<html>..."
com.cnn.www	t5	html	"<html>..."
com.cnn.www	t6	html	"<html>..."
com.example.www	t5	html	"<html>..."

Column Family: anchor			
Row Key	Timestamp	Qualifier	Value
com.cnn.www	t8	cnnsi.com	"CNN"
com.cnn.www	t5	my.look.ca	"CNN.com"

Figure 1-4. Physical structure of a Webtable

Data Files and Index Files

The primary goal of a database system is to store data and to allow quick access to it. But how is the data organized? Why do we need a database management system and not just a bunch of files? How does file organization improve efficiency?

Database systems do use files for storing the data, but instead of relying on filesystem hierarchies of directories and files for locating records, they compose files using implementation-specific formats. The main reasons to use specialized file organization over flat files are:

Storage efficiency
> Files are organized in a way that minimizes storage overhead per stored data record.

Access efficiency
> Records can be located in the smallest possible number of steps.

Update efficiency
> Record updates are performed in a way that minimizes the number of changes on disk.

Database systems store *data records*, consisting of multiple fields, in tables, where each table is usually represented as a separate file. Each record in the table can be looked up using a *search key*. To locate a record, database systems use *indexes*: auxiliary data structures that allow it to efficiently locate data records without scanning an entire table on every access. Indexes are built using a subset of fields identifying the record.

A database system usually separates *data files* and *index files*: data files store data records, while index files store record metadata and use it to locate records in data files. Index files are typically smaller than the data files. Files are partitioned into *pages*, which typically have the size of a single or multiple disk blocks. Pages can be organized as sequences of records or as a *slotted pages* (see "Slotted Pages" on page 52).

New records (insertions) and updates to the existing records are represented by key/value pairs. Most modern storage systems *do not* delete data from pages explicitly. Instead, they use *deletion markers* (also called *tombstones*), which contain deletion metadata, such as a key and a timestamp. Space occupied by the records *shadowed* by their updates or deletion markers is reclaimed during garbage collection, which reads the pages, writes the live (i.e., nonshadowed) records to the new place, and discards the shadowed ones.

Data Files

Data files (sometimes called *primary files*) can be implemented as *index-organized tables* (IOT), *heap-organized tables* (heap files), or *hash-organized tables* (hashed files).

Records in heap files are not required to follow any particular order, and most of the time they are placed in a write order. This way, no additional work or file reorganization is required when new pages are appended. Heap files require additional index structures, pointing to the locations where data records are stored, to make them searchable.

In hashed files, records are stored in buckets, and the hash value of the key determines which bucket a record belongs to. Records in the bucket can be stored in append order or sorted by key to improve lookup speed.

Index-organized tables (IOTs) store data records in the index itself. Since records are stored in key order, range scans in IOTs can be implemented by sequentially scanning its contents.

Storing data records in the index allows us to reduce the number of disk seeks by at least one, since after traversing the index and locating the searched key, we do not have to address a separate file to find the associated data record.

When records are stored in a separate file, index files hold *data entries*, uniquely identifying data records and containing enough information to locate them in the data file. For example, we can store file *offsets* (sometimes called *row locators*), locations of data records in the data file, or bucket IDs in the case of hash files. In index-organized tables, data entries hold actual data records.

Index Files

An index is a structure that organizes data records on disk in a way that facilitates efficient retrieval operations. Index files are organized as specialized structures that map keys to locations in data files where the records identified by these keys (in the case of heap files) or primary keys (in the case of index-organized tables) are stored.

An index on a *primary* (data) file is called the *primary index*. In most cases we can also assume that the primary index is built over a primary key or a set of keys identified as primary. All other indexes are called *secondary*.

Secondary indexes can point directly to the data record, or simply store its primary key. A pointer to a data record can hold an offset to a heap file or an index-organized table. Multiple secondary indexes can point to the same record, allowing a single data record to be identified by different fields and located through different indexes. While primary index files hold a unique entry per search key, secondary indexes may hold several entries per search key [GARCIAMOLINA08].

If the order of data records follows the search key order, this index is called *clustered* (also known as clustering). Data records in the clustered case are usually stored in the same file or in a *clustered file*, where the key order is preserved. If the data is stored in a separate file, and its order does not follow the key order, the index is called *nonclustered* (sometimes called unclustered).

Figure 1-5 shows the difference between the two approaches:

- a) An index-organized table, where data records are stored directly in the index file.
- b) An index file storing the offsets and a separate file storing data records.

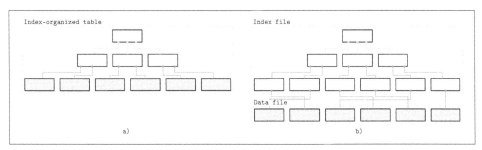

Figure 1-5. Storing data records in an index file versus storing offsets to the data file (index segments shown in white; segments holding data records shown in gray)

 Index-organized tables store information in index order and are clustered by definition. Primary indexes are *most often* clustered. Secondary indexes are nonclustered by definition, since they're used to facilitate access by keys other than the primary one. Clustered indexes can be both index-organized or have separate index and data files.

Many database systems have an inherent and explicit *primary key*, a set of columns that uniquely identify the database record. In cases when the primary key is not specified, the storage engine can create an *implicit* primary key (for example, MySQL InnoDB adds a new auto-increment column and fills in its values automatically).

This terminology is used in different kinds of database systems: relational database systems (such as MySQL and PostgreSQL), Dynamo-based NoSQL stores (such as Apache Cassandra (*https://databass.dev/links/119*) and in Riak (*https://databass.dev/links/120*)), and document stores (such as MongoDB). There can be some project-specific naming, but most often there's a clear mapping to this terminology.

Primary Index as an Indirection

There are different opinions in the database community on whether data records should be referenced directly (through file offset) or via the primary key index.[4]

Both approaches have their pros and cons and are better discussed in the scope of a complete implementation. By referencing data directly, we can reduce the number of disk seeks, but have to pay a cost of updating the pointers whenever the record is updated or relocated during a maintenance process. Using indirection in the form of a primary index allows us to reduce the cost of pointer updates, but has a higher cost on a read path.

Updating just a couple of indexes might work if the workload mostly consists of reads, but this approach does not work well for write-heavy workloads with multiple indexes. To reduce the costs of pointer updates, instead of payload offsets, some implementations use primary keys for indirection. For example, MySQL InnoDB uses a primary index and performs two lookups: one in the secondary index, and one in a primary index when performing a query [TARIQ11]. This adds an overhead of a primary index lookup instead of following the offset directly from the secondary index.

Figure 1-6 shows how the two approaches are different:

- a) Two indexes reference data entries directly from secondary index files.
- b) A secondary index goes through the indirection layer of a primary index to locate the data entries.

---

4 The original post that has stirred up the discussion was controversial and one-sided, but you can refer to the presentation comparing MySQL and PostgreSQL index and storage formats (*https://databass.dev/links/121*), which references the original source as well.

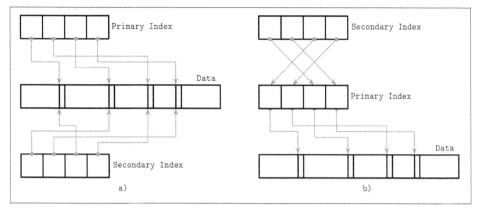

Figure 1-6. Referencing data tuples directly (a) versus using a primary index as indirection (b)

It is also possible to use a hybrid approach and store both data file offsets and primary keys. First, you check if the data offset is still valid and pay the extra cost of going through the primary key index if it has changed, updating the index file after finding a new offset.

Buffering, Immutability, and Ordering

A storage engine is based on some data structure. However, these structures do not describe the semantics of caching, recovery, transactionality, and other things that storage engines add on top of them.

In the next chapters, we will start the discussion with B-Trees (see "Ubiquitous B-Trees" on page 33) and try to understand why there are so many B-Tree variants, and why new database storage structures keep emerging.

Storage structures have three common variables: they use *buffering* (or avoid using it), use *immutable* (or mutable) files, and store values *in order* (or out of order). Most of the distinctions and optimizations in storage structures discussed in this book are related to one of these three concepts.

Buffering

This defines whether or not the storage structure chooses to collect a certain amount of data in memory before putting it on disk. Of course, every on-disk structure has to use buffering to *some* degree, since the smallest unit of data transfer to and from the disk is a *block*, and it is desirable to write full blocks. Here, we're talking about avoidable buffering, something storage engine implementers *choose* to do. One of the first optimizations we discuss in this book is adding in-memory buffers to B-Tree nodes to amortize I/O costs (see "Lazy B-Trees" on page 114). However, this is not the only way we can apply buffering.

For example, two-component LSM Trees (see "Two-component LSM Tree" on page 132), despite their similarities with B-Trees, use buffering in an entirely different way, and combine buffering with immutability.

Mutability (or immutability)

This defines whether or not the storage structure reads parts of the file, updates them, and writes the updated results at the same location in the file. Immutable structures are *append-only*: once written, file contents are not modified. Instead, modifications are appended to the end of the file. There are other ways to implement immutability. One of them is *copy-on-write* (see "Copy-on-Write" on page 112), where the modified page, holding the updated version of the record, is written to the *new* location in the file, instead of its original location. Often the distinction between LSM and B-Trees is drawn as immutable against in-place update storage, but there are structures (for example, "Bw-Trees" on page 120) that are inspired by B-Trees but are immutable.

Ordering

This is defined as whether or not the *data records* are stored in the key order in the pages on disk. In other words, the keys that sort closely are stored in contiguous segments on disk. Ordering often defines whether or not we can efficiently scan the *range* of records, not only locate the individual data records. Storing data out of order (most often, in insertion order) opens up for some write-time optimizations. For example, Bitcask (see "Bitcask" on page 153) and WiscKey (see "WiscKey" on page 154) store data records directly in append-only files.

Of course, a brief discussion of these three concepts is not enough to show their power, and we'll continue this discussion throughout the rest of the book.

Summary

In this chapter, we've discussed the architecture of a database management system and covered its primary components.

To highlight the importance of disk-based structures and their difference from in-memory ones, we discussed memory- and disk-based stores. We came to the conclusion that disk-based structures are important for both types of stores, but are used for different purposes.

To understand how access patterns influence database system design, we discussed column- and row-oriented database management systems and the primary factors that set them apart from each other. To start a conversation about *how the data is stored*, we covered data and index files.

Lastly, we introduced three core concepts: buffering, immutability, and ordering. We will use them throughout this book to highlight properties of the storage engines that use them.

Further Reading

If you'd like to learn more about the concepts mentioned in this chapter, you can refer to the following sources:

Database architecture
> Hellerstein, Joseph M., Michael Stonebraker, and James Hamilton. 2007. "Architecture of a Database System." *Foundations and Trends in Databases* 1, no. 2 (February): 141-259. *https://doi.org/10.1561/1900000002.*

Column-oriented DBMS
> Abadi, Daniel, Peter Boncz, Stavros Harizopoulos, Stratos Idreaos, and Samuel Madden. 2013. *The Design and Implementation of Modern Column-Oriented Database Systems.* Hanover, MA: Now Publishers Inc.

In-memory DBMS
> Faerber, Frans, Alfons Kemper, and Per-Åke Alfons. 2017. *Main Memory Database Systems.* Hanover, MA: Now Publishers Inc.

CHAPTER 2

B-Tree Basics

In the previous chapter, we separated storage structures in two groups: *mutable* and *immutable* ones, and identified immutability as one of the core concepts influencing their design and implementation. Most of the mutable storage structures use an *in-place update* mechanism. During insert, delete, or update operations, data records are updated directly in their locations in the target file.

Storage engines often allow multiple versions of the same data record to be present in the database; for example, when using multiversion concurrency control (see "Multiversion Concurrency Control" on page 99) or slotted page organization (see "Slotted Pages" on page 52). For the sake of simplicity, for now we assume that each key is associated only with one data record, which has a unique location.

One of the most popular storage structures is a B-Tree. Many open source database systems are B-Tree based, and over the years they've proven to cover the majority of use cases.

B-Trees are not a recent invention: they were introduced by Rudolph Bayer and Edward M. McCreight back in 1971 and gained popularity over the years. By 1979, there were already quite a few variants of B-Trees. Douglas Comer collected and systematized some of them [COMER79].

Before we dive into B-Trees, let's first talk about why we should consider alternatives to traditional search trees, such as, for example, binary search trees, 2-3-Trees, and AVL Trees [KNUTH98]. For that, let's recall what binary search trees are.

Binary Search Trees

A *binary search tree* (BST) is a sorted in-memory data structure, used for efficient key-value lookups. BSTs consist of multiple nodes. Each tree node is represented by a key, a value associated with this key, and two child pointers (hence the name binary). BSTs start from a single node, called a *root node*. There can be only one root in the tree. Figure 2-1 shows an example of a binary search tree.

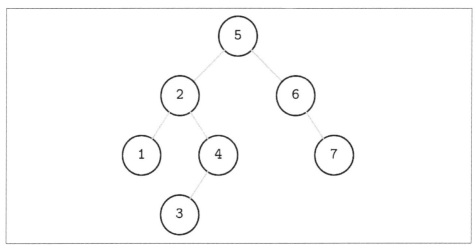

Figure 2-1. Binary search tree

Each node splits the search space into left and right *subtrees*, as Figure 2-2 shows: a node key is *greater than* any key stored in its left subtree and *less than* any key stored in its right subtree [SEDGEWICK11].

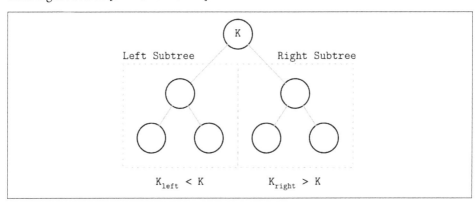

Figure 2-2. Binary tree node invariants

Following left pointers from the root of the tree down to the leaf level (the level where nodes have no children) locates the node holding the smallest key within the tree and a value associated with it. Similarly, following right pointers locates the node holding the largest key within the tree and a value associated with it. Values are allowed to be stored in all nodes in the tree. Searches start from the root node, and may terminate before reaching the bottom level of the tree if the searched key was found on a higher level.

Tree Balancing

Insert operations do not follow any specific pattern, and element insertion might lead to the situation where the tree is unbalanced (i.e., one of its branches is longer than the other one). The worst-case scenario is shown in Figure 2-3 (b), where we end up with a *pathological* tree, which looks more like a linked list, and instead of desired logarithmic complexity, we get linear, as illustrated in Figure 2-3 (a).

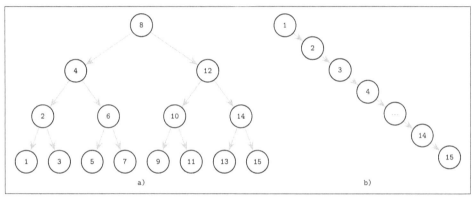

Figure 2-3. Balanced (a) and unbalanced or pathological (b) tree examples

This example might slightly exaggerate the problem, but it illustrates why the tree needs to be balanced: even though it's somewhat unlikely that all the items end up on one side of the tree, at least some of them certainly will, which will significantly slow down searches.

The *balanced* tree is defined as one that has a height of $\log_2$ N, where N is the total number of items in the tree, and the difference in height between the two subtrees is not greater than one[1] [KNUTH98]. Without balancing, we lose performance benefits of the binary search tree structure, and allow insertions and deletions order to determine tree shape.

---

1 This property is imposed by AVL Trees and several other data structures. More generally, binary search trees keep the difference in heights between subtrees within a small constant factor.

In the balanced tree, following the left or right node pointer reduces the search space in half on average, so lookup complexity is logarithmic: $O(\log_2 N)$. If the tree is not balanced, worst-case complexity goes up to $O(N)$, since we might end up in the situation where all elements end up on one side of the tree.

Instead of adding new elements to one of the tree branches and making it longer, while the other one remains empty (as shown in Figure 2-3 (b)), the tree is *balanced* after each operation. Balancing is done by reorganizing nodes in a way that minimizes tree height and keeps the number of nodes on each side within bounds.

One of the ways to keep the tree balanced is to perform a rotation step after nodes are added or removed. If the insert operation leaves a branch unbalanced (two consecutive nodes in the branch have only one child), we can *rotate* nodes around the middle one. In the example shown in Figure 2-4, during rotation the middle node (3), known as a rotation *pivot*, is promoted one level higher, and its parent becomes its right child.

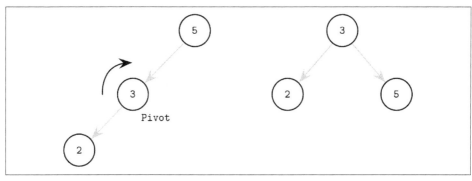

Figure 2-4. Rotation step example

Trees for Disk-Based Storage

As previously mentioned, unbalanced trees have a worst-case complexity of $O(N)$. Balanced trees give us an average $O(\log_2 N)$. At the same time, due to low *fanout* (fanout is the maximum allowed number of children per node), we have to perform balancing, relocate nodes, and update pointers rather frequently. Increased maintenance costs make BSTs impractical as on-disk data structures [NIEVERGELT74].

If we wanted to maintain a BST on disk, we'd face several problems. One problem is locality: since elements are added in random order, there's no guarantee that a newly created node is written close to its parent, which means that node child pointers may span across several disk pages. We can improve the situation to a certain extent by modifying the tree layout and using paged binary trees (see "Paged Binary Trees" on page 33).

Another problem, closely related to the cost of following child pointers, is tree height. Since binary trees have a fanout of just two, height is a binary logarithm of the number of the elements in the tree, and we have to perform $O(\log_2 N)$ seeks to locate the searched element and, subsequently, perform the same number of disk transfers. 2-3-Trees and other low-fanout trees have a similar limitation: while they are useful as in-memory data structures, small node size makes them impractical for external storage [COMER79].

A naive on-disk BST implementation would require as many disk seeks as comparisons, since there's no built-in concept of locality. This sets us on a course to look for a data structure that would exhibit this property.

Considering these factors, a version of the tree that would be better suited for disk implementation has to exhibit the following properties:

- *High fanout* to improve locality of the neighboring keys.
- *Low height* to reduce the number of seeks during traversal.

 Fanout and height are inversely correlated: the higher the fanout, the lower the height. If fanout is high, each node can hold more children, reducing the number of nodes and, subsequently, reducing height.

Disk-Based Structures

We've talked about memory and disk-based storage (see "Memory- Versus Disk-Based DBMS" on page 10) in general terms. We can draw the same distinction for specific data structures: some are better suited to be used on disk and some work better in memory.

As we have discussed, not every data structure that satisfies space and complexity requirements can be effectively used for on-disk storage. Data structures used in databases have to be adapted to account for persistent medium limitations.

On-disk data structures are often used when the amounts of data are so large that keeping an entire dataset in memory is impossible or not feasible. Only a fraction of the data can be *cached* in memory at any time, and the rest has to be stored on disk in a manner that allows efficiently accessing it.

Hard Disk Drives

Most traditional algorithms were developed when spinning disks were the most wide-spread persistent storage medium, which significantly influenced their design. Later, new developments in storage media, such as flash drives, inspired new algorithms and modifications to the existing ones, exploiting the capabilities of the new hardware. These days, new types of data structures are emerging, optimized to work with nonvolatile byte-addressable storage (for example, [XIA17] [KANNAN18]).

On spinning disks, *seeks* increase costs of random reads because they require disk rotation and mechanical head movements to position the read/write head to the desired location. However, once the expensive part is done, reading or writing contiguous bytes (i.e., sequential operations) is *relatively* cheap.

The smallest transfer unit of a spinning drive is a *sector*, so when some operation is performed, at least an entire sector can be read or written. Sector sizes typically range from 512 bytes to 4 Kb.

Head positioning is the most expensive part of an operation on the HDD. This is one of the reasons we often hear about the positive effects of *sequential* I/O: reading and writing contiguous memory segments from disk.

Solid State Drives

Solid state drives (SSDs) do not have moving parts: there's no disk that spins, or head that has to be positioned for the read. A typical SSD is built of *memory cells*, connected into *strings* (typically 32 to 64 cells per string), strings are combined into *arrays*, arrays are combined into *pages*, and pages are combined into *blocks* [LARRIVEE15].

Depending on the exact technology used, a cell can hold one or multiple bits of data. Pages vary in size between devices, but typically their sizes range from 2 to 16 Kb. Blocks typically contain 64 to 512 pages. Blocks are organized into planes and, finally, planes are placed on a *die*. SSDs can have one or more dies. Figure 2-5 shows this hierarchy.

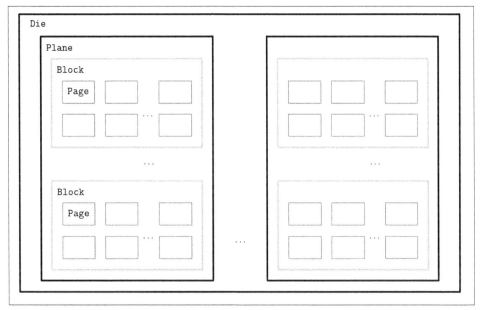

Figure 2-5. SSD organization schematics

The smallest unit that can be written (programmed) or read is a page. However, we can only make changes to the empty memory cells (i.e., to ones that have been erased before the write). The smallest erase entity is not a page, but a block that holds multiple pages, which is why it is often called an *erase block*. Pages in an empty block have to be written sequentially.

The part of a flash memory controller responsible for mapping page IDs to their physical locations, tracking empty, written, and discarded pages, is called the Flash Translation Layer (FTL) (see "Flash Translation Layer" on page 157 for more about FTL). It is also responsible for *garbage collection*, during which FTL finds blocks it can safely erase. Some blocks might still contain live pages. In this case, it relocates live pages from these blocks to new locations and remaps page IDs to point there. After this, it erases the now-unused blocks, making them available for writes.

Since in both device types (HDDs and SSDs) we are addressing chunks of memory rather than individual bytes (i.e., accessing data block-wise), most operating systems have a *block device* abstraction [CESATI05]. It hides an internal disk structure and buffers I/O operations internally, so when we're reading a *single word* from a block device, the *whole block* containing it is read. This is a constraint we cannot ignore and should always take into account when working with disk-resident data structures.

In SSDs, we don't have a strong emphasis on random versus sequential I/O, as in HDDs, because the difference in latencies between random and sequential reads is not as large. There is *still* some difference caused by prefetching, reading contiguous pages, and internal parallelism [GOOSSAERT14].

Even though garbage collection is usually a background operation, its effects may negatively impact write performance, especially in cases of random and unaligned write workloads.

Writing only full blocks, and combining subsequent writes to the same block, can help to reduce the number of required I/O operations. We discuss buffering and immutability as ways to achieve that in later chapters.

On-Disk Structures

Besides the cost of disk access itself, the main limitation and design condition for building efficient on-disk structures is the fact that the smallest unit of disk operation is a block. To follow a pointer to the specific location within the block, we have to fetch an entire block. Since we already have to do that, we can change the layout of the data structure to take advantage of it.

We've mentioned pointers several times throughout this chapter already, but this word has slightly different semantics for on-disk structures. On disk, most of the time we manage the data layout manually (unless, for example, we're using memory mapped files (*https://databass.dev/links/64*)). This is still similar to regular pointer operations, but we have to compute the target pointer addresses and follow the pointers explicitly.

Most of the time, on-disk offsets are precomputed (in cases when the pointer is written on disk before the part it points to) or cached in memory until they are flushed on the disk. Creating long dependency chains in on-disk structures greatly increases code and structure complexity, so it is preferred to keep the number of pointers and their spans to a minimum.

In summary, on-disk structures are designed with their target storage specifics in mind and generally optimize for fewer disk accesses. We can do this by improving locality, optimizing the internal representation of the structure, and reducing the number of out-of-page pointers.

In "Binary Search Trees" on page 26, we came to the conclusion that *high fanout* and *low height* are desired properties for an optimal on-disk data structure. We've also just discussed additional space overhead coming from pointers, and maintenance overhead from remapping these pointers as a result of balancing. B-Trees combine these ideas: increase node fanout, and reduce tree height, the number of node pointers, and the frequency of balancing operations.

Paged Binary Trees

Laying out a binary tree by grouping nodes into pages, as Figure 2-6 shows, improves the situation with locality. To find the next node, it's only necessary to follow a pointer in an already fetched page. However, there's still some overhead incurred by the nodes and pointers between them. Laying the structure out on disk and its further maintenance are nontrivial endeavors, especially if keys and values are not presorted and added in random order. Balancing requires page reorganization, which in turn causes pointer updates.

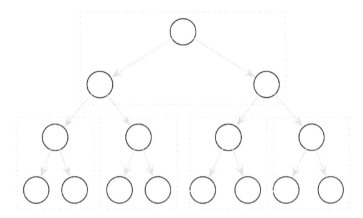

Figure 2-6. Paged binary trees

Ubiquitous B-Trees

> We are braver than a bee, and a… longer than a tree…
>
> —Winnie the Pooh

B-Trees can be thought of as a vast catalog room in the library: you first have to pick the correct cabinet, then the correct shelf in that cabinet, then the correct drawer on the shelf, and then browse through the cards in the drawer to find the one you're searching for. Similarly, a B-Tree builds a hierarchy that helps to navigate and locate the searched items quickly.

As we discussed in "Binary Search Trees" on page 26, B-Trees build upon the foundation of balanced search trees and are different in that they have higher fanout (have more child nodes) and smaller height.

In most of the literature, binary tree nodes are drawn as circles. Since each node is responsible just for one key and splits the range into two parts, this level of detail is sufficient and intuitive. At the same time, B-Tree nodes are often drawn as rectangles, and pointer blocks are also shown explicitly to highlight the relationship between child nodes and separator keys. Figure 2-7 shows binary tree, 2-3-Tree, and B-Tree nodes side by side, which helps to understand the similarities and differences between them.

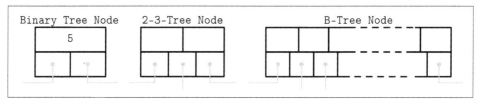

Figure 2-7. Binary tree, 2-3-Tree, and B-Tree nodes side by side

Nothing prevents us from depicting binary trees in the same way. Both structures have similar pointer-following semantics, and differences start showing in how the balance is maintained. Figure 2-8 shows that and hints at similarities between BSTs and B-Trees: in both cases, keys split the tree into subtrees, and are used for navigating the tree and finding searched keys. You can compare it to Figure 2-1.

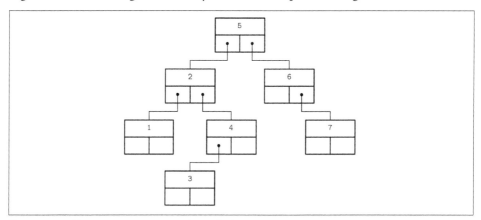

Figure 2-8. Alternative representation of a binary tree

B-Trees are *sorted*: keys inside the B-Tree nodes are stored in order. Because of that, to locate a searched key, we can use an algorithm like binary search. This also implies that lookups in B-Trees have logarithmic complexity. For example, finding a searched key among 4 billion (4×10^9) items takes about 32 comparisons (see "B-Tree Lookup Complexity" on page 37 for more on this subject). If we had to make a disk seek for each one of these comparisons, it would significantly slow us down, but since B-Tree nodes store dozens or even hundreds of items, we only have to make one disk seek per level jump. We'll discuss a lookup algorithm in more detail later in this chapter.

Using B-Trees, we can efficiently execute both *point* and *range* queries. Point queries, expressed by the equality (=) predicate in most query languages, locate a single item. On the other hand, range queries, expressed by comparison (<, >, ≤, and ≥) predicates, are used to query multiple data items in order.

B-Tree Hierarchy

B-Trees consist of multiple nodes. Each node holds up to N keys and N + 1 pointers to the child nodes. These nodes are logically grouped into three groups:

Root node
> This has no parents and is the top of the tree.

Leaf nodes
> These are the bottom layer nodes that have no child nodes.

Internal nodes
> These are all other nodes, connecting root with leaves. There is usually more than one level of internal nodes.

This hierarchy is shown in Figure 2-9.

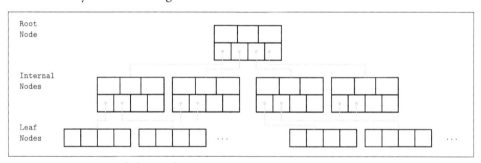

Figure 2-9. B-Tree node hierarchy

Since B-Trees are a *page* organization technique (i.e., they are used to organize and navigate fixed-size pages), we often use terms *node* and *page* interchangeably.

The relation between the node capacity and the number of keys it actually holds is called *occupancy*.

B-Trees are characterized by their *fanout*: the number of keys stored in each node. Higher fanout helps to amortize the cost of structural changes required to keep the tree balanced and to reduce the number of seeks by storing keys and pointers to child nodes in a single block or multiple consecutive blocks. Balancing operations (namely, *splits* and *merges*) are triggered when the nodes are full or nearly empty.

B⁺-Trees

We're using the term *B-Tree* as an umbrella for a family of data structures that share all or most of the mentioned properties. A more precise name for the described data structure is B⁺-Tree. [KNUTH98] refers to trees with a high fanout as *multiway* trees.

B-Trees allow storing values on any level: in root, internal, and leaf nodes. B⁺-Trees store values *only* in leaf nodes. Internal nodes store only *separator keys* used to guide the search algorithm to the associated value stored on the leaf level.

Since values in B⁺-Trees are stored only on the leaf level, all operations (inserting, updating, removing, and retrieving data records) affect only leaf nodes and propagate to higher levels only during splits and merges.

B⁺-Trees became widespread, and we refer to them as B-Trees, similar to other literature the subject. For example, in [GRAEFE11] B⁺-Trees are referred to as a default design, and MySQL InnoDB refers to its B⁺-Tree implementation as B-tree.

Separator Keys

Keys stored in B-Tree nodes are called *index entries*, *separator keys*, or *divider cells*. They split the tree into *subtrees* (also called *branches* or *subranges*), holding corresponding key ranges. Keys are stored in sorted order to allow binary search. A subtree is found by locating a key and following a corresponding pointer from the higher to the lower level.

The first pointer in the node points to the subtree holding items *less than* the first key, and the last pointer in the node points to the subtree holding items *greater than or equal* to the last key. Other pointers are reference subtrees *between* the two keys: $K_{i-1} \leq K_s < K_i$, where K is a set of keys, and K_s is a key that belongs to the subtree. Figure 2-10 shows these invariants.

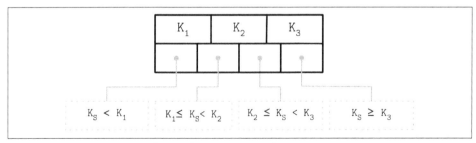

Figure 2-10. How separator keys split a tree into subtrees

Some B-Tree variants also have sibling node pointers, most often on the leaf level, to simplify range scans. These pointers help avoid going back to the parent to find the next sibling. Some implementations have pointers in both directions, forming a double-linked list on the leaf level, which makes the reverse iteration possible.

What sets B-Trees apart is that, rather than being built from top to bottom (as binary search trees), they're constructed the other way around—from bottom to top. The number of leaf nodes grows, which increases the number of internal nodes and tree height.

Since B-Trees reserve extra space inside nodes for future insertions and updates, tree storage utilization can get as low as 50%, but is usually considerably higher. Higher occupancy does not influence B-Tree performance negatively.

B-Tree Lookup Complexity

B-Tree lookup complexity can be viewed from two standpoints: the number of block transfers and the number of comparisons done during the lookup.

In terms of number of transfers, the logarithm base is N (number of keys per node). There are N times more nodes on each new level, and following a child pointer reduces the search space by the factor of N. During lookup, at most $\log_N$ M (where M is a total number of items in the B-Tree) pages are addressed to find a searched key. The number of child pointers that have to be followed on the root-to-leaf pass is also equal to the number of levels, in other words, the height h of the tree.

From the perspective of number of comparisons, the logarithm base is 2, since searching a key inside each node is done using binary search. Every comparison halves the search space, so complexity is $\log_2$ M.

Knowing the distinction between the number of seeks and the number of comparisons helps us gain the intuition about how searches are performed and understand what lookup complexity is, from both perspectives.

In textbooks and articles,[2] B-Tree lookup complexity is generally referenced as log M. Logarithm base is generally not used in complexity analysis, since changing the base simply adds a constant factor (*https://databass.dev/links/65*), and multiplication by a constant factor does not change complexity. For example, given the nonzero constant factor c, O(|c| × n) == O(n) [KNUTH97].

---

2 For example, [KNUTH98].

B-Tree Lookup Algorithm

Now that we have covered the structure and internal organization of B-Trees, we can define algorithms for lookups, insertions, and removals. To find an item in a B-Tree, we have to perform a single traversal from root to leaf. The objective of this search is to find a searched key or its predecessor. Finding an exact match is used for point queries, updates, and deletions; finding its predecessor is useful for range scans and inserts.

The algorithm starts from the root and performs a binary search, comparing the searched key with the keys stored in the root node until it finds the first separator key that is greater than the searched value. This locates a searched subtree. As we've discussed previously, index keys split the tree into subtrees with boundaries *between* two neighboring keys. As soon as we find the subtree, we follow the pointer that corresponds to it and continue the same search process (locate the separator key, follow the pointer) until we reach a target leaf node, where we either find the searched key or conclude it is not present by locating its predecessor.

On each level, we get a more detailed view of the tree: we start on the most coarse-grained level (the root of the tree) and descend to the next level where keys represent more precise, detailed ranges, until we finally reach leaves, where the data records are located.

During the point query, the search is done after finding or failing to find the searched key. During the range scan, iteration starts from the closest found key-value pair and continues by following sibling pointers until the end of the range is reached or the range predicate is exhausted.

Counting Keys

Across the literature, you can find different ways to describe key and child offset counts. [BAYER72] mentions the device-dependent natural number k that represents an optimal page size. Pages, in this case, can hold between k and 2k keys, but can be partially filled and hold at least k + 1 and at most 2k + 1 pointers to child nodes. The root page can hold between 1 and 2k keys. Later, a number l is introduced, and it is said that any nonleaf page can have l + 1 keys.

Other sources, for example [GRAEFE11], describe nodes that can hold up to N *separator keys* and N + 1 *pointers*, with otherwise similar semantics and invariants.

Both approaches bring us to the same result, and differences are only used to emphasize the contents of each source. In this book, we stick to N as the number of keys (or key-value pairs, in the case of the leaf nodes) for clarity.

B-Tree Node Splits

To insert the value into a B-Tree, we first have to locate the target leaf and find the insertion point. For that, we use the algorithm described in the previous section. After the leaf is located, the key and value are appended to it. Updates in B-Trees work by locating a target leaf node using a lookup algorithm and associating a new value with an existing key.

If the target node doesn't have enough room available, we say that the node has *overflowed* [NICHOLS66] and has to be split in two to fit the new data. More precisely, the node is split if the following conditions hold:

- For leaf nodes: if the node can hold up to N key-value pairs, and inserting one more key-value pair brings it *over* its maximum capacity N.
- For nonleaf nodes: if the node can hold up to N + 1 pointers, and inserting one more pointer brings it *over* its maximum capacity N + 1.

Splits are done by allocating the new node, transferring half the elements from the splitting node to it, and adding its first key and pointer to the parent node. In this case, we say that the key is *promoted*. The index at which the split is performed is called the *split point* (also called the midpoint). All elements after the split point (including split point in the case of leaf node split) are transferred to the newly created sibling node, and the rest of the elements remain in the splitting node.

If the parent node is full and does not have space available for the promoted key and pointer to the newly created node, it has to be split as well. This operation might propagate recursively all the way to the root.

As soon as the tree reaches its capacity (i.e., split propagates all the way up to the root), we have to split the root node. When the root node is split, a new root, holding a split point key, is allocated. The old root (now holding only half the entries) is demoted to the next level along with its newly created sibling, increasing the tree height by one. The tree height changes when the root node is split and the new root is allocated, or when two nodes are merged to form a new root. On the leaf and internal node levels, the tree only grows *horizontally*.

Figure 2-11 shows a fully occupied *leaf* node during insertion of the new element 11. We draw the line in the middle of the full node, leave half the elements in the node, and move the rest of elements to the new one. A split point value is placed into the parent node to serve as a separator key.

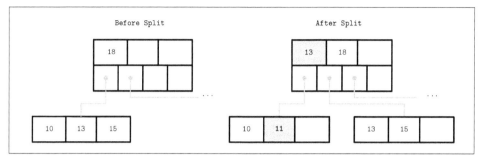

Figure 2-11. Leaf node split during the insertion of 11. New element and promoted key are shown in gray.

Figure 2-12 shows the split process of a fully occupied *nonleaf* (i.e., root or internal) node during insertion of the new element 11. To perform a split, we first create a new node and move elements starting from index N/2 + 1 to it. The split point key is promoted to the parent.

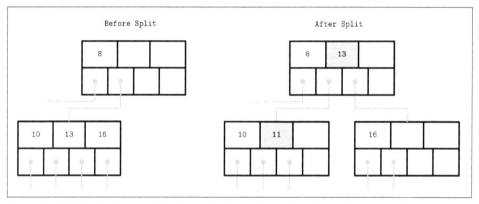

Figure 2-12. Nonleaf node split during the insertion of 11. New element and promoted key are shown in gray.

Since nonleaf node splits are always a manifestation of splits propagating from the levels below, we have an additional pointer (to the newly created node on the next level). If the parent does not have enough space, it has to be split as well.

It doesn't matter whether the leaf or nonleaf node is split (i.e., whether the node holds keys and values or just the keys). In the case of leaf split, keys are moved together with their associated values.

When the split is done, we have two nodes and have to pick the correct one to finish insertion. For that, we can use the separator key invariants. If the inserted key is less than the promoted one, we finish the operation by inserting to the split node. Otherwise, we insert to the newly created one.

To summarize, node splits are done in four steps:

1. Allocate a new node.
2. Copy half the elements from the splitting node to the new one.
3. Place the new element into the corresponding node.
4. At the parent of the split node, add a separator key and a pointer to the new node.

B-Tree Node Merges

Deletions are done by first locating the target leaf. When the leaf is located, the key and the value associated with it are removed.

If neighboring nodes have too few values (i.e., their occupancy falls under a threshold), the sibling nodes are merged. This situation is called *underflow*. [BAYER72] describes two underflow scenarios: if two adjacent nodes have a common parent and their contents fit into a single node, their contents should be merged (concatenated); if their contents do not fit into a single node, keys are redistributed between them to restore balance (see "Rebalancing" on page 70). More precisely, two nodes are merged if the following conditions hold:

- For leaf nodes: if a node can hold up to N key-value pairs, and a combined number of key-value pairs in two neighboring nodes is less than or equal to N.
- For nonleaf nodes: if a node can hold up to N + 1 pointers, and a combined number of pointers in two neighboring nodes is less than or equal to N + 1.

Figure 2-13 shows the merge during deletion of element 16. To do this, we move elements from one of the siblings to the other one. Generally, elements from the *right* sibling are moved to the *left* one, but it can be done the other way around as long as the key order is preserved.

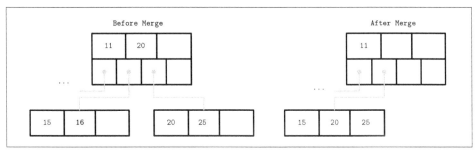

Figure 2-13. Leaf node merge

Figure 2-14 shows two sibling nonleaf nodes that have to be merged during deletion of element 10. If we combine their elements, they fit into one node, so we can have one node instead of two. During the merge of nonleaf nodes, we have to pull the corresponding separator key from the parent (i.e., demote it). The number of pointers is reduced by one because the merge is a result of the propagation of the pointer deletion from the lower level, caused by the page removal. Just as with splits, merges can propagate all the way to the root level.

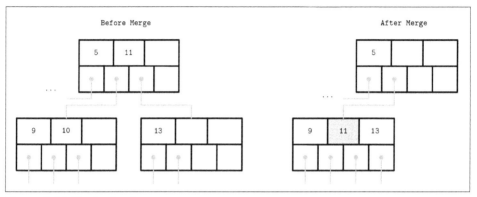

Figure 2-14. Nonleaf node merge

To summarize, node merges are done in three steps, assuming the element is already removed:

1. Copy all elements from the *right* node to the *left* one.
2. Remove the *right* node pointer from the parent (or *demote* it in the case of a nonleaf merge).
3. Remove the right node.

One of the techniques often implemented in B-Trees to reduce the number of splits and merges is rebalancing, which we discuss in "Rebalancing" on page 70.

Summary

In this chapter, we started with a motivation to create specialized structures for on-disk storage. Binary search trees might have similar complexity characteristics, but still fall short of being suitable for disk because of low fanout and a large number of relocations and pointer updates caused by balancing. B-Trees solve both problems by increasing the number of items stored in each node (high fanout) and less frequent balancing operations.

After that, we discussed internal B-Tree structure and outlines of algorithms for lookup, insert, and delete operations. Split and merge operations help to restructure the tree to keep it balanced while adding and removing elements. We keep the tree depth to a minimum and add items to the existing nodes while there's still some free space in them.

We can use this knowledge to create in-memory B-Trees. To create a disk-based implementation, we need to go into details of how to lay out B-Tree nodes on disk and compose on-disk layout using data-encoding formats.

Further Reading

If you'd like to learn more about the concepts mentioned in this chapter, you can refer to the following sources:

Binary search trees
> Sedgewick, Robert and Kevin Wayne. 2011. *Algorithms (4th Ed.).* Boston: Pearson.

> Knuth, Donald E. 1997. *The Art of Computer Programming, Volume 2 (3rd Ed.): Seminumerical Algorithms.* Boston: Addison-Wesley Longman.

Algorithms for splits and merges in B-Trees
> Elmasri, Ramez and Shamkant Navathe. 2011. *Fundamentals of Database Systems (6th Ed.).* Boston: Pearson.

> Silberschatz, Abraham, Henry F. Korth, and S. Sudarshan. 2010. *Database Systems Concepts (6th Ed.).* New York: McGraw-Hill.

CHAPTER 3

File Formats

With the basic semantics of B-Trees covered, we are now ready to explore how exactly B-Trees and other structures are implemented on disk. We access the disk in a way that is different from how we access main memory: from an application developer's perspective, memory accesses are mostly transparent. Because of virtual memory [BHATTACHARJEE17], we do not have to manage offsets manually. Disks are accessed using system calls (see *https://databass.dev/links/54*). We usually have to specify the offset inside the target file, and then interpret on-disk representation into a form suitable for main memory.

This means that efficient on-disk structures have to be designed with this distinction in mind. To do that, we have to come up with a file format that's easy to construct, modify, and interpret. In this chapter, we'll discuss general principles and practices that help us to design all sorts of on-disk structures, not only B-Trees.

There are numerous possibilities for B-Tree implementations, and here we discuss several useful techniques. Details may vary between implementations, but the general principles remain the same. Understanding the basic mechanics of B-Trees, such as splits and merges, is necessary, but they are insufficient for the actual implementation. There are many things that have to play together for the final result to be useful.

The semantics of pointer management in on-disk structures are somewhat different from in-memory ones. It is useful to think of on-disk B-Trees as a page management mechanism: algorithms have to compose and navigate *pages*. Pages and pointers to them have to be calculated and placed accordingly.

Since most of the complexity in B-Trees comes from mutability, we discuss details of page layouts, splitting, relocations, and other concepts applicable to mutable data structures. Later, when talking about LSM Trees (see "LSM Trees" on page 130), we focus on sorting and maintenance, since that's where most LSM complexity comes from.

Motivation

Creating a file format is in many ways similar to how we create data structures in languages with an unmanaged memory model. We allocate a block of data and slice it any way we like, using fixed-size primitives and structures. If we want to reference a larger chunk of memory or a structure with variable size, we use pointers.

Languages with an unmanaged memory model allow us to allocate more memory any time we need (within reasonable bounds) without us having to think or worry about whether or not there's a contiguous memory segment available, whether or not it is fragmented, or what happens after we free it. On disk, we have to take care of garbage collection and fragmentation ourselves.

Data layout is much less important in memory than on disk. For a disk-resident data structure to be efficient, we need to lay out data on disk in ways that allow quick access to it, and consider the specifics of a persistent storage medium, come up with binary data formats, and find a means to serialize and deserialize data efficiently.

Anyone who has ever used a low-level language such as C without additional libraries knows the constraints. Structures have a predefined size and are allocated and freed explicitly. Manually implementing memory allocation and tracking is even more challenging, since it is only possible to operate with memory segments of predefined size, and it is necessary to track which segments are already released and which ones are still in use.

When storing data in main memory, most of the problems with memory layout do not exist, are easier to solve, or can be solved using third-party libraries. For example, handling variable-length fields and oversize data is much more straightforward, since we can use memory allocation and pointers, and do not need to lay them out in any special way. There still are cases when developers design specialized main memory data layouts to take advantage of CPU cache lines, prefetching, and other hardware-related specifics, but this is mainly done for optimization purposes [FOWLER11].

Even though the operating system and filesystem take over some of the responsibilities, implementing on-disk structures requires attention to more details and has more pitfalls.

Binary Encoding

To store data on disk efficiently, it needs to be encoded using a format that is compact and easy to serialize and deserialize. When talking about binary formats, you hear the word *layout* quite often. Since we do not have primitives such as `malloc` and `free`, but only `read` and `write`, we have to think of accesses differently and prepare data accordingly.

Here, we discuss the main principles used to create efficient page layouts. These principles apply to any binary format: you can use similar guidelines to create file and serialization formats or communication protocols.

Before we can organize records into pages, we need to understand how to represent keys and data records in binary form, how to combine multiple values into more complex structures, and how to implement variable-size types and arrays.

Primitive Types

Keys and values have a *type*, such as `integer`, `date`, or `string`, and can be represented (serialized to and deserialized from) in their raw binary forms.

Most numeric data types are represented as fixed-size values. When working with multibyte numeric values, it is important to use the same *byte-order* (*endianness*) for both encoding and decoding. Endianness determines the sequential order of bytes:

Big-endian
> The order starts from the most-significant byte (MSB), followed by the bytes in *decreasing* significance order. In other words, MSB has the *lowest* address.

Little-endian
> The order starts from the least-significant byte (LSB), followed by the bytes in *increasing* significance order.

Figure 3-1 illustrates this. The hexadecimal 32-bit integer `0xAABBCCDD`, where AA is the MSB, is shown using both big- and little-endian byte order.

Figure 3-1. Big- and little-endian byte order. The most significant byte is shown in gray. Addresses, denoted by a, grow from left to right.

For example, to reconstruct a 64-bit integer with a corresponding byte order, RocksDB has platform-specific definitions that help to identify target platform byte order (*https://databass.dev/links/55*).[1] If the target platform endianness does not match value endianness (EncodeFixed64WithEndian (*https://databass.dev/links/56*) looks up kLittleEndian value and compares it with value endianness), it reverses the bytes using EndianTransform (*https://databass.dev/links/57*), which reads values byte-wise in reverse order and appends them to the result.

Records consist of primitives like numbers, strings, booleans, and their combinations. However, when transferring data over the network or storing it on disk, we can only use byte sequences. This means that, in order to send or write the record, we have to *serialize* it (convert it to an interpretable sequence of bytes) and, before we can use it after receiving or reading, we have to *deserialize* it (translate the sequence of bytes back to the original record).

In binary data formats, we always start with primitives that serve as building blocks for more complex structures. Different numeric types may vary in size. byte value is 8 bits, short is 2 bytes (16 bits), int is 4 bytes (32 bits), and long is 8 bytes (64 bits).

Floating-point numbers (such as float and double) are represented by their *sign*, *fraction*, and *exponent*. The IEEE Standard for Binary Floating-Point Arithmetic (*https://ieeexplore.ieee.org/document/30711*) (IEEE 754) standard describes widely accepted floating-point number representation. A 32-bit float represents a single-precision value. For example, a floating-point number 0.15652 has a binary representation, as shown in Figure 3-2. The first 23 bits represent a fraction, the following 8 bits represent an exponent, and 1 bit represents a sign (whether or not the number is negative).

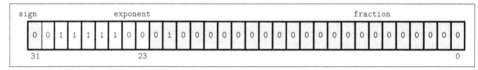

Figure 3-2. Binary representation of single-precision float number

Since a floating-point value is calculated using fractions, the number this representation yields is just an approximation. Discussing a complete conversion algorithm is out of the scope of this book, and we only cover representation basics.

The double represents a double-precision floating-point value [SAVARD05]. Most programming languages have means for encoding and decoding floating-point values to and from their binary representation in their standard libaries.

---

1 Depending on the platform (macOS, Solaris, Aix, or one of the BSD flavors, or Windows), the kLittleEndian variable is set to whether or not the platform supports little-endian.

Strings and Variable-Size Data

All primitive numeric types have a fixed size. Composing more complex values together is much like struct[2] in C. You can combine primitive values into structures and use fixed-size arrays or pointers to other memory regions.

Strings and other variable-size data types (such as arrays of fixed-size data) can be serialized as a number, representing the length of the array or string, followed by size bytes: the actual data. For strings, this representation is often called *UCSD String* or *Pascal String* (*https://databass.dev/links/59*), named after the popular implementation of the Pascal programming language. We can express it in pseudocode as follows:

```
String
{
    size    uint_16
    data    byte[size]
}
```

An alternative to Pascal strings is *null-terminated strings*, where the reader consumes the string byte-wise until the end-of-string symbol is reached. The Pascal string approach has several advantages: it allows finding out a length of a string in constant time, instead of iterating through string contents, and a language-specific string can be composed by slicing size bytes from memory and passing the byte array to a string constructor.

Bit-Packed Data: Booleans, Enums, and Flags

Booleans can be represented either by using a single byte, or encoding true and false as 1 and 0 values. Since a boolean has only two values, using an entire byte for its representation is wasteful, and developers often batch boolean values together in groups of eight, each boolean occupying just one bit. We say that every 1 bit is *set* and every 0 bit is *unset* or *empty*.

Enums (*https://databass.dev/links/60*), short for *enumerated types*, can be represented as integers and are often used in binary formats and communication protocols. Enums are used to represent often-repeated low-cardinality values. For example, we can encode a B-Tree node type using an enum:

```
enum NodeType {
    ROOT,     // 0x00h
    INTERNAL, // 0x01h
    LEAF      // 0x02h
};
```

---

2 It's worth noting that compilers can add padding to structures, which is also architecture dependent. This may break the assumptions about the exact byte offsets and locations. You can read more about structure packing here: *https://databass.dev/links/58*.

Another closely related concept is *flags*, kind of a combination of packed booleans and enums. Flags can represent nonmutually exclusive named boolean parameters. For example, we can use flags to denote whether or not the page holds value cells, whether the values are fixed-size or variable-size, and whether or not there are overflow pages associated with this node. Since every bit represents a flag value, we can only use power-of-two values for masks (since powers of two in binary always have a single set bit; for example, 2^3 == 8 == 1000b, 2^4 == 16 == 0001 0000b, etc.):

```
int IS_LEAF_MASK        = 0x01h; // bit #1
int VARIABLE_SIZE_VALUES = 0x02h; // bit #2
int HAS_OVERFLOW_PAGES  = 0x04h; // bit #3
```

Just like packed booleans, flag values can be read and written from the packed value using *bitmasks* and bitwise operators. For example, in order to set a bit responsible for one of the flags, we can use bitwise OR (|) and a bitmask. Instead of a bitmask, we can use *bitshift* (<<) and a bit index. To unset the bit, we can use bitwise AND (&) and the bitwise negation operator (~). To test whether or not the bit n is set, we can compare the result of a bitwise AND with 0:

```
// Set the bit
flags |= HAS_OVERFLOW_PAGES;
flags |= (1 << 2);

// Unset the bit
flags &= ~HAS_OVERFLOW_PAGES;
flags &= ~(1 << 2);

// Test whether or not the bit is set
is_set = (flags & HAS_OVERFLOW_PAGES) != 0;
is_set = (flags & (1 << 2)) != 0;
```

General Principles

Usually, you start designing a file format by deciding how the addressing is going to be done: whether the file is going to be split into same-sized pages, which are represented by a single block or multiple contiguous blocks. Most in-place update storage structures use pages of the same size, since it significantly simplifies read and write access. Append-only storage structures often write data page-wise, too: records are appended one after the other and, as soon as the page fills up in memory, it is flushed on disk.

The file usually starts with a fixed-size *header* and may end with a fixed-size *trailer*, which hold auxiliary information that should be accessed quickly or is required for decoding the rest of the file. The rest of the file is split into pages. Figure 3-3 shows this file organization schematically.

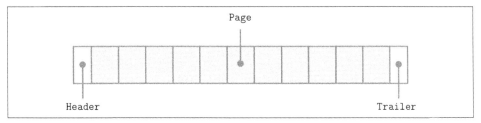

Figure 3-3. File organization

Many data stores have a fixed schema, specifying the number, order, and type of fields the table can hold. Having a fixed schema helps to reduce the amount of data stored on disk: instead of repeatedly writing field names, we can use their positional identifiers.

If we wanted to design a format for the company directory, storing names, birth dates, tax numbers, and genders for each employee, we could use several approaches. We could store the fixed-size fields (such as birth date and tax number) in the head of the structure, followed by the variable-size ones:

```
Fixed-size fields:
| (4 bytes) employee_id          |
| (4 bytes) tax_number           |
| (3 bytes) date                 |
| (1 byte)  gender               |
| (2 bytes) first_name_length    |
| (2 bytes) last_name_length     |

Variable-size fields:
| (first_name_length bytes) first_name |
| (last_name_length bytes) last_name   |
```

Now, to access `first_name`, we can slice `first_name_length` bytes after the fixed-size area. To access `last_name`, we can locate its starting position by checking the sizes of the variable-size fields that precede it. To avoid calculations involving multiple fields, we can encode both *offset* and *length* to the fixed-size area. In this case, we can locate any variable-size field separately.

Building more complex structures usually involves building hierarchies: fields composed out of primitives, cells composed of fields, pages composed of cells, sections composed of pages, regions composed of sections, and so on. There are no strict rules you have to follow here, and it all depends on what kind of data you need to create a format for.

Database files often consist of multiple parts, with a lookup table aiding navigation and pointing to the start offsets of these parts written either in the file header, trailer, or in the separate file.

Page Structure

Database systems store data records in data and index files. These files are partitioned into fixed-size units called *pages*, which often have a size of multiple filesystem blocks. Page sizes usually range from 4 to 16 Kb.

Let's take a look at the example of an on-disk B-Tree node. From a structure perspective, in B-Trees, we distinguish between the *leaf nodes* that hold keys and data records pairs, and *nonleaf nodes* that hold keys and pointers to other nodes. Each B-Tree node occupies one page or multiple pages linked together, so in the context of B-Trees the terms *node* and *page* (and even *block*) are often used interchangeably.

The original B-Tree paper [BAYER72] describes a simple page organization for fixed-size data records, where each page is just a concatenation of triplets, as shown in Figure 3-4: keys are denoted by k, associated values are denoted by v, and pointers to child pages are denoted by p.

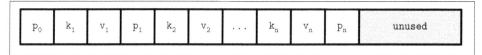

Figure 3-4. Page organization for fixed-size records

This approach is easy to follow, but has some downsides:

- Appending a key anywhere but the right side requires relocating elements.
- It doesn't allow managing or accessing variable-size records efficiently and works only for fixed-size data.

Slotted Pages

When storing variable-size records, the main problem is free space management: reclaiming the space occupied by removed records. If we attempt to put a record of size n into the space previously occupied by the record of size m, unless m == n or we can find another record that has a size exactly m - n, this space will remain unused. Similarly, a segment of size m cannot be used to store a record of size k if k is larger than m, so it will be inserted without reclaiming the unused space.

To simplify space management for variable-size records, we can split the page into fixed-size segments. However, we end up wasting space if we do that, too. For example, if we use a segment size of 64 bytes, unless the record size is a multiple of 64, we waste 64 - (n modulo 64) bytes, where n is the size of the inserted record. In other words, unless the record is a multiple of 64, one of the blocks will be only partially filled.

Space reclamation can be done by simply rewriting the page and moving the records around, but we need to preserve record offsets, since out-of-page pointers might be using these offsets. It is desirable to do that while minimizing space waste, too.

To summarize, we need a page format that allows us to:

- Store variable-size records with a minimal overhead.
- Reclaim space occupied by the removed records.
- Reference records in the page without regard to their exact locations.

To efficiently store variable-size records such as strings, binary large objects (BLOBs), etc., we can use an organization technique called *slotted page* (i.e., a page with slots) [SILBERSCHATZ10] or *slot directory* [RAMAKRISHNAN03]. This approach is used by many databases, for example, PostgreSQL (*https://databass.dev/links/61*).

We organize the page into a collection of *slots* or *cells* and split out pointers and cells in two independent memory regions residing on different sides of the page. This means that we only need to reorganize pointers addressing the cells to preserve the order, and deleting a record can be done either by nullifying its pointer or removing it.

A slotted page has a fixed-size header that holds important information about the page and cells (see "Page Header" on page 61). Cells may differ in size and can hold arbitrary data: keys, pointers, data records, etc. Figure 3-5 shows a slotted page organization, where every page has a maintenance region (header), cells, and pointers to them.

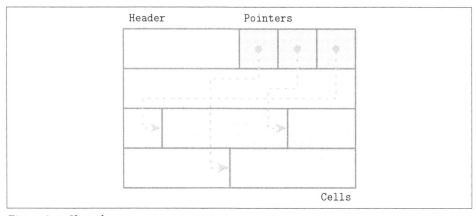

Figure 3-5. Slotted page

Let's see how this approach fixes the problems we stated in the beginning of this section:

- Minimal overhead: the only overhead incurred by slotted pages is a pointer array holding offsets to the exact positions where the records are stored.

- Space reclamation: space can be reclaimed by defragmenting and rewriting the page.

- Dynamic layout: from outside the page, slots are referenced only by their IDs, so the exact location is internal to the page.

Cell Layout

Using flags, enums, and primitive values, we can start designing the cell layout, then combine cells into pages, and compose a tree out of the pages. On a cell level, we have a distinction between key and key-value cells. Key cells hold a separator key and a pointer to the page *between* two neighboring pointers. Key-value cells hold keys and data records associated with them.

We assume that all cells within the page are uniform (for example, all cells can hold either just keys or both keys and values; similarly, all cells hold either fixed-size or variable-size data, but not a mix of both). This means we can store metadata describing cells once on the page level, instead of duplicating it in every cell.

To compose a key cell, we need to know:

- Cell type (can be inferred from the page metadata)
- Key size
- ID of the child page this cell is pointing to
- Key bytes

A variable-size key cell layout might look something like this (a fixed-size one would have no size specifier on the cell level):

```
0                4                8
+----------------+----------------+-------------+
| [int] key_size | [int] page_id  | [bytes] key |
+----------------+----------------+-------------+
```

We have grouped fixed-size data fields together, followed by key_size bytes. This is not strictly necessary but can simplify offset calculation, since all fixed-size fields can be accessed by using static, precomputed offsets, and we need to calculate the offsets only for the variable-size data.

The key-value cells hold data records instead of the child page IDs. Otherwise, their structure is similar:

- Cell type (can be inferred from page metadata)
- Key size
- Value size
- Key bytes
- Data record bytes

```
0              1                5 ...
+--------------+----------------+
| [byte] flags | [int] key_size |
+--------------+----------------+

5                9                          .. + key_size
+----------------+--------------------+----------------------+
| [int] value_size |    [bytes] key   | [bytes] data_record  |
+----------------+--------------------+----------------------+
```

You might have noticed the distinction between the *offset* and *page ID* here. Since pages have a fixed size and are managed by the page cache (see "Buffer Management" on page 81), we only need to store the page ID, which is later translated to the actual offset in the file using the lookup table. *Cell offsets* are page-local and are relative to the page start offset: this way we can use a smaller cardinality integer to keep the representation more compact.

Variable-Size Data

It is not necessary for the key and value in the cell to have a fixed size. Both the key and value can have a variable size. Their locations can be calculated from the fixed-size cell header using offsets.

To locate the key, we skip the header and read key_size bytes. Similarly, to locate the value, we can skip the header plus key_size more bytes and read value_size bytes.

There are different ways to do the same; for example, by storing a total size and calculating the value size by subtraction. It all boils down to having enough information to slice the cell into subparts and reconstruct the encoded data.

Combining Cells into Slotted Pages

To organize cells into pages, we can use the *slotted page* technique that we discussed in "Page Structure" on page 52. We append cells to the right side of the page (toward its end) and keep cell offsets/pointers in the left side of the page, as shown in Figure 3-6.

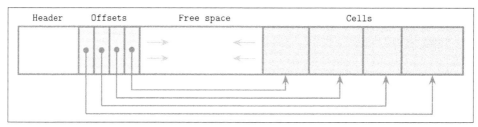

Figure 3-6. Offset and cell growth direction

Keys can be inserted out of order and their logical sorted order is kept by sorting cell offset pointers in key order. This design allows appending cells to the page with minimal effort, since cells don't have to be relocated during insert, update, or delete operations.

Let's consider an example of a page that holds names. Two names are added to the page, and their insertion order is: *Tom* and *Leslie*. As you can see in Figure 3-7, their *logical* order (in this case, alphabetical), does *not* match *insertion* order (order in which they were appended to the page). Cells are laid out in insertion order, but offsets are re-sorted to allow using binary search.

Figure 3-7. Records appended in random order: Tom, Leslie

Now, we'd like to add one more name to this page: *Ron*. New data is appended at the upper boundary of the free space of the page, but cell offsets have to preserve the lexicographical key order: *Leslie, Ron, Tom*. To do that, we have to reorder cell offsets: pointers after the *insertion point* are shifted to the right to make space for the new pointer to the Ron cell, as you can see in Figure 3-8.

Figure 3-8. Appending one more record: Ron

Managing Variable-Size Data

Removing an item from the page does not have to remove the actual cell and shift other cells to reoccupy the freed space. Instead, the cell can be marked as deleted and an in-memory *availability list* can be updated with the amount of freed memory and a pointer to the freed value. The availability list stores offsets of freed segments and their sizes. When inserting a new cell, we first check the availability list to find if there's a segment where it may fit. You can see an example of the fragmented page with available segments in Figure 3-9.

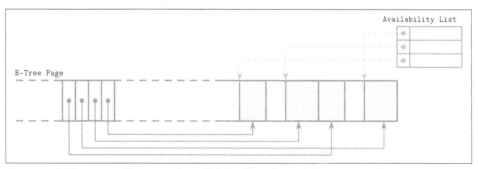

Figure 3-9. Fragmented page and availability list. Occupied pages are shown in gray. Dotted lines represent pointers to unoccupied memory regions from the availability list.

SQLite calls unoccupied segments *freeblocks* and stores a pointer to the first freeblock in the page header (*https://databass.dev/links/62*). Additionally, it stores a total number of available bytes within the page to quickly check whether or not we can fit a new element into the page after defragmenting it.

Fit is calculated based on the *strategy*:

First fit

> This might cause a larger overhead, since the space remaining after reusing the first suitable segment might be too small to fit any other cell, so it will be effectively wasted.

Best fit

For best fit, we try to find a segment for which insertion leaves the smallest remainder.

If we cannot find enough consecutive bytes to fit the new cell but there are enough fragmented bytes available, live cells are read and rewritten, defragmenting the page and reclaiming space for new writes. If there's not enough free space even after defragmentation, we have to create an overflow page (see "Overflow Pages" on page 65).

 To improve locality (especially when keys are small in size), some implementations store keys and values separately on the leaf level. Keeping keys together can improve the locality during the search. After the searched key is located, its value can be found in a value cell with a corresponding index. With variable-size keys, this requires us to calculate and store an additional value cell pointer.

In summary, to simplify B-Tree layout, we assume that each node occupies a single page. A page consists of a fixed-size header, cell pointer block, and cells. Cells hold keys and pointers to the pages representing child nodes or associated data records. B-Trees use simple pointer hierarchies: page identifiers to locate the child nodes in the tree file, and cell offsets to locate cells within the page.

Versioning

Database systems constantly evolve, and developers work to add features, and to fix bugs and performance issues. As a result of that, the binary file format can change. Most of the time, any storage engine version has to support more than one serialization format (e.g., current and one or more legacy formats for backward compatibility). To support that, we have to be able to find out which version of the file we're up against.

This can be done in several ways. For example, Apache Cassandra is using version prefixes in filenames. This way, you can tell which version the file has without even opening it. As of version 4.0, a data file name has the na prefix, such as *na-1-big-Data.db*. Older files have different prefixes: files written in version 3.0 have the ma prefix.

Alternatively, the version can be stored in a separate file. For example, PostgreSQL (*https://databass.dev/links/63*) stores the version in the *PG_VERSION* file.

The version can also be stored directly in the index file header. In this case, a part of the header (or an entire header) has to be encoded in a format that does not change between versions. After finding out which version the file is encoded with, we can create a version-specific reader to interpret the contents. Some file formats identify the version using magic numbers, which we discuss in more detail in "Magic Numbers" on page 62.

Checksumming

Files on disk may get damaged or corrupted by software bugs and hardware failures. To identify these problems preemptively and avoid propagating corrupt data to other subsystems or even nodes, we can use checksums and cyclic redundancy checks (CRCs).

Some sources make no distinction between cryptographic and noncryptographic hash functions, CRCs, and checksums. What they all have in common is that they reduce a large chunk of data to a small number, but their use cases, purposes, and guarantees are different.

Checksums provide the weakest form of guarantee and aren't able to detect corruption in multiple bits. They're usually computed by using XOR with parity checks or summation [KOOPMAN15].

CRCs can help detect burst errors (e.g., when multiple consecutive bits got corrupted) and their implementations usually use lookup tables and polynomial division [STONE98]. Multibit errors are crucial to detect, since a significant percentage of failures in communication networks and storage devices manifest this way.

 Noncryptographic hashes and CRCs should not be used to verify whether or not the data has been tampered with. For this, you should always use strong cryptographic hashes designed for security. The main goal of CRC is to make sure that there were no unintended and accidental changes in data. These algorithms are not designed to resist attacks and intentional changes in data.

Before writing the data on disk, we compute its checksum and write it together with the data. When reading it back, we compute the checksum again and compare it with the written one. If there's a checksum mismatch, we know that corruption has occurred and we should not use the data that was read.

Since computing a checksum over the whole file is often impractical and it is unlikely we're going to read the entire content every time we access it, page checksums are usually computed on pages and placed in the page header. This way, checksums can be more robust (since they are performed on a small subset of the data), and the whole file doesn't have to be discarded if corruption is contained in a single page.

Summary

In this chapter, we learned about binary data organization: how to serialize primitive data types, combine them into cells, build slotted pages out of cells, and navigate these structures.

We learned how to handle variable-size data types such as strings, byte sequences, and arrays, and compose special cells that hold a size of values contained in them.

We discussed the slotted page format, which allows us to reference individual cells from outside the page by cell ID, store records in the insertion order, and preserve the key order by sorting cell offsets.

These principles can be used to compose binary formats for on-disk structures and network protocols.

Further Reading

If you'd like to learn more about the concepts mentioned in this chapter, you can refer to the following sources:

File organization techniques

Folk, Michael J., Greg Riccardi, and Bill Zoellick. 1997. *File Structures: An Object-Oriented Approach with C++ (3rd Ed.)*. Boston: Addison-Wesley Longman.

Giampaolo, Dominic. 1998. *Practical File System Design with the Be File System (1st Ed.)*. San Francisco: Morgan Kaufmann.

Vitter, Jeffrey Scott. 2008. "Algorithms and data structures for external memory." *Foundations and Trends in Theoretical Computer Science* 2, no. 4 (January): 305-474. *https://doi.org/10.1561/0400000014*.

CHAPTER 4

Implementing B-Trees

In the previous chapter, we talked about general principles of binary format composition, and learned how to create cells, build hierarchies, and connect them to pages using pointers. These concepts are applicable for both in-place update and append-only storage structures. In this chapter, we discuss some concepts specific to B-Trees.

The sections in this chapter are split into three logical groups. First, we discuss organization: how to establish relationships between keys and pointers, and how to implement headers and links between pages.

Next, we discuss processes that occur during root-to-leaf descends, namely how to perform binary search and how to collect breadcrumbs and keep track of parent nodes in case we later have to split or merge nodes.

Lastly, we discuss optimization techniques (rebalancing, right-only appends, and bulk loading), maintenance processes, and garbage collection.

Page Header

The page header holds information about the page that can be used for navigation, maintenance, and optimizations. It usually contains flags that describe page contents and layout, number of cells in the page, lower and upper offsets marking the empty space (used to append cell offsets and data), and other useful metadata.

For example, PostgreSQL (*https://databass.dev/links/12*) stores the page size and layout version in the header. In MySQL InnoDB (*https://databass.dev/links/13*), page header holds the number of heap records, level, and some other implementation-specific values. In SQLite (*https://databass.dev/links/14*), page header stores the number of cells and a rightmost pointer.

Magic Numbers

One of the values often placed in the file or page header is a magic number. Usually, it's a multibyte block, containing a constant value that can be used to signal that the block represents a page, specify its kind, or identify its version.

Magic numbers are often used for validation and sanity checks [GIAMPAOLO98]. It's very improbable that the byte sequence at a random offset would exactly match the magic number. If it did match, there's a good chance the offset is correct. For example, to verify that the page is loaded and aligned correctly, during write we can place the magic number 50 41 47 45 (hex for PAGE) into the header. During the read, we validate the page by comparing the four bytes from the read header with the expected byte sequence.

Sibling Links

Some implementations store forward and backward links, pointing to the left and right sibling pages. These links help to locate neighboring nodes without having to ascend back to the parent. This approach adds some complexity to split and merge operations, as the sibling offsets have to be updated as well. For example, when a non-rightmost node is split, its right sibling's backward pointer (previously pointing to the node that was split) has to be re-bound to point to the newly created node.

In Figure 4-1 you can see that to locate a sibling node, unless the siblings are linked, we have to refer to the parent node. This operation might ascend all the way up to the root, since the direct parent can only help to address *its* own children. If we store sibling links directly in the header, we can simply follow them to locate the previous or next node on the same level.

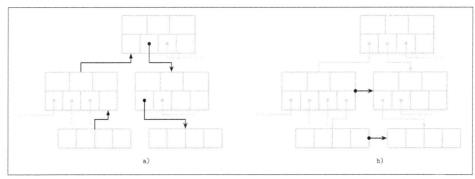

Figure 4-1. Locating a sibling by following parent links (a) versus sibling links (b)

One of the downsides of storing sibling links is that they have to be updated during splits and merges. Since updates have to happen in a sibling node, not in a splitting/merging node, it may require additional locking. We discuss how sibling links can be useful in a concurrent B-Tree implementation in "Blink-Trees" on page 107.

Rightmost Pointers

B-Tree separator keys have strict invariants: they're used to split the tree into subtrees and navigate them, so there is always one more pointer to child pages than there are keys. That's where the +1 mentioned in "Counting Keys" on page 38 is coming from.

In "Separator Keys" on page 36, we described separator key invariants. In many implementations, nodes look more like the ones displayed in Figure 4-2: each separator key has a child pointer, while the last pointer is stored separately, since it's not paired with any key. You can compare this to Figure 2-10.

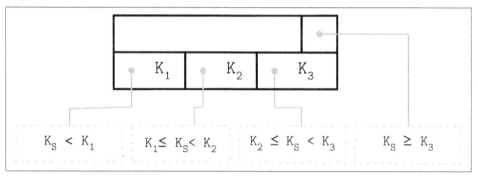

Figure 4-2. Rightmost pointer

This extra pointer can be stored in the header as, for example, it is implemented in SQLite (*https://databass.dev/links/16*).

If the rightmost child is split and the new cell is appended to its parent, the rightmost child pointer has to be reassigned. As shown in Figure 4-3, after the split, the cell appended to the parent (shown in gray) holds the promoted key and points to the split node. The pointer to the new node is assigned instead of the previous rightmost pointer. A similar approach is described and implemented in SQLite.[1]

---

1 You can find this algorithm in the `balance_deeper` function in the project repository (*https://databass.dev/links/15*).

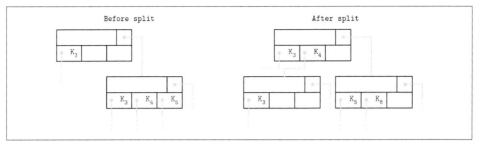

Figure 4-3. Rightmost pointer update during node split. The promoted key is shown in gray.

Node High Keys

We can take a slightly different approach and store the rightmost pointer in the cell along with the node *high key*. The high key represents the highest possible key that can be present in the subtree under the current node. This approach is used by PostgreSQL and is called B^{link}-Trees (for concurrency implications of this approach, see "Blink-Trees" on page 107).

B-Trees have N keys (denoted with K_t) and N + 1 pointers (denoted with P_t). In each subtree, keys are bounded by $K_{t-1} \leq K_s < K_t$. The $K_0 = -\infty$ is implicit and is not present in the node.

B^{link}-Trees add a K_{N+1} key to each node. It specifies an upper bound of keys that can be stored in the subtree to which the pointer P_N points, and therefore is an upper bound of values that can be stored in the current subtree. Both approaches are shown in Figure 4-4: (a) shows a node *without* a high key, and (b) shows a node with a high key.

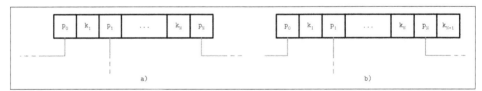

Figure 4-4. B-Trees without (a) and with (b) a high key

In this case, pointers can be stored pairwise, and each cell can have a corresponding pointer, which might simplify rightmost pointer handling as there are not as many edge cases to consider.

In Figure 4-5, you can see schematic page structure for both approaches and how the search space is split differently for these cases: going up to $+\infty$ in the first case, and up to the upper bound of K_3 in the second.

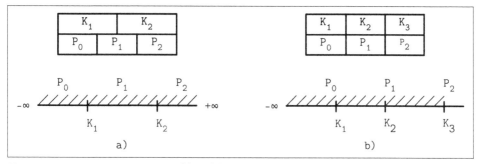

Figure 4-5. Using +∞ as a virtual key (a) versus storing the high key (b)

Overflow Pages

Node size and tree fanout values are fixed and do not change dynamically. It would also be difficult to come up with a value that would be universally optimal: if variable-size values are present in the tree and they are large enough, only a few of them can fit into the page. If the values are tiny, we end up wasting the reserved space.

The B-Tree algorithm specifies that every node keeps a specific number of items. Since some values have different sizes, we may end up in a situation where, according to the B-Tree algorithm, the node is not *full* yet, but there's *no more free space* on the fixed-size *page* that holds this node. Resizing the page requires copying already written data to the new region and is often impractical. However, we still need to find a way to increase or extend the page size.

To implement variable-size nodes without copying data to the new contiguous region, we can build nodes from multiple linked pages. For example, the default page size is 4 K, and after inserting a few values, its data size has grown over 4 K. Instead of allowing arbitrary sizes, nodes are allowed to grow in 4 K increments, so we allocate a 4 K extension page and link it from the original one. These linked page extensions are called *overflow pages*. For clarity, we call the original page the *primary page* in the scope of this section.

Most B-Tree implementations allow storing only up to a fixed number of payload bytes in the B-Tree node directly and *spilling* the rest to the overflow page. This value is calculated by dividing the node size by fanout. Using this approach, we cannot end up in a situation where the page has no free space, as it will always have at least `max_payload_size` bytes. For more information on overflow pages in SQLite, see the SQLite source code repository (*https://databass.dev/links/16*); also check out the MySQL InnoDB documentation (*https://databass.dev/links/17*).

When the inserted payload is larger than `max_payload_size`, the node is checked for whether or not it already has any associated overflow pages. If an overflow page already exists and has enough space available, extra bytes from the payload are spilled there. Otherwise, a new overflow page is allocated.

In Figure 4-6, you can see a primary page and an overflow page with records pointing from the primary page to the overflow one, where their payload continues.

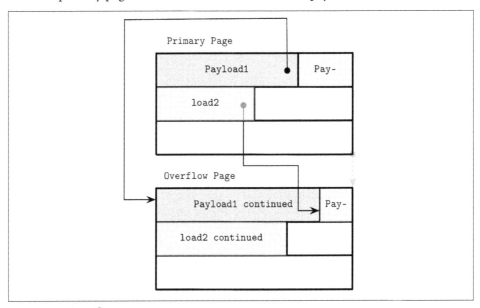

Figure 4-6. Overflow pages

Overflow pages require some extra bookkeeping, since they may get fragmented as well as primary pages, and we have to be able to reclaim this space to write new data, or discard the overflow page if it's not needed anymore.

When the first overflow page is allocated, its page ID is stored in the header of the primary page. If a single overflow page is not enough, multiple overflow pages are linked together by storing the next overflow page ID in the previous one's header. Several pages may have to be traversed to locate the overflow part for the given payload.

Since keys usually have high cardinality, storing a portion of a key makes sense, as most of the comparisons can be made on the trimmed key part that resides in the primary page.

For data records, we have to locate their overflow parts to return them to the user. However, this doesn't matter much, since it's an infrequent operation. If all data records are oversize, it is worth considering specialized blob storage for large values.

Binary Search

We've already discussed the B-Tree lookup algorithm (see "B-Tree Lookup Algorithm" on page 38) and mentioned that we locate a searched key within the node using the *binary search* algorithm. Binary search works *only* for sorted data. If keys are not ordered, they can't be binary searched. This is why keeping keys in order and maintaining a sorted invariant is essential.

The binary search algorithm receives an array of sorted items and a searched key, and returns a number. If the returned number is positive, we know that the searched key was found and the number specifies its position in the input array. A negative return value indicates that the searched key is not present in the input array and gives us an *insertion point*.

The insertion point is the index of the first element that is *greater than* the given key. An absolute value of this number is the index at which the searched key can be inserted to preserve order. Insertion can be done by shifting elements over one position, starting from an insertion point, to make space for the inserted element [SEDGE-WICK11].

The majority of searches on higher levels do not result in exact matches, and we're interested in the search direction, in which case we have to find the first value that is greater than the searched one and follow the corresponding child link into the associated subtree.

Binary Search with Indirection Pointers

Cells in the B-Tree page are stored in the insertion order, and only cell offsets preserve the logical element order. To perform binary search through page cells, we pick the middle cell offset, follow its pointer to locate the cell, compare the key from this cell with the searched key to decide whether the search should continue left or right, and continue this process recursively until the searched element or the insertion point is found, as shown in Figure 4-7.

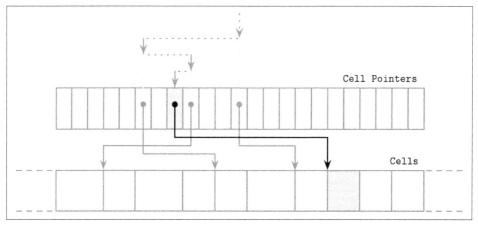

Figure 4-7. Binary search with indirection pointers. The searched element is shown in gray. Dotted arrows represent binary search through cell pointers. Solid lines represent accesses that follow the cell pointers, necessary to compare the cell value with a searched key.

Propagating Splits and Merges

As we've discussed in previous chapters, B-Tree splits and merges can propagate to higher levels. For that, we need to be able to traverse a chain back to the root node from the splitting leaf or a pair of merging leaves.

B-Tree nodes may include parent node pointers. Since pages from lower levels are always paged in when they're referenced from a higher level, it is not even necessary to persist this information on disk.

Just like sibling pointers (see "Sibling Links" on page 62), parent pointers have to be updated whenever the parent changes. This happens in all the cases when the separator key with the page identifier is transferred from one node to another: during the parent node splits, merges, or rebalancing of the parent node.

Some implementations (for example, WiredTiger (*https://databass.dev/links/20*)) use parent pointers for leaf traversal to avoid deadlocks, which may happen when using sibling pointers (see [MILLER78], [LEHMAN81]). Instead of using sibling pointers to traverse leaf nodes, the algorithm employs parent pointers, much like we saw in Figure 4-1.

To address and locate a sibling, we can follow a pointer from the parent node and recursively descend back to the lower level. Whenever we reach the end of the parent node after traversing all the siblings sharing the parent, the search continues upward recursively, eventually reaching up to the root and continuing back down to the leaf level.

Breadcrumbs

Instead of storing and maintaining parent node pointers, it is possible to keep track of nodes traversed on the path to the target leaf node, and follow the chain of parent nodes in reverse order in case of cascading splits during inserts, or merges during deletes.

During operations that may result in structural changes of the B-Tree (insert or delete), we first traverse the tree from the root to the leaf to find the target node and the insertion point. Since we do not always know up front whether or not the operation will result in a split or merge (at least not until the target leaf node is located), we have to collect *breadcrumbs*.

Breadcrumbs contain references to the nodes followed from the root and are used to backtrack them in reverse when propagating splits or merges. The most natural data structure for this is a stack. For example, PostgreSQL stores breadcrumbs in a stack, internally referenced as BTStack.[2]

If the node is split or merged, breadcrumbs can be used to find insertion points for the keys pulled to the parent and to walk back up the tree to propagate structural changes to the higher-level nodes, if necessary. This stack is maintained in memory.

Figure 4-8 shows an example of root-to-leaf traversal, collecting breadcrumbs containing pointers to the visited nodes and cell indices. If the target leaf node is split, the item on top of the stack is popped to locate its immediate parent. If the parent node has enough space, a new cell is appended to it at the cell index from the breadcrumb (assuming the index is still valid). Otherwise, the parent node is split as well. This process continues recursively until either the stack is empty and we have reached the root, or there was no split on the level.

---

2 You can read more about it in the project repository: *https://databass.dev/links/21*.

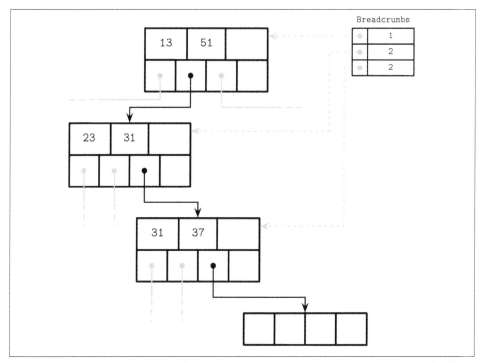

Figure 4-8. Breadcrumbs collected during lookup, containing traversed nodes and cell indices. Dotted lines represent logical links to visited nodes. Numbers in the breadcrumbs table represent indices of the followed child pointers.

Rebalancing

Some B-Tree implementations attempt to postpone split and merge operations to amortize their costs by *rebalancing* elements within the level, or moving elements from more occupied nodes to less occupied ones for as long as possible before finally performing a split or merge. This helps to improve node occupancy and may reduce the number of levels within the tree at a potentially higher maintenance cost of rebalancing.

Load balancing can be performed during insert and delete operations [GRAEFE11]. To improve space utilization, instead of splitting the node on overflow, we can transfer some of the elements to one of the sibling nodes and make space for the insertion. Similarly, during delete, instead of merging the sibling nodes, we may choose to move some of the elements from the neighboring nodes to ensure the node is at least half full.

B*-Trees keep distributing data between the neighboring nodes until both siblings are full [KNUTH98]. Then, instead of splitting a single node into two half-empty ones, the algorithm splits two nodes into three nodes, each of which is two-thirds full. SQLite uses this variant in the implementation (*https://databass.dev/links/22*). This approach improves an average occupancy by postponing splits, but requires additional tracking and balancing logic. Higher utilization also means more efficient searches, because the height of the tree is smaller and fewer pages have to be traversed on the path to the searched leaf.

Figure 4-9 shows distributing elements between the neighboring nodes, where the left sibling contains more elements than the right one. Elements from the more occupied node are moved to the less occupied one. Since balancing changes the min/max invariant of the sibling nodes, we have to update keys and pointers at the parent node to preserve it.

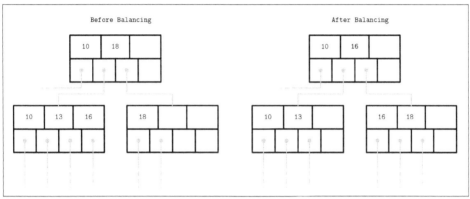

Figure 4-9. B-Tree balancing: Distributing elements between the more occupied node and the less occupied one

Load balancing is a useful technique used in many database implementations. For example, SQLite implements the *balance-siblings* algorithm (*https://databass.dev/links/23*), which is somewhat close to what we have described in this section. Balancing might add some complexity to the code, but since its use cases are isolated, it can be implemented as an optimization at a later stage.

Right-Only Appends

Many database systems use auto-incremented monotonically increasing values as primary index keys. This case opens up an opportunity for an optimization, since all the insertions are happening toward the end of the index (in the rightmost leaf), so most of the splits occur on the rightmost node on each level. Moreover, since the keys are monotonically incremented, given that the ratio of appends versus updates and deletes is low, nonleaf pages are also less fragmented than in the case of randomly ordered keys.

PostgreSQL is calling this case a *fastpath* (*https://databass.dev/links/24*). When the inserted key is strictly greater than the first key in the rightmost page, and the rightmost page has enough space to hold the newly inserted entry, the new entry is inserted into the appropriate location in the cached rightmost leaf, and the whole read path can be skipped.

SQLite has a similar concept and calls it *quickbalance* (*https://databass.dev/links/25*). When the entry is inserted on the far right end and the target node is full (i.e., it becomes the largest entry in the tree upon insertion), instead of rebalancing or splitting the node, it allocates the new rightmost node and adds its pointer to the parent (for more on implementing balancing in SQLite, see "Rebalancing" on page 70). Even though this leaves the newly created page nearly empty (instead of half empty in the case of a node split), it is very likely that the node will get filled up shortly.

Bulk Loading

If we have presorted data and want to bulk load it, or have to rebuild the tree (for example, for defragmentation), we can take the idea with right-only appends even further. Since the data required for tree creation is already sorted, during bulk loading we only need to append the items at the rightmost location in the tree.

In this case, we can avoid splits and merges altogether and compose the tree from the bottom up, writing it out level by level, or writing out higher-level nodes as soon as we have enough pointers to already written lower-level nodes.

One approach for implementing bulk loading is to write presorted data on the leaf level page-wise (rather then inserting individual elements). After the leaf page is written, we propagate its first key to the parent and use a normal algorithm for building higher B-Tree levels [RAMAKRISHNAN03]. Since appended keys are given in the sorted order, all splits in this case occur on the rightmost node.

Since B-Trees are always built starting from the bottom (leaf) level, the complete leaf level can be written out before any higher-level nodes are composed. This allows having all child pointers at hand by the time the higher levels are constructed. The main benefits of this approach are that we do not have to perform any splits or merges on disk and, at the same time, have to keep only a minimal part of the tree (i.e., all parents of the currently filling leaf node) in memory for the time of construction.

Immutable B-Trees can be created in the same manner but, unlike mutable B-Trees, they require no space overhead for subsequent modifications, since all operations on a tree are final. All pages can be completely filled up, improving occupancy and resulting into better performance.

Compression

Storing the raw, uncompressed data can induce significant overhead, and many databases offer ways to compress it to save space. The apparent trade-off here is between access speed and compression ratio: larger compression ratios can improve data size, allowing you to fetch more data in a single access, but might require more RAM and CPU cycles to compress and decompress it.

Compression can be done at different granularity levels. Even though compressing entire files can yield better compression ratios, it has limited application as a whole file has to be recompressed on an update, and more granular compression is usually better-suited for larger datasets. Compressing an entire index file is both impractical and hard to implement efficiently: to address a particular page, the whole file (or its section containing compression metadata) has to be accessed (in order to locate a compressed section), decompressed, and made available.

An alternative is to compress data page-wise. It fits our discussion well, since the algorithms we've been discussing so far use fixed-size pages. Pages can be compressed and uncompressed independently from one another, allowing you to couple compression with page loading and flushing. However, a compressed page in this case can occupy only a fraction of a disk block and, since transfers are usually done in units of disk blocks, it might be necessary to page in extra bytes [RAY95]. In Figure 4-10, you can see a compressed page (a) taking less space than the disk block. When we load this page, we also page in additional bytes that belong to the other page. With pages that span multiple disk blocks, like (b) in the same image, we have to read an additional block.

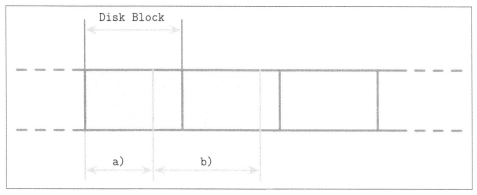

Figure 4-10. Compression and block padding

Another approach is to compress data only, either row-wise (compressing entire data records) or column-wise (compressing columns individually). In this case, page management and compression are decoupled.

Most of the open source databases reviewed while writing this book have pluggable compression methods, using available libraries such as Snappy (*https://databass.dev/links/26*), zLib (*https://databass.dev/links/27*), lz4 (*https://databass.dev/links/28*), and many others.

As compression algorithms yield different results depending on a dataset and potential objectives (e.g., compression ratio, performance, or memory overhead), we will not go into comparison and implementation details in this book. There are many overviews available that evaluate different compression algorithms for different block sizes (for example, Squash Compression Benchmark (*https://databass.dev/links/29*)), usually focusing on four metrics: memory overhead, compression performance, decompression performance, and compression ratio. These metrics are important to consider when picking a compression library.

Vacuum and Maintenance

So far we've been mostly talking about user-facing operations in B-Trees. However, there are other processes that happen in parallel with queries that maintain storage integrity, reclaim space, reduce overhead, and keep pages in order. Performing these operations in the background allows us to save some time and avoid paying the price of cleanup during inserts, updates, and deletes.

The described design of slotted pages (see "Slotted Pages" on page 52) requires maintenance to be performed on pages to keep them in good shape. For example, subsequent splits and merges in internal nodes or inserts, updates, and deletes on the leaf level can result in a page that has enough *logical* space but does not have enough *contiguous* space, since it is fragmented. Figure 4-11 shows an example of such a situation: the page still has some logical space available, but it's fragmented and is split between the two deleted (garbage) records and some remaining free space between the header/cell pointers and cells.

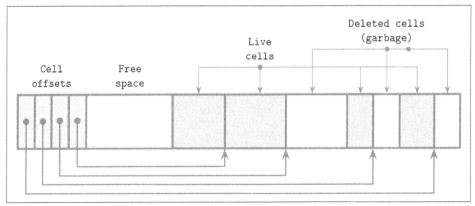

Figure 4-11. An example of a fragmented page

B-Trees are navigated from the root level. Data records that can be reached by following pointers down from the root node are *live* (addressable). Nonaddressable data records are said to be *garbage*: these records are not referenced anywhere and cannot be read or interpreted, so their contents are as good as nullified.

You can see this distinction in Figure 4-11: cells that still have pointers to them are addressable, unlike the removed or overwritten ones. Zero-filling of garbage areas is often skipped for performance reasons, as eventually these areas are overwritten by the new data anyway.

Fragmentation Caused by Updates and Deletes

Let's consider under which circumstances pages get into the state where they have nonaddressable data and have to be compacted. On the leaf level, deletes only remove cell offsets from the header, leaving the cell itself intact. After this is done, the cell is not *addressable* anymore, its contents will not appear in the query results, and nullifying it or moving neighboring cells is not necessary.

When the page is split, only offsets are trimmed and, since the rest of the page is not addressable, cells whose offsets were truncated are not reachable, so they will be overwritten whenever the new data arrives, or garbage-collected when the vacuum process kicks in.

 Some databases rely on garbage collection, and leave removed and updated cells in place for multiversion concurrency control (see "Multiversion Concurrency Control" on page 99). Cells remain accessible for the concurrently executing transactions until the update is complete, and can be collected as soon as no other thread accesses them. Some databases maintain structures that track *ghost* records, which are collected as soon as all transactions that may have seen them complete [WEIKUM01].

Since deletes only discard cell offsets and do not relocate remaining cells or physically remove the target cells to occupy the freed space, freed bytes might end up scattered across the page. In this case, we say that the page is *fragmented* and requires defragmentation.

To make a write, we often need a contiguous block of free bytes where the cell fits. To put the freed fragments back together and fix this situation, we have to *rewrite* the page.

Insert operations leave tuples in their insertion order. This does not have as significant an impact, but having naturally sorted tuples can help with cache prefetch during sequential reads.

Updates are mostly applicable to the leaf level: internal page keys are used for guided navigation and only define subtree boundaries. Additionally, updates are performed on a per-key basis, and generally do not result in structural changes in the tree, apart from the creation of overflow pages. On the leaf level, however, update operations do not change cell order and attempt to avoid page rewrite. This means that multiple versions of the cell, only one of which is addressable, may end up being stored.

Page Defragmentation

The process that takes care of space reclamation and page rewrites is called *compaction*, *vacuum*, or just *maintenance*. Page rewrites can be done synchronously on write if the page does not have enough free physical space (to avoid creating unnecessary overflow pages), but compaction is mostly referred to as a distinct, asynchronous process of walking through pages, performing garbage collection, and rewriting their contents.

This process reclaims the space occupied by dead cells, and rewrites cells in their logical order. When pages are rewritten, they may also get relocated to new positions in the file. Unused in-memory pages become available and are returned to the page cache. IDs of the newly available on-disk pages are added to the *free page list* (sometimes called a *freelist*[3]). This information has to be persisted to survive node crashes and restarts, and to make sure free space is not lost or leaked.

Summary

In this chapter, we discussed the concepts specific to on-disk B-Tree implementations, such as:

Page header
    What information is usually stored there.

Rightmost pointers
    These are not paired with separator keys, and how to handle them.

High keys
    Determine the maximum allowed key that can be stored in the node.

Overflow pages
    Allow you to store oversize and variable-size records using fixed-size pages.

---

3 For example, SQLite maintains a list of pages (*https://databass.dev/links/30*) that are not used by the database, where *trunk* pages are held in a linked list and hold addresses of freed pages.

After that, we went through some details related to root-to-leaf traversals:

- How to perform binary search with indirection pointers
- How to keep track of tree hierarchies using parent pointers or breadcrumbs

Lastly, we went through some optimization and maintenance techniques:

Rebalancing
Moves elements between neighboring nodes to reduce a number of splits and merges.

Right-only appends
Appends the new rightmost cell instead of splitting it under the assumption that it will quickly fill up.

Bulk loading
A technique for efficiently building B-Trees from scratch from sorted data.

Garbage collection
A process that rewrites pages, puts cells in key order, and reclaims space occupied by unaddressable cells.

These concepts should bridge the gap between the basic B-Tree algorithm and a real-world implementation, and help you better understand how B-Tree–based storage systems work.

Further Reading

If you'd like to learn more about the concepts mentioned in this chapter, you can refer to the following sources:

Disk-based B-Trees
Graefe, Goetz. 2011. "Modern B-Tree Techniques." *Foundations and Trends in Databases* 3, no. 4 (April): 203-402. *https://doi.org/10.1561/1900000028.*

Healey, Christopher G. 2016. *Disk-Based Algorithms for Big Data (1st Ed.).* Boca Raton: CRC Press.

CHAPTER 5

Transaction Processing and Recovery

In this book, we've taken a bottom-up approach to database system concepts: we first learned about storage structures. Now, we're ready to move to the higher-level components responsible for buffer management, lock management, and recovery, which are the prerequisites for understanding database transactions.

A *transaction* is an indivisible logical unit of work in a database management system, allowing you to represent multiple operations as a single step. Operations executed by transactions include reading and writing database records. A database transaction has to preserve atomicity, consistency, isolation, and durability. These properties are commonly referred as *ACID* [HAERDER83]:

Atomicity

Transaction steps are *indivisible*, which means that either *all* the steps associated with the transaction execute successfully or none of them do. In other words, transactions should not be applied partially. Each transaction can either *commit* (make all changes from write operations executed during the transaction visible), or *abort* (roll back all transaction side effects that haven't yet been made visible). Commit is a final operation. After an abort, the transaction can be retried.

Consistency

Consistency is an application-specific guarantee; a transaction should only bring the database from one valid state to another valid state, maintaining all database invariants (such as constraints, referential integrity, and others). Consistency is the most weakly defined property, possibly because it is the only property that is controlled by the user and not only by the database itself.

Isolation

Multiple concurrently executing transactions should be able to run without interference, as if there were no other transactions executing at the same time.

Isolation defines *when* the changes to the database state may become visible, and what changes may become visible to the concurrent transactions. Many databases use isolation levels that are weaker than the given definition of isolation for performance reasons. Depending on the methods and approaches used for concurrency control, changes made by a transaction may or may not be visible to other concurrent transactions (see "Isolation Levels" on page 96).

Durability

Once a transaction has been committed, all database state modifications have to be persisted on disk and be able to survive power outages, system failures, and crashes.

Implementing transactions in a database system, in addition to a storage structure that organizes and persists data on disk, requires several components to work together. On the node locally, the *transaction manager* coordinates, schedules, and tracks transactions and their individual steps.

The *lock manager* guards access to these resources and prevents concurrent accesses that would violate data integrity. Whenever a lock is requested, the lock manager checks if it is already held by any other transaction in shared or exclusive mode, and grants access to it if the requested access level results in no contradiction. Since exclusive locks can be held by at most one transaction at any given moment, other transactions requesting them have to wait until locks are released, or abort and retry later. As soon as the lock is released or whenever the transaction terminates, the lock manager notifies one of the pending transactions, letting it acquire the lock and continue.

The *page cache* serves as an intermediary between persistent storage (disk) and the rest of the storage engine. It stages state changes in main memory and serves as a cache for the pages that haven't been synchronized with persistent storage. All changes to a database state are first applied to the cached pages.

The *log manager* holds a history of operations (log entries) applied to cached pages but not yet synchronized with persistent storage to guarantee they won't be lost in case of a crash. In other words, the log is used to reapply these operations and reconstruct the cached state during startup. Log entries can also be used to undo changes done by the aborted transactions.

Distributed (multipartition) transactions require additional coordination and remote execution. We discuss distributed transaction protocols in Chapter 13.

Buffer Management

Most databases are built using a two-level memory hierarchy: slower persistent storage (disk) and faster main memory (RAM). To reduce the number of accesses to persistent storage, pages are *cached* in memory. When the page is requested again by the storage layer, its cached copy is returned.

Cached pages available in memory can be reused under the assumption that no other process has modified the data on disk. This approach is sometimes referenced as *virtual disk* [BAYER72]. A virtual disk read accesses physical storage only if no copy of the page is already available in memory. A more common name for the same concept is *page cache* or *buffer pool*. The page cache is responsible for caching pages read from disk in memory. In case of a database system crash or unorderly shutdown, cached contents are lost.

Since the term *page cache* better reflects the purpose of this structure, this book defaults to this name. The term *buffer pool* sounds like its primary purpose is to pool and reuse *empty* buffers, without sharing their contents, which can be a useful part of a page cache or even as a separate component, but does not reflect the entire purpose as precisely.

The problem of caching pages is not limited in scope to databases. Operating systems have the concept of a page cache, too. Operating systems utilize *unused* memory segments to transparently cache disk contents to improve performance of I/O syscalls.

Uncached pages are said to be *paged in* when they're loaded from disk. If any changes are made to the cached page, it is said to be *dirty*, until these changes are *flushed* back on disk.

Since the memory region where cached pages are held is usually substantially smaller than an entire dataset, the page cache eventually fills up and, in order to page in a new page, one of the cached pages has to be *evicted*.

In Figure 5-1, you can see the relation between the logical representation of B-Tree pages, their cached versions, and the pages on disk. The page cache loads pages into free slots out of order, so there's no direct mapping between how pages are ordered on disk and in memory.

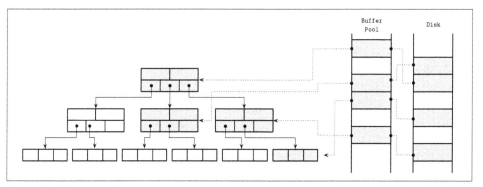

Figure 5-1. Page cache

The primary functions of a page cache can be summarized as:

- It keeps cached page contents in memory.
- It allows modifications to on-disk pages to be *buffered* together and performed against their cached versions.
- When a requested page isn't present in memory and there's enough space available for it, it is *paged in* by the page cache, and its cached version is returned.
- If an already cached page is requested, its cached version is returned.
- If there's not enough space available for the new page, some other page is *evicted* and its contents are *flushed* to disk.

Bypassing the Kernel Page Cache

Many database systems open files using O_DIRECT flag (*https://databass.dev/links/31*). This flag allows I/O system calls to bypass the kernel page cache, access the disk directly, and use database-specific buffer management. This is sometimes frowned upon by the operating systems folks.

Linus Torvalds has criticized (*https://databass.dev/links/32*) usage of O_DIRECT since it's not asynchronous and has no readahead or other means for instructing the kernel about access patterns. However, until operating systems start offering better mechanisms, O_DIRECT is still going to be useful.

We can gain some control over how the kernel evicts pages from its cache is by using fadvise (*https://databass.dev/links/33*), but this only allows us to ask the kernel to consider our opinion and does not guarantee it will actually happen. To avoid syscalls when performing I/O, we can use memory mapping, but then we lose control over caching.

Caching Semantics

All changes made to buffers are kept in memory until they are eventually written back to disk. As no other process is allowed to make changes to the backing file, this synchronization is a one-way process: from memory to disk, and not vice versa. The page cache allows the database to have more control over memory management and disk accesses. You can think of it as an application-specific equivalent of the kernel page cache: it accesses the block device directly, implements similar functionality, and serves a similar purpose. It abstracts disk accesses and decouples logical write operations from the physical ones.

Caching pages helps to keep the tree partially in memory without making additional changes to the algorithm and materializing objects in memory. All we have to do is replace disk accesses by the calls to the page cache.

When the storage engine accesses (in other words, requests) the page, we first check if its contents are already cached, in which case the cached page contents are returned. If the page contents are not yet cached, the cache translates the logical page address or page number to its physical address, loads its contents in memory, and returns its cached version to the storage engine. Once returned, the buffer with cached page contents is said to be *referenced*, and the storage engine has to hand it back to the page cache or dereference it once it's done. The page cache can be instructed to avoid evicting pages by *pinning* them.

If the page is modified (for example, a cell was appended to it), it is marked as dirty. A dirty flag set on the page indicates that its contents are out of sync with the disk and have to be flushed for durability.

Cache Eviction

Keeping caches populated is good: we can serve more reads without going to persistent storage, and more same-page writes can be buffered together. However, the page cache has a limited capacity and, sooner or later, to serve the new contents, old pages have to be evicted. If page contents are in sync with the disk (i.e., were already flushed or were never modified) and the page is not pinned or referenced, it can be evicted right away. Dirty pages have to be *flushed* before they can be evicted. Referenced pages should not be evicted while some other thread is using them.

Since triggering a flush on every eviction might be bad for performance, some databases use a separate background process that cycles through the dirty pages that are likely to be evicted, updating their disk versions. For example, PostgreSQL has a background flush writer (*https://databass.dev/links/34*) that does just that.

Another important property to keep in mind is *durability*: if the database has crashed, all data that was not flushed is lost. To make sure that all changes are persisted, flushes are coordinated by the *checkpoint* process. The checkpoint process controls the write-ahead log (WAL) and page cache, and ensures that they work in lockstep. Only log records associated with operations applied to cached pages that were flushed can be discarded from the WAL. Dirty pages cannot be evicted until this process completes.

This means there is always a trade-off between several objectives:

- Postpone flushes to reduce the number of disk accesses
- Preemptively flush pages to allow quick eviction
- Pick pages for eviction and flush in the optimal order
- Keep cache size within its memory bounds
- Avoid losing the data as it is not persisted to the primary storage

We explore several techniques that help us to improve the first three characteristics while keeping us within the boundaries of the other two.

Locking Pages in Cache

Having to perform disk I/O on each read or write is impractical: subsequent reads may request the same page, just as subsequent writes may modify the same page. Since B-Tree gets "narrower" toward the top, higher-level nodes (ones that are closer to the root) are hit for most of the reads. Splits and merges also eventually propagate to the higher-level nodes. This means there's always at least a part of a tree that can significantly benefit from being cached.

We can "lock" pages that have a high probability of being used in the nearest time. Locking pages in the cache is called *pinning*. Pinned pages are kept in memory for a longer time, which helps to reduce the number of disk accesses and improve performance [GRAEFE11].

Since each lower B-Tree node level has exponentially more nodes than the higher one, and higher-level nodes represent just a small fraction of the tree, this part of the tree can reside in memory permanently, and other parts can be paged in on demand. This means that, in order to perform a query, we won't have to make h disk accesses (as discussed in "B-Tree Lookup Complexity" on page 37, h is the height of the tree), but only hit the disk for the lower levels, for which pages are not cached.

Operations performed against a subtree may result in structural changes that contradict each other—for example, multiple delete operations causing merges followed by writes causing splits, or vice versa. Likewise for structural changes that propagate from different subtrees (structural changes occurring close to each other in time, in different parts of the tree, propagating up). These operations can be buffered together by applying changes only in memory, which can reduce the number of disk writes and amortize the operation costs, since only one write can be performed instead of multiple writes.

Prefetching and Immediate Eviction

The page cache also allows the storage engine to have fine-grained control over prefetching and eviction. It can be instructed to load pages ahead of time, before they are accessed. For example, when the leaf nodes are traversed in a range scan, the next leaves can be preloaded. Similarly, if a maintenance process loads the page, it can be evicted immediately after the process finishes, since it's unlikely to be useful for the in-flight queries. Some databases, for example, PostgreSQL (*https://databass.dev/ links/35*), use a circular buffer (in other words, FIFO page replacement policy) for large sequential scans.

Page Replacement

When cache capacity is reached, to load new pages, old ones have to be evicted. However, unless we evict pages that are least likely to be accessed again soon, we might end up loading them several times subsequently even though we could've just kept them in memory for all that time. We need to find a way to estimate the likelihood of subsequent page access to optimize this.

For this, we can say that pages should be evicted according to the *eviction policy* (also sometimes called the *page-replacement* policy). It attempts to find pages that are least likely to be accessed again any time soon. When the page is evicted from the cache, the new page can be loaded in its place.

For a page cache implementation to be performant, it needs an efficient page-replacement algorithm. An ideal page-replacement strategy would require a crystal ball that would predict the order in which pages are going to be accessed and evict only pages that will not be touched for the longest time. Since requests do not necessarily follow any specific pattern or distribution, precisely predicting behavior can be complicated, but using a right page replacement strategy can help to reduce the number of evictions.

It seems logical that we can reduce the number of evictions by simply using a larger cache. However, this does not appear to be the case. One of the examples demonstrating this dilemma this is called *Bélády's anomaly* [BEDALY69]. It shows that increasing the number of pages might increase the number of evictions if the used page-replacement algorithm is not optimal. When pages that might be required soon are evicted and then loaded again, pages start competing for space in the cache. Because of that, we need to wisely consider the algorithm we're using, so that it would improve the situation, not make it worse.

FIFO and LRU

The most naïve page-replacement strategy is first in, first out (*FIFO*). FIFO maintains a queue of page IDs in their insertion order, adding new pages to the tail of the queue. Whenever the page cache is full, it takes the element from the head of the queue to find the page that was paged in at the farthest point in time. Since it does not account for subsequent page accesses, only for page-in events, this proves to be impractical for the most real-world systems. For example, the root and topmost-level pages are paged in first and, according to this algorithm, are the first candidates for eviction, even though it's clear from the tree structure that these pages are likely to paged in again soon, if not immediately.

A natural extension of the FIFO algorithm is *least-recently used* (LRU) [TANEN-BAUM14]. It also maintains a queue of eviction candidates in insertion order, but allows you to place a page back to the tail of the queue on repeated accesses, as if this was the first time it was paged in. However, updating references and relinking nodes on every access can become expensive in a concurrent environment.

There are other LRU-based cache eviction strategies. For example, 2Q (Two-Queue LRU) maintains two queues and puts pages into the first queue during the initial access and moves them to the second *hot* queue on subsequent accesses, allowing you to distinguish between the recently and frequently accessed pages [JONSON94]. LRU-K identifies frequently referenced pages by keeping track of the last K accesses, and using this information to estimate access times on a page basis [ONEIL93].

CLOCK

In some situations, efficiency may be more important than precision. *CLOCK* algorithm variants are often used as compact, cache-friendly, and concurrent alternatives to LRU [SOUNDARARARJAN06]. Linux, for example, uses a variant of the CLOCK algorithm (*https://databass.dev/links/36*).

CLOCK-sweep holds references to pages and associated access bits in a circular buffer. Some variants use counters (*https://databass.dev/links/37*) instead of bits to account for frequency. Every time the page is accessed, its access bit is set to 1. The algorithm works by going around the circular buffer, checking access bits:

- If the access bit is 1, and the page is unreferenced, it is set to 0, and the next page is inspected.

- If the access bit is already 0, the page becomes a *candidate* and is scheduled for eviction.

- If the page is currently referenced, its access bit remains unchanged. It is assumed that the access bit of an accessed page cannot be 0, so it cannot be evicted. This makes referenced pages less likely to be replaced.

Figure 5-2 shows a circular buffer with access bits.

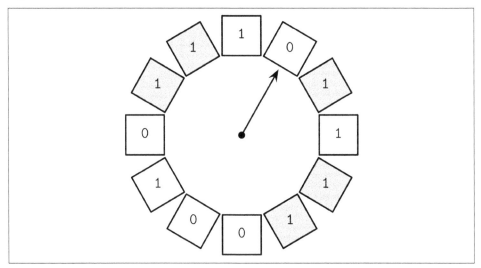

Figure 5-2. CLOCK-sweep example. Counters for currently referenced pages are shown in gray. Counters for unreferenced pages are shown in white. The arrow points to the element that will be checked next.

An advantage of using a circular buffer is that both the clock hand pointer and contents can be modified using compare-and-swap operations, and do not require additional locking mechanisms. The algorithm is easy to understand and implement and is often used in both textbooks [TANENBAUM14] and real-wold systems.

LRU is not always the best replacement strategy for a database system. Sometimes, it may be more practical to consider *usage frequency* rather than *recency* as a predictive factor. In the end, for a database system under a heavy load, recency might not be very indicative as it only represents the order in which items were accessed.

LFU

To improve the situation, we can start tracking *page reference events* rather than *page-in events*. One of the approaches allowing us to do this tracks least-frequently used (LFU) pages.

TinyLFU, a frequency-based page-eviction policy [EINZIGER17], does precisely this: instead of evicting pages based on *page-in recency*, it orders pages by *usage frequency*. It is implemented in the popular Java library called Caffeine (*https://databass.dev/links/38*).

TinyLFU uses a frequency histogram [CORMODE11] to maintain compact cache access history, since preserving an entire history might be prohibitively expensive for practical purposes.

Elements can be in one of the three queues:

- *Admission*, maintaining newly added elements, implemented using LRU policy.
- *Probation*, holding elements most likely to get evicted.
- *Protected*, holding elements that are to stay in the queue for a longer time.

Rather than choosing which elements to evict every time, this approach chooses which ones to promote for retention. Only the items that have a frequency larger than the item that would be evicted as a result of promoting them, can be moved to the probation queue. On subsequent accesses, items can get moved from probation to the protected queue. If the protected queue is full, one of the elements from it may have to be placed back into probation. More frequently accessed items have a higher chance of retention, and less frequently used ones are more likely to be evicted.

Figure 5-3 shows the logical connections between the admission, probation, and protected queues, the frequency filter, and eviction.

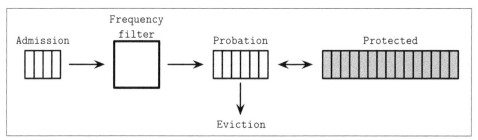

Figure 5-3. TinyLFU admission, protected, and probation queues

There are many other algorithms that can be used for optimal cache eviction. The choice of a page-replacement strategy has a significant impact on latency and the number of performed I/O operations, and has to be taken into consideration.

Recovery

Database systems are built on top of several hardware and software layers that can have their own stability and reliability problems. Database systems themselves, as well as the underlying software and hardware components, may fail. Database implementers have to consider these failure scenarios and make sure that the data that was "promised" to be written is, in fact, written.

A *write-ahead log* (WAL for short, also known as a *commit log*) is an append-only auxiliary disk-resident structure used for crash and transaction recovery. The page cache allows buffering changes to page contents in memory. Until the cached contents are flushed back to disk, the only disk-resident copy preserving the operation history is stored in the WAL. Many database systems use append-only write-ahead logs; for example, PostgreSQL (*https://databass.dev/links/39*) and MySQL (*https://data bass.dev/links/40*).

The main functionality of a write-ahead log can be summarized as:

- Allow the page cache to buffer updates to disk-resident pages while ensuring durability semantics in the larger context of a database system.
- Persist all operations on disk until the cached copies of pages affected by these operations are synchronized on disk. Every operation that modifies the database state has to be logged on disk *before* the contents of the associated pages can be modified.
- Allow lost in-memory changes to be reconstructed from the operation log in case of a crash.

In addition to this functionality, the write-ahead log plays an important role in transaction processing. It is hard to overstate the importance of the WAL as it ensures that data makes it to the persistent storage and is available in case of a crash, as uncommitted data is replayed from the log and the pre-crash database state is fully restored. In this section, we will often refer to ARIES (Algorithm for Recovery and Isolation Exploiting Semantics), a state-of-the-art recovery algorithm that is widely used and cited [MOHAN92].

PostgreSQL Versus fsync()

PostgreSQL uses checkpoints to ensure that index and data files have been updated with all information up to a certain record in the logfile. Flushing all dirty (modified) pages at once is done periodically by the checkpoint process. Synchronizing dirty page contents with disk is done by making the fsync() kernel call, which is supposed to sync dirty pages to disk, and unset the *dirty* flag on the kernel pages. As you would expect, fsync returns with an error if it isn't able to flush pages on disk.

In Linux and a few other operating systems, fsync unsets the dirty flag *even* from unsuccessfully flushed pages after I/O errors. Additionally, errors will be reported only to the file descriptors that were open at the time of failure, so fsync will *not* return any errors that have occurred *before* the descriptor it was called upon was opened [CORBET18].

Since the checkpointer doesn't keep all files open at any given point in time, it may happen that it misses error notifications. Because dirty page flags are cleared, the checkpointer will assume that data has successfully made it on disk while, in fact, it might have not been written.

A combination of these behaviors can be a source of data loss or database corruption in the presence of potentially recoverable failures. Such behaviors can be difficult to detect and some of the states they lead to may be unrecoverable. Sometimes, even triggering such behavior can be nontrivial. When working on recovery mechanisms, we should always take extra care and think through and attempt to test every possible failure scenario.

Log Semantics

The write-ahead log is append-only and its written contents are immutable, so all writes to the log are sequential. Since the WAL is an immutable, append-only data structure, readers can safely access its contents up to the latest write threshold while the writer continues appending data to the log tail.

The WAL consists of log records. Every record has a unique, monotonically increasing *log sequence number* (LSN). Usually, the LSN is represented by an internal counter or a timestamp. Since log records do not necessarily occupy an entire disk block, their contents are cached in the *log buffer* and are flushed on disk in a *force* operation. Forces happen as the log buffers fill up, and can be requested by the transaction manager or a page cache. All log records have to be flushed on disk in LSN order.

Besides individual operation records, the WAL holds records indicating transaction completion. A transaction can't be considered committed until the log is forced up to the LSN of its commit record.

To make sure the system can continue functioning correctly after a crash during rollback or recovery, some systems use *compensation log records* (CLR) during undo and store them in the log.

The WAL is usually coupled with a primary storage structure by the interface that allows *trimming* it whenever a *checkpoint* is reached. Logging is one of the most critical correctness aspects of the database, which is somewhat tricky to get right: even the slightest disagreements between log trimming and ensuring that the data has made it to the primary storage structure may cause data loss.

Checkpoints are a way for a log to know that log records up to a certain mark are fully persisted and aren't required anymore, which significantly reduces the amount of work required during the database startup. A process that forces *all* dirty pages to be flushed on disk is generally called a *sync checkpoint*, as it fully synchronizes the primary storage structure.

Flushing the entire contents on disk is rather impractical and would require pausing all running operations until the checkpoint is done, so most database systems implement *fuzzy checkpoints*. In this case, the `last_checkpoint` pointer stored in the log header contains the information about the last successful checkpoint. A fuzzy checkpoint begins with a special `begin_checkpoint` log record specifying its start, and ends with `end_checkpoint` log record, containing information about the dirty pages, and the contents of a transaction table. Until all the pages specified by this record are flushed, the checkpoint is considered to be *incomplete*. Pages are flushed asynchronously and, once this is done, the `last_checkpoint` record is updated with the LSN of the `begin_checkpoint` record and, in case of a crash, the recovery process will start from there [MOHAN92].

Operation Versus Data Log

Some database systems, for example System R [CHAMBERLIN81], use *shadow paging*: a copy-on-write technique ensuring data durability and transaction atomicity. New contents are placed into the new unpublished *shadow* page and made visible with a pointer flip, from the old page to the one holding updated contents.

Any state change can be represented by a before-image and an after-image or by corresponding redo and undo operations. Applying a *redo* operation to a *before-image* produces an *after-image*. Similarly, applying an *undo* operation to an *after-image* produces a *before-image*.

We can use a physical log (that stores complete page state or byte-wise changes to it) or a logical log (that stores operations that have to be performed against the current state) to move records or pages from one state to the other, both backward and forward in time. It is important to track the *exact* state of the pages that physical and logical log records can be applied to.

Physical logging records before and after images, requiring entire pages affected by the operation to be logged. A logical log specifies which operations have to be applied to the page, such as `"insert a data record X for key Y"`, and a corresponding undo operation, such as `"remove the value associated with Y"`.

In practice, many database systems use a combination of these two approaches, using logical logging to perform an undo (for concurrency and performance) and physical logging to perform a redo (to improve recovery time) [MOHAN92].

Steal and Force Policies

To determine when the changes made in memory have to be flushed on disk, database management systems define steal/no-steal and force/no-force policies. These policies are *mostly* applicable to the page cache, but they're better discussed in the context of recovery, since they have a significant impact on which recovery approaches can be used in combination with them.

A recovery method that allows flushing a page modified by the transaction even before the transaction has committed is called a *steal* policy. A *no-steal* policy does not allow flushing any uncommitted transaction contents on disk. To *steal* a dirty page here means flushing its in-memory contents to disk and loading a different page from disk in its place.

A *force* policy requires all pages modified by the transactions to be flushed on disk *before* the transaction commits. On the other hand, a *no-force* policy allows a transaction to commit even if some pages modified during this transaction were not yet flushed on disk. To *force* a dirty page here means to flush it on disk before the commit.

Steal and force policies are important to understand, since they have implications for transaction undo and redo. *Undo* rolls back updates to forced pages for committed transactions, while *redo* applies changes performed by committed transactions on disk.

Using the *no-steal* policy allows implementing recovery using only redo entries: old copy is contained in the page on disk and modification is stored in the log [WEI-KUM01]. With *no-force*, we potentially can buffer several updates to pages by *deferring* them. Since page contents have to be cached in memory for that time, a larger page cache may be needed.

When the *force* policy is used, crash recovery doesn't need any additional work to reconstruct the results of committed transactions, since pages modified by these transactions are already flushed. A major drawback of using this approach is that transactions take longer to commit due to the necessary I/O.

More generally, *until* the transaction commits, we need to have enough information to undo its results. If any pages touched by the transaction are flushed, we need to keep undo information in the log until it commits to be able to roll it back. Otherwise, we have to keep redo records in the log until it commits. In both cases, transaction *cannot* commit until either undo or redo records are written to the logfile.

ARIES

ARIES is a *steal/no-force* recovery algorithm. It uses physical redo to improve performance during recovery (since changes can be installed quicker) and logical undo to improve concurrency during normal operation (since logical undo operations can be applied to pages independently). It uses WAL records to implement *repeating history* during recovery, to completely reconstruct the database state before undoing uncommitted transactions, and creates compensation log records during undo [MOHAN92].

When the database system restarts after the crash, recovery proceeds in three phases:

1. The *analysis* phase identifies dirty pages in the page cache and transactions that were in progress at the time of a crash. Information about dirty pages is used to identify the starting point for the redo phase. A list of in-progress transactions is used during the undo phase to roll back incomplete transactions.

2. The *redo* phase repeats the history up to the point of a crash and restores the database to the previous state. This phase is done for incomplete transactions as well as ones that were committed but whose contents weren't flushed to persistent storage.

3. The *undo* phase rolls back all incomplete transactions and restores the database to the last consistent state. All operations are rolled back in reverse chronological order. In case the database crashes again during recovery, operations that undo transactions are logged as well to avoid repeating them.

ARIES uses LSNs for identifying log records, tracks pages modified by running transactions in the dirty page table, and uses physical redo, logical undo, and fuzzy checkpointing. Even though the paper describing this system was released in 1992, most concepts, approaches, and paradigms are still relevant in transaction processing and recovery today.

Concurrency Control

When discussing database management system architecture in "DBMS Architecture" on page 8, we mentioned that the transaction manager and lock manager work together to handle *concurrency control*. Concurrency control is a set of techniques for handling interactions between concurrently executing transactions. These techniques can be roughly grouped into the following categories:

Optimistic concurrency control (OCC)
    Allows transactions to execute concurrent read and write operations, and determines whether or not the result of the combined execution is serializable. In other words, transactions do not block each other, maintain histories of their operations, and check these histories for possible conflicts before commit. If execution results in a conflict, one of the conflicting transactions is aborted.

Multiversion concurrency control (MVCC)
    Guarantees a consistent view of the database at some point in the past identified by the timestamp by allowing multiple timestamped versions of the record to be present. MVCC can be implemented using validation techniques, allowing only one of the updating or committing transactions to win, as well as with lockless techniques such as timestamp ordering, or lock-based ones, such as two-phase locking.

Pessimistic (also known as conservative) concurrency control (PCC)
    There are both lock-based and nonlocking conservative methods, which differ in how they manage and grant access to shared resources. Lock-based approaches require transactions to maintain locks on database records to prevent other transactions from modifying locked records and assessing records that are being modified until the transaction releases its locks. Nonlocking approaches maintain

read and write operation lists and restrict execution, depending on the schedule of unfinished transactions. Pessimistic schedules can result in a deadlock when multiple transactions wait for each other to release a lock in order to proceed.

In this chapter, we concentrate on node-local concurrency control techniques. In Chapter 13, you can find information about distributed transactions and other approaches, such as deterministic concurrency control (see "Distributed Transactions with Calvin" on page 266).

Before we can further discuss concurrency control, we need to define a set of problems we're trying to solve and discuss how transaction operations overlap and what consequences this overlapping has.

Serializability

Transactions consist of read and write operations executed against the database state, and business logic (transformations, applied to the read contents). A *schedule* is a list of operations required to execute a set of transactions from the database-system perspective (i.e., only ones that interact with the database state, such as read, write, commit, or abort operations), since all other operations are assumed to be side-effect free (in other words, have no impact on the database state) [GARCIAMOLINA08].

A schedule is *complete* if contains all operations from every transaction executed in it. *Correct* schedules are logical equivalents to the original lists of operations, but their parts can be executed in parallel or get reordered for optimization purposes, as long as this does not violate ACID properties and the correctness of the results of individual transactions [WEIKUM01].

A schedule is said to be *serial* when transactions in it are executed completely independently and without any interleaving: every preceding transaction is fully executed before the next one starts. Serial execution is easy to reason about, as contrasted with all possible interleavings between several multistep transactions. However, always executing transactions one after another would significantly limit the system throughput and hurt performance.

We need to find a way to execute transaction operations concurrently, while maintaining the correctness and simplicity of a serial schedule. We can achieve this with *serializable* schedules. A schedule is serializable if it is equivalent to *some* complete serial schedule over the same set of transactions. In other words, it produces the same result as if we executed a set of transactions one after another in *some* order. Figure 5-4 shows three concurrent transactions, and possible execution histories (3! = 6 possibilities, in every possible order).

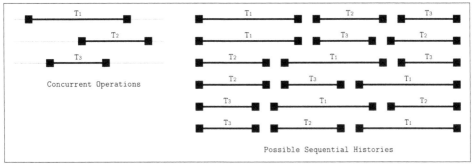

Figure 5-4. Concurrent transactions and their possible sequential execution histories

Transaction Isolation

Transactional database systems allow different isolation levels. An *isolation level* specifies how and when parts of the transaction can and should become visible to other transactions. In other words, isolation levels describe the degree to which transactions are isolated from other concurrently executing transactions, and what kinds of anomalies can be encountered during execution.

Achieving isolation comes at a cost: to prevent incomplete or temporary writes from propagating over transaction boundaries, we need additional coordination and synchronization, which negatively impacts the performance.

Read and Write Anomalies

The SQL standard [MELTON06] refers to and describes *read anomalies* that can occur during execution of concurrent transactions: dirty, nonrepeatable, and phantom reads.

A *dirty read* is a situation in which a transaction can read uncommitted changes from other transactions. For example, transaction T_1 updates a user record with a new value for the address field, and transaction T_2 reads the updated address before T_1 commits. Transaction T_1 aborts and rolls back its execution results. However, T_2 has already been able to read this value, so it has accessed the value that has never been committed.

A *nonrepeatable read* (sometimes called a fuzzy read) is a situation in which a transaction queries the *same row* twice and gets different results. For example, this can happen even if transaction T_1 reads a row, then transaction T_2 modifies it *and commits* this change. If T_1 requests the same row again before finishing its execution, the result will differ from the previous run.

If we use range reads during the transaction (i.e., read not a single data record, but a range of records), we might see *phantom records*. A *phantom read* is when a transaction queries the same *set of rows* twice and receives different results. It is similar to a nonrepeatable read, but holds for range queries.

There are also *write anomalies* with similar semantics: lost update, dirty write, and write skew.

A *lost update* occurs when transactions T_1 and T_2 both attempt to update the value of V. T_1 and T_2 read the value of V. T_1 updates V and commits, and T_2 updates V after that and commits as well. Since the transactions are not aware about each other's existence, if both of them are allowed to commit, the results of T_1 will be overwritten by the results of T_2, and the update from T_1 will be lost.

A *dirty write* is a situation in which one of the transactions takes an uncommitted value (i.e., dirty read), modifies it, and saves it. In other words, when transaction results are based on the values that have never been committed.

A *write skew* occurs when each individual transaction respects the required invariants, but their combination does not satisfy these invariants. For example, transactions T_1 and T_2 modify values of two accounts A_1 and A_2. A_1 starts with 100$ and A_2 starts with 150$. The account value is allowed to be negative, as long as the sum of the two accounts is nonnegative: A_1 + A_2 >= 0. T_1 and T_2 each attempt to withdraw 200$ from A_1 and A_2, respectively. Since at the time these transactions start A_1 + A_2 = 250$, 250$ is available in total. Both transactions assume they're preserving the invariant and are allowed to commit. After the commit, A_1 has -100$ and A_2 has -50$, which clearly violates the requirement to keep a sum of the accounts positive [FEKETE04].

Isolation Levels

The lowest (in other words, weakest) isolation level is *read uncommitted*. Under this isolation level, the transactional system allows one transaction to observe uncommitted changes of other concurrent transactions. In other words, dirty reads are allowed.

We can avoid some of the anomalies. For example, we can make sure that any read performed by the specific transaction can only read *already committed* changes. However, it is not guaranteed that if the transaction attempts to read the same data record once again at a later stage, it will see the same value. If there was a committed modification between two reads, two queries in the same transaction would yield different results. In other words, dirty reads are not permitted, but phantom and nonrepeatable reads are. This isolation level is called *read committed*. If we further disallow nonrepeatable reads, we get a *repeatable read* isolation level.

The strongest isolation level is serializability. As we already discussed in "Serializability" on page 94, it guarantees that transaction outcomes will appear in *some* order as if transactions were executed *serially* (i.e., without overlapping in time). Disallowing concurrent execution would have a substantial negative impact on the database performance. Transactions can get reordered, as long as their internal invariants hold and can be executed concurrently, but their outcomes have to appear in *some* serial order.

Figure 5-5 shows isolation levels and the anomalies they allow.

	Dirty	Non-Repeatable	Phantom
Read Uncommitted	Allowed	Allowed	Allowed
Read Committed	-	Allowed	Allowed
Repeatable Read	-	-	Allowed
Serializable	-	-	-

Figure 5-5. Isolation levels and allowed anomalies

Transactions that do not have dependencies can be executed in any order since their results are fully independent. Unlike linearizability (which we discuss in the context of distributed systems; see "Linearizability" on page 223), serializability is a property of *multiple* operations executed in *arbitrary* order. It does not imply or attempt to impose any particular order on executing transactions. *Isolation* in ACID terms means serializability [BAILIS14a]. Unfortunately, implementing serializability requires coordination. In other words, transactions executing concurrently have to coordinate to preserve invariants and impose a serial order on conflicting executions [BAILIS14b].

Some databases use *snapshot isolation*. Under snapshot isolation, a transaction can observe the state changes performed by all transactions that were committed by the time it has started. Each transaction takes a snapshot of data and executes queries against it. This snapshot cannot change during transaction execution. The transaction commits only if the values it has modified did *not* change while it was executing. Otherwise, it is aborted and rolled back.

If two transactions attempt to modify the same value, only one of them is allowed to commit. This precludes a *lost update* anomaly. For example, transactions T_1 and T_2 both attempt to modify V. They read the current value of V from the snapshot that contains changes from all transactions that were committed before they started. Whichever transaction attempts to commit first, will commit, and the other one will have to abort. The failed transactions will retry instead of overwriting the value.

A *write skew* anomaly is possible under snapshot isolation, since if two transactions read from local state, modify independent records, and preserve local invariants, they both are allowed to commit [FEKETE04]. We discuss snapshot isolation in more detail in the context of distributed transactions in "Distributed Transactions with Percolator" on page 272.

Optimistic Concurrency Control

Optimistic concurrency control assumes that transaction conflicts occur rarely and, instead of using locks and blocking transaction execution, we can validate transactions to prevent read/write conflicts with concurrently executing transactions and ensure serializability before committing their results. Generally, transaction execution is split into three phases [WEIKUM01]:

Read phase
> The transaction executes its steps in its own private context, without making any of the changes visible to other transactions. After this step, all transaction dependencies (*read set*) are known, as well as the side effects the transaction produces (*write set*).

Validation phase
> Read and write sets of concurrent transactions are checked for the presence of possible conflicts between their operations that might violate serializability. If some of the data the transaction was reading is now out-of-date, or it would overwrite some of the values written by transactions that committed during its read phase, its private context is cleared and the read phase is restarted. In other words, the validation phase determines whether or not committing the transaction preserves ACID properties.

Write phase
> If the validation phase hasn't determined any conflicts, the transaction can commit its write set from the private context to the database state.

Validation can be done by checking for conflicts with the transactions that have already been committed (*backward-oriented*), or with the transactions that are currently in the validation phase (*forward-oriented*). Validation and write phases of different transactions should be done atomically. No transaction is allowed to commit while some other transaction is being validated. Since validation and write phases are generally shorter than the read phase, this is an acceptable compromise.

Backward-oriented concurrency control ensures that for any pair of transactions T_1 and T_2, the following properties hold:

- T_1 was committed before the read phase of T_2 began, so T_2 is allowed to commit.

- T_1 was committed before the T_2 write phase, and the write set of T_1 doesn't intersect with the T_2 read set. In other words, T_1 hasn't written any values T_2 should have seen.

- The read phase of T_1 has completed before the read phase of T_2, and the write set of T_2 doesn't intersect with the read or write sets of T_1. In other words, transactions have operated on independent sets of data records, so both are allowed to commit.

This approach is efficient if validation usually succeeds and transactions don't have to be retried, since retries have a significant negative impact on performance. Of course, optimistic concurrency still has a *critical section*, which transactions can enter one at a time. Another approach that allows nonexclusive ownership for some operations is to use readers-writer locks (to allow shared access for readers) and upgradeable locks (to allow conversion of shared locks to exclusive when needed).

Multiversion Concurrency Control

Multiversion concurrency control is a way to achieve transactional consistency in database management systems by allowing multiple record versions and using monotonically incremented transaction IDs or timestamps. This allows reads and writes to proceed with a minimal coordination on the storage level, since reads can continue accessing older values until the new ones are committed.

MVCC distinguishes between *committed* and *uncommitted* versions, which correspond to value versions of committed and uncommitted transactions. The last committed version of the value is assumed to be *current*. Generally, the goal of the transaction manager in this case is to have at most one uncommitted value at a time.

Depending on the isolation level implemented by the database system, read operations may or may not be allowed to access uncommitted values [WEIKUM01]. Multiversion concurrency can be implemented using locking, scheduling, and conflict resolution techniques (such as two-phase locking), or timestamp ordering. One of the major use cases for MVCC for implementing snapshot isolation [HELLERSTEIN07].

Pessimistic Concurrency Control

Pessimistic concurrency control schemes are more conservative than optimistic ones. These schemes determine transaction conflicts while they're running and block or abort their execution.

One of the simplest pessimistic (lock-free) concurrency control schemes is *timestamp ordering*, where each transaction has a timestamp. Whether or not transaction operations are allowed to be executed is determined by whether or not any transaction with a *later* timestamp has already been committed. To implement that, the transaction manager has to maintain `max_read_timestamp` and `max_write_timestamp` per value, describing read and write operations executed by concurrent transactions.

Read operations that attempt to read a value with a timestamp lower than `max_write_timestamp` cause the transaction they belong to be aborted, since there's already a newer value, and allowing this operation would violate the transaction order.

Similarly, *write* operations with a timestamp lower than `max_read_timestamp` would conflict with a more recent read. However, *write* operations with a timestamp lower than `max_write_timestamp` are allowed, since we can safely ignore the outdated written values. This conjecture is commonly called the *Thomas Write Rule* [THOMAS79]. As soon as read or write operations are performed, the corresponding maximum timestamp values are updated. Aborted transactions restart with a *new* timestamp, since otherwise they're guaranteed to be aborted again [RAMAKRISHNAN03].

Lock-Based Concurrency Control

Lock-based concurrency control schemes are a form of pessimistic concurrency control that uses explicit locks on the database objects rather than resolving schedules, like protocols such as timestamp ordering do. Some of the downsides of using locks are contention and scalability issues [REN16].

One of the most widespread lock-based techniques is *two-phase locking* (2PL), which separates lock management into two phases:

- The *growing phase* (also called the *expanding phase*), during which all locks required by the transaction are acquired and no locks are released.

- The *shrinking phase*, during which all locks acquired during the growing phase are released.

A rule that follows from these two definitions is that a transaction cannot acquire any locks as soon as it has released at least one of them. It's important to note that 2PL does not preclude transactions from executing steps during either one of these phases; however, some 2PL variants (such as conservative 2PL) do impose these limitations.

 Despite similar names, two-phase locking is a concept that is entirely different from two-phase commit (see "Two-Phase Commit" on page 259). Two-phase commit is a protocol used for distributed multipartition transactions, while two-phase locking is a concurrency control mechanism often used to implement serializability.

Deadlocks

In locking protocols, transactions attempt to acquire locks on the database objects and, in case a lock cannot be granted immediately, a transaction has to wait until the lock is released. A situation may occur when two transactions, while attempting to acquire locks they require in order to proceed with execution, end up waiting for each other to release the other locks they hold. This situation is called a *deadlock*.

Figure 5-6 shows an example of a deadlock: T_1 holds lock L_1 and waits for lock L_2 to be released, while T_2 holds lock L_2 and waits for L_1 to be released.

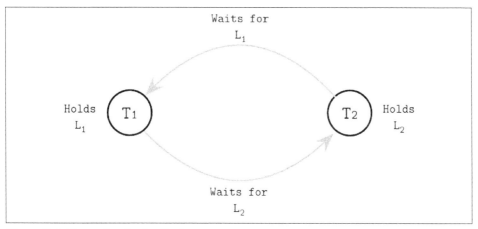

Figure 5-6. Example of a deadlock

The simplest way to handle deadlocks is to introduce timeouts and abort long-running transactions under the assumption that they might be in a deadlock. Another strategy, conservative 2PL, requires transactions to acquire all the locks before they can execute any of their operations and abort if they cannot. However, these approaches significantly limit system concurrency, and database systems mostly use a transaction manager to *detect* or *avoid* (in other words, prevent) deadlocks.

Detecting deadlocks is generally done using a *waits-for graph*, which tracks relationships between the in-flight transactions and establishes waits-for relationships between them.

Cycles in this graph indicate the presence of a deadlock: transaction T_1 is waiting for T_2 which, in turn, waits for T_1. Deadlock detection can be done *periodically* (once per time interval) or *continuously* (every time the waits-for graph is updated) [WEI-KUM01]. One of the transactions (usually, the one that attempted to acquire the lock more recently) is aborted.

To *avoid* deadlocks and restrict lock acquisition to cases that will not result in a deadlock, the transaction manager can use transaction timestamps to determine their *priority*. A lower timestamp usually implies higher priority and vice versa.

If transaction T_1 attempts to acquire a lock currently held by T_2, and T_1 has higher priority (it started before T_2), we can use one of the following restrictions to avoid deadlocks [RAMAKRISHNAN03]:

Wait-die
> T_1 is allowed to block and *wait* for the lock. Otherwise, T_1 is aborted and restarted. In other words, a transaction can be blocked only by a transaction with a higher timestamp.

Wound-wait
> T_2 is aborted and restarted (T_1 *wounds* T_2). Otherwise (if T_2 has started before T_1), T_1 is allowed to wait. In other words, a transaction can be blocked only by a transaction with a lower timestamp.

Transaction processing requires a scheduler to handle deadlocks. At the same time, latches (see "Latches" on page 103) rely on the programmer to ensure that deadlocks cannot happen and do not rely on deadlock avoidance mechanisms.

Locks

If two transactions are submitted concurrently, modifying overlapping segments of data, neither one of them should observe partial results of the other one, hence maintaining logical consistency. Similarly, two threads from the same transaction have to observe the same database contents, and have access to each other's data.

In transaction processing, there's a distinction between the mechanisms that guard the logical and physical data integrity. The two concepts responsible logical and physical integrity are, correspondingly, *locks* and *latches*. The naming is somewhat unfortunate since what's called a latch here is usually referred to as a lock in systems programming, but we'll clarify the distinction and implications in this section.

Locks are used to isolate and schedule overlapping transactions and manage database contents but not the internal storage structure, and are acquired on the key. Locks can guard either a specific key (whether it's existing or nonexisting) or a range of keys. Locks are generally stored and managed outside of the tree implementation and represent a higher-level concept, managed by the database lock manager.

Locks are more heavyweight than latches and are held for the duration of the transaction.

Latches

On the other hand, latches guard the *physical* representation: leaf page contents are modified during insert, update, and delete operations. Nonleaf page contents and a tree structure are modified during operations resulting in splits and merges that propagate from leaf under- and overflows. Latches guard the physical tree representation (page contents and the tree structure) during these operations and are obtained on the page level. Any page has to be latched to allow safe concurrent access to it. Lockless concurrency control techniques still have to use latches.

Since a single modification on the leaf level might propagate to higher levels of the B-Tree, latches might have to be obtained on multiple levels. Executing queries should not be able to observe pages in an inconsistent state, such as incomplete writes or partial node splits, during which data might be present in both the source and target node, or not yet propagated to the parent.

The same rules apply to parent or sibling pointer updates. A general rule is to hold a latch for the smallest possible duration—namely, when the page is read or updated—to increase concurrency.

Interferences between concurrent operations can be roughly grouped into three categories:

- *Concurrent reads*, when several threads access the same page without modifying it.
- *Concurrent updates*, when several threads attempt to make modifications to the same page.
- *Reading while writing*, when one of the threads is trying to modify the page contents, and the other one is trying to access the same page for a read.

These scenarios also apply to accesses that overlap with database maintenance (such as background processes, as described in "Vacuum and Maintenance" on page 74).

Readers-writer lock

The simplest latch implementation would grant exclusive read/write access to the requesting thread. However, most of the time, we do not need to isolate *all* the processes from each other. For example, reads can access pages concurrently without causing any trouble, so we only need to make sure that multiple concurrent *writers* do not overlap, and *readers* do not overlap with *writers*. To achieve this level of granularity, we can use a *readers-writer lock* or RW lock.

An RW lock allows multiple readers to access the object concurrently, and only writers (which we usually have fewer of) have to obtain exclusive access to the object. Figure 5-7 shows the compatibility table for readers-writer locks: only readers can share lock ownership, while all other combinations of readers and writers should obtain exclusive ownership.

	Reader	Writer
Reader	Shared	Exclusive
Writer	Exclusive	Exclusive

Figure 5-7. Readers-writer lock compatibility table

In Figure 5-8 (a), we have multiple readers accessing the object, while the writer is waiting for its turn, since it can't modify the page while readers access it. In Figure 5-8 (b), `writer 1` holds an exclusive lock on the object, while another writer and three readers have to wait.

Figure 5-8. Readers-writer locks

Since two overlapping reads attempting to access the same page do not require synchronization other than preventing the page from being fetched from disk by the page cache twice, reads can be safely executed concurrently in shared mode. As soon as writes come into play, we need to isolate them from both concurrent reads and other writes.

Busy-Wait and Queueing Techniques

To manage shared access to pages, we can either use blocking algorithms, which deschedule threads and wake them up as soon as they can proceed, or use busy-wait algorithms. Busy-wait algorithms allow threads to wait for insignificant amounts of time instead of handing control back to the scheduler.

Queuing is usually implemented using compare-and-swap instructions, used to perform operations guaranteeing lock acquisition and queue update atomicity. If the queue is empty, the thread obtains access immediately. Otherwise, the thread appends itself to the waiting queue and spins on the variable that can be updated only by the thread preceding it in the queue. This helps to reduce the amount of CPU traffic for lock acquisition and release [MELLORCRUMMEY91].

Latch crabbing

The most straightforward approach for latch acquisition is to grab all the latches on the way from the root to the target leaf. This creates a concurrency bottleneck and can be avoided in most cases. The time during which a latch is held should be minimized. One of the optimizations that can be used to achieve that is called *latch crabbing* (or latch coupling) [RAMAKRISHNAN03].

Latch crabbing is a rather simple method that allows holding latches for less time and releasing them as soon as it's clear that the executing operation does not require them anymore. On the read path, as soon as the child node is located and its latch is acquired, the parent node's latch can be released.

During insert, the parent latch can be released if the operation is guaranteed not to result in structural changes that can propagate to it. In other words, the parent latch can be released if the child node is not full.

Similarly, during deletes, if the child node holds enough elements and the operation will not cause sibling nodes to merge, the latch on the parent node is released.

Figure 5-9 shows a root-to-leaf pass during insert:

- a) The write latch is acquired on the root level.
- b) The next-level node is located, and its write latch is acquired. The node is checked for potential structural changes. Since the node is not full, the parent latch can be released.
- c) The operation descends to the next level. The write latch is acquired, the target leaf node is checked for potential structural changes, and the parent latch is released.

This approach is optimistic: most insert and delete operations do not cause structural changes that propagate multiple levels up. In fact, the probability of structural changes decreases at higher levels. Most of the operations only require the latch on the target node, and the number of cases when the parent latch has to be retained is relatively small.

If the child page is still not loaded in the page cache, we can either latch a future loading page, or release a parent latch and restart the root-to-leaf pass after the page is loaded to reduce contention. Restarting root-to-leaf traversal sounds rather expensive, but in reality, we have to perform it rather infrequently, and can employ mechanisms to detect whether or not there were any structural changes at higher levels since the time of traversal [GRAEFE10].

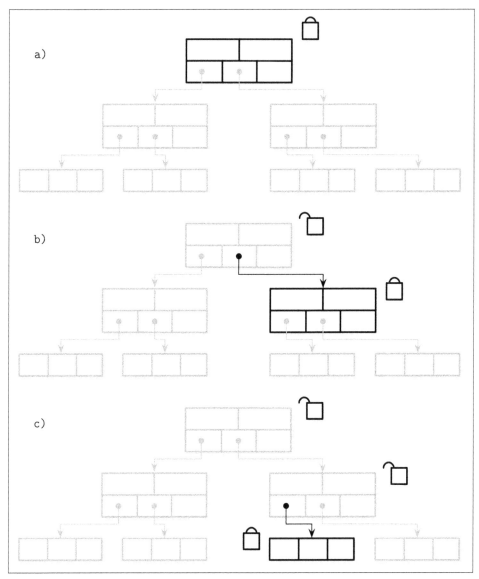

Figure 5-9. Latch crabbing during insert

Latch Upgrading and Pointer Chasing

Instead of acquiring latches during traversal in an exclusive mode right away, *latch upgrading* can be employed instead. This approach involves acquisition of shared locks along the search path and *upgrading* them to exclusive locks when necessary.

Write operations first acquire exclusive locks only at the leaf level. If the leaf has to be split or merged, the algorithm walks up the tree and attempts to *upgrade* a shared lock that the parent holds, acquiring exclusive ownership of latches for the affected portion of the tree (i.e., nodes that will also be split or merged as a result of that operation). Since multiple threads might attempt to acquire exclusive locks on one of the higher levels, one of them has to wait or restart.

You might have noticed that the mechanisms described so far all start by acquiring a latch on the root node. Every request has to go through the root node, and it quickly becomes a bottleneck. At the same time, the root is always the last to be split, since all of its children have to fill up first. This means that the root node can *always* be latched optimistically, and the price of a retry (*pointer chasing*) is seldom paid.

Blink-Trees

B^{link}-Trees build on top of B*-Trees (see "Rebalancing" on page 70) and add *high keys* (see "Node High Keys" on page 64) and *sibling link* pointers [LEHMAN81]. A high key indicates the highest possible subtree key. Every node but root in a B^{link}-Tree has two pointers: a child pointer descending from the parent and a sibling link from the left node residing on the same level.

B^{link}-Trees allow a state called *half-split*, where the node is already referenced by the sibling pointer, but not by the child pointer from its parent. Half-split is identified by checking the node high key. If the search key exceeds the high key of the node (which violates the high key invariant), the lookup algorithm concludes that the structure has been changed concurrently and follows the sibling link to proceed with the search.

The pointer has to be quickly added to the parent guarantee the best performance, but the search process doesn't have to be aborted and restarted, since all elements in the tree are accessible. The advantage here is that we do not have to hold the parent lock when descending to the child level, even if the child is going to be split: we can make a new node visible through its sibling link and update the parent pointer lazily without sacrificing correctness [GRAEFE10].

While this is slightly less efficient than descending directly from the parent and requires accessing an extra page, this results in correct root-to-leaf descent while simplifying concurrent access. Since splits are a relatively infrequent operation and B-Trees rarely shrink, this case is exceptional, and its cost is insignificant. This approach has quite a few benefits: it reduces contention, prevents holding a parent lock during splits, and reduces the number of locks held during tree structure modification to a constant number. More importantly, it allows reads concurrent to structural tree changes, and prevents deadlocks otherwise resulting from concurrent modifications ascending to the parent nodes.

Summary

In this chapter, we discussed the storage engine components responsible for transaction processing and recovery. When implementing transaction processing, we are presented with two problems:

- To improve efficiency, we need to allow concurrent transaction execution.
- To preserve correctness, we have to ensure that concurrently executing transactions preserve ACID properties.

Concurrent transaction execution can cause different kinds of read and write anomalies. Presence or absence of these anomalies is described and limited by implementing different isolation levels. Concurrency control approaches determine how transactions are scheduled and executed.

The page cache is responsible for reducing the number of disk accesses: it caches pages in memory and allows read and write access to them. When the cache reaches its capacity, pages are evicted and flushed back on disk. To make sure that unflushed changes are not lost in case of node crashes and to support transaction rollback, we use write-ahead logs. The page cache and write-ahead logs are coordinated using force and steal policies, ensuring that every transaction can be executed efficiently and rolled back without sacrificing durability.

Further Reading

If you'd like to learn more about the concepts mentioned in this chapter, you can refer to the following sources:

Transaction processing and recovery, generally

Weikum, Gerhard, and Gottfried Vossen. 2001. *Transactional Information Systems: Theory, Algorithms, and the Practice of Concurrency Control and Recovery.* San Francisco: Morgan Kaufmann Publishers Inc.

Bernstein, Philip A. and Eric Newcomer. 2009. *Principles of Transaction Processing.* San Francisco: Morgan Kaufmann.

Graefe, Goetz, Guy, Wey & Sauer, Caetano. 2016. "Instant Recovery with Write-Ahead Logging: Page Repair, System Restart, Media Restore, and System Failover, (2nd Ed.)" in *Synthesis Lectures on Data Management* 8, 1-113. 10.2200/S00710ED2V01Y201603DTM044.

Mohan, C., Don Haderle, Bruce Lindsay, Hamid Pirahesh, and Peter Schwarz. 1992. "ARIES: a transaction recovery method supporting fine-granularity locking and partial rollbacks using write-ahead logging." *Transactions on Database Systems* 17, no. 1 (March): 94-162. *https://doi.org/10.1145/128765.128770.*

Concurrency control in B-Trees

Wang, Paul. 1991. "An In-Depth Analysis of Concurrent B-Tree Algorithms." MIT Technical Report. *https://apps.dtic.mil/dtic/tr/fulltext/u2/a232287.pdf.*

Goetz Graefe. 2010. A survey of B-tree locking techniques. ACM Trans. Database Syst. 35, 3, Article 16 (July 2010), 26 pages.

Parallel and concurrent data structures

McKenney, Paul E. 2012. "Is Parallel Programming Hard, And, If So,What Can You Do About It?" *https://arxiv.org/abs/1701.00854.*

Herlihy, Maurice and Nir Shavit. 2012. *The Art of Multiprocessor Programming, Revised Reprint (1st Ed.).* San Francisco: Morgan Kaufmann.

Chronological developments in the field of transaction processing

Diaconu, Cristian, Craig Freedman, Erik Ismert, Per-Åke Larson, Pravin Mittal, Ryan Stonecipher, Nitin Verma, and Mike Zwilling. 2013. "Hekaton: SQL Server's Memory-Optimized OLTP Engine." In *Proceedings of the 2013 ACM SIGMOD International Conference on Management of Data (SIGMOD '13)*, 1243-1254. New York: Association for Computing Machinery. *https://doi.org/10.1145/2463676.2463710.*

Kimura, Hideaki. 2015. "FOEDUS: OLTP Engine for a Thousand Cores and NVRAM." In *Proceedings of the 2015 ACM SIGMOD International Conference on*

Management of Data (SIGMOD '15), 691-706. *https://doi.org/10.1145/2723372.2746480.*

Yu, Xiangyao, Andrew Pavlo, Daniel Sanchez, and Srinivas Devadas. 2016. "Tic-Toc: Time Traveling Optimistic Concurrency Control." In *Proceedings of the 2016 International Conference on Management of Data (SIGMOD '16), 1629-1642. https://doi.org/10.1145/2882903.2882935.*

Kim, Kangnyeon, Tianzheng Wang, Ryan Johnson, and Ippokratis Pandis. 2016. "ERMIA: Fast Memory-Optimized Database System for Heterogeneous Work-loads." In *Proceedings of the 2016 International Conference on Management of Data (SIGMOD '16), 1675-1687. https://doi.org/10.1145/2882903.2882905.*

Lim, Hyeontaek, Michael Kaminsky, and David G. Andersen. 2017. "Cicada: Dependably Fast Multi-Core In-Memory Transactions." In *Proceedings of the 2017 ACM International Conference on Management of Data (SIGMOD '17), 21-35. https://doi.org/10.1145/3035918.3064015.*

CHAPTER 6

B-Tree Variants

B-Tree variants have a few things in common: tree structure, balancing through splits and merges, and lookup and delete algorithms. Other details, related to concurrency, on-disk page representation, links between sibling nodes, and maintenance processes, may vary between implementations.

In this chapter, we'll discuss several techniques that can be used to implement efficient B-Trees and structures that employ them:

- *Copy-on-write B-Trees* are structured like B-Trees, but their nodes are immutable and are not updated in place. Instead, pages are copied, updated, and written to new locations.

- *Lazy B-Trees* reduce the number of I/O requests from subsequent same-node writes by *buffering* updates to nodes. In the next chapter, we also cover two-component LSM trees (see "Two-component LSM Tree" on page 132), which take buffering a step further to implement fully immutable B-Trees.

- *FD-Trees* take a different approach to buffering, somewhat similar to LSM Trees (see "LSM Trees" on page 130). FD-Trees buffer updates in a small B-Tree. As soon as this tree fills up, its contents are written into an immutable run. Updates propagate between *levels* of immutable runs in a cascading manner, from higher levels to lower ones.

- *Bw-Trees* separate B-Tree nodes into several smaller parts that are written in an append-only manner. This reduces costs of small writes by batching updates to the different nodes together.

- *Cache-oblivious B-Trees* allow treating on-disk data structures in a way that is very similar to how we build in-memory ones.

Copy-on-Write

Some databases, rather than building complex latching mechanisms, use the *copy-on-write* technique to guarantee data integrity in the presence of concurrent operations. In this case, whenever the page is about to be modified, its contents are copied, the copied page is modified instead of the original one, and a parallel tree hierarchy is created.

Old tree versions remain accessible for readers that run concurrently to the writer, while writers accessing modified pages have to wait until preceding write operations are complete. After the new page hierarchy is created, the pointer to the topmost page is atomically updated. In Figure 6-1, you can see a new tree being created parallel to the old one, reusing the untouched pages.

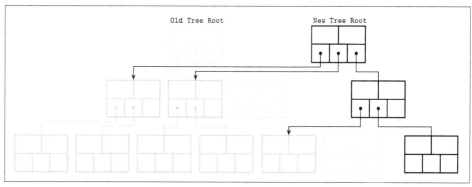

Figure 6-1. Copy-on-write B-Trees

An obvious downside of this approach is that it requires more space (even though old versions are retained only for brief time periods, since pages can be reclaimed immediately after concurrent operations using the old pages complete) and processor time, as entire page contents have to be copied. Since B-Trees are generally shallow, the simplicity and advantages of this approach often still outweigh the downsides.

The biggest advantage of this approach is that readers require no synchronization, because written pages are immutable and can be accessed without additional latching. Since writes are performed against copied pages, readers do not block writers. No operation can observe a page in an incomplete state, and a system crash cannot leave pages in a corrupted state, since the topmost pointer is switched only when all page modifications are done.

Implementing Copy-on-Write: LMDB

One of the storage engines using copy-on-write is the Lightning Memory-Mapped Database (LMDB (*https://databass.dev/links/85*)), which is a key-value store used by the OpenLDAP project. Due to its design and architecture, LMDB doesn't require a page cache, a write-ahead log, checkpointing, or compaction.[1]

LMDB is implemented as a single-level data store, which means that read and write operations are satisfied directly through the memory map, without additional application-level caching in between. This also means that pages require no additional materialization and reads can be served directly from the memory map without copying data to the intermediate buffer. During the update, every branch node on the path from the root to the target leaf is copied and potentially modified: nodes for which updates propagate are changed, and the rest of the nodes remain intact.

LMDB holds only two versions (*https://databass.dev/links/88*) of the root node: the latest version, and the one where new changes are going to be committed. This is sufficient since all writes have to go through the root node. After the new root is created, the old one becomes unavailable for new reads and writes. As soon as the reads referencing old tree sections complete, their pages are reclaimed and can be reused. Because of LMDB's append-only design, it does not use sibling pointers and has to ascend back to the parent node during sequential scans.

With this design, leaving stale data in copied nodes is impractical: there is already a copy that can be used for MVCC and satisfy ongoing read transactions. The database structure is inherently multiversioned, and readers can run without any locks as they do not interfere with writers in any way.

Abstracting Node Updates

To update the page on disk, one way or the other, we have to first update its in-memory representation. However, there are a few ways to represent a node in memory: we can access the cached version of the node directly, do it through the wrapper object, or create its in-memory representation native to the implementation language.

In languages with an unmanaged memory model, raw binary data stored in B-Tree nodes can be reinterpreted and native pointers can be used to manipulate it. In this case, the node is defined in terms of structures, which use raw binary data behind the

---

[1] To learn more about LMDB, see the code comments (*https://databass.dev/links/86*) and the presentation (*https://databass.dev/links/87*).

pointer and runtime casts. Most often, they point to the memory area managed by the page cache or use memory mapping.

Alternatively, B-Tree nodes can be materialized into objects or structures native to the language. These structures can be used for inserts, updates, and deletes. During flush, changes are applied to pages in memory and, subsequently, on disk. This approach has the advantage of simplifying concurrent accesses since changes to underlying raw pages are managed separately from accesses to intermediate objects, but results in a higher memory overhead, since we have to store two versions (raw binary and language-native) of the same page in memory.

The third approach is to provide access to the buffer backing the node through the wrapper object that materializes changes in the B-Tree as soon as they're performed. This approach is most often used in languages with a managed memory model. Wrapper objects apply the changes to the backing buffers.

Managing on-disk pages, their cached versions, and their in-memory representations separately allows them to have different life cycles. For example, we can buffer insert, update, and delete operations, and reconcile changes made in memory with the original on-disk versions during reads.

Lazy B-Trees

Some algorithms (in the scope of this book, we call them lazy B-Trees[2]) reduce costs of updating the B-Tree and use more lightweight, concurrency- and update-friendly in-memory structures to buffer updates and propagate them with a delay.

WiredTiger

Let's take a look at how we can use buffering to implement a lazy B-Tree. For that, we can materialize B-Tree nodes in memory as soon as they are paged in and use this structure to store updates until we're ready to flush them.

A similar approach is used by WiredTiger (*https://databass.dev/links/89*), a now-default MongoDB storage engine. Its row store B-Tree implementation uses different formats for in-memory and on-disk pages. Before in-memory pages are persisted, they have to go through the reconciliation process.

---

2 This is not a commonly recognized name, but since the B-Tree variants we're discussing here share one property—buffering B-Tree updates in intermediate structures instead of applying them to the tree directly—we'll use the term *lazy*, which rather precisely defines this property.

In Figure 6-2, you can see a schematic representation of WiredTiger pages and their composition in a B-Tree. A *clean* page consists of just an index, initially constructed from the on-disk page image. Updates are first saved into the *update buffer*.

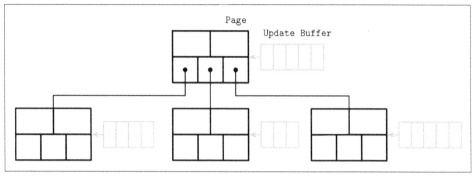

Figure 6-2. WiredTiger: high-level overview

Update buffers are accessed during reads: their contents are merged with the original on-disk page contents to return the most recent data. When the page is flushed, update buffer contents are reconciled with page contents and persisted on disk, over-writing the original page. If the size of the reconciled page is greater than the maximum, it is split into multiple pages. Update buffers are implemented using skiplists, which have a complexity similar to search trees [PAPADAKIS93] but have a better concurrency profile [PUGH90a].

Figure 6-3 shows that both clean and dirty pages in WiredTiger have in-memory versions, and reference a base image on disk. Dirty pages have an update buffer in addition to that.

The main advantage here is that the page updates and structural modifications (splits and merges) are performed by the background thread, and read/write processes do not have to wait for them to complete.

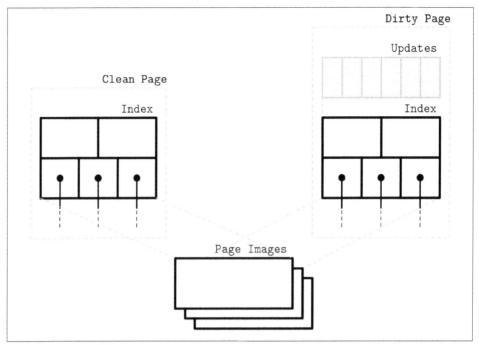

Figure 6-3. WiredTiger pages

Lazy-Adaptive Tree

Rather than buffering updates to individual nodes, we can group nodes into subtrees, and attach an update buffer for batching operations *to each subtree*. Update buffers in this case will track all operations performed against the subtree top node and its descendants. This algorithm is called *Lazy-Adaptive Tree* (LA-Tree) [AGRAWAL09].

When inserting a data record, a new entry is first added to the root node update buffer. When this buffer becomes full, it is emptied by copying and propagating the changes to the buffers in the lower tree levels. This operation can continue recursively if the lower levels fill up as well, until it finally reaches the leaf nodes.

In Figure 6-4, you see an LA-Tree with cascaded buffers for nodes grouped in corresponding subtrees. Gray boxes represent changes that propagated from the root buffer.

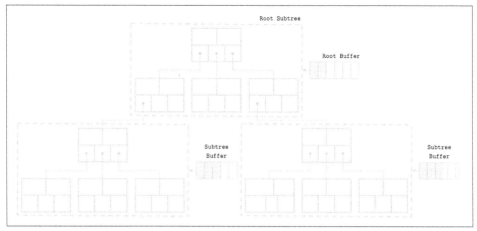

Figure 6-4. LA-Tree

Buffers have hierarchical dependencies and are *cascaded*: all the updates propagate from higher-level buffers to the lower-level ones. When the updates reach the leaf level, batched insert, update, and delete operations are performed there, applying all changes to the tree contents and its structure at once. Instead of performing subsequent updates on pages separately, pages can be updated in a single run, requiring fewer disk accesses and structural changes, since splits and merges propagate to the higher levels in batches as well.

The buffering approaches described here optimize tree update time by batching write operations, but in slightly different ways. Both algorithms require additional lookups in in-memory buffering structures and merge/reconciliation with stale disk data.

FD-Trees

Buffering is one of the ideas that is widely used in database storage: it helps to avoid many small random writes and performs a single larger write instead. On HDDs, random writes are slow because of the head positioning. On SSDs, there are no moving parts, but the extra write I/O imposes an additional garbage collection penalty.

Maintaining a B-Tree requires a lot of random writes—leaf-level writes, splits, and merges propagating to the parents—but what if we could avoid random writes and node updates altogether?

So far we've discussed buffering updates to individual nodes or groups of nodes by creating auxiliary buffers. An alternative approach is to group updates targeting *different nodes* together by using append-only storage and merge processes, an idea that has also inspired LSM Trees (see "LSM Trees" on page 130). This means that any write we perform does not require locating a target node for the write: all updates are simply appended. One of the examples of using this approach for indexing is called Flash Disk Tree (FD-Tree) [LI10].

An FD-Tree consists of a small mutable *head tree* and multiple immutable sorted runs. This approach limits the surface area, where random write I/O is required, to the head tree: a small B-Tree buffering the updates. As soon as the head tree fills up, its contents are transferred to the immutable *run*. If the size of the newly written run exceeds the threshold, its contents are merged with the next level, gradually propagating data records from upper to lower levels.

Fractional Cascading

To maintain pointers between the levels, FD-Trees use a technique called *fractional cascading* [CHAZELLE86]. This approach helps to reduce the cost of locating an item in the cascade of sorted arrays: you perform log n steps to find the searched item in the first array, but subsequent searches are significantly cheaper, since they start the search from the closest match from the previous level.

Shortcuts between the levels are made by building *bridges* between the neighbor-level arrays to minimize the *gaps*: element groups without pointers from higher levels. Bridges are built by *pulling* elements from lower levels to the higher ones, if they don't already exist there, and pointing to the location of the pulled element in the lower-level array.

Since [CHAZELLE86] solves a search problem in computational geometry, it describes bidirectional bridges, and an algorithm for restoring the gap size invariant that we won't be covering here. We describe only the parts that are applicable to database storage and FD-Trees in particular.

We could create a mapping from every element of the higher-level array to the closest element on the next level, but that would cause too much overhead for pointers and their maintenance. If we were to map only the items that already exist on a higher level, we could end up in a situation where the gaps between the elements are too large. To solve this problem, we pull every Nth item from the lower-level array to the higher one.

For example, if we have multiple sorted arrays:

```
A1 = [12, 24, 32, 34, 39]
A2 = [22, 25, 28, 30, 35]
A3 = [11, 16, 24, 26, 30]
```

We can bridge the gaps between elements by pulling every other element from the array with a higher index to the one with a lower index in order to simplify searches:

```
A1 = [12, 24, 25, 30, 32, 34, 39]
A2 = [16, 22, 25, 26, 28, 30, 35]
A3 = [11, 16, 24, 26, 30]
```

Now, we can use these pulled elements to create *bridges* (or *fences* as the FD-Tree paper calls them): pointers from higher-level elements to their counterparts on the lower levels, as Figure 6-5 shows.

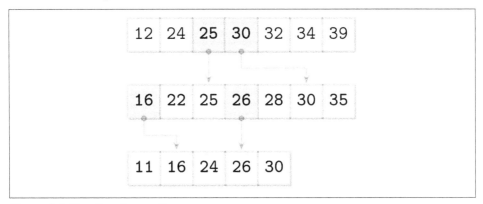

Figure 6-5. Fractional cascading

To search for elements in *all* these arrays, we perform a binary search on the highest level, and the search space on the next level is reduced significantly, since now we are forwarded to the approximate location of the searched item by following a bridge. This allows us to connect multiple sorted runs and reduce the costs of searching in them.

Logarithmic Runs

An FD-Tree combines fractional cascading with creating *logarithmically sized sorted runs*: immutable sorted arrays with sizes increasing by a factor of k, created by merging the previous level with the current one.

The highest-level run is created when the head tree becomes full: its leaf contents are written to the first level. As soon as the head tree fills up again, its contents are merged with the first-level items. The merged result replaces the old version of the first run. The lower-level runs are created when the sizes of the higher-level ones reach a threshold. If a lower-level run already exists, it is replaced by the result of merging its contents with the contents of a higher level. This process is quite similar to compaction in LSM Trees, where immutable table contents are merged to create larger tables.

Figure 6-6 shows a schematic representation of an FD-Tree, with a head B-Tree on the top, two logarithmic runs L1 and L2, and bridges between them.

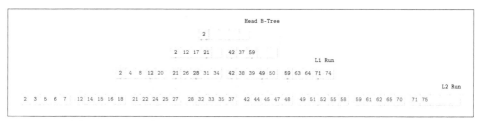

Figure 6-6. Schematic FD-Tree overview

To keep items in all sorted runs addressable, FD-Trees use an adapted version of fractional cascading, where *head elements* from lower-level pages are propagated as pointers to the higher levels. Using these pointers, the cost of searching in lower-level trees is reduced, since the search was already partially done on a higher level and can continue from the closest match.

Since FD-Trees do not update pages in place, and it may happen that data records for the same key are present on several levels, the FD-Trees delete work by inserting tombstones (the FD-Tree paper calls them *filter entries*) that indicate that the data record associated with a corresponding key is marked for deletion, and all data records for that key in the lower levels have to be discarded. When tombstones propagate all the way to the lowest level, they can be discarded, since it is guaranteed that there are no items they can shadow anymore.

Bw-Trees

Write amplification is one of the most significant problems with in-place update implementations of B-Trees: subsequent updates to a B-Tree page may require updating a disk-resident page copy on every update. The second problem is space amplification: we reserve extra space to make updates possible. This also means that for each transferred *useful* byte carrying the requested data, we have to transfer some empty bytes and the rest of the page. The third problem is complexity in solving concurrency problems and dealing with latches.

To solve all three problems at once, we have to take an approach entirely different from the ones we've discussed so far. Buffering updates helps with write and space amplification, but offers no solution to concurrency issues.

We can batch updates to different nodes by using append-only storage, link nodes together into chains, and use an in-memory data structure that allows *installing* pointers between the nodes with a single compare-and-swap operation, making the tree lock-free. This approach is called a *Buzzword-Tree* (Bw-Tree) [LEVANDOSKI14] .

Update Chains

A Bw-Tree writes a *base node* separately from its modifications. Modifications (*delta nodes*) form a chain: a linked list from the newest modification, through older ones, with the base node in the end. Each update can be stored separately, without needing to rewrite the existing node on disk. Delta nodes can represent inserts, updates (which are indistinguishable from inserts), or deletes.

Since the sizes of base and delta nodes are unlikely to be page aligned, it makes sense to store them contiguously, and because neither base nor delta nodes are modified during update (all modifications just prepend a node to the existing linked list), we do not need to reserve any extra space.

Having a node as a logical, rather than physical, entity is an interesting paradigm change: we do not need to pre-allocate space, require nodes to have a fixed size, or even keep them in contiguous memory segments. This certainly has a downside: during a read, all deltas have to be traversed and applied to the base node to reconstruct the actual node state. This is somewhat similar to what LA-Trees do (see "Lazy-Adaptive Tree" on page 116): keeping updates separate from the main structure and replaying them on read.

Taming Concurrency with Compare-and-Swap

It would be quite costly to maintain an on-disk tree structure that allows prepending items to child nodes: it would require us to constantly update parent nodes with pointers to the freshest delta. This is why Bw-Tree nodes, consisting of a chain of deltas and the base node, have logical identifiers and use an in-memory *mapping table* from the identifiers to their locations on disk. Using this mapping also helps us to get rid of latches: instead of having exclusive ownership during write time, the Bw-Tree uses compare-and-swap operations on physical offsets in the mapping table.

Figure 6-7 shows a simple Bw-Tree. Each logical node consists of a single base node and multiple linked delta nodes.

Figure 6-7. Bw-Tree. Dotted lines represent virtual links between the nodes, resolved using the mapping table. Solid lines represent actual data pointers between the nodes.

To update a Bw-Tree node, the algorithm executes the following steps:

1. The target logical *leaf* node is located by traversing the tree from root to leaf. The mapping table contains virtual links to target base nodes or the latest delta nodes in the update chain.

2. A new delta node is created with a pointer to the base node (or to the latest delta node) located during step 1.

3. The mapping table is updated with a pointer to the new delta node created during step 2.

An update operation during step 3 can be done using compare-and-swap, which is an atomic operation, so all reads, concurrent to the pointer update, are ordered either *before* or *after* the write, without blocking either the readers or the writer. Reads ordered *before* follow the old pointer and do not see the new delta node, since it was not yet installed. Reads ordered *after* follow the new pointer, and observe the update. If two threads attempt to install a new delta node to the same logical node, only one of them can succeed, and the other one has to retry the operation.

Structural Modification Operations

A Bw-Tree is logically structured like a B-Tree, which means that nodes still might grow to be too large (overflow) or shrink to be almost empty (underflow) and require structure modification operations (SMOs), such as splits and merges. The semantics of splits and merges here are similar to those of B-Trees (see "B-Tree Node Splits" on page 39 and "B-Tree Node Merges" on page 41), but their implementation is different.

Split SMOs start by consolidating the logical contents of the splitting node, applying deltas to its base node, and creating a new page containing elements to the right of the split point. After this, the process proceeds in two steps [WANG18]:

1. *Split*—A special *split delta* node is appended to the splitting node to notify the readers about the ongoing split. The split delta node holds a midpoint separator key to invalidate records in the splitting node, and a link to the new logical sibling node.

2. *Parent update*—At this point, the situation is similar to that of the B^{link}-Tree *half-split* (see "Blink-Trees" on page 107), since the node is available through the split delta node pointer, but is not yet referenced by the parent, and readers have to go through the old node and then traverse the sibling pointer to reach the newly created sibling node. A new node is added as a child to the parent node, so that readers can directly reach it instead of being redirected through the splitting node, and the split completes.

Updating the parent pointer is a performance optimization: all nodes and their elements remain accessible even if the parent pointer is never updated. Bw-Trees are latch-free, so any thread can encounter an incomplete SMO. The thread is required to cooperate by picking up and finishing a multistep SMO before proceeding. The next thread will follow the installed parent pointer and won't have to go through the sibling pointer.

Merge SMOs work in a similar way:

1. *Remove sibling*—A special *remove delta* node is created and appended to the *right* sibling, indicating the start of the merge SMO and marking the right sibling for deletion.

2. *Merge*—A *merge delta* node is created on the *left* sibling to point to the contents of the right sibling and making it a logical part of the left sibling.

3. *Parent update*—At that point, the right sibling node contents are accessible from the left one. To finish the merge process, the link to the right sibling has to be removed from the parent.

Concurrent SMOs require an additional *abort delta* node to be installed on the parent to prevent concurrent splits and merges [WANG18]. An abort delta works similarly to a write lock: only one thread can have write access at a time, and any thread that attempts to append a new record to this delta node will abort. On SMO completion, the abort delta can be removed from the parent.

The Bw-Tree height grows during the root node splits. When the root node gets too big, it is split in two, and a new root is created in place of the old one, with the old root and a newly created sibling as its children.

Consolidation and Garbage Collection

Delta chains can get arbitrarily long without any additional action. Since reads are getting more expensive as the delta chain gets longer, we need to try to keep the delta chain length within reasonable bounds. When it reaches a configurable threshold, we rebuild the node by merging the base node contents with all of the deltas, consolidating them to one new base node. The new node is then written to the new location on disk and the node pointer in the mapping table is updated to point to it. We discuss this process in more detail in "LLAMA and Mindful Stacking" on page 160, as the underlying log-structured storage is responsible for garbage collection, node consolidation, and relocation.

As soon as the node is consolidated, its old contents (the base node and all of the delta nodes) are no longer addressed from the mapping table. However, we cannot free the memory they occupy right away, because some of them might be still used by ongoing operations. Since there are no latches held by readers (readers did not have to pass through or register at any sort of barrier to access the node), we need to find other means to track live pages.

To separate threads that might have encountered a specific node from those that couldn't have possibly seen it, Bw-Trees use a technique known as *epoch-based recla-mation*. If some nodes and deltas are removed from the mapping table due to consoli-dations that replaced them during some epoch, original nodes are preserved until every reader that started during the same epoch or the earlier one is finished. After that, they can be safely garbage collected, since later readers are guaranteed to have never seen those nodes, as they were not addressable by the time those readers started.

The Bw-Tree is an interesting B-Tree variant, making improvements on several important aspects: write amplification, nonblocking access, and cache friendliness. A modified version was implemented in Sled (*https://databass.dev/links/90*), an experi-mental storage engine. The CMU Database Group has developed an in-memory ver-sion of the Bw-Tree called OpenBw-Tree (*https://databass.dev/links/91*) and released a practical implementation guide [WANG18].

We've only touched on higher-level Bw-Tree concepts related to B-Trees in this chap-ter, and we continue the discussion about them in "LLAMA and Mindful Stacking" on page 160, including the discussion about the underlying log-structured storage.

Cache-Oblivious B-Trees

Block size, node size, cache line alignments, and other configurable parameters influ-ence B-Tree performance. A new class of data structures called *cache-oblivious struc-tures* [DEMAINE02] give asymptotically optimal performance regardless of the underlying memory hierarchy and a need to tune these parameters. This means that the algorithm is not required to know the sizes of the cache lines, filesystem blocks, and disk pages. Cache-oblivious structures are designed to perform well without modification on multiple machines with different configurations.

So far, we've been mostly looking at B-Trees from a two-level memory hierarchy (with the exception of LMDB described in "Copy-on-Write" on page 112). B-Tree nodes are stored in disk-resident pages, and the page cache is used to allow efficient access to them in main memory.

The two levels of this hierarchy are *page cache* (which is faster, but is limited in space) and *disk* (which is generally slower, but has a larger capacity) [AGGARWAL88]. Here, we have only two parameters, which makes it rather easy to design algorithms as we only have to have two level-specific code modules that take care of all the details relevant to that level.

The disk is partitioned into blocks, and data is transferred between disk and cache in blocks: even when the algorithm has to locate a single item within the block, an entire block has to be loaded. This approach is *cache-aware*.

When developing performance-critical software, we often program for a more complex model, taking into consideration CPU caches, and sometimes even disk hierarchies (like hot/cold storage or build HDD/SSD/NVM hierarchies, and phase off data from one level to the other). Most of the time such efforts are difficult to generalize. In "Memory- Versus Disk-Based DBMS" on page 10, we talked about the fact that accessing disk is several orders of magnitude slower than accessing main memory, which has motivated database implementers to optimize for this difference.

Cache-oblivious algorithms allow reasoning about data structures in terms of a two-level memory model while providing the benefits of a multilevel hierarchy model. This approach allows having no platform-specific parameters, yet guarantees that the number of transfers between the two levels of the hierarchy is within a constant factor. If the data structure is optimized to perform optimally for any two levels of memory hierarchy, it also works optimally for the two *adjacent* hierarchy levels. This is achieved by working at the highest cache level as much as possible.

van Emde Boas Layout

A cache-oblivious B-Tree consists of a static B-Tree and a packed array structure [BENDER05]. A static B-Tree is built using the *van Emde Boas* layout. It splits the tree at the middle level of the edges. Then each subtree is split recursively in a similar manner, resulting in subtrees of sqr(N) size. The key idea of this layout is that any recursive tree is stored in a contiguous block of memory.

In Figure 6-8, you can see an example of a van Emde Boas layout. Nodes, logically grouped together, are placed closely together. On top, you can see a logical layout representation (i.e., how nodes form a tree), and on the bottom you can see how tree nodes are laid out in memory and on disk.

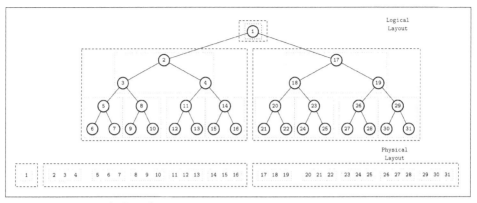

Figure 6-8. van Emde Boas layout

To make the data structure dynamic (i.e., allow inserts, updates, and deletes), cache-oblivious trees use a *packed array* data structure, which uses contiguous memory segments for storing elements, but contains gaps reserved for future inserted elements. Gaps are spaced based on the *density threshold*. Figure 6-9 shows a packed array structure, where elements are spaced to create gaps.

Figure 6-9. Packed array

This approach allows inserting items into the tree with fewer relocations. Items have to be relocated just to create a gap for the newly inserted element, if the gap is not already present. When the packed array becomes too densely or sparsely populated, the structure has to be rebuilt to grow or shrink the array.

The static tree is used as an index for the bottom-level packed array, and has to be updated in accordance with relocated elements to point to correct elements on the bottom level.

This is an interesting approach, and ideas from it can be used to build efficient B-Tree implementations. It allows constructing on-disk structures in ways that are very similar to how main memory ones are constructed. However, as of the date of writing, I'm not aware of any nonacademic cache-oblivious B-Tree implementations.

A possible reason for that is an assumption that when cache loading is abstracted away, while data is loaded and written back in blocks, paging and eviction still have a negative impact on the result. Another possible reason is that in terms of block transfers, the complexity of cache-oblivious B-Trees is the same as their cache-aware counterpart. This may change when more efficient nonvolatile byte-addressable storage devices become more widespread.

Summary

The original B-Tree design has several shortcomings that might have worked well on spinning disks, but make it less efficient when used on SSDs. B-Trees have high *write amplification* (caused by page rewrites) and high *space overhead* since B-Trees have to reserve space in nodes for future writes.

Write amplification can be reduced by using *buffering*. Lazy B-Trees, such as WiredTiger and LA-Trees, attach in-memory buffers to individual nodes or groups of nodes to reduce the number of required I/O operations by buffering subsequent updates to pages in memory.

To reduce space amplification, FD-Trees use *immutability*: data records are stored in the immutable sorted *runs*, and the size of a mutable B-Tree is limited.

Bw-Trees solve space amplification by using immutability, too. B-Tree nodes and updates to them are stored in separate on-disk locations and persisted in the log-structured store. Write amplification is reduced compared to the original B-Tree design, since reconciling contents that belong to a single logical node is relatively infrequent. Bw-Trees do not require latches for protecting pages from concurrent accesses, as the virtual pointers between the logical nodes are stored in memory.

Further Reading

If you'd like to learn more about the concepts mentioned in this chapter, you can refer to the following sources:

Copy-on-Write B-Trees
Driscoll, J. R., N. Sarnak, D. D. Sleator, and R. E. Tarjan. 1986. "Making data structures persistent." In *Proceedings of the eighteenth annual ACM symposium on Theory of computing (STOC '86)*, 109-121. *https://dx.doi.org/ 10.1016/0022-0000(89)90034-2.*

Lazy-Adaptive Trees
Agrawal, Devesh, Deepak Ganesan, Ramesh Sitaraman, Yanlei Diao, and Shashi Singh. 2009. "Lazy-Adaptive Tree: an optimized index structure for flash devices." *Proceedings of the VLDB Endowment* 2, no. 1 (January): 361-372. *https://doi.org/ 10.14778/1687627.1687669.*

FD-Trees
Li, Yinan, Bingsheng He, Robin Jun Yang, Qiong Luo, and Ke Yi. 2010. "Tree Indexing on Solid State Drives." *Proceedings of the VLDB Endowment* 3, no. 1-2 (September): 1195-1206. *https://doi.org/10.14778/1920841.1920990.*

Bw-Trees
Wang, Ziqi, Andrew Pavlo, Hyeontaek Lim, Viktor Leis, Huanchen Zhang, Michael Kaminsky, and David G. Andersen. 2018. "Building a Bw-Tree Takes More Than Just Buzz Words." *Proceedings of the 2018 International Conference on Management of Data (SIGMOD '18)*, 473–488. *https://doi.org/ 10.1145/3183713.3196895*

Levandoski, Justin J., David B. Lomet, and Sudipta Sengupta. 2013. "The Bw-Tree: A B-tree for new hardware platforms." In *Proceedings of the 2013 IEEE International Conference on Data Engineering (ICDE '13)*, 302-313. IEEE. *https:// doi.org/10.1109/ICDE.2013.6544834.*

Cache-Oblivious B-Trees
Bender, Michael A., Erik D. Demaine, and Martin Farach-Colton. 2005. "Cache-Oblivious B-Trees." *SIAM Journal on Computing* 35, no. 2 (August): 341-358. *https://doi.org/10.1137/S0097539701389956.*

CHAPTER 7

Log-Structured Storage

Accountants don't use erasers or they end up in jail.

—Pat Helland

When accountants have to modify the record, instead of erasing the existing value, they create a new record with a correction. When the quarterly report is published, it may contain minor modifications, correcting the previous quarter results. To derive the bottom line, you have to go through the records and calculate a subtotal [HELLAND15].

Similarly, immutable storage structures do not allow modifications to the existing files: tables are written once and are never modified again. Instead, new records are appended to the new file and, to find the final value (or conclude its absence), records have to be reconstructed from multiple files. In contrast, mutable storage structures modify records on disk in place.

Immutable data structures are often used in functional programming languages and are getting more popular because of their safety characteristics: once created, an immutable structure doesn't change, all of its references can be accessed concurrently, and its integrity is guaranteed by the fact that it cannot be modified.

On a high level, there is a strict distinction between how data is treated inside a storage structure and outside of it. Internally, immutable files can hold multiple copies, more recent ones overwriting the older ones, while mutable files generally hold only the most recent value instead. When accessed, immutable files are processed, redundant copies are reconciled, and the most recent ones are returned to the client.

As do other books and papers on the subject, we use B-Trees as a typical example of mutable structure and *Log-Structured Merge Trees* (LSM Trees) as an example of an immutable structure. Immutable LSM Trees use append-only storage and merge reconciliation, and B-Trees locate data records on disk and update pages at their original offsets in the file.

In-place update storage structures are optimized for read performance [GRAEFE04]: after locating data on disk, the record can be returned to the client. This comes at the expense of write performance: to update the data record in place, it first has to be located on disk. On the other hand, append-only storage is optimized for write performance. Writes do not have to locate records on disk to overwrite them. However, this is done at the expense of reads, which have to retrieve multiple data record versions and reconcile them.

So far we've mostly talked about mutable storage structures. We've touched on the subject of immutability while discussing copy-on-write B-Trees (see "Copy-on-Write" on page 112), FD-Trees (see "FD-Trees" on page 117), and Bw-Trees (see "Bw-Trees" on page 120). But there are more ways to implement immutable structures.

Because of the structure and construction approach taken by mutable B-Trees, most I/O operations during reads, writes, and maintenance are *random*. Each write operation first needs to locate a page that holds a data record and only then can modify it. B-Trees require node splits and merges that relocate already written records. After some time, B-Tree pages may require maintenance. Pages are fixed in size, and some free space is reserved for future writes. Another problem is that even when only one cell in the page is modified, an entire page has to be rewritten.

There are alternative approaches that can help to mitigate these problems, make some of the I/O operations sequential, and avoid page rewrites during modifications. One of the ways to do this is to use immutable structures. In this chapter, we'll focus on LSM Trees: how they're built, what their properties are, and how they are different from B-Trees.

LSM Trees

When talking about B-Trees, we concluded that space overhead and write amplification can be improved by using buffering. Generally, there are two ways buffering can be applied in different storage structures: to postpone propagating writes to disk-resident pages (as we've seen with "FD-Trees" on page 117 and "WiredTiger" on page 114), and to make write operations sequential.

One of the most popular immutable on-disk storage structures, LSM Tree uses buffering and append-only storage to achieve sequential writes. The LSM Tree is a variant of a disk-resident structure similar to a B-Tree, where nodes are fully occupied, optimized for sequential disk access. This concept was first introduced in a paper by Patrick O'Neil and Edward Cheng [ONEIL96]. Log-structured merge trees take their name from log-structured filesystems, which write all modifications on disk in a log-like file [ROSENBLUM92].

LSM Trees write immutable files and merge them together over time. These files usually contain an index of their own to help readers efficiently locate data. Even though LSM Trees are often presented as an alternative to B-Trees, it is common for B-Trees to be used as the internal indexing structure for an LSM Tree's immutable files.

The word "merge" in LSM Trees indicates that, due to their immutability, tree contents are merged using an approach similar to merge sort. This happens during maintenance to reclaim space occupied by the redundant copies, and during reads, before contents can be returned to the user.

LSM Trees defer data file writes and buffer changes in a memory-resident table. These changes are then propagated by writing their contents out to the immutable disk files. All data records remain accessible in memory until the files are fully persisted.

Keeping data files immutable favors sequential writes: data is written on the disk in a single pass and files are append-only. Mutable structures can pre-allocate blocks in a single pass (for example, indexed sequential access method (ISAM) [RAMAKRISHNAN03] [LARSON81]), but subsequent accesses still require random reads and writes. Immutable structures allow us to lay out data records sequentially to prevent fragmentation. Additionally, immutable files have higher *density*: we do not reserve any extra space for data records that are going to be written later, or for the cases when updated records require more space than the originally written ones.

Since files are immutable, insert, update, and delete operations do not need to locate data records on disk, which significantly improves write performance and throughput. Instead, duplicate contents are allowed, and conflicts are resolved during the read time. LSM Trees are particularly useful for applications where writes are far more common than reads, which is often the case in modern data-intensive systems, given ever-growing amounts of data and ingest rates.

Reads and writes do not intersect by design, so data on disk can be read and written without segment locking, which significantly simplifies concurrent access. In contrast, mutable structures employ hierarchical locks and latches (you can find more information about locks and latches in "Concurrency Control" on page 93) to ensure on-disk data structure integrity, and allow multiple concurrent readers but require exclusive subtree ownership for writers. LSM-based storage engines use linearizable in-memory views of data and index files, and only have to guard concurrent access to the structures managing them.

Both B-Trees and LSM Trees require some housekeeping to optimize performance, but for different reasons. Since the number of allocated files steadily grows, LSM Trees have to merge and rewrite files to make sure that the smallest possible number of files is accessed during the read, as requested data records might be spread across multiple files. On the other hand, mutable files may have to be rewritten partially or wholly to decrease fragmentation and reclaim space occupied by updated or deleted records. Of course, the exact scope of work done by the housekeeping process heavily depends on the concrete implementation.

LSM Tree Structure

We start with ordered LSM Trees [ONEIL96], where files hold sorted data records. Later, in "Unordered LSM Storage" on page 152, we'll also discuss structures that allow storing data records in insertion order, which has some obvious advantages on the write path.

As we just discussed, LSM Trees consist of smaller memory-resident and larger disk-resident components. To write out immutable file contents on disk, it is necessary to first *buffer* them in memory and *sort* their contents.

A memory-resident component (often called a *memtable*) is mutable: it buffers data records and serves as a target for read and write operations. Memtable contents are persisted on disk when its size grows up to a configurable threshold. Memtable updates incur no disk access and have no associated I/O costs. A separate write-ahead log file, similar to what we discussed in "Recovery" on page 88, is required to guarantee durability of data records. Data records are appended to the log and committed in memory before the operation is acknowledged to the client.

Buffering is done in memory: all read and write operations are applied to a memory-resident table that maintains a sorted data structure allowing concurrent access, usually some form of an in-memory sorted tree, or any data structure that can give similar performance characteristics.

Disk-resident components are built by *flushing* contents buffered in memory to disk. Disk-resident components are used only for reads: buffered contents are persisted, and files are never modified. This allows us to think in terms of simple operations: writes against an in-memory table, and reads against disk and memory-based tables, merges, and file removals.

Throughout this chapter, we will be using the word *table* as a shortcut for *disk-resident table*. Since we're discussing semantics of a storage engine, this term is not ambiguous with a *table* concept in the wider context of a database management system.

Two-component LSM Tree

We distinguish between two- and multicomponent LSM Trees. *Two-component LSM Trees* have only one disk component, comprised of immutable segments. The disk component here is organized as a B-Tree, with 100% node occupancy and read-only pages.

Memory-resident tree contents are flushed on disk in parts. During a flush, for each flushed in-memory subtree, we find a corresponding subtree on disk and write out the merged contents of a memory-resident segment and disk-resident subtree into the new segment on disk. Figure 7-1 shows in-memory and disk-resident trees before a merge.

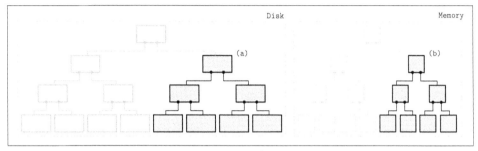

Figure 7-1. Two-component LSM Tree before a flush. Flushing memory- and disk-resident segments are shown in gray.

After the subtree is flushed, superseded memory-resident and disk-resident subtrees are discarded and replaced with the result of their merge, which becomes addressable from the preexisting sections of the disk-resident tree. Figure 7-2 shows the result of a merge process, already written to the new location on disk and attached to the rest of the tree.

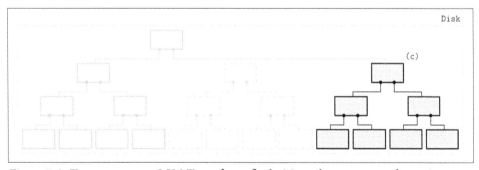

Figure 7-2. Two-component LSM Tree after a flush. Merged contents are shown in gray. Boxes with dashed lines depict discarded on-disk segments.

A merge can be implemented by advancing iterators reading the disk-resident leaf nodes and contents of the in-memory tree in lockstep. Since both sources are sorted, to produce a sorted merged result, we only need to know the *current* values of both iterators during each step of the merge process.

This approach is a logical extension and continuation of our conversation on immutable B-Trees. Copy-on-write B-Trees (see "Copy-on-Write" on page 112) use B-Tree structure, but their nodes are not fully occupied, and they require copying pages on the root-leaf path and creating a *parallel* tree structure. Here, we do something similar, but since we buffer writes in memory, we amortize the costs of the disk-resident tree update.

When implementing subtree merges and flushes, we have to make sure of three things:

1. *As soon as* the flush process starts, all new writes have to go to the new memtable.

2. *During* the subtree flush, both the disk-resident and flushing memory-resident subtree have to remain accessible for reads.

3. *After* the flush, publishing merged contents, and discarding unmerged disk- and memory-resident contents have to be performed atomically.

Even though two-component LSM Trees can be useful for maintaining index files, no implementations are known to the author as of time of writing. This can be explained by the write amplification characteristics of this approach: merges are relatively frequent, as they are triggered by memtable flushes.

Multicomponent LSM Trees

Let's consider an alternative design, multicomponent LSM Trees that have more than just one disk-resident table. In this case, entire memtable contents are flushed in a single run.

It quickly becomes evident that after multiple flushes we'll end up with multiple disk-resident tables, and their number will only grow over time. Since we do not always know exactly which tables are holding required data records, we might have to access multiple files to locate the searched data.

Having to read from multiple sources instead of just one might get expensive. To mitigate this problem and keep the number of tables to minimum, a periodic merge process called *compaction* (see "Maintenance in LSM Trees" on page 141) is triggered. Compaction picks several tables, reads their contents, merges them, and writes the merged result out to the new combined file. Old tables are discarded simultaneously with the appearance of the new merged table.

Figure 7-3 shows the multicomponent LSM Tree data life cycle. Data is first buffered in a memory-resident component. When it gets too large, its contents are flushed on disk to create disk-resident tables. Later, multiple tables are merged together to create larger tables.

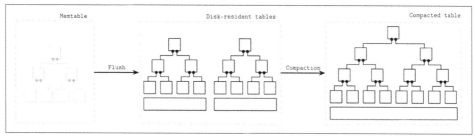

Figure 7-3. Multicomponent LSM Tree data life cycle

The rest of this chapter is dedicated to multicomponent LSM Trees, building blocks, and their maintenance processes.

In-memory tables

Memtable flushes can be triggered periodically, or by using a size threshold. Before it can be flushed, the memtable has to be *switched*: a new memtable is allocated, and it becomes a target for all new writes, while the old one moves to the flushing state. These two steps have to be performed atomically. The flushing memtable remains available for reads until its contents are fully flushed. After this, the old memtable is discarded in favor of a newly written disk-resident table, which becomes available for reads.

In Figure 7-4, you see the components of the LSM Tree, relationships between them, and operations that fulfill transitions between them:

Current memtable
    Receives writes and serves reads.

Flushing memtable
    Available for reads.

On-disk flush target
    Does not participate in reads, as its contents are incomplete.

Flushed tables
    Available for reads as soon as the flushed memtable is discarded.

Compacting tables
    Currently merging disk-resident tables.

Compacted tables
    Created from flushed or other compacted tables.

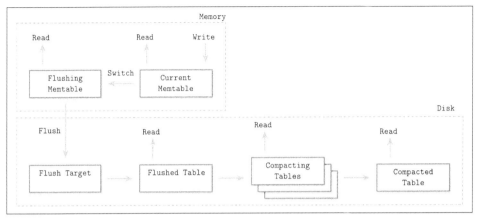

Figure 7-4. LSM component structure

Data is already sorted in memory, so a disk-resident table can be created by sequentially writing out memory-resident contents to disk. During a flush, both the flushing memtable and the current memtable are available for read.

Until the memtable is fully flushed, the only disk-resident version of its contents is stored in the write-ahead log. When memtable contents are fully flushed on disk, the log can be *trimmed*, and the log section, holding operations applied to the flushed memtable, can be discarded.

Updates and Deletes

In LSM Trees, insert, update, and delete operations do not require locating data records on disk. Instead, redundant records are reconciled during the read.

Removing data records from the memtable is not enough, since other disk or memory resident tables may hold data records for the same key. If we were to implement deletes by just removing items from the memtable, we would end up with deletes that either have no impact or would *resurrect* the previous values.

Let's consider an example. The flushed disk-resident table contains data record v1 associated with a key k1, and the memtable holds its new value v2:

```
Disk Table        Memtable
| k1 | v1 |        | k1 | v2 |
```

If we just remove v2 from the memtable and flush it, we effectively resurrect v1, since it becomes the only value associated with that key:

```
Disk Table        Memtable
| k1 | v1 |          ∅
```

Because of that, deletes need to be recorded *explicitly*. This can be done by inserting a special *delete entry* (sometimes called a *tombstone* or a *dormant certificate*), indicating removal of the data record associated with a specific key:

```
Disk Table        Memtable
| k1 | v1 |        | k1 | <tombstone> |
```

The reconciliation process picks up tombstones, and filters out the shadowed values.

Sometimes it might be useful to remove a consecutive range of keys rather than just a single key. This can be done using *predicate deletes*, which work by appending a delete entry with a predicate that sorts according to regular record-sorting rules. During reconciliation, data records matching the predicate are skipped and not returned to the client.

Predicates can take a form of DELETE FROM table WHERE key ≥ "k2" AND key < "k4" and can receive any range matchers. Apache Cassandra implements this approach and calls it *range tombstones*. A range tombstone covers a range of keys rather than just a single key.

When using range tombstones, resolution rules have to be carefully considered because of overlapping ranges and disk-resident table boundaries. For example, the following combination will hide data records associated with k2 and k3 from the final result:

```
Disk Table 1       Disk Table 2
| k1 | v1 |         | k2 | <start_tombstone_inclusive> |
| k2 | v2 |         | k4 | <end_tombstone_exclusive>   |
| k3 | v3 |
| k4 | v4 |
```

LSM Tree Lookups

LSM Trees consist of multiple components. During lookups, more than one component is usually accessed, so their contents have to be merged and reconciled before they can be returned to the client. To better understand the merge process, let's see how tables are iterated during the merge and how conflicting records are combined.

Merge-Iteration

Since contents of disk-resident tables are sorted, we can use a multiway merge-sort algorithm. For example, we have three sources: two disk-resident tables and one memtable. Usually, storage engines offer a *cursor* or an *iterator* to navigate through file contents. This cursor holds the offset of the last consumed data record, can be checked for whether or not iteration has finished, and can be used to retrieve the next data record.

A multiway merge-sort uses a *priority queue*, such as *min-heap* [SEDGEWICK11], that holds up to N elements (where N is the number of iterators), which sorts its contents and prepares the next-in-line smallest element to be returned. The head of each iterator is placed into the queue. An element in the head of the queue is then the minimum of all iterators.

 A priority queue is a data structure used for maintaining an ordered queue of items. While a regular queue retains items in order of their addition (first in, first out), a priority queue re-sorts items on insertion and the item with the highest (or lowest) priority is placed in the head of the queue. This is particularly useful for merge-iteration, since we have to output elements in a sorted order.

When the smallest element is removed from the queue, the iterator associated with it is checked for the next value, which is then placed into the queue, which is re-sorted to preserve the order.

Since all iterator contents are sorted, reinserting a value from the iterator that held the previous smallest value of all iterator heads also preserves an invariant that the queue still holds the smallest elements from all iterators. Whenever one of the iterators is exhausted, the algorithm proceeds without reinserting the next iterator head. The algorithm continues until either query conditions are satisfied or all iterators are exhausted.

Figure 7-5 shows a schematic representation of the merge process just described: head elements (light gray items in source tables) are placed to the priority queue. Elements from the priority queue are returned to the output iterator. The resulting output is sorted.

It may happen that we encounter more than one data record for the same key during merge-iteration. From the priority queue and iterator invariants, we know that if each iterator only holds a single data record per key, and we end up with multiple records for the same key in the queue, these data records must have come from the different iterators.

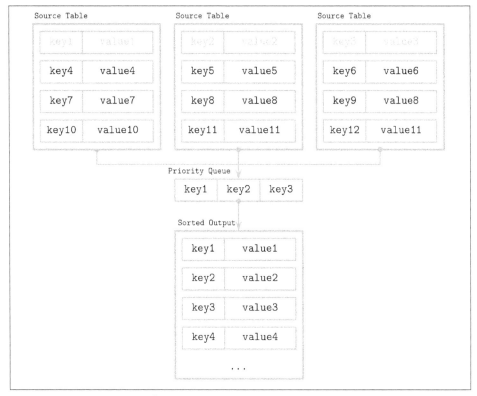

Figure 7-5. LSM merge mechanics

Let's follow through one example step-by-step. As input data, we have iterators over two disk-resident tables:

```
Iterator 1:         Iterator 2:
{k2: v1} {k4: v2}   {k1: v3} {k2: v4} {k3: v5}
```

The priority queue is filled from the iterator heads:

```
Iterator 1:         Iterator 2:          Priority queue:
{k4: v2}            {k2: v4} {k3: v5}    {k1: v3} {k2: v1}
```

Key k1 is the smallest key in the queue and is appended to the result. Since it came from Iterator 2, we refill the queue from it:

```
Iterator 1:         Iterator 2:     Priority queue:      Merged Result:
{k4: v2}            {k3: v5}        {k2: v1} {k2: v4}     {k1: v3}
```

Now, we have *two* records for the k2 key in the queue. We can be sure there are no other records with the same key in any iterator because of the aforementioned invariants. Same-key records are merged and appended to the merged result.

The queue is refilled with data from both iterators:

```
Iterator 1:        Iterator 2:        Priority queue:      Merged Result:
{}                 {}                 {k3: v5} {k4: v2}     {k1: v3} {k2: v4}
```

Since all iterators are now empty, we append the remaining queue contents to the output:

```
Merged Result:
   {k1: v3} {k2: v4} {k3: v5} {k4: v2}
```

In summary, the following steps have to be repeated to create a combined iterator:

1. Initially, fill the queue with the first items from each iterator.

2. Take the smallest element (head) from the queue.

3. Refill the queue from the corresponding iterator, unless this iterator is exhausted.

In terms of complexity, merging iterators is the same as merging sorted collections. It has O(N) memory overhead, where N is the number of iterators. A sorted collection of iterator heads is maintained with O(log N) (average case) [KNUTH98].

Reconciliation

Merge-iteration is just a single aspect of what has to be done to merge data from multiple sources. Another important aspect is *reconciliation* and *conflict resolution* of the data records associated with the same key.

Different tables might hold data records for the same key, such as updates and deletes, and their contents have to be reconciled. The priority queue implementation from the preceding example must be able to allow multiple values associated with the same key and trigger reconciliation.

 An operation that inserts the record to the database if it does not exist, and updates an existing one otherwise, is called an *upsert*. In LSM Trees, insert and update operations are indistinguishable, since they do not attempt to locate data records previously associated with the key in all sources and reassign its value, so we can say that we *upsert* records by default.

To reconcile data records, we need to understand which one of them takes precedence. Data records hold metadata necessary for this, such as timestamps. To establish the order between the items coming from multiple sources and find out which one is more recent, we can compare their timestamps.

Records shadowed by the records with higher timestamps are not returned to the client or written during compaction.

Maintenance in LSM Trees

Similar to mutable B-Trees, LSM Trees require maintenance. The nature of these processes is heavily influenced by the invariants these algorithms preserve.

In B-Trees, the maintenance process collects unreferenced cells and defragments the pages, reclaiming the space occupied by removed and shadowed records. In LSM Trees, the number of disk-resident tables is constantly growing, but can be reduced by triggering periodic compaction.

Compaction picks multiple disk-resident tables, iterates over their entire contents using the aforementioned merge and reconciliation algorithms, and writes out the results into the newly created table.

Since disk-resident table contents are sorted, and because of the way merge-sort works, compaction has a theoretical memory usage upper bound, since it should only hold iterator heads in memory. All table contents are consumed sequentially, and the resulting merged data is also written out sequentially. These details may vary between implementations due to additional optimizations.

Compacting tables remain available for reads until the compaction process finishes, which means that for the duration of compaction, it is required to have enough free space available on disk for a compacted table to be written.

At any given time, multiple compactions can be executed in the system. However, these concurrent compactions usually work on nonintersecting sets of tables. A compaction writer can both merge several tables into one and partition one table into multiple tables.

Tombstones and Compaction

Tombstones represent an important piece of information required for correct reconciliation, as some other table might still hold an outdated data record shadowed by the tombstone.

During compaction, tombstones are not dropped right away. They are preserved until the storage engine can be certain that no data record for the same key with a smaller timestamp is present in any other table. RocksDB keeps tombstones until they reach the bottommost level (*https://databass.dev/links/74*). Apache Cassandra keeps tombstones until the GC (garbage collection) grace period is reached (*https://databass.dev/ links/75*) because of the eventually consistent nature of the database, ensuring that other nodes observe the tombstone. Preserving tombstones during compaction is important to avoid data resurrection.

Leveled compaction

Compaction opens up multiple opportunities for optimizations, and there are many different compaction strategies. One of the frequently implemented compaction strategies is called *leveled compaction*. For example, it is used by RocksDB (*https://databass.dev/links/76*).

Leveled compaction separates disk-resident tables into *levels*. Tables on each level have target sizes, and each level has a corresponding *index* number (identifier). Somewhat counterintuitively, the level with the highest index is called the *bottommost* level. For clarity, this section avoids using terms *higher* and *lower level* and uses the same qualifiers for *level index*. That is, since 2 is larger than 1, level 2 has a higher index than level 1. The terms *previous* and *next* have the same order semantics as level indexes.

Level-0 tables are created by flushing memtable contents. Tables in level 0 may contain overlapping key ranges. As soon as the number of tables on level 0 reaches a threshold, their contents are merged, creating new tables for level 1.

Key ranges for the tables on level 1 and all levels with a higher index do not overlap, so level-0 tables have to be partitioned during compaction, split into ranges, and merged with tables holding corresponding key ranges. Alternatively, compaction can include *all* level-0 and level-1 tables, and output partitioned level-1 tables.

Compactions on the levels with the higher indexes pick tables from two consecutive levels with overlapping ranges and produce a new table on a higher level. Figure 7-6 schematically shows how the compaction process migrates data between the levels. The process of compacting level-1 and level-2 tables will produce a new table on level 2. Depending on how tables are partitioned, multiple tables from one level can be picked for compaction.

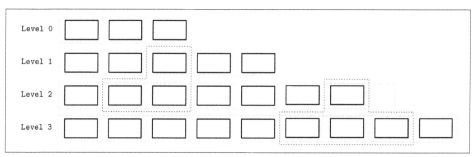

Figure 7-6. Compaction process. Gray boxes with dashed lines represent currently compacting tables. Level-wide boxes represent the target data size limit on the level. Level 1 is over the limit.

Keeping different key ranges in the distinct tables reduces the number of tables accessed during the read. This is done by inspecting the table metadata and filtering out the tables whose ranges do not contain a searched key.

Each level has a limit on the table size and the maximum number of tables. As soon as the number of tables on level 1 or any level with a higher index reaches a threshold, tables from the *current* level are merged with tables on the *next* level holding the overlapping key range.

Sizes grow exponentially between the levels: tables on each next level are exponentially larger than tables on the previous one. This way, the freshest data is always on the level with the lowest index, and older data gradually migrates to the higher ones.

Size-tiered compaction

Another popular compaction strategy is called *size-tiered compaction*. In size-tiered compaction, rather than grouping disk-resident tables based on their level, they're grouped by size: smaller tables are grouped with smaller ones, and bigger tables are grouped with bigger ones.

Level 0 holds the smallest tables that were either flushed from memtables or created by the compaction process. When the tables are compacted, the resulting merged table is written to the level holding tables with corresponding sizes. The process continues recursively incrementing levels, compacting and promoting larger tables to higher levels, and demoting smaller tables to lower levels.

One of the problems with size-tiered compaction is called *table starvation*: if compacted tables are still small enough after compaction (e.g., records were shadowed by the tombstones and did not make it to the merged table), higher levels may get starved of compaction and their tombstones will not be taken into consideration, increasing the cost of reads. In this case, compaction has to be forced for a level, even if it doesn't contain enough tables.

There are other commonly implemented compaction strategies that might optimize for different workloads. For example, Apache Cassandra also implements a *time window* compaction strategy (*https://databass.dev/links/77*), which is particularly useful for time-series workloads with records for which time-to-live is set (in other words, items have to be expired after a given time period).

The time window compaction strategy takes write timestamps into consideration and allows dropping entire files that hold data for an already expired time range without requiring us to compact and rewrite their contents.

Read, Write, and Space Amplification

When implementing an optimal compaction strategy, we have to take multiple factors into consideration. One approach is to reclaim space occupied by duplicate records and reduce space overhead, which results in higher write amplification caused by rewriting tables continuously. The alternative is to avoid rewriting the data continuously, which increases read amplification (overhead from reconciling data records associated with the same key during the read), and space amplification (since redundant records are preserved for a longer time).

 One of the big disputes in the database community is whether B-Trees or LSM Trees have lower write amplification. It is extremely important to understand the *source* of write amplification in both cases. In B-Trees, it comes from writeback operations and subsequent updates to the same node. In LSM Trees, write amplification is caused by migrating data from one file to the other during compaction. Comparing the two directly may lead to incorrect assumptions.

In summary, when storing data on disk in an immutable fashion, we face three problems:

Read amplification
    Resulting from a need to address multiple tables to retrieve data.

Write amplification
    Caused by continuous rewrites by the compaction process.

Space amplification
    Arising from storing multiple records associated with the same key.

We'll be addressing each one of these throughout the rest of the chapter.

RUM Conjecture

One of the popular cost models for storage structures takes three factors into consideration: *Read*, *Update*, and *Memory* overheads. It is called RUM Conjecture [ATHA-NASSOULIS16].

RUM Conjecture states that reducing two of these overheads inevitably leads to change for the worse in the third one, and that optimizations can be done only at the expense of one of the three parameters. We can compare different storage engines in terms of these three parameters to understand which ones they optimize for, and which potential trade-offs this may imply.

An ideal solution would provide the lowest read cost while maintaining low memory and write overheads, but in reality, this is not achievable, and we are presented with a trade-off.

B-Trees are read-optimized. Writes to the B-Tree require locating a record on disk, and subsequent writes to the same page might have to update the page on disk multiple times. Reserved extra space for future updates and deletes increases space overhead.

LSM Trees do not require locating the record on disk during write and do not reserve extra space for future writes. There is still some space overhead resulting from storing redundant records. In a default configuration, reads are more expensive, since multiple tables have to be accessed to return complete results. However, optimizations we discuss in this chapter help to mitigate this problem.

As we've seen in the chapters about B-Trees, and will see in this chapter, there are ways to improve these characteristics by applying different optimizations.

This cost model is not perfect, as it does not take into account other important metrics such as latency, access patterns, implementation complexity, maintenance overhead, and hardware-related specifics. Higher-level concepts important for distributed databases, such as consistency implications and replication overhead, are also not considered. However, this model can be used as a first approximation and a rule of thumb as it helps understand what the *storage engine* has to offer.

Implementation Details

We've covered the basic dynamics of LSM Trees: how data is read, written, and compacted. However, there are some other things that many LSM Tree implementations have in common that are worth discussing: how memory- and disk-resident tables are implemented, how secondary indexes work, how to reduce the number of disk-resident tables accessed during read and, finally, new ideas related to log-structured storage.

Sorted String Tables

So far we've discussed the hierarchical and logical structure of LSM Trees (that they consist of multiple memory- and disk-resident components), but have not yet discussed how disk-resident tables are implemented and how their design plays together with the rest of the system.

Disk-resident tables are often implemented using *Sorted String Tables* (SSTables). As the name suggests, data records in SSTables are sorted and laid out in key order. SSTables usually consist of two components: index files and data files. Index files are implemented using some structure allowing logarithmic lookups, such as B-Trees, or constant-time lookups, such as hashtables.

Since data files hold records in key order, using hashtables for indexing does not prevent us from implementing range scans, as a hashtable is only accessed to locate the first key in the range, and the range itself can be read from the data file sequentially while the range predicate still matches.

The index component holds keys and data entries (offsets in the data file where the actual data records are located). The data component consists of concatenated key-value pairs. The cell design and data record formats we discussed in Chapter 3 are largely applicable to SSTables. The main difference here is that cells are written sequentially and are not modified during the life cycle of the SSTable. Since the index files hold pointers to the data records stored in the data file, their offsets have to be known by the time the index is created.

During compaction, data files can be read sequentially without addressing the index component, as data records in them are already ordered. Since tables merged during compaction have the same order, and merge-iteration is order-preserving, the resulting merged table is also created by writing data records sequentially in a single run. As soon as the file is fully written, it is considered immutable, and its disk-resident contents are not modified.

SSTable-Attached Secondary Indexes

One of the interesting developments in the area of LSM Tree indexing is *SSTable-Attached Secondary Indexes* (SASI) implemented in Apache Cassandra. To allow indexing table contents not just by the primary key, but also by any other field, index structures and their life cycles are coupled with the SSTable life cycle, and an index is created per SSTable. When the memtable is flushed, its contents are written to disk, and secondary index files are created along with the SSTable primary key index.

Since LSM Trees buffer data in memory and indexes have to work for memory-resident contents as well as the disk-resident ones, SASI maintains a separate in-memory structure, indexing memtable contents.

During a read, primary keys of searched records are located by searching and merging index contents, and data records are merged and reconciled similar to how lookups usually work in LSM Trees.

One of the advantages of piggybacking the SSTable life cycle is that indexes can be created during memtable flush or compaction.

Bloom Filters

The source of read amplification in LSM Trees is that we have to address multiple disk-resident tables for the read operation to complete. This happens because we do not always know up front whether or not a disk-resident table contains a data record for the searched key.

One of the ways to prevent table lookup is to store its key range (smallest and largest keys stored in the given table) in metadata, and check if the searched key belongs to the range of that table. This information is imprecise and can only tell us if the data record *can* be present in the table. To improve this situation, many implementations, including Apache Cassandra (*https://databass.dev/links/78*) and RocksDB (*https://databass.dev/links/79*), use a data structure called a *Bloom filter*.

 Probabilistic data structures are generally more space efficient than their "regular" counterparts. For example, to check set membership, cardinality (find out the number of distinct elements in a set), or frequency (find out how many times a certain element has been encountered), we would have to store all set elements and go through the entire dataset to find the result. Probabilistic structures allow us to store approximate information and perform queries that yield results with an element of uncertainty. Some commonly known examples of such data structures are a Bloom filter (for set membership), HyperLogLog (for cardinality estimation) [FLAJO-LET12], and Count-Min Sketch (for frequency estimation) [COR-MODE12].

A *Bloom filter*, conceived by Burton Howard Bloom in 1970 [BLOOM70], is a space-efficient probabilistic data structure that can be used to test whether the element is a member of the set or not. It can produce false-positive matches (say that the element is a member of the set, while it is not present there), but cannot produce false negatives (if a negative match is returned, the element is guaranteed not to be a member of the set).

In other words, a Bloom filter can be used to tell if the key *might be in the table* or *is definitely not in the table*. Files for which a Bloom filter returns a negative match are skipped during the query. The rest of the files are accessed to find out if the data record is actually present. Using Bloom filters associated with disk-resident tables helps to significantly reduce the number of tables accessed during a read.

A Bloom filter uses a large bit array and multiple hash functions. Hash functions are applied to keys of the records in the table to find indices in the bit array, bits for which are set to 1. Bits set to 1 in all positions determined by the hash functions indicate a *presence* of the key in the set. During lookup, when checking for element presence in a Bloom filter, hash functions are calculated for the key again and, if bits determined by *all* hash functions are 1, we return the positive result stating that item is a member of the set with a certain probability. If at least one of the bits is 0, we can precisely say that element is not present in the set.

Hash functions applied to different keys can return the same bit position and result in a *hash collision*, and 1 bits only imply that *some* hash function has yielded this bit position for *some* key.

Probability of false positives is managed by configuring the size of the bit set and the number of hash functions: in a larger bit set, there's a smaller chance of collision; similarly, having more hash functions, we can check more bits and have a more precise outcome.

The larger bit set occupies more memory, and computing results of more hash functions may have a negative performance impact, so we have to find a reasonable middle ground between acceptable probability and incurred overhead. Probability can be calculated from the expected set size. Since tables in LSM Trees are immutable, set size (number of keys in the table) is known up front.

Let's take a look at a simple example, shown in Figure 7-7. We have a 16-way bit array and 3 hash functions, which yield values 3, 5, and 10 for key1. We now set bits at these positions. The next key is added and hash functions yield values of 5, 8, and 14 for key2, for which we set bits, too.

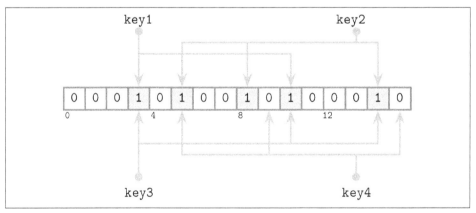

Figure 7-7. Bloom filter

Now, we're trying to check whether or not key3 is present in the set, and hash functions yield 3, 10, and 14. Since all three bits were set when adding key1 and key2, we have a situation in which the Bloom filter returns a false positive: key3 was never appended there, yet all of the calculated bits are set. However, since the Bloom filter only claims that element *might* be in the table, this result is acceptable.

If we try to perform a lookup for key4 and receive values of 5, 9, and 15, we find that only bit 5 is set, and the other two bits are unset. If even one of the bits is unset, we know for sure that the element was never appended to the filter.

Skiplist

There are many different data structures for keeping sorted data in memory, and one that has been getting more popular recently because of its simplicity is called a *skiplist* [PUGH90b]. Implementation-wise, a skiplist is not much more complex than a singly-linked list, and its probabilistic complexity guarantees are close to those of search trees.

Skiplists do not require rotation or relocation for inserts and updates, and use probabilistic balancing instead. Skiplists are generally less cache-friendly than in-memory B-Trees, since skiplist nodes are small and randomly allocated in memory. Some implementations improve the situation by using unrolled linked lists (*https://data bass.dev/links/80*).

A skiplist consists of a series of nodes of a different *height*, building linked hierarchies allowing to skip ranges of items. Each node holds a key, and, unlike the nodes in a linked list, some nodes have more than just one successor. A node of height h is linked *from* one or more predecessor nodes of a height *up to* h. Nodes on the lowest level can be linked from nodes of any height.

Node height is determined by a random function and is computed during insert. Nodes that have the same height form a *level*. The number of levels is capped to avoid infinite growth, and a maximum height is chosen based on how many items can be held by the structure. There are exponentially fewer nodes on each next level.

Lookups work by following the node pointers on the highest level. As soon as the search encounters the node that holds a key that is *greater than* the searched one, its predecessor's link to the node on the next level is followed. In other words, if the searched key is *greater than* the current node key, the search continues forward. If the searched key is *smaller than* the current node key, the search continues from the predecessor node on the next level. This process is repeated recursively until the searched key or its predecessor is located.

For example, searching for key 7 in the skiplist shown in Figure 7-8 can be done as follows:

1. Follow the pointer on the highest level, to the node that holds key 10.

2. Since the searched key 7 is *smaller than* 10, the next-level pointer from the head node is followed, locating a node holding key 5.

3. The highest-level pointer on this node is followed, locating the node holding key 10 again.

4. The searched key 7 is *smaller than* 10, and the next-level pointer from the node holding key 5 is followed, locating a node holding the searched key 7.

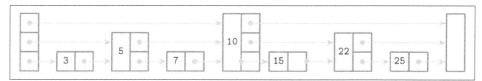

Figure 7-8. Skiplist

During insert, an insertion point (node holding a key or its predecessor) is found using the aforementioned algorithm, and a new node is created. To build a tree-like hierarchy and keep balance, the height of the node is determined using a random number, generated based on a probability distribution. Pointers in predecessor nodes holding keys *smaller than* the key in a newly created node are linked to point to that node. Their higher-level pointers remain intact. Pointers in the newly created node are linked to corresponding successors on each level.

During delete, forward pointers of the removed node are placed to predecessor nodes on corresponding levels.

We can create a concurrent version of a skiplist by implementing a linearizability scheme that uses an additional `fully_linked` flag that determines whether or not the node pointers are fully updated. This flag can be set using compare-and-swap [HER-LIHY10]. This is required because the node pointers have to be updated on multiple levels to fully restore the skiplist structure.

In languages with an unmanaged memory model, reference counting or *hazard pointers* can be used to ensure that currently referenced nodes are not freed while they are accessed concurrently [RUSSEL12]. This algorithm is deadlock-free, since nodes are always accessed from higher levels.

Apache Cassandra uses skiplists for the secondary index memtable implementation (*https://databass.dev/links/81*). WiredTiger uses skiplists for some in-memory operations.

Disk Access

Since most of the table contents are disk-resident, and storage devices generally allow accessing data blockwise, many LSM Tree implementations rely on the page cache for disk accesses and intermediate caching. Many techniques described in "Buffer Management" on page 81, such as page eviction and pinning, still apply to log-structured storage.

The most notable difference is that in-memory contents are immutable and therefore require no additional locks or latches for concurrent access. Reference counting is applied to make sure that currently accessed pages are not evicted from memory, and in-flight requests complete before underlying files are removed during compaction.

Another difference is that data records in LSM Trees are not necessarily page aligned, and pointers can be implemented using absolute offsets rather than page IDs for addressing. In Figure 7-9, you can see records with contents that are not aligned with disk blocks. Some records cross the page boundaries and require loading several pages in memory.

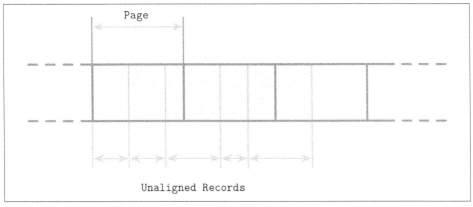

Figure 7-9. Unaligned data records

Compression

We've discussed compression already in context of B-Trees (see "Compression" on page 73). Similar ideas are also applicable to LSM Trees. The main difference here is that LSM Tree tables are immutable, and are generally written in a single pass. When compressing data page-wise, compressed pages are not page aligned, as their sizes are smaller than that of uncompressed ones.

To be able to address compressed pages, we need to keep track of the address boundaries when writing their contents. We could fill compressed pages with zeros, aligning them to the page size, but then we'd lose the benefits of compression.

To make compressed pages addressable, we need an indirection layer which stores offsets and sizes of compressed pages. Figure 7-10 shows the mapping between compressed and uncompressed blocks. Compressed pages are *always* smaller than the originals, since otherwise there's no point in compressing them.

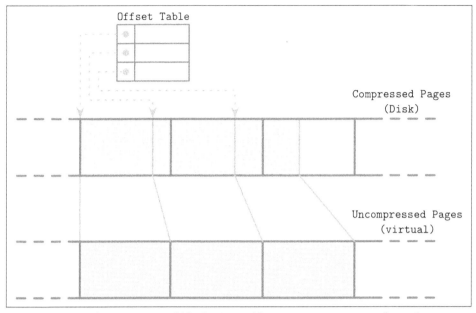

Figure 7-10. Reading compressed blocks. Dotted lines represent pointers from the map-ping table to the offsets of compressed pages on disk. Uncompressed pages generally reside in the page cache.

During compaction and flush, compressed pages are appended sequentially, and compression information (the original uncompressed page offset and the actual com-pressed page offset) is stored in a separate file segment. During the read, the com-pressed page offset and its size are looked up, and the page can be uncompressed and materialized in memory.

Unordered LSM Storage

Most of the storage structures discussed so far store data *in order*. Mutable and immutable B-Tree pages, sorted runs in FD-Trees, and SSTables in LSM Trees store data records in key order. The order in these structures is preserved differently: B-Tree pages are updated in place, FD-Tree runs are created by merging contents of two runs, and SSTables are created by buffering and sorting data records in memory.

In this section, we discuss structures that store records in random order. Unordered stores generally do not require a separate log and allow us to reduce the cost of writes by storing data records in insertion order.

Bitcask

Bitcask (*https://databass.dev/links/82*), one of the storage engines used in Riak (*https://databass.dev/links/83*), is an unordered log-structured storage engine [SHEEHY10b]. Unlike the log-structured storage implementations discussed so far, it *does not* use memtables for buffering, and stores data records directly in logfiles.

To make values searchable, Bitcask uses a data structure called *keydir*, which holds references to the *latest* data records for the corresponding keys. Old data records may still be present on disk, but are not referenced from keydir, and are garbage-collected during compaction. Keydir is implemented as an in-memory hashmap and has to be rebuilt from the logfiles during startup.

During a *write*, a key and a data record are appended to the logfile sequentially, and the pointer to the newly written data record location is placed in keydir.

Reads check the keydir to locate the searched key and follow the associated pointer to the logfile, locating the data record. Since at any given moment there can be only one value associated with the key in the keydir, point queries do not have to merge data from multiple sources.

Figure 7-11 shows mapping between the keys and records in data files in Bitcask. Logfiles hold data records, and keydir points to the latest *live* data record associated with each key. Shadowed records in data files (ones that were superseded by later writes or deletes) are shown in gray.

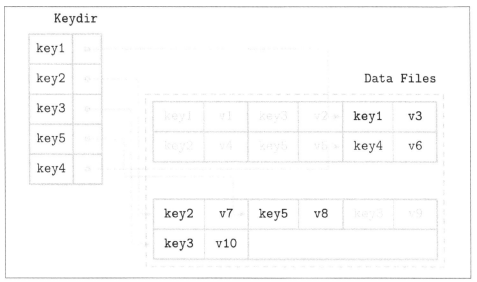

Figure 7-11. Mapping between keydir and data files in Bitcask. Solid lines represent pointers from the key to the latest value associated with it. Shadowed key/value pairs are shown in light gray.

During compaction, contents of all logfiles are read sequentially, merged, and written to a new location, preserving only *live* data records and discarding the shadowed ones. Keydir is updated with new pointers to relocated data records.

Data records are stored directly in logfiles, so a separate write-ahead log doesn't have to be maintained, which reduces both space overhead and write amplification. A downside of this approach is that it offers only point queries and doesn't allow range scans, since items are unordered both in keydir and in data files.

Advantages of this approach are simplicity and great point query performance. Even though multiple versions of data records exist, only the latest one is addressed by keydir. However, having to keep all keys in memory and rebuilding keydir on startup are limitations that might be a deal breaker for some use cases. While this approach is great for point queries, it does not offer any support for range queries.

WiscKey

Range queries are important for many applications, and it would be great to have a storage structure that could have the write and space advantages of unordered storage, while still allowing us to perform range scans.

WiscKey [LU16] decouples sorting from garbage collection by keeping the keys sorted in LSM Trees, and keeping data records in unordered append-only files called *vLogs* (value logs). This approach can solve two problems mentioned while discussing Bitcask: a need to keep all keys in memory and to rebuild a hashtable on startup.

Figure 7-12 shows key components of WiscKey, and mapping between keys and log files. vLog files hold unordered data records. Keys are stored in sorted LSM Trees, pointing to the latest data records in the logfiles.

Since keys are typically much smaller than the data records associated with them, compacting them is significantly more efficient. This approach can be particularly useful for use cases with a low rate of updates and deletes, where garbage collection won't free up as much disk space.

The main challenge here is that because vLog data is unsorted, range scans require random I/O. WiscKey uses internal SSD parallelism to prefetch blocks in parallel during range scans and reduce random I/O costs. In terms of block transfers, the costs are still high: to fetch a single data record during the range scan, the entire page where it is located has to be read.

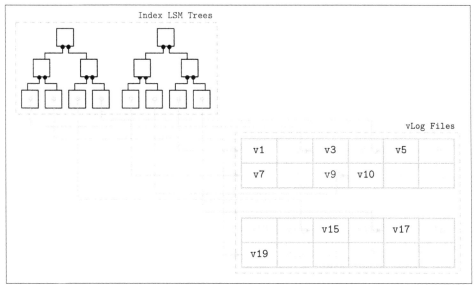

Figure 7-12. Key components of WiscKey: index LSM Trees and vLog files, and relationships between them. Shadowed records in data files (ones that were superseded by later writes or deletes) are shown in gray. Solid lines represent pointers from the key in the LSM tree to the latest value in the log file.

During compaction, vLog file contents are read sequentially, merged, and written to a new location. Pointers (values in a key LSM Tree) are updated to point to these new locations. To avoid scanning entire vLog contents, WiscKey uses `head` and `tail` pointers, holding information about vLog segments that hold live keys.

Since data in vLog is unsorted and contains no liveness information, the key tree has to be scanned to find which values are still live. Performing these checks during garbage collection introduces additional complexity: traditional LSM Trees can resolve file contents during compaction without addressing the key index.

Concurrency in LSM Trees

The main concurrency challenges in LSM Trees are related to switching *table views* (collections of memory- and disk-resident tables that change during flush and compaction) and log synchronization. Memtables are also generally accessed concurrently (except core-partitioned stores such as ScyllaDB), but concurrent in-memory data structures are out of the scope of this book.

During flush, the following rules have to be followed:

- The new memtable has to become available for reads and writes.
- The old (flushing) memtable has to remain visible for reads.
- The flushing memtable has to be written on disk.
- Discarding a flushed memtable and making a flushed disk-resident table have to be performed as an atomic operation.
- The write-ahead log segment, holding log entries of operations applied to the flushed memtable, has to be discarded.

For example, Apache Cassandra solves these problems by using operation order barriers (*https://databass.dev/links/84*): all operations that were accepted for write will be waited upon prior to the memtable flush. This way the flush process (serving as a consumer) knows which other processes (acting as producers) depend on it.

More generally, we have the following synchronization points:

Memtable switch
> After this, all writes go only to the new memtable, making it primary, while the old one is still available for reads.

Flush finalization
> Replaces the old memtable with a flushed disk-resident table in the table view.

Write-ahead log truncation
> Discards a log segment holding records associated with a flushed memtable.

These operations have severe correctness implications. Continuing writes to the old memtable might result in data loss; for example, if the write is made into a memtable section that was already flushed. Similarly, failing to leave the old memtable available for reads until its disk-resident counterpart is ready will result in incomplete results.

During compaction, the table view is also changed, but here the process is slightly more straightforward: old disk-resident tables are discarded, and the compacted version is added instead. Old tables have to remain accessible for reads until the new one is fully written and is ready to replace them for reads. Situations in which the same tables participate in multiple compactions running in parallel have to be avoided as well.

In B-Trees, log truncation has to be coordinated with flushing dirty pages from the page cache to guarantee durability. In LSM Trees, we have a similar requirement: writes are buffered in a memtable, and their contents are not durable until fully flushed, so log truncation has to be coordinated with memtable flushes. As soon as the flush is complete, the log manager is given the information about the latest flushed log segment, and its contents can be safely discarded.

Not synchronizing log truncations with flushes will also result in data loss: if a log segment is discarded before the flush is complete, and the node crashes, log contents will not be replayed, and data from this segment won't be restored.

Log Stacking

Many modern filesystems are log structured: they buffer writes in a memory segment and flush its contents on disk when it becomes full in an append-only manner. SSDs use log-structured storage, too, to deal with small random writes, minimize write overhead, improve wear leveling, and increase device lifetime.

Log-structured storage (LSS) systems started gaining popularity around the time SSDs were becoming more affordable. LSM Trees and SSDs are a good match, since sequential workloads and append-only writes help to reduce amplification from in-place updates, which negatively affect performance on SSDs.

If we stack multiple log-structured systems on top each other, we can run into several problems that we were trying to solve using LSS, including write amplification, fragmentation, and poor performance. At the very least, we need to keep the SSD flash translation layer and the filesystem in mind when developing our applications [YANG14].

Flash Translation Layer

Using a log-structuring mapping layer in SSDs is motivated by two factors: small random writes have to be batched together in a physical page, and the fact that SSDs work by using program/erase cycles. Writes can be done only into previously *erased* pages. This means that a page cannot be *programmed* (in other words, written) unless it is empty (in other words, was *erased*).

A *single* page cannot be erased, and only *groups* of pages in a *block* (typically holding 64 to 512 pages) can be erased together. Figure 7-13 shows a schematic representation of pages, grouped into blocks. The flash translation layer (FTL) translates logical page addresses to their physical locations and keeps track of page states (live, discarded, or empty). When FTL runs out of free pages, it has to perform garbage collection and erase discarded pages.

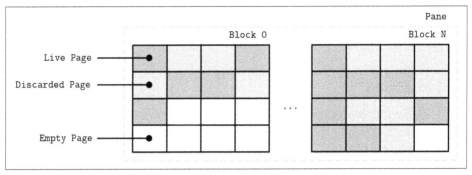

Figure 7-13. SSD pages, grouped into blocks

There are no guarantees that all pages in the block that is about to be erased are discarded. Before the block can be erased, FTL has to relocate its *live* pages to one of the blocks containing empty pages. Figure 7-14 shows the process of moving live pages from one block to new locations.

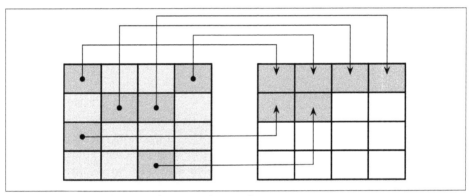

Figure 7-14. Page relocation during garbage collection

When all live pages are relocated, the block can be safely erased, and its empty pages become available for writes. Since FTL is aware of page states and state transitions and has all the necessary information, it is also responsible for SSD *wear leveling*.

Wear leveling distributes the load evenly across the medium, avoiding hotspots, where blocks fail prematurely because of a high number of program-erase cycles. It is required, since flash memory cells can go through only a limited number of program-erase cycles, and using memory cells evenly helps to extend the lifetime of the device.

In summary, the motivation for using log-structured storage on SSDs is to amortize I/O costs by batching small random writes together, which generally results in a smaller number of operations and, subsequently, reduces the number of times the garbage collection is triggered.

Filesystem Logging

On top of that, we get filesystems, many of which also use logging techniques for write buffering to reduce write amplification and use the underlying hardware optimally.

Log stacking manifests in a few different ways. First, each layer has to perform its own bookkeeping, and most often the underlying log does not expose the information necessary to avoid duplicating the efforts.

Figure 7-15 shows a mapping between a higher-level log (for example, the application) and a lower-level log (for example, the filesystem) resulting in redundant logging and different garbage collection patterns [YANG14]. Misaligned segment writes can make the situation even worse, since discarding a higher-level log segment may cause fragmentation and relocation of the neighboring segments' parts.

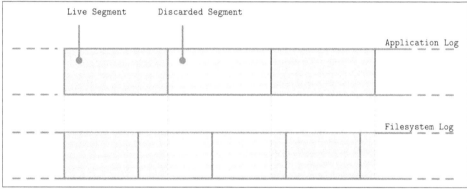

Figure 7-15. Misaligned writes and discarding of a higher-level log segment

Because layers do not communicate LSS-related scheduling (for example, discarding or relocating segments), lower-level subsystems might perform redundant operations on discarded data or the data that is about to be discarded. Similarly, because there's no single, standard segment size, it may happen that unaligned higher-level segments occupy multiple lower-level segments. All these overheads can be reduced or completely avoided.

Even though we say that log-structured storage is all about sequential I/O, we have to keep in mind that database systems may have multiple write streams (for example, log writes parallel to data record writes) [YANG14]. When considered on a hardware level, interleaved sequential write streams may not translate into the same sequential pattern: blocks are not necessarily going to be placed in write order. Figure 7-16 shows multiple streams overlapping in time, writing records that have sizes not aligned with the underlying hardware page size.

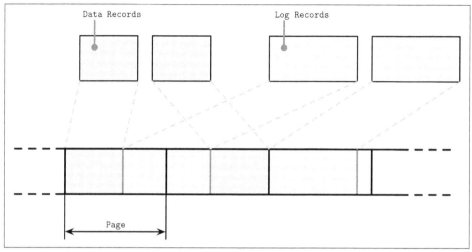

Figure 7-16. Unaligned multistream writes

This results in fragmentation that we tried to avoid. To reduce interleaving, some database vendors recommend keeping the log on a separate device to isolate work-loads and be able to reason about their performance and access patterns independently. However, it is more important to keep partitions aligned to the underlying hardware [INTEL14] and keep writes aligned to page size [KIM12].

LLAMA and Mindful Stacking

> Well, you'll never believe this, but that llama you're looking at was once a human being. And not just any human being. That guy was an emperor. A rich, powerful ball of charisma.
>
> —Kuzco from *The Emperor's New Groove*

In "Bw-Trees" on page 120, we discussed an immutable B-Tree version called Bw-Tree. Bw-Tree is layered on top of a *latch-free, log-structured, access-method aware* (LLAMA) storage subsystem. This layering allows Bw-Trees to grow and shrink dynamically, while leaving garbage collection and page management transparent for the tree. Here, we're most interested in the *access-method aware* part, demonstrating the benefits of coordination between the software layers.

To recap, a *logical* Bw-Tree node consists of a linked list of *physical* delta nodes, a chain of updates from the newest one to the oldest one, ending in a base node. Logical nodes are linked using an in-memory mapping table, pointing to the location of the latest update on disk. Keys and values are added to and removed from the logical nodes, but their physical representations remain immutable.

Log-structured storage buffers node updates (delta nodes) together in 4 Mb flush buffers. As soon as the page fills up, it's flushed on disk. Periodically, garbage collection reclaims space occupied by the unused delta and base nodes, and relocates the live ones to free up fragmented pages.

Without access-method awareness, interleaved delta nodes that belong to different logical nodes will be written in their insertion order. Bw-Tree awareness in LLAMA allows for the consolidation of several delta nodes into a single contiguous physical location. If two updates in delta nodes *cancel* each other (for example, an insert followed by delete), their *logical* consolidation can be performed as well, and only the latter delete can be persisted.

LSS garbage collection can also take care of consolidating the logical Bw-Tree node contents. This means that garbage collection will not only reclaim the free space, but also significantly reduce the physical node fragmentation. If garbage collection only rewrote several delta nodes contiguously, they would still take the same amount of space, and readers would need to perform the work of applying the delta updates to the base node. At the same time, if a higher-level system consolidated the nodes and wrote them contiguously to the new locations, LSS would *still* have to garbage-collect the old versions.

By being aware of Bw-Tree semantics, several deltas may be rewritten as a single base node with all deltas already applied *during* garbage collection. This reduces the total space used to represent this Bw-Tree node and the latency required to read the page while reclaiming the space occupied by discarded pages.

You can see that, when considered carefully, stacking can yield many benefits. It is not necessary to always build tightly coupled single-level structures. Good APIs and exposing the right information can significantly improve efficiency.

Open-Channel SSDs

An alternative to stacking software layers is to skip all indirection layers and use the hardware directly. For example, it is possible to avoid using a filesystem and flash translation layer by developing for Open-Channel SSDs. This way, we can avoid at least two layers of logs and have more control over wear-leveling, garbage collection, data placement, and scheduling. One of the implementations that uses this approach is LOCS (LSM Tree-based KV Store on Open-Channel SSD) [WANG13]. Another example using Open-Channel SSDs is LightNVM, implemented in the Linux kernel [BJØRLING17].

The flash translation layer usually handles data placement, garbage collection, and page relocation. Open-Channel SSDs expose their internals, drive management, and

I/O scheduling without needing to go through the FTL. While this certainly requires much more attention to detail from the developer's perspective, this approach may yield significant performance improvements. You can draw a parallel with using the O_DIRECT flag to bypass the kernel page cache, which gives better control, but requires manual page management.

Software Defined Flash (SDF) [OUYANG14], a hardware/software codesigned Open-Channel SSDs system, exposes an asymmetric I/O interface that takes SSD specifics into consideration. Sizes of read and write units are different, and write unit size corresponds to erase unit size (block), which greatly reduces write amplification. This setting is ideal for log-structured storage, since there's only one software layer that performs garbage collection and relocates pages. Additionally, developers have access to internal SSD parallelism, since every channel in SDF is exposed as a separate block device, which can be used to further improve performance.

Hiding complexity behind a simple API might sound compelling, but can cause complications in cases in which software layers have different semantics. Exposing *some* underlying system internals may be beneficial for better integration.

Summary

Log-structured storage is used everywhere: from the flash translation layer, to filesystems and database systems. It helps to reduce write amplification by batching small random writes together in memory. To reclaim space occupied by removed segments, LSS periodically triggers garbage collection.

LSM Trees take some ideas from LSS and help to build index structures managed in a log-structured manner: writes are batched in memory and flushed on disk; shadowed data records are cleaned up during compaction.

It is important to remember that many software layers use LSS, and make sure that layers are stacked optimally. Alternatively, we can skip the filesystem level altogether and access hardware directly.

Further Reading

If you'd like to learn more about the concepts mentioned in this chapter, you can refer to the following sources:

Overview

Luo, Chen, and Michael J. Carey. 2019. "LSM-based Storage Techniques: A Survey." *The VLDB Journal https://doi.org/10.1007/s00778-019-00555-y.*

LSM Trees

O'Neil, Patrick, Edward Cheng, Dieter Gawlick, and Elizabeth O'Neil. 1996. "The log-structured merge-tree (LSM-tree)." *Acta Informatica* 33, no. 4: 351-385. *https://doi.org/10.1007/s002360050048.*

Bitcask

Justin Sheehy, David Smith. "Bitcask: A Log-Structured Hash Table for Fast Key/Value Data." 2010.

WiscKey

Lanyue Lu, Thanumalayan Sankaranarayana Pillai, Hariharan Gopalakrishnan, Andrea C. Arpaci-Dusseau, and Remzi H. Arpaci-Dusseau. 2017. "WiscKey: Separating Keys from Values in SSD-Conscious Storage." ACM Trans. Storage 13, 1, Article 5 (March 2017), 28 pages.

LOCS

Peng Wang, Guangyu Sun, Song Jiang, Jian Ouyang, Shiding Lin, Chen Zhang, and Jason Cong. 2014. "An efficient design and implementation of LSM-tree based key-value store on open-channel SSD." In Proceedings of the Ninth European Conference on Computer Systems (EuroSys '14). ACM, New York, NY, USA, Article 16, 14 pages.

LLAMA

Justin Levandoski, David Lomet, and Sudipta Sengupta. 2013. "LLAMA: a cache/storage subsystem for modern hardware." Proc. VLDB Endow. 6, 10 (August 2013), 877-888.

Part I Conclusion

In Part I, we've been talking about storage engines. We started from high-level database system architecture and classification, learned how to implement on-disk storage structures, and how they fit into the full picture with other components.

We've seen several storage structures, starting from B-Trees. The discussed structures do not represent an entire field, and there are many other interesting developments. However, these examples are still a good illustration of the three properties we identified at the beginning of this part: *buffering*, *immutability*, and *ordering*. These properties are useful for describing, memorizing, and expressing different aspects of the storage structures.

Figure I-1 summarizes the discussed storage structures and shows whether or not they're using these properties.

Adding in-memory buffers always has a positive impact on write amplification. In in-place update structures like WiredTiger and LA-Trees, in-memory buffering helps to amortize the cost of multiple same-page writes by combining them. In other words, buffering helps to reduce write amplification.

In immutable structures, such as multicomponent LSM Trees and FD-Trees, buffering has a similar positive effect, but at a cost of future rewrites when moving data from one immutable level to the other. In other words, using immutability may lead to deferred write amplification. At the same time, using immutability has a positive impact on concurrency and space amplification, since most of the discussed immutable structures use fully occupied pages.

When using immutability, unless we *also* use buffering, we end up with unordered storage structures like Bitcask and WiscKey (with the exception of copy-on-write B-Trees, which copy, re-sort, and relocate their pages). WiscKey stores *only keys* in sorted LSM Trees and allows retrieving records in key order using the key index. In Bw-Trees, *some* of the nodes (ones that were consolidated) hold data records in key order, while the rest of the logical Bw-Tree nodes may have their delta updates scattered across different pages.

	Buffered	Mutable	Ordered
B+Trees	No	Yes	Yes
WiredTiger	Yes	Yes	Yes
LA-Trees	Yes	Yes	Yes
COW B-Trees	No	No	Yes
2C LSM Trees	Yes	No	Yes
MC LSM Trees	Yes	No	Yes
FD-Trees	Yes	No	Yes
BitCask	No	No	No
WiscKey	Yes(1)	No	Yes(1)
BW-Trees	No	No	No(2)

Figure I-1. Buffering, immutability, and ordering properties of discussed storage structures. (1) WiscKey uses buffering only for keeping keys sorted order. (2) Only consolidated nodes in Bw-Trees hold ordered records.

You see that these three properties can be mixed and matched in order to achieve the desired characteristics. Unfortunately, storage engine design usually involves trade-offs: you increase the cost of one operation in favor of the other.

Using this knowledge, you should be able to start looking closer at the code of most modern database systems. Some of the code references and starting points can be found across the entire book. Knowing and understanding the terminology will make this process easier for you.

Many modern database systems are powered by probabilistic data structures [FLAJO-LET12] [CORMODE04], and there's new research being done on bringing ideas from machine learning into database systems [KRASKA18]. We're about to experience further changes in research and industry as nonvolatile and byte-addressable storage becomes more prevalent and widely available [VENKATARAMAN11].

Knowing the fundamental concepts described in this book should help you to understand and implement newer research, since it borrows from, builds upon, and is inspired by the same concepts. The major advantage of knowing the theory and history is that there's nothing entirely new and, as the narrative of this book shows, progress is incremental.

Distributed Systems

A distributed system is one in which the failure of a computer you didn't even know existed can render your own computer unusable.

—Leslie Lamport

Without distributed systems, we wouldn't be able to make phone calls, transfer money, or exchange information over long distances. We use distributed systems daily. Sometimes, even without acknowledging it: any client/server application is a distributed system.

For many modern software systems, *vertical* scaling (scaling by running the same software on a bigger, faster machine with more CPU, RAM, or faster disks) isn't viable. Bigger machines are more expensive, harder to replace, and may require special maintenance. An alternative is to scale *horizontally*: to run software on multiple machines connected over the network and working as a single logical entity.

Distributed systems might differ both in size, from a handful to hundreds of machines, and in characteristics of their participants, from small handheld or sensor devices to high-performance computers.

The time when database systems were mainly running on a single node is long gone, and most modern database systems have multiple nodes connected in clusters to increase storage capacity, improve performance, and enhance availability.

Even though some of the theoretical breakthroughs in distributed computing aren't new, most of their practical application happened relatively recently. Today, we see increasing interest in the subject, more research, and new development being done.

Basic definitions

In a distributed system, we have several *participants* (sometimes called *processes*, *nodes*, or *replicas*). Each participant has its own local *state*. Participants communicate by exchanging *messages* using communication *links* between them.

Processes can access the time using a *clock*, which can be *logical* or *physical*. Logical clocks are implemented using a kind of monotonically growing counter. Physical clocks, also called *wall clocks*, are bound to a notion of time in the physical world and are accessible through process-local means; for example, through an operating system.

It's impossible to talk about distributed systems without mentioning the inherent difficulties caused by the fact that its parts are located apart from each other. Remote processes communicate through links that can be slow and unreliable, which makes knowing the exact state of the remote process more complicated.

Most of the research in the distributed systems field is related to the fact that nothing is entirely reliable: communication channels may delay, reorder, or fail to deliver the messages; processes may pause, slow down, crash, go out of control, or suddenly stop responding.

There are many themes in common in the fields of concurrent and distributed programming, since CPUs are tiny distributed systems with links, processors, and communication protocols. You'll see many parallels with concurrent programming in "Consistency Models" on page 222. However, most of the primitives can't be reused directly because of the costs of communication between remote parties, and the unreliability of links and processes.

To overcome the difficulties of the distributed environment, we need to use a particular class of algorithms, *distributed algorithms*, which have notions of local and remote state and execution and work despite unreliable networks and component failures. We describe algorithms in terms of *state* and *steps* (or *phases*), with *transitions* between them. Each process executes the algorithm steps locally, and a combination of local executions and process interactions constitutes a distributed algorithm.

Distributed algorithms describe the local behavior and interaction of multiple independent nodes. Nodes communicate by sending messages to each other. Algorithms define participant roles, exchanged messages, states, transitions, executed steps, properties of the delivery medium, timing assumptions, failure models, and other characteristics that describe processes and their interactions.

Distributed algorithms serve many different purposes:

Coordination
   A process that supervises the actions and behavior of several workers.

Cooperation
   Multiple participants relying on one another for finishing their tasks.

Dissemination
   Processes cooperating in spreading the information to all interested parties quickly and reliably.

Consensus
   Achieving agreement among multiple processes.

In this book, we talk about algorithms in the context of their usage and prefer a practical approach over purely academic material. First, we cover all necessary abstractions, the processes and the connections between them, and progress to building more complex communication patterns. We start with UDP, where the sender doesn't have any guarantees on whether or not its message has reached its destination; and finally, to achieve consensus, where multiple processes agree on a specific value.

CHAPTER 8

Introduction and Overview

What makes distributed systems inherently different from single-node systems? Let's take a look at a simple example and try to see. In a single-threaded program, we define variables and the execution process (a set of steps).

For example, we can define a variable and perform simple arithmetic operations over it:

```
int x = 1;
x += 2;
x *= 2;
```

We have a single execution history: we declare a variable, increment it by two, then multiply it by two, and get the result: 6. Let's say that, instead of having one execution thread performing these operations, we have two threads that have read and write access to variable x.

Concurrent Execution

As soon as two execution threads are allowed to access the variable, the exact outcome of the concurrent step execution is unpredictable, unless the steps are synchronized between the threads. Instead of a single possible outcome, we end up with four, as Figure 8-1 shows.[1]

---

1 Interleaving, where the multiplier reads before the adder, is left out for brevity, since it yields the same result as a).

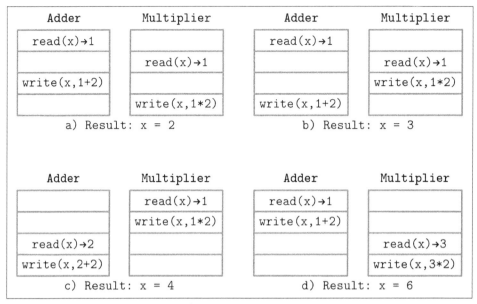

Figure 8-1. Possible interleavings of concurrent executions

- a) x = 2, if both threads read an initial value, the adder writes its value, but it is overwritten with the multiplication result.
- b) x = 3, if both threads read an initial value, the multiplier writes its value, but it is overwritten with the addition result.
- c) x = 4, if the multiplier can read the initial value and execute its operation before the adder starts.
- d) x = 6, if the adder can read the initial value and execute its operation before the multiplier starts.

Even before we can cross a single node boundary, we encounter the first problem in distributed systems: *concurrency*. Every concurrent program has some properties of a distributed system. Threads access the shared state, perform some operations locally, and propagate the results back to the shared variables.

To define execution histories precisely and reduce the number of possible outcomes, we need *consistency models*. Consistency models describe concurrent executions and establish an order in which operations can be executed and made visible to the participants. Using different consistency models, we can constraint or relax the number of states the system can be in.

There is a lot of overlap in terminology and research in the areas of distributed systems and concurrent computing, but there are also some differences. In a concurrent system, we can have *shared memory*, which processors can use to exchange the information. In a distributed system, each processor has its local state and participants communicate by passing messages.

Concurrent and Parallel

We often use the terms *concurrent* and *parallel* computing interchangeably, but these concepts have a slight semantic difference. When two sequences of steps execute concurrently, both of them are in progress, but only one of them is executed at any moment. If two sequences execute in parallel, their steps can be executed simultaneously. Concurrent operations overlap in time, while parallel operations are executed by multiple processors [WEIKUM01].

Joe Armstrong, creator of the Erlang programming language, gave an example (*https://databass.dev/links/44*): concurrent execution is like having two queues to a single coffee machine, while parallel execution is like having two queues to two coffee machines. That said, the vast majority of sources use the term concurrency to describe systems with several parallel execution threads, and the term parallelism is rarely used.

Shared State in a Distributed System

We can try to introduce some notion of shared memory to a distributed system, for example, a single source of information, such as database. Even if we solve the problems with concurrent access to it, we still cannot guarantee that all processes are in sync.

To access this database, processes have to go over the communication medium by sending and receiving messages to query or modify the state. However, what happens if one of the processes does not receive a response from the database for a longer time? To answer this question, we first have to define what *longer* even means. To do this, the system has to be described in terms of *synchrony*: whether the communication is fully asynchronous, or whether there are some timing assumptions. These timing assumptions allow us to introduce operation timeouts and retries.

We do not know whether the database hasn't responded because it's overloaded, unavailable, or slow, or because of some problems with the network on the way to it. This describes a *nature* of a crash: processes may crash by failing to participate in further algorithm steps, having a temporary failure, or by omitting some of the messages. We need to define a *failure model* and describe ways in which failures can occur before we decide how to treat them.

A property that describes system reliability and whether or not it can continue operating correctly in the presence of failures is called *fault tolerance*. Failures are inevitable, so we need to build systems with reliable components, and eliminating a single point of failure in the form of the aforementioned single-node database can be the first step in this direction. We can do this by introducing some *redundancy* and adding a backup database. However, now we face a different problem: how do we keep *multiple copies* of shared state in sync?

So far, trying to introduce shared state to our simple system has left us with more questions than answers. We now know that sharing state is not as simple as just introducing a database, and have to take a more granular approach and describe interactions in terms of independent processes and passing messages between them.

Fallacies of Distributed Computing

In an ideal case, when two computers talk over the network, everything works just fine: a process opens up a connection, sends the data, gets responses, and everyone is happy. Assuming that operations always succeed and nothing can go wrong is dangerous, since when something does break and our assumptions turn out to be wrong, systems behave in ways that are hard or impossible to predict.

Most of the time, assuming that the *network is reliable* is a reasonable thing to do. It has to be reliable to at least some extent to be useful. We've all been in the situation when we tried to establish a connection to the remote server and got a `Network is Unreachable` error instead. But even if it is possible to establish a connection, a successful *initial* connection to the server does not guarantee that the link is stable, and the connection can get interrupted at any time. The message might've reached the remote party, but the response could've gotten lost, or the connection was interrupted before the response was delivered.

Network switches break, cables get disconnected, and network configurations can change at any time. We should build our system by handling all of these scenarios gracefully.

A connection can be stable, but we can't expect remote calls to be as fast as the local ones. We should make as few assumptions about latency as possible and never assume that *latency is zero*. For our message to reach a remote server, it has to go through several software layers, and a physical medium such as optic fiber or a cable. All of these operations are not instantaneous.

Michael Lewis, in his *Flash Boys* book (Simon and Schuster), tells a story about companies spending millions of dollars to reduce latency by several milliseconds to able to access stock exchanges faster than the competition. This is a great example of using latency as a competitive advantage, but it's worth mentioning that, according to some other studies, such as [BARTLETT16], the chance of stale-quote arbitrage (the ability to profit from being able to know prices and execute orders faster than the competition) doesn't give fast traders the ability to exploit markets.

Learning our lessons, we've added retries, reconnects, and removed the assumptions about instantaneous execution, but this still turns out not to be enough. When increasing the number, rates, and sizes of exchanged messages, or adding new processes to the existing network, we should not assume that *bandwidth is infinite*.

 In 1994, Peter Deutsch published a now-famous list of assertions, titled "Fallacies of distributed computing," describing the aspects of distributed computing that are easy to overlook. In addition to network reliability, latency, and bandwidth assumptions, he describes some other problems. For example, network security, the possible presence of adversarial parties, intentional and unintentional topology changes that can break our assumptions about presence and location of specific resources, transport costs in terms of both time and resources, and, finally, the existence of a single authority having knowledge and control over the entire network.

Deutsch's list of distributed computing fallacies is pretty exhaustive, but it focuses on what can go wrong when we send messages from one process to another through the link. These concerns are valid and describe the most general and low-level complications, but unfortunately, there are many other assumptions we make about the distributed systems while designing and implementing them that can cause problems when operating them.

Processing

Before a remote process can send a response to the message it just received, it needs to perform some work locally, so we cannot assume that *processing is instantaneous*. Taking network latency into consideration is not enough, as operations performed by the remote processes aren't immediate, either.

Moreover, there's no guarantee that processing starts as soon as the message is delivered. The message may land in the pending queue on the remote server, and will have to wait there until all the messages that arrived before it are processed.

Nodes can be located closer or further from one another, have different CPUs, amounts of RAM, different disks, or be running different software versions and configurations. We cannot expect them to process requests at the same rate. If we have to wait for several remote servers working in parallel to respond to complete the task, the execution as a whole is as slow as the slowest remote server.

Contrary to the widespread belief, *queue capacity is not infinite* and piling up more requests won't do the system any good. *Backpressure* is a strategy that allows us to cope with producers that publish messages at a rate that is faster than the rate at which consumers can process them by slowing down the producers. Backpressure is one of the least appreciated and applied concepts in distributed systems, often built post hoc instead of being an integral part of the system design.

Even though increasing the queue capacity might sound like a good idea and can help to pipeline, parallelize, and effectively schedule requests, nothing is happening to the messages while they're sitting in the queue and waiting for their turn. Increasing the queue size may negatively impact latency, since changing it has no effect on the processing rate.

In general, process-local queues are used to achieve the following goals:

Decoupling
Receipt and processing are separated in time and happen independently.

Pipelining
Requests in different stages are processed by independent parts of the system. The subsystem responsible for receiving messages doesn't have to block until the previous message is fully processed.

Absorbing short-time bursts
System load tends to vary, but request inter-arrival times are hidden from the component responsible for request processing. Overall system latency increases because of the time spent in the queue, but this is usually still better than responding with a failure and retrying the request.

Queue size is workload- and application-specific. For relatively stable workloads, we can size queues by measuring task processing times and the average time each task spends in the queue before it is processed, and making sure that latency remains within acceptable bounds while throughput increases. In this case, queue sizes are relatively small. For unpredictable workloads, when tasks get submitted in bursts, queues should be sized to account for bursts and high load as well.

The remote server can work through requests quickly, but it doesn't mean that we always get a positive response from it. It can respond with a failure: it couldn't make a write, the searched value was not present, or it could've hit a bug. In summary, even the most favorable scenario still requires some attention from our side.

Clocks and Time

> Time is an illusion. Lunchtime doubly so.
>
> —Ford Prefect, *The Hitchhiker's Guide to the Galaxy*

Assuming that clocks on remote machines run in sync can also be dangerous. Combined with *latency is zero* and *processing is instantaneous*, it leads to different idiosyncrasies, especially in time-series and real-time data processing. For example, when collecting and aggregating data from participants with a different perception of time, you should understand time drifts between them and normalize times accordingly, rather than relying on the source timestamp. Unless you use specialized high-precision time sources, you should not rely on timestamps for synchronization or ordering. Of course this doesn't mean we cannot or should not rely on time at all: in the end, any synchronous system uses *local* clocks for timeouts.

It's essential to always account for the possible time differences between the processes and the time required for the messages to get delivered and processed. For example, Spanner (see "Distributed Transactions with Spanner" on page 268) uses a special time API that returns a timestamp and uncertainty bounds to impose a strict transaction order. Some failure-detection algorithms rely on a shared notion of time and a guarantee that the clock drift is always within allowed bounds for correctness [GUPTA01].

Besides the fact that clock synchronization in a distributed system is hard, the *current* time is constantly changing: you can request a current POSIX timestamp from the operating system, and request another *current* timestamp after executing several steps, and the two will be different. This is a rather obvious observation, but understanding both a source of time and which exact moment the timestamp captures is crucial.

Understanding whether the clock source is monotonic (i.e., that it won't ever go backward) and how much the scheduled time-related operations might drift can be helpful, too.

State Consistency

Most of the previous assumptions fall into the *almost always false* category, but there are some that are better described as *not always true*: when it's easy to take a mental shortcut and simplify the model by thinking of it a specific way, ignoring some tricky edge cases.

Distributed algorithms do not always guarantee strict state consistency. Some approaches have looser constraints and allow state divergence between replicas, and rely on *conflict resolution* (an ability to detect and resolve diverged states within the system) and *read-time data repair* (bringing replicas back in sync during reads in cases where they respond with different results). You can find more information about these concepts in Chapter 12. Assuming that the state is fully consistent across the nodes may lead to subtle bugs.

An eventually consistent distributed database system might have the logic to handle replica disagreement by querying a quorum of nodes during reads, but assume that the database schema and the view of the cluster are strongly consistent. Unless we enforce consistency of this information, relying on that assumption may have severe consequences.

For example, there was a bug in Apache Cassandra (*https://databass.dev/links/46*), caused by the fact that schema changes propagate to servers at different times. If you tried to read from the database while the schema was propagating, there was a chance of corruption, since one server encoded results assuming one schema and the other one decoded them using a different schema.

Another example is a bug caused by the divergent view of the ring (*https://data bass.dev/links/47*): if one of the nodes assumes that the other node holds data records for a key, but this other node has a different view of the cluster, reading or writing the data can result in misplacing data records or getting an empty response while data records are in fact happily present on the other node.

It is better to think about the possible problems in advance, even if a complete solution is costly to implement. By understanding and handling these cases, you can embed safeguards or change the design in a way that makes the solution more natural.

Local and Remote Execution

Hiding complexity behind an API might be dangerous. For example, if you have an iterator over the local dataset, you can reasonably predict what's going on behind the scenes, even if the storage engine is unfamiliar. Understanding the process of iteration over the remote dataset is an entirely different problem: you need to understand consistency and delivery semantics, data reconciliation, paging, merges, concurrent access implications, and many other things.

Simply hiding both behind the same interface, however useful, might be misleading. Additional API parameters may be necessary for debugging, configuration, and observability. We should always keep in mind that *local and remote execution are not the same* [WALDO96].

The most apparent problem with hiding remote calls is latency: remote invocation is many times more costly than the local one, since it involves two-way network transport, serialization/deserialization, and many other steps. Interleaving local and blocking remote calls may lead to performance degradation and unintended side effects [VINOSKI08].

Need to Handle Failures

It's OK to start working on a system assuming that all nodes are up and functioning normally, but thinking this is the case all the time is dangerous. In a long-running system, nodes can be taken down for maintenance (which usually involves a graceful shutdown) or crash for various reasons: software problems, out-of-memory killer

[KERRISK10], runtime bugs, hardware issues, etc. Processes do fail, and the best thing you can do is be prepared for failures and understand how to handle them.

If the remote server doesn't respond, we do not always know the exact reason for it. It could be caused by the crash, a network failure, the remote process, or the link to it being slow. Some distributed algorithms use *heartbeat protocols* and *failure detectors* to form a hypothesis about which participants are alive and reachable.

Network Partitions and Partial Failures

When two or more servers cannot communicate with each other, we call the situation *network partition*. In "Perspectives on the CAP Theorem" [GILBERT12], Seth Gilbert and Nancy Lynch draw a distinction between the case when two participants cannot communicate with each other and when several groups of participants are isolated from one another, cannot exchange messages, and proceed with the algorithm.

General unreliability of the network (packet loss, retransmission, latencies that are hard to predict) are *annoying but tolerable*, while network partitions can cause much more trouble, since independent groups can proceed with execution and produce conflicting results. Network links can also fail asymmetrically: messages can still be getting delivered from one process to the other one, but not vice versa.

To build a system that is robust in the presence of failure of one or multiple processes, we have to consider cases of *partial failures* [TANENBAUM06] and how the system can continue operating even though a part of it is unavailable or functioning incorrectly.

Failures are hard to detect and aren't always visible in the same way from different parts of the system. When designing highly available systems, one should always think about edge cases: what if we did replicate the data, but received no acknowledgments? Do we need to retry? Is the data still going to be available for reads on the nodes that have sent acknowledgments?

Murphy's Law[2] tells us that the failures do happen. Programming folklore adds that the failures will happen in the worst way possible, so our job as distributed systems engineers is to make sure we reduce the number of scenarios where things go wrong and prepare for failures in a way that contains the damage they can cause.

It's impossible to prevent all failures, but we can still build a resilient system that functions correctly in their presence. The best way to design for failures is to test for them. It's close to impossible to think through every possible failure scenario and predict the behaviors of multiple processes. Setting up testing harnesses that create partitions,

---

2 Murphy's Law is an adage that can be summarized as "Anything that can go wrong, will go wrong," which was popularized and is often used as an idiom in popular culture.

simulate bit rot [GRAY05], increase latencies, diverge clocks, and magnify relative processing speeds is the best way to go about it. Real-world distributed system setups can be quite adversarial, unfriendly, and "creative" (however, in a very hostile way), so the testing effort should attempt to cover as many scenarios as possible.

 Over the last few years, we've seen a few open source projects that help to recreate different failure scenarios. Toxiproxy (*https://data bass.dev/links/48*) can help to simulate network problems: limit the bandwidth, introduce latency, timeouts, and more. Chaos Monkey (*https://databass.dev/links/49*) takes a more radical approach and exposes engineers to production failures by randomly shutting down services. CharybdeFS (*https://databass.dev/links/50*) helps to simulate filesystem and hardware errors and failures. You can use these tools to test your software and make sure it behaves correctly in the presence of these failures. CrashMonkey (*https://data bass.dev/links/122*), a filesystem agnostic record-replay-and-test framework, helps test data and metadata consistency for persistent files.

When working with distributed systems, we have to take fault tolerance, resilience, possible failure scenarios, and edge cases seriously. Similar to "given enough eyeballs, all bugs are shallow," (*https://databass.dev/links/51*) we can say that a large enough cluster will eventually hit every possible issue. At the same time, given enough testing, we will be able to eventually find every existing problem.

Cascading Failures

We cannot always wholly isolate failures: a process tipping over under a high load increases the load for the rest of cluster, making it even more probable for the other nodes to fail. *Cascading failures* can propagate from one part of the system to the other, increasing the scope of the problem.

Sometimes, cascading failures can even be initiated by perfectly good intentions. For example, a node was offline for a while and did not receive the most recent updates. After it comes back online, helpful peers would like to help it to catch up with recent happenings and start streaming the data it's missing over to it, exhausting network resources or causing the node to fail shortly after the startup.

To protect a system from propagating failures and treat failure scenarios gracefully, *circuit breakers* can be used. In electrical engineering, circuit breakers protect expensive and hard-to-replace parts from overload or short circuit by interrupting the current flow. In software development, circuit breakers monitor failures and allow fallback mechanisms that can protect the system by steering away from the failing service, giving it some time to recover, and handling failing calls gracefully.

When the connection to one of the servers fails or the server does not respond, the client starts a reconnection loop. By that point, an overloaded server already has a hard time catching up with new connection requests, and client-side retries in a tight loop don't help the situation. To avoid that, we can use a *backoff* strategy. Instead of retrying immediately, clients wait for some time. Backoff can help us to avoid amplifying problems by scheduling retries and increasing the time window between subsequent requests.

Backoff is used to increase time periods between requests from a single client. However, different clients using the same backoff strategy can produce substantial load as well. To prevent *different* clients from retrying all at once after the backoff period, we can introduce *jitter*. Jitter adds small random time periods to backoff and reduces the probability of clients waking up and retrying at the same time.

Hardware failures, bit rot, and software errors can result in corruption that can propagate through standard delivery mechanisms. For example, corrupted data records can get replicated to the other nodes if they are not validated. Without validation mechanisms in place, a system can propagate corrupted data to the other nodes, potentially overwriting noncorrupted data records. To avoid that, we should use checksumming and validation to verify the integrity of any content exchanged between the nodes.

Overload and hotspotting can be avoided by planning and coordinating execution. Instead of letting peers execute operation steps independently, we can use a coordinator that prepares an execution plan based on the available resources and predicts the load based on the past execution data available to it.

In summary, we should always consider cases in which failures in one part of the system can cause problems elsewhere. We should equip our systems with circuit breakers, backoff, validation, and coordination mechanisms. Handling small isolated problems is always more straightforward than trying to recover from a large outage.

We've just spent an entire section discussing problems and potential failure scenarios in distributed systems, but we should see this as a warning and not as something that should scare us away.

Understanding what can go wrong, and carefully designing and testing our systems makes them more robust and resilient. Being aware of these issues can help you to identify and find potential sources of problems during development, as well as debug them in production.

Distributed Systems Abstractions

When talking about programming languages, we use common terminology and define our programs in terms of functions, operators, classes, variables, and pointers. Having a common vocabulary helps us to avoid inventing new words every time we describe anything. The more precise and less ambiguous our definitions are, the easier it is for our listeners to understand us.

Before we move to algorithms, we first have to cover the distributed systems vocabulary: definitions you'll frequently encounter in talks, books, and papers.

Links

Networks are not reliable: messages can get lost, delayed, and reordered. Now, with this thought in our minds, we will try to build several communication protocols. We'll start with the least reliable and robust ones, identifying the states they can be in, and figuring out the possible additions to the protocol that can provide better guarantees.

Fair-loss link

We can start with two *processes*, connected with a *link*. Processes can send messages to each other, as shown in Figure 8-2. Any communication medium is imperfect, and messages can get lost or delayed.

Let's see what kind of guarantees we can get. After the message M is sent, from the senders' perspective, it can be in one of the following states:

- Not *yet* delivered to process B (but will be, at some point in time)
- Irrecoverably lost during transport
- Successfully delivered to the remote process

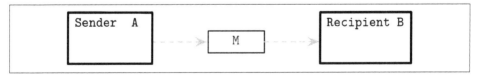

Figure 8-2. Simplest, unreliable form of communication

Notice that the sender does not have any way to find out if the message is already delivered. In distributed systems terminology, this kind of link is called *fair-loss*. The properties of this kind of link are:

Fair loss
> If both sender and recipient are correct and the sender keeps retransmitting the message infinitely many times, it will eventually be delivered.[3]

Finite duplication
> Sent messages won't be delivered infinitely many times.

No creation
> A link will not come up with messages; in other words, it won't deliver the message that was never sent.

A fair-loss link is a useful abstraction and a first building block for communication protocols with strong guarantees. We can assume that this link is not losing messages between communicating parties *systematically* and doesn't create new messages. But, at the same time, we cannot entirely rely on it. This might remind you of the User Datagram Protocol (UDP) (*https://databass.dev/links/52*), which allows us to send messages from one process to the other, but does not have reliable delivery semantics on the protocol level.

Message acknowledgments

To improve the situation and get more clarity in terms of message status, we can introduce *acknowledgments*: a way for the recipient to notify the sender that it has received the message. For that, we need to use bidirectional communication channels and add some means that allow us to distinguish differences between the messages; for example, *sequence numbers*, which are unique monotonically increasing message identifiers.

It is enough to have a *unique* identifier for every message. Sequence numbers are just a particular case of a unique identifier, where we achieve uniqueness by drawing identifiers from a counter. When using hash algorithms to identify messages uniquely, we should account for possible collisions and make sure we can still disambiguate messages.

---

3 A more precise definition is that if a correct process A sends a message to a correct process B infinitely often, it will be delivered infinitely often ([CACHIN11]).

Now, process A can send a message M(n), where n is a monotonically increasing message counter. As soon as B receives the message, it sends an acknowledgment ACK(n) back to A. Figure 8-3 shows this form of communication.

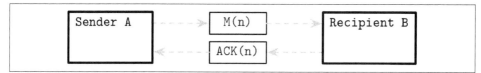

Figure 8-3. Sending a message with an acknowledgment

The acknowledgment, as well as the original message, may get lost on the way. The number of states the message can be in changes slightly. Until A receives an acknowledgment, the message is still in one of the three states we mentioned previously, but as soon as A receives the acknowledgment, it can be confident that the message is delivered to B.

Message retransmits

Adding acknowledgments is *still* not enough to call this communication protocol reliable: a sent message may still get lost, or the remote process may fail before acknowledging it. To solve this problem and provide delivery guarantees, we can try *retransmits* instead. Retransmits are a way for the sender to retry a potentially failed operation. We say *potentially* failed, because the sender doesn't really know whether it has failed or not, since the type of link we're about to discuss does *not* use acknowledgments.

After process A sends message M, it waits until timeout T is triggered and tries to send the same message again. Assuming the link between processes stays intact, network partitions between the processes are not infinite, and not *all* packets are lost, we can state that, from the sender's perspective, the message is either not *yet* delivered to process B or is successfully delivered to process B. Since A keeps trying to send the message, we can say that it *cannot* get irrecoverably lost during transport.

In distributed systems terminology, this abstraction is called a *stubborn link*. It's called stubborn because the sender keeps resending the message again and again indefinitely, but, since this sort of abstraction would be highly impractical, we need to combine retries with acknowledgments.

Problem with retransmits

Whenever we send the message, until we receive an acknowledgment from the remote process, we do not know whether it has already been processed, it will be processed shortly, it has been lost, or the remote process has crashed before receiving it— any one of these states is possible. We can retry the operation and send the message again, but this can result in message duplicates. Processing duplicates is only safe if the operation we're about to perform is idempotent.

An *idempotent* operation is one that can be executed multiple times, yielding the same result without producing additional side effects. For example, a server shutdown operation can be idempotent, the first call initiates the shutdown, and all subsequent calls do not produce any additional effects.

If every operation was idempotent, we could think less about delivery semantics, rely more on retransmits for fault tolerance, and build systems in an entirely reactive way: triggering an action as a response to some signal, without causing unintended side effects. However, operations are not necessarily idempotent, and merely assuming that they are might lead to cluster-wide side effects. For example, charging a customer's credit card is not idempotent, and charging it multiple times is definitely undesirable.

Idempotence is particularly important in the presence of partial failures and network partitions, since we cannot always find out the exact status of a remote operation—whether it has succeeded, failed, or will be executed shortly—and we just have to wait longer. Since guaranteeing that each executed operation is idempotent is an unrealistic requirement, we need to provide guarantees *equivalent* to idempotence without changing the underlying operation semantics. To achieve this, we can use *deduplication* and avoid processing messages more than once.

Message order

Unreliable networks present us with two problems: messages can arrive out of order and, because of retransmits, some messages may arrive more than once. We have already introduced sequence numbers, and we can use these message identifiers on the recipient side to ensure *first-in, first-out* (FIFO) ordering. Since every message has a sequence number, the receiver can track:

- $n_{consecutive}$, specifying the highest sequence number, up to which it has seen all messages. Messages up to this number can be put back in order.

- $n_{processed}$, specifying the highest sequence number, up to which messages were put back in their original order and *processed*. This number can be used for deduplication.

If the received message has a nonconsecutive sequence number, the receiver puts it into the reordering buffer. For example, it receives a message with a sequence number 5 after receiving one with 3, and we know that 4 is still missing, so we need to put 5 aside until 4 comes, and we can reconstruct the message order. Since we're building on top of a fair-loss link, we assume that messages between $n_{consecutive}$ and n_{max_seen} will eventually be delivered.

The recipient can safely discard the messages with sequence numbers up to $n_{consecutive}$ that it receives, since they're guaranteed to be already delivered.

Deduplication works by checking if the message with a sequence number n has already been *processed* (passed down the stack by the receiver) and discarding already processed messages.

In distributed systems terms, this type of link is called a *perfect link*, which provides the following guarantees [CACHIN11]:

Reliable delivery
> Every message sent *once* by the correct process A to the correct process B, will *eventually* be delivered.

No duplication
> No message is delivered more than once.

No creation
> Same as with other types of links, it can only deliver the messages that were actually sent.

This might remind you of the TCP[4] protocol (however, reliable delivery in TCP is guaranteed only in the scope of a single session). Of course, this model is just a simplified representation we use for illustration purposes only. TCP has a much more sophisticated model for dealing with acknowledgments, which groups acknowledgments and reduces the protocol-level overhead. In addition, TCP has selective acknowledgments, flow control, congestion control, error detection, and many other features that are out of the scope of our discussion.

Exactly-once delivery

> There are only two hard problems in distributed systems: 2. Exactly-once delivery 1. Guaranteed order of messages 2. Exactly-once delivery.
>
> —Mathias Verraes

There have been many discussions about whether or not *exactly-once delivery* is possible. Here, semantics and precise wording are essential. Since there might be a link failure preventing the message from being delivered from the first try, most of the real-world systems employ *at-least-once delivery*, which ensures that the sender retries until it receives an acknowledgment, otherwise the message is not considered to be received. Another delivery semantic is *at-most-once*: the sender sends the message and doesn't expect any delivery confirmation.

---

4 See *https://databass.dev/links/53.*

The TCP protocol works by breaking down messages into packets, transmitting them one by one, and stitching them back together on the receiving side. TCP might attempt to retransmit some of the packets, and more than one transmission attempt may succeed. Since TCP marks each packet with a sequence number, even though some packets were transmitted more than once, it can deduplicate the packets and guarantee that the recipient will see the message and *process* it only once. In TCP, this guarantee is valid only for a *single session*: if the message is acknowledged and processed, but the sender didn't receive the acknowledgment before the connection was interrupted, the application is not aware of this delivery and, depending on its logic, it might attempt to send the message once again.

This means that exactly-once *processing* is what's interesting here since duplicate *deliveries* (or packet transmissions) have no side effects and are merely an artifact of the best effort by the link. For example, if the database node has only *received* the record, but hasn't *persisted* it, delivery has occurred, but it'll be of no use unless the record can be retrieved (in other words, unless it was both delivered and processed).

For the exactly-once guarantee to hold, nodes should have a *common knowledge* [HALPERN90]: everyone knows about some fact, and everyone knows that everyone else also knows about that fact. In simplified terms, nodes have to agree on the state of the record: both nodes agree that it either *was* or *was not* persisted. As you will see later in this chapter, this is theoretically impossible, but in practice we still use this notion by relaxing coordination requirements.

Any misunderstanding about whether or not exactly-once delivery is possible most likely comes from approaching the problem from different protocol and abstraction levels and the definition of "delivery." It's not possible to build a reliable link without ever transferring any message more than once, but we can create the illusion of exactly-once delivery from the sender's perspective by *processing* the message once and ignoring duplicates.

Now, as we have established the means for reliable communication, we can move ahead and look for ways to achieve uniformity and agreement between processes in the distributed system.

Two Generals' Problem

One of the most prominent descriptions of an agreement in a distributed system is a thought experiment widely known as the *Two Generals' Problem*.

This thought experiment shows that it is impossible to achieve an agreement between two parties if communication is *asynchronous* in the presence of link failures. Even though TCP exhibits properties of a perfect link, it's important to remember that perfect links, despite the name, do not guarantee *perfect* delivery. They also can't guarantee that participants will be alive the whole time, and are concerned only with transport.

Imagine two armies, led by two generals, preparing to attack a fortified city. The armies are located on two sides of the city and can succeed in their siege only if they attack simultaneously.

The generals can communicate by sending messengers, and already have devised an attack plan. The only thing they now have to agree on is whether or not to carry out the plan. Variants of this problem are when one of the generals has a higher rank, but needs to make sure the attack is coordinated; or that the generals need to agree on the exact time. These details do not change the problem definition: the generals have to come to an agreement.

The army generals only have to agree on the fact that they both will proceed with the attack. Otherwise, the attack cannot succeed. General A sends a message MSG(N), stating an intention to proceed with the attack at a specified time, *if* the other party agrees to proceed as well.

After A sends the messenger, he doesn't know whether the messenger has arrived or not: the messenger can get captured and fail to deliver the message. When general B receives the message, he has to send an acknowledgment ACK(MSG(N)). Figure 8-4 shows that a message is sent one way and acknowledged by the other party.

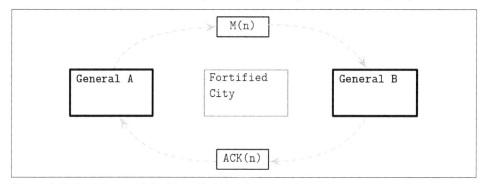

Figure 8-4. Two Generals' Problem illustrated

The messenger carrying this acknowledgment might get captured or fail to deliver it, as well. B doesn't have any way of knowing if the messenger has successfully delivered the acknowledgment.

To be sure about it, B has to wait for ACK(ACK(MSG(N))), a second-order acknowledgment stating that A received an acknowledgment for the acknowledgment.

No matter how many further confirmations the generals send to each other, they will always be one ACK away from knowing if they can safely proceed with the attack. The generals are doomed to wonder if the message carrying this last acknowledgment has reached the destination.

Notice that we did not make any timing assumptions: communication between generals is fully asynchronous. There is no upper time bound set on how long the generals can take to respond.

FLP Impossibility

In a paper by Fisher, Lynch, and Paterson, the authors describe a problem famously known as the *FLP Impossibility Problem* [FISCHER85] (derived from the first letters of authors' last names), wherein they discuss a form of consensus in which processes start with an initial value and attempt to agree on a new value. After the algorithm completes, this new value has to be the same for all nonfaulty processes.

Reaching an agreement on a specific value is straightforward if the network is entirely reliable; but in reality, systems are prone to many different sorts of failures, such as message loss, duplication, network partitions, and slow or crashed processes.

A consensus protocol describes a system that, given multiple processes starting at its *initial state*, brings all of the processes to the *decision state*. For a consensus protocol to be correct, it has to preserve three properties:

Agreement
> The decision the protocol arrives at has to be unanimous: each process decides on some value, and this has to be the same for all processes. Otherwise, we have not reached a consensus.

Validity
> The agreed value has to be *proposed* by one of the participants, which means that the system should not just "come up" with the value. This also implies nontriviality of the value: processes should not always decide on some predefined default value.

Termination
> An agreement is final only if there are no processes that did not reach the decision state.

[FISCHER85] assumes that processing is entirely asynchronous; there's no shared notion of time between the processes. Algorithms in such systems cannot be based on timeouts, and there's no way for a process to find out whether the other process has crashed or is simply running too slow. The paper shows that, given these assumptions, there exists no protocol that can guarantee consensus in a bounded time. No completely asynchronous consensus algorithm can tolerate the unannounced crash of even a single remote process.

If we do not consider an upper time bound for the process to complete the algorithm steps, process failures can't be reliably detected, and there's no deterministic algorithm to reach a consensus.

However, FLP Impossibility does not mean we have to pack our things and go home, as reaching consensus is not possible. It only means that we cannot always reach consensus in an asynchronous system in bounded time. In practice, systems exhibit at least some degree of synchrony, and the solution to this problem requires a more refined model.

System Synchrony

From FLP Impossibility, you can see that the timing assumption is one of the critical characteristics of the distributed system. In an *asynchronous system*, we do not know the relative speeds of processes, and cannot guarantee message delivery in a bounded time or a particular order. The process might take indefinitely long to respond, and process failures can't always be reliably detected.

The main criticism of asynchronous systems is that these assumptions are not realistic: processes can't have *arbitrarily* different processing speeds, and links don't take *indefinitely* long to deliver messages. Relying on time both simplifies reasoning and helps to provide upper-bound timing guarantees.

It is not always possible to solve a consensus problem in an asynchronous model [FISCHER85]. Moreover, designing an efficient asynchronous algorithm is not always achievable, and for some tasks the practical solutions are more likely to be time-dependent [ARJOMANDI83].

These assumptions can be loosened up, and the system can be considered to be *synchronous*. For that, we introduce the notion of timing. It is much easier to reason about the system under the synchronous model. It assumes that processes are progressing at comparable rates, that transmission delays are bounded, and message delivery cannot take arbitrarily long.

A synchronous system can also be represented in terms of synchronized process-local clocks: there is an upper time bound in time difference between the two process-local time sources [CACHIN11].

Designing systems under a synchronous model allows us to use timeouts. We can build more complex abstractions, such as leader election, consensus, failure detection, and many others on top of them. This makes the best-case scenarios more robust, but results in a failure if the timing assumptions don't hold up. For example, in the Raft consensus algorithm (see "Raft" on page 300), we may end up with multiple processes believing they're leaders, which is resolved by forcing the lagging process to accept the other process as a leader; failure-detection algorithms (see

Chapter 9) can wrongly identify a live process as failed or vice versa. When designing our systems, we should make sure to consider these possibilities.

Properties of both asynchronous and synchronous models can be combined, and we can think of a system as *partially synchronous*. A partially synchronous system exhibits some of the properties of the synchronous system, but the bounds of message delivery, clock drift, and relative processing speeds might not be exact and hold only *most of the time* [DWORK88].

Synchrony is an essential property of the distributed system: it has an impact on performance, scalability, and general solvability, and has many factors necessary for the correct functioning of our systems. Some of the algorithms we discuss in this book operate under the assumptions of synchronous systems.

Failure Models

We keep mentioning *failures*, but so far it has been a rather broad and generic concept that might capture many meanings. Similar to how we can make different timing assumptions, we can assume the presence of different types of failures. A *failure model* describes exactly how processes can crash in a distributed system, and algorithms are developed using these assumptions. For example, we can assume that a process can crash and never recover, or that it is expected to recover after some time passes, or that it can fail by spinning out of control and supplying incorrect values.

In distributed systems, processes rely on one another for executing an algorithm, so failures can result in incorrect execution across the whole system.

We'll discuss multiple failure models present in distributed systems, such as *crash*, *omission*, and *arbitrary* faults. This list is not exhaustive, but it covers most of the cases applicable and important in real-life systems.

Crash Faults

Normally, we expect the process to be executing all steps of an algorithm correctly. The simplest way for a process to crash is by *stopping* the execution of any further steps required by the algorithm and not sending any messages to other processes. In other words, the process *crashes*. Most of the time, we assume a *crash-stop* process abstraction, which prescribes that, once the process has crashed, it remains in this state.

This model does not assume that it is impossible for the process to recover, and does not discourage recovery or try to prevent it. It only means that the algorithm *does not rely* on recovery for correctness or liveness. Nothing prevents processes from recovering, catching up with the system state, and participating in the *next* instance of the algorithm.

Failed processes are not able to continue participating in the current round of negotiations during which they failed. Assigning the recovering process a new, different identity does not make the model equivalent to crash-recovery (discussed next), since most algorithms use predefined lists of processes and clearly define failure semantics in terms of how many failures they can tolerate [CACHIN11].

Crash-recovery is a different process abstraction, under which the process stops executing the steps required by the algorithm, but recovers at a later point and tries to execute further steps. The possibility of recovery requires introducing a durable state and recovery protocol into the system [SKEEN83]. Algorithms that allow crash-recovery need to take all possible recovery states into consideration, since the recovering process may attempt to continue execution from the last step known to it.

Algorithms, aiming to exploit recovery, have to take both state and identity into account. Crash-recovery, in this case, can also be viewed as a special case of omission failure, since from the other process's perspective there's no distinction between the process that was unreachable and the one that has crashed and recovered.

Omission Faults

Another failure model is *omission fault*. This model assumes that the process skips some of the algorithm steps, or is not able to execute them, or this execution is not visible to other participants, or it cannot send or receive messages to and from other participants. Omission fault captures network partitions between the processes caused by faulty network links, switch failures, or network congestion. Network partitions can be represented as omissions of messages between individual processes or process groups. A crash can be simulated by completely omitting any messages to and from the process.

When the process is operating slower than the other participants and sends responses much later than expected, for the rest of the system it may look like it is forgetful. Instead of stopping completely, a slow node attempts to send its results out of sync with other nodes.

Omission failures occur when the algorithm that was supposed to execute certain steps either skips them or the results of this execution are not visible. For example, this may happen if the message is lost on the way to the recipient, and the sender fails to send it again and continues to operate as if it was successfully delivered, even though it was irrecoverably lost. Omission failures can also be caused by intermittent hangs, overloaded networks, full queues, etc.

Arbitrary Faults

The hardest class of failures to overcome is *arbitrary* or *Byzantine* faults: a process continues executing the algorithm steps, but in a way that contradicts the algorithm (for example, if a process in a consensus algorithm decides on a value that no other participant has ever proposed).

Such failures can happen due to bugs in software, or due to processes running different versions of the algorithm, in which case failures are easier to find and understand. It can get much more difficult when we do not have control over all processes, and one of the processes is intentionally misleading other processes.

You might have heard of Byzantine fault tolerance from the airspace industry: airplane and spacecraft systems do not take responses from subcomponents at face value and cross-validate their results. Another widespread application is cryptocurrencies [GILAD17], where there is no central authority, different parties control the nodes, and adversary participants have a material incentive to forge values and attempt to game the system by providing faulty responses.

Handling Failures

We can *mask* failures by forming process groups and introducing redundancy into the algorithm: even if one of the processes fails, the user will not notice this failure [CHRISTIAN91].

There might be some performance penalty related to failures: normal execution relies on processes being responsive, and the system has to fall back to the slower execution path for error handling and correction. Many failures can be prevented on the software level by code reviews, extensive testing, ensuring message delivery by introducing timeouts and retries, and making sure that steps are executed in order locally.

Most of the algorithms we're going to cover here assume the crash-failure model and work around failures by introducing redundancy. These assumptions help to create algorithms that perform better and are easier to understand and implement.

Summary

In this chapter, we discussed some of the distributed systems terminology and introduced some basic concepts. We've talked about the inherent difficulties and complications caused by the unreliability of the system components: links may fail to deliver messages, processes may crash, or the network may get partitioned.

This terminology should be enough for us to continue the discussion. The rest of the book talks about the *solutions* commonly used in distributed systems: we think back to what can go wrong and see what options we have available.

Further Reading

If you'd like to learn more about the concepts mentioned in this chapter, you can refer to the following sources:

Distributed systems abstractions, failure models, and timing assumptions

Lynch, Nancy A. 1996. *Distributed Algorithms*. San Francisco: Morgan Kaufmann.

Tanenbaum, Andrew S. and Maarten van Steen. 2006. *Distributed Systems: Principles and Paradigms* (2nd Ed). Boston: Pearson.

Cachin, Christian, Rachid Guerraoui, and Lus Rodrigues. 2011. *Introduction to Reliable and Secure Distributed Programming* (2nd Ed.). New York: Springer.

Failure Detection

If a tree falls in a forest and no one is around to hear it, does it make a sound?

—Unknown Author

In order for a system to appropriately react to failures, failures should be detected in a timely manner. A faulty process might get contacted even though it won't be able to respond, increasing latencies and reducing overall system availability.

Detecting failures in asynchronous distributed systems (i.e., without making any timing assumptions) is extremely difficult as it's impossible to tell whether the process has crashed, or is running slowly and taking an indefinitely long time to respond. We discussed a problem related to this one in "FLP Impossibility" on page 189.

Terms such as *dead*, *failed*, and *crashed* are usually used to describe a process that has stopped executing its steps completely. Terms such as *unresponsive*, *faulty*, and *slow* are used to describe *suspected* processes, which may actually be dead.

Failures may occur on the *link* level (messages between processes are lost or delivered slowly), or on the *process* level (the process crashes or is running slowly), and slowness may not always be distinguishable from failure. This means there's always a trade-off between wrongly suspecting alive processes as dead (producing *false-positives*), and delaying marking an unresponsive process as dead, giving it the benefit of doubt and expecting it to respond eventually (producing *false-negatives*).

A *failure detector* is a local subsystem responsible for identifying failed or unreachable processes to exclude them from the algorithm and guarantee liveness while preserving safety.

Liveness and safety are the properties that describe an algorithm's ability to solve a specific problem and the correctness of its output. More formally, *liveness* is a property that guarantees that a specific intended event *must* occur. For example, if one of the processes has failed, a failure detector *must* detect that failure. *Safety* guarantees that unintended events will *not* occur. For example, if a failure detector has marked a process as dead, this process had to be, in fact, dead [LAMPORT77] [RAYNAL99] [FREILING11].

From a practical perspective, excluding failed processes helps to avoid unnecessary work and prevents error propagation and cascading failures, while reducing availability when excluding potentially suspected alive processes.

Failure-detection algorithms should exhibit several essential properties. First of all, every nonfaulty member should eventually notice the process failure, and the algorithm should be able to make progress and eventually reach its final result. This property is called *completeness*.

We can judge the quality of the algorithm by its *efficiency*: how fast the failure detector can identify process failures. Another way to do this is to look at the *accuracy* of the algorithm: whether or not the process failure was precisely detected. In other words, an algorithm is *not* accurate if it falsely accuses a live process of being failed or is not able to detect the existing failures.

We can think of the relationship between efficiency and accuracy as a tunable parameter: a more efficient algorithm might be less precise, and a more accurate algorithm is usually less efficient. It is provably impossible to build a failure detector that is both accurate and efficient. At the same time, failure detectors are allowed to produce false-positives (i.e., falsely identify live processes as failed and vice versa) [CHANDRA96].

Failure detectors are an essential prerequisite and an integral part of many consensus and atomic broadcast algorithms, which we'll be discussing later in this book.

Many distributed systems implement failure detectors by using *heartbeats*. This approach is quite popular because of its simplicity and strong completeness. Algorithms we discuss here assume the absence of Byzantine failures: processes do not attempt to intentionally lie about their state or states of their neighbors.

Heartbeats and Pings

We can query the state of remote processes by triggering one of two periodic processes:

- We can trigger a ping, which sends messages to remote processes, checking if they are still alive by expecting a response within a specified time period.

- We can trigger a *heartbeat* when the process is actively notifying its peers that it's still running by sending messages to them.

We'll use pings as an example here, but the same problem can be solved using heartbeats, producing similar results.

Each process maintains a list of other processes (alive, dead, and suspected ones) and updates it with the last response time for each process. If a process fails to respond to a ping message for a longer time, it is marked as *suspected*.

Figure 9-1 shows the normal functioning of a system: process P1 is querying the state of neighboring node P2, which responds with an acknowledgment.

Figure 9-1. Pings for failure detection: normal functioning, no message delays

In contrast, Figure 9-2 shows how acknowledgment messages are delayed, which might result in marking the active process as down.

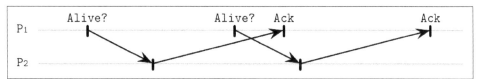

Figure 9-2. Pings for failure detection: responses are delayed, coming after the next message is sent

Many failure-detection algorithms are based on heartbeats and timeouts. For example, Akka, a popular framework for building distributed systems, has an implementation of a deadline failure detector (*https://databass.dev/links/41*), which uses heartbeats and reports a process failure if it has failed to register within a fixed time interval.

This approach has several potential downsides: its precision relies on the careful selection of ping frequency and timeout, and it does not capture process visibility from the perspective of other processes (see "Outsourced Heartbeats" on page 198).

Timeout-Free Failure Detector

Some algorithms avoid relying on timeouts for detecting failures. For example, Heartbeat, a *timeout-free* failure detector [AGUILERA97], is an algorithm that only counts heartbeats and allows the application to detect process failures based on the data in the heartbeat counter vectors. Since this algorithm is timeout-free, it operates under *asynchronous* system assumptions.

The algorithm assumes that any two correct processes are connected to each other with a *fair path*, which contains only fair links (i.e., if a message is sent over this link infinitely often, it is also received infinitely often), and each process is aware of the existence of *all* other processes in the network.

Each process maintains a list of neighbors and counters associated with them. Processes start by sending heartbeat messages to their neighbors. Each message contains a path that the heartbeat has traveled so far. The initial message contains the first sender in the path and a unique identifier that can be used to avoid broadcasting the same message multiple times.

When the process receives a new heartbeat message, it increments counters for all participants present in the path and sends the heartbeat to the ones that are not present there, appending itself to the path. Processes stop propagating messages as soon as they see that all the known processes have already received it (in other words, process IDs appear in the path).

Since messages are propagated through different processes, and heartbeat paths contain aggregated information received from the neighbors, we can (correctly) mark an unreachable process as alive even when the direct link between the two processes is faulty.

Heartbeat counters represent a global and normalized view of the system. This view captures how the heartbeats are propagated relative to one another, allowing us to compare processes. However, one of the shortcomings of this approach is that interpreting heartbeat counters may be quite tricky: we need to pick a threshold that can yield reliable results. Unless we can do that, the algorithm will falsely mark active processes as suspected.

Outsourced Heartbeats

An alternative approach, used by the Scalable Weakly Consistent Infection-style Process Group Membership Protocol (SWIM) [GUPTA01] is to use *outsourced heartbeats* to improve reliability using information about the process liveness from the perspective of its neighbors. This approach does not require processes to be aware of all other processes in the network, only a subset of connected peers.

As shown in Figure 9-3, process P_1 sends a ping message to process P_2. P_2 doesn't respond to the message, so P_1 proceeds by selecting multiple random members (P_3 and P_4). These random members try sending heartbeat messages to P_2 and, if it responds, forward acknowledgments back to P_1.

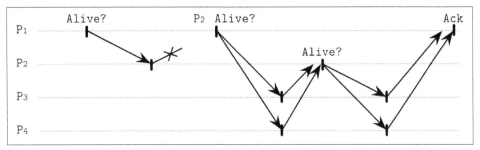

Figure 9-3. "Outsourcing" heartbeats

This allows accounting for both direct and indirect reachability. For example, if we have processes P_1, P_2, and P_3, we can check the state of P_3 from the perspective of both P_1 and P_2.

Outsourced heartbeats allow reliable failure detection by distributing responsibility for deciding across the group of members. This approach does not require broadcasting messages to a broad group of peers. Since outsourced heartbeat requests can be triggered in parallel, this approach can collect more information about suspected processes quickly, and allow us to make more accurate decisions.

Phi-Accrual Failure Detector

Instead of treating node failure as a binary problem, where the process can be only in two states: up or down, a *phi-accrual* (φ-accrual) failure detector [HAYASHIBARA04] has a continuous scale, capturing the probability of the monitored process's crash. It works by maintaining a sliding window, collecting arrival times of the most recent heartbeats from the peer processes. This information is used to approximate arrival time of the *next* heartbeat, compare this approximation with the actual arrival time, and compute the *suspicion level* φ: how certain the failure detector is about the failure, given the current network conditions.

The algorithm works by collecting and sampling arrival times, creating a view that can be used to make a reliable judgment about node health. It uses these samples to compute the value of φ: if this value reaches a threshold, the node is marked as down. This failure detector dynamically adapts to changing network conditions by adjusting the scale on which the node can be marked as a suspect.

From the architecture perspective, a phi-accrual failure detector can be viewed as a combination of three subsystems:

Monitoring
Collecting liveness information through pings, heartbeats, or request-response sampling.

Interpretation
   Making a decision on whether or not the process should be marked as suspected.

Action
   A callback executed whenever the process is marked as suspected.

The monitoring process collects and stores data samples (which are assumed to follow a normal distribution) in a fixed-size window of heartbeat arrival times. Newer arrivals are added to the window, and the oldest heartbeat data points are discarded.

Distribution parameters are estimated from the sampling window by determining the mean and variance of samples. This information is used to compute the probability of arrival of the message within t time units after the previous one. Given this information, we compute ϕ, which describes how likely we are to make a correct decision about a process's liveness. In other words, how likely it is to make a mistake and receive a heartbeat that will contradict the calculated assumptions.

This approach was developed by researchers from the Japan Advanced Institute of Science and Technology, and is now used in many distributed systems; for example, Cassandra (*https://databass.dev/links/42*) and Akka (*https://databass.dev/links/43*) (along with the aforementioned deadline failure detector).

Gossip and Failure Detection

Another approach that avoids relying on a single-node view to make a decision is a gossip-style failure detection service [VANRENESSE98], which uses *gossip* (see "Gossip Dissemination" on page 250) to collect and distribute states of neighboring processes.

Each member maintains a list of other members, their *heartbeat counters*, and timestamps, specifying when the heartbeat counter was incremented for the last time. Periodically, each member increments its heartbeat counter and distributes its list to a random neighbor. Upon the message receipt, the neighboring node merges the list with its own, updating heartbeat counters for the other neighbors.

Nodes also periodically check the list of states and heartbeat counters. If any node did not update its counter for long enough, it is considered failed. This timeout period should be chosen carefully to minimize the probability of false-positives. How often members have to communicate with each other (in other words, worst-case bandwidth) is capped, and can grow at most linearly with a number of processes in the system.

Figure 9-4 shows three communicating processes sharing their heartbeat counters:

- a) All three can communicate and update their timestamps.
- b) P3 isn't able to communicate with P1, but its timestamp t_6 can still be propagated through P2.
- c) P3 crashes. Since it doesn't send updates anymore, it is detected as failed by other processes.

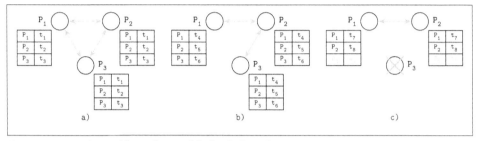

Figure 9-4. Replicated heartbeat table for failure detection

This way, we can detect crashed nodes, as well as the nodes that are unreachable by any other cluster member. This decision is reliable, since the view of the cluster is an aggregate from multiple nodes. If there's a link failure between the two hosts, heartbeats can still propagate through other processes. Using gossip for propagating system states increases the number of messages in the system, but allows information to spread more reliably.

Reversing Failure Detection Problem Statement

Since propagating the information about failures is not always possible, and propagating it by notifying every member might be expensive, one of the approaches, called *FUSE* (failure notification service) [DUNAGAN04], focuses on reliable and cheap failure propagation that works even in cases of network partitions.

To detect process failures, this approach arranges all active processes in groups. If one of the groups becomes unavailable, all participants detect the failure. In other words, every time a single process failure is detected, it is converted and propagated as a *group failure*. This allows detecting failures in the presence of any pattern of disconnects, partitions, and node failures.

Processes in the group periodically send ping messages to other members, querying whether they're still alive. If one of the members cannot respond to this message because of a crash, network partition, or link failure, the member that has initiated this ping will, in turn, stop responding to ping messages itself.

Figure 9-5 shows four communicating processes:

- a) Initial state: all processes are alive and can communicate.
- b) P_2 crashes and stops responding to ping messages.
- c) P_4 detects the failure of P_2 and stops responding to ping messages itself.
- d) Eventually, P_1 and P_3 notice that both P_1 and P_2 do not respond, and process failure propagates to the entire group.

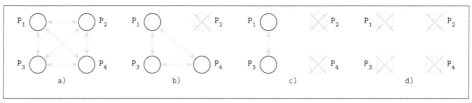

Figure 9-5. FUSE failure detection

All failures are propagated through the system from the source of failure to all other participants. Participants gradually stop responding to pings, converting from the individual node failure to the group failure.

Here, we use the absence of communication as a means of propagation. An advantage of using this approach is that every member is guaranteed to learn about group failure and adequately react to it. One of the downsides is that a link failure separating a single process from other ones can be converted to the group failure as well, but this can be seen as an advantage, depending on the use case. Applications can use their own definitions of propagated failures to account for this scenario.

Summary

Failure detectors are an essential part of any distributed system. As shown by the FLP Impossibility result, no protocol can guarantee consensus in an asynchronous system. Failure detectors help to augment the model, allowing us to solve a consensus problem by making a trade-off between accuracy and completeness. One of the significant findings in this area, proving the usefulness of failure detectors, was described in [CHANDRA96], which shows that solving consensus is possible even with a failure detector that makes an infinite number of mistakes.

We've covered several algorithms for failure detection, each using a different approach: some focus on detecting failures by direct communication, some use broadcast or gossip for spreading the information around, and some opt out by using quiescence (in other words, absence of communication) as a means of propagation. We now know that we can use heartbeats or pings, hard deadlines, or continuous scales. Each one of these approaches has its own upsides: simplicity, accuracy, or precision.

Further Reading

If you'd like to learn more about the concepts mentioned in this chapter, you can refer to the following sources:

Failure detection and algorithms

Chandra, Tushar Deepak and Sam Toueg. 1996. "Unreliable failure detectors for reliable distributed systems." *Journal of the ACM* 43, no. 2 (March): 225-267. *https://doi.org/10.1145/226643.226647.*

Freiling, Felix C., Rachid Guerraoui, and Petr Kuznetsov. 2011. "The failure detector abstraction." *ACM Computing Surveys* 43, no. 2 (January): Article 9. *https://doi.org/10.1145/1883612.1883616.*

Phan-Ba, Michael. 2015. "A literature review of failure detection within the context of solving the problem of distributed consensus." *https://www.cs.ubc.ca/~bestchai/theses/michael-phan-ba-msc-essay-2015.pdf*

CHAPTER 10

Leader Election

Synchronization can be quite costly: if each algorithm step involves contacting each other participant, we can end up with a significant communication overhead. This is particularly true in large and geographically distributed networks. To reduce synchronization overhead and the number of message round-trips required to reach a decision, some algorithms rely on the existence of the *leader* (sometimes called *coordinator*) process, responsible for executing or coordinating steps of a distributed algorithm.

Generally, processes in distributed systems are uniform, and any process can take over the leadership role. Processes assume leadership for long periods of time, but this is not a permanent role. Usually, the process remains a leader until it crashes. After the crash, any other process can start a new election round, assume leadership, if it gets elected, and continue the failed leader's work.

The *liveness* of the election algorithm guarantees that *most of the time* there will be a leader, and the election will eventually complete (i.e., the system should not be in the election state indefinitely).

Ideally, we'd like to assume *safety*, too, and guarantee there may be *at most one* leader at a time, and completely eliminate the possibility of a *split brain* situation (when two leaders serving the same purpose are elected but unaware of each other). However, in practice, many leader election algorithms violate this agreement.

Leader processes can be used, for example, to achieve a total order of messages in a broadcast. The leader collects and holds the global state, receives messages, and disseminates them among the processes. It can also be used to coordinate system reorganization after the failure, during initialization, or when important state changes happen.

Election is triggered when the system initializes, and the leader is elected for the first time, or when the previous leader crashes or fails to communicate. Election has to be deterministic: exactly one leader has to emerge from the process. This decision needs to be effective for all participants.

Even though leader election and distributed locking (i.e., exclusive ownership over a shared resource) might look alike from a theoretical perspective, they are slightly different. If one process holds a lock for executing a critical section, it is unimportant for other processes to know who exactly is holding a lock right now, as long as the liveness property is satisfied (i.e., the lock will be eventually released, allowing others to acquire it). In contrast, the elected process has some special properties and has to be known to all other participants, so the newly elected leader has to notify its peers about its role.

If a distributed locking algorithm has any sort of preference toward some process or group of processes, it will eventually starve nonpreferred processes from the shared resource, which contradicts the liveness property. In contrast, the leader can remain in its role until it stops or crashes, and long-lived leaders are preferred.

Having a stable leader in the system helps to avoid state synchronization between remote participants, reduce the number of exchanged messages, and drive execution from a single process instead of requiring peer-to-peer coordination. One of the potential problems in systems with a notion of leadership is that the leader can become a bottleneck. To overcome that, many systems partition data in non-intersecting independent replica sets (see "Database Partitioning" on page 270). Instead of having a single system-wide leader, each replica set has its own leader. One of the systems that uses this approach is Spanner (see "Distributed Transactions with Spanner" on page 268).

Because every leader process will eventually fail, failure has to be detected, reported, and reacted upon: a system has to elect another leader to replace the failed one.

Some algorithms, such as ZAB (see "Zookeeper Atomic Broadcast (ZAB)" on page 283), Multi-Paxos (see "Multi-Paxos" on page 291), or Raft (see "Raft" on page 300), use temporary leaders to reduce the number of messages required to reach an agreement between the participants. However, these algorithms use their own algorithm-specific means for leader election, failure detection, and resolving conflicts between the competing leader processes.

Bully Algorithm

One of the leader election algorithms, known as the *bully algorithm*, uses process ranks to identify the new leader. Each process gets a unique rank assigned to it. During the election, the process with the highest rank becomes a leader [GARCIAMOLINA82].

This algorithm is known for its simplicity. The algorithm is named *bully* because the highest-ranked node "bullies" other nodes into accepting it. It is also known as *monarchial* leader election: the highest-ranked sibling becomes a monarch after the previous one ceases to exist.

Election starts if one of the processes notices that there's no leader in the system (it was never initialized) or the previous leader has stopped responding to requests, and proceeds in three steps:[1]

1. The process sends election messages to processes with higher identifiers.

2. The process waits, allowing higher-ranked processes to respond. If no higher-ranked process responds, it proceeds with step 3. Otherwise, the process notifies the highest-ranked process it has heard from, and allows it to proceed with step 3.

3. The process assumes that there are no active processes with a higher rank, and notifies all lower-ranked processes about the new leader.

Figure 10-1 illustrates the bully leader election algorithm:

- a) Process 3 notices that the previous leader 6 has crashed and starts a new election by sending `Election` messages to processes with higher identifiers.
- b) 4 and 5 respond with `Alive`, as they have a higher rank than 3.
- c) 3 notifies the highest-ranked process 5 that has responded during this round.
- d) 5 is elected as a new leader. It broadcasts `Elected` messages, notifying lower-ranked processes about the election results.

---

1 These steps describe the *modified* bully election algorithm [KORDAFSHARI05] as it's more compact and clear.

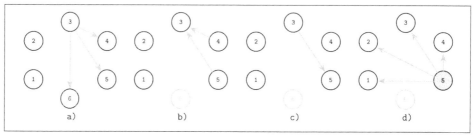

Figure 10-1. Bully algorithm: previous leader (6) fails and process 3 starts the new election

One of the apparent problems with this algorithm is that it violates the safety guarantee (that at most one leader can be elected at a time) in the presence of network partitions. It is quite easy to end up in the situation where nodes get split into two or more independently functioning subsets, and each subset elects its leader. This situation is called *split brain*.

Another problem with this algorithm is a strong preference toward high-ranked nodes, which becomes an issue if they are unstable and can lead to a permanent state of reelection. An unstable high-ranked node proposes itself as a leader, fails shortly thereafter, wins reelection, fails again, and the whole process repeats. This problem can be solved by distributing host quality metrics and taking them into consideration during the election.

Next-In-Line Failover

There are many versions of the bully algorithm that improve its various properties. For example, we can use multiple next-in-line alternative processes as a failover to shorten reelections [GHOLIPOUR09].

Each elected leader provides a list of failover nodes. When one of the processes detects a leader failure, it starts a new election round by sending a message to the highest-ranked *alternative* from the list provided by the failed leader. If one of the proposed alternatives is up, it becomes a new leader without having to go through the complete election round.

If the process that has detected the leader failure is itself the highest ranked process from the list, it can notify the processes about the new leader right away.

Figure 10-2 shows the process with this optimization in place:

- a) 6, a leader with designated alternatives {5,4}, crashes. 3 notices this failure and contacts 5, the alternative from the list with the highest rank.

- b) 5 responds to 3 that it's alive to prevent it from contacting other nodes from the alternatives list.
- c) 5 notifies other nodes that it's a new leader.

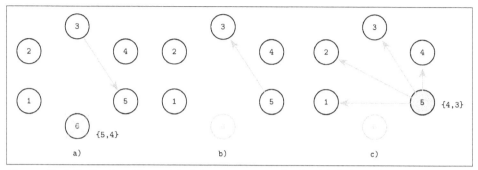

Figure 10-2. Bully algorithm with failover: previous leader (6) fails and process 3 starts the new election by contacting the highest-ranked alternative

As a result, we require fewer steps during the election if the next-in-line process is alive.

Candidate/Ordinary Optimization

Another algorithm attempts to lower requirements on the number of messages by splitting the nodes into two subsets, *candidate* and *ordinary*, where only one of the candidate nodes can eventually become a leader [MURSHED12].

The ordinary process initiates election by contacting candidate nodes, collecting responses from them, picking the highest-ranked alive candidate as a new leader, and then notifying the rest of the nodes about the election results.

To solve the problem with multiple simultaneous elections, the algorithm proposes to use a tiebreaker variable δ, a process-specific delay, varying significantly between the nodes, that allows one of the nodes to initiate the election before the other ones. The tiebreaker time is generally greater than the message round-trip time. Nodes with higher priorities have a lower δ, and vice versa.

Figure 10-3 shows the steps of the election process:

- a) Process 4 from the ordinary set notices the failure of leader process 6. It starts a new election round by contacting all remaining processes from the candidate set.
- b) Candidate processes respond to notify 4 that they're still alive.
- c) 4 notifies all processes about the new leader: 2.

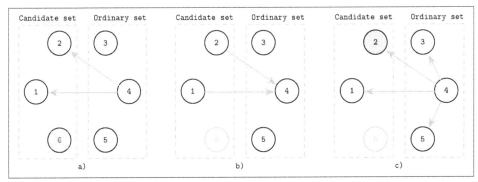

Figure 10-3. Candidate/ordinary modification of the bully algorithm: previous leader (6) fails and process 4 starts the new election

Invitation Algorithm

An *invitation algorithm* allows processes to "invite" other processes to join their groups instead of trying to outrank them. This algorithm allows multiple leaders *by definition*, since each group has its own leader.

Each process starts as a leader of a new group, where the only member is the process itself. Group leaders contact peers that do not belong to their groups, inviting them to join. If the peer process is a leader itself, two groups are merged. Otherwise, the contacted process responds with a group leader ID, allowing two group leaders to establish contact and merge groups in fewer steps.

Figure 10-4 shows the execution steps of the invitation algorithm:

- a) Four processes start as leaders of groups containing one member each. 1 invites 2 to join its group, and 3 invites 4 to join its group.

- b) 2 joins a group with process 1, and 4 joins a group with process 3. 1, the leader of the first group, contacts 3, the leader of the other group. Remaining group members (4, in this case) are notified about the new group leader.

- c) Two groups are merged and 1 becomes a leader of an extended group.

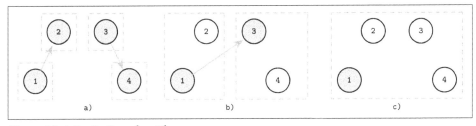

Figure 10-4. Invitation algorithm

Since groups are merged, it doesn't matter whether the process that suggested the group merge becomes a new leader or the other one does. To keep the number of messages required to merge groups to a minimum, a leader of a larger group can become a leader for a new group. This way only the processes from the smaller group have to be notified about the change of leader.

Similar to the other discussed algorithms, this algorithm allows processes to settle in multiple groups and have multiple leaders. The invitation algorithm allows creating process groups and merging them without having to trigger a new election from scratch, reducing the number of messages required to finish the election.

Ring Algorithm

In the ring algorithm [CHANG79], all nodes in the system form a ring and are aware of the ring topology (i.e., their predecessors and successors in the ring). When the process detects the leader failure, it starts the new election. The election message is forwarded across the ring: each process contacts its successor (the next node closest to it in the ring). If this node is unavailable, the process skips the unreachable node and attempts to contact the nodes after it in the ring, until eventually one of them responds.

Nodes contact their siblings, following around the ring and collecting the live node set, adding themselves to the set before passing it over to the next node, similar to the failure-detection algorithm described in "Timeout-Free Failure Detector" on page 197, where nodes append their identifiers to the path before passing it to the next node.

The algorithm proceeds by fully traversing the ring. When the message comes back to the node that started the election, the highest-ranked node from the live set is chosen as a leader. In Figure 10-5, you can see an example of such a traversal:

- a) Previous leader 6 has failed and each process has a view of the ring from its perspective.

- b) 3 initiates an election round by starting traversal. On each step, there's a set of nodes traversed on the path so far. 5 can't reach 6, so it skips it and goes straight to 1.

- c) Since 5 was the node with the highest rank, 3 initiates another round of messages, distributing the information about the new leader.

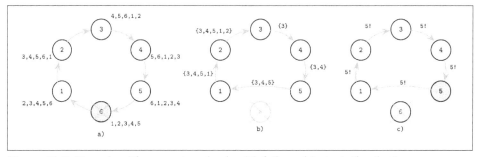

Figure 10-5. Ring algorithm: previous leader (6) fails and 3 starts the election process

Variants of this algorithm include collecting a single highest-ranked identifier instead of a set of active nodes to save space: since the max function is commutative, it is enough to know a current maximum. When the algorithm comes back to the node that has started the election, the last known highest identifier is circulated across the ring once again.

Since the ring can be partitioned in two or more parts, with each part potentially electing its own leader, this approach doesn't hold a safety property, either.

As you can see, for a system with a leader to function correctly, we need to know the status of the current leader (whether it is alive or not), since to keep processes organized and for execution to continue, the leader has to be alive and reachable to perform its duties. To detect leader crashes, we can use failure-detection algorithms (see Chapter 9).

Summary

Leader election is an important subject in distributed systems, since using a designated leader helps to reduce coordination overhead and improve the algorithm's performance. Election rounds might be costly but, since they're infrequent, they do not have a negative impact on the overall system performance. A single leader can become a bottleneck, but most of the time this is solved by partitioning data and using per-partition leaders or using different leaders for different actions.

Unfortunately, all the algorithms we've discussed in this chapter are prone to the split brain problem: we can end up with two leaders in independent subnets that are not aware of each other's existence. To avoid split brain, we have to obtain a cluster-wide majority of votes.

Many consensus algorithms, including Multi-Paxos and Raft, rely on a leader for coordination. But isn't leader election the same as consensus? To elect a leader, we need to reach a consensus about its identity. If we can reach consensus about the leader identity, we can use the same means to reach consensus on anything else [ABRAHAM13].

The identity of a leader may change without processes knowing about it, so the question is whether the process-local knowledge about the leader is still valid. To achieve that, we need to combine leader election with failure detection. For example, the *stable leader election* algorithm uses rounds with a unique stable leader and timeout-based failure detection to guarantee that the leader can retain its position for as long as it doesn't crash and is accessible [AGUILERA01].

Algorithms that rely on leader election often *allow* the existence of multiple leaders and attempt to resolve conflicts between the leaders as quickly as possible. For example, this is true for Multi-Paxos (see "Multi-Paxos" on page 291), where only one of the two conflicting leaders (proposers) can proceed, and these conflicts are resolved by collecting a second quorum, guaranteeing that the values from two different proposers won't be accepted.

In Raft (see "Raft" on page 300), a leader can discover that its term is out-of-date, which implies the presence of a different leader in the system, and update its term to the more recent one.

In both cases, having a leader is a way to ensure *liveness* (if the current leader has failed, we need a new one), and processes should not take indefinitely long to understand whether or not it has really failed. Lack of *safety* and allowing multiple leaders is a performance optimization: algorithms can proceed with a replication phase, and *safety* is guaranteed by detecting and resolving the conflicts.

We discuss consensus and leader election in the context of consensus in more detail in Chapter 14.

Further Reading

If you'd like to learn more about the concepts mentioned in this chapter, you can refer to the following sources:

Leader election algorithms

> Lynch, Nancy and Boaz Patt-Shamir. 1993. "Distributed algorithms." *Lecture notes for 6.852*. Cambridge, MA: MIT.

> Attiya, Hagit and Jennifer Welch. 2004. *Distributed Computing: Fundamentals, Simulations and Advanced Topics*. USA: John Wiley & Sons.

> Tanenbaum, Andrew S. and Maarten van Steen. 2006. *Distributed Systems: Principles and Paradigms* (2nd Ed.). Upper Saddle River, NJ: Prentice-Hall.

CHAPTER 11

Replication and Consistency

Before we move on to discuss consensus and atomic commitment algorithms, let's put together the last piece required for their in-depth understanding: *consistency models*. Consistency models are important, since they explain visibility semantics and behavior of the system in the presence of multiple copies of data.

Fault tolerance is a property of a system that can continue operating correctly in the presence of failures of its components. Making a system fault-tolerant is not an easy task, and it may be difficult to add fault tolerance to the existing system. The primary goal is to remove a single point of failure from the system and make sure that we have redundancy in mission-critical components. Usually, redundancy is entirely transparent for the user.

A system can continue operating correctly by storing multiple copies of data so that, when one of the machines fails, the other one can serve as a failover. In systems with a single source of truth (for example, primary/replica databases), failover can be done explicitly, by promoting a replica to become a new master. Other systems do not require explicit reconfiguration and ensure consistency by collecting responses from multiple participants during read and write queries.

Data *replication* is a way of introducing redundancy by maintaining multiple copies of data in the system. However, since updating multiple copies of data atomically is a problem equivalent to consensus [MILOSEVIC11], it might be quite costly to perform this operation for *every* operation in the database. We can explore some more cost-effective and flexible ways to make data *look* consistent from the user's perspective, while allowing some degree of divergence between participants.

Replication is particularly important in multidatacenter deployments. Geo-replication, in this case, serves multiple purposes: it increases availability and the ability to withstand a failure of one or more datacenters by providing redundancy. It can also help to reduce the latency by placing a copy of data physically closer to the client.

When data records are modified, their copies have to be updated accordingly. When talking about replication, we care most about three events: *write*, *replica update*, and *read*. These operations trigger a sequence of events initiated by the client. In some cases, updating replicas can happen after the write has finished from the client perspective, but this still does not change the fact that the client has to be able to observe operations in a particular order.

Achieving Availability

We've talked about the fallacies of distributed systems and have identified many things that can go wrong. In the real world, nodes aren't always alive or able to communicate with one another. However, intermittent failures should not impact *availability*: from the user's perspective, the system as a whole has to continue operating as if nothing has happened.

System availability is an incredibly important property: in software engineering, we always strive for high availability, and try to minimize downtime. Engineering teams brag about their uptime metrics. We care so much about availability for several reasons: software has become an integral part of our society, and many important things cannot happen without it: bank transactions, communication, travel, and so on.

For companies, lack of availability can mean losing customers or money: you can't shop in the online store if it's down, or transfer the money if your bank's website isn't responding.

To make the system highly available, we need to design it in a way that allows handling failures or unavailability of one or more participants gracefully. For that, we need to introduce redundancy and replication. However, as soon as we add redundancy, we face the problem of keeping several copies of data in sync and have to implement recovery mechanisms.

Infamous CAP

Availability is a property that measures the ability of the system to serve a response for every request successfully. The theoretical definition of availability mentions eventual response, but of course, in a real-world system, we'd like to avoid services that take indefinitely long to respond.

Ideally, we'd like every operation to be *consistent*. Consistency is defined here as atomic or *linearizable* consistency (see "Linearizability" on page 223). Linearizable history can be expressed as a sequence of instantaneous operations that preserves the original operation order. Linearizability simplifies reasoning about the possible system states and makes a distributed system appear as if it was running on a single machine.

We would like to achieve both consistency and availability while tolerating network partitions. The network can get split into several parts where processes are not able to communicate with each other: some of the messages sent between partitioned nodes won't reach their destinations.

Availability requires any nonfailing node to deliver results, while consistency requires results to be linearizable. CAP conjecture, formulated by Eric Brewer, discusses trade-offs between Consistency, Availability, and Partition tolerance [BREWER00].

Availability requirement is impossible to satisfy in an asynchronous system, and we cannot implement a system that simultaneously guarantees both *availability* and *consistency* in the presence of *network partitions* [GILBERT02]. We can build systems that guarantee strong consistency while providing *best effort* availability, or guarantee availability while providing *best effort* consistency [GILBERT12]. Best effort here implies that if everything works, the system will not *purposefully* violate any guarantees, but guarantees are allowed to be weakened and violated in the case of network partitions.

In other words, CAP describes a continuum of potential choices, where on different sides of the spectrum we have systems that are:

Consistent and partition tolerant
   CP systems prefer failing requests to serving potentially inconsistent data.

Available and partition tolerant
   AP systems loosen the consistency requirement and allow serving potentially inconsistent values during the request.

An example of a CP system is an implementation of a consensus algorithm, requiring a majority of nodes for progress: always consistent, but might be unavailable in the case of a network partition. A database always accepting writes and serving reads as long as even a single replica is up is an example of an AP system, which may end up losing data or serving inconsistent results.

PACELEC conjecture [ABADI12], an extension of CAP, states that in presence of network partitions there's a choice between consistency and availability (PAC). Else (E), even if the system is running normally, we *still* have to make a choice between latency and consistency.

Use CAP Carefully

It's important to note that CAP discusses *network partitions* rather than *node crashes* or any other type of failure (such as crash-recovery). A node, partitioned from the rest of the cluster, can serve inconsistent requests, but a crashed node will not respond at all. On the one hand, this implies that it's not necessary to have any nodes down to face consistency problems. On the other hand, this isn't the case in the real world: there are many different failure scenarios (some of which can be simulated with network partitions).

CAP implies that we can face consistency problems even if all the nodes are up, but there are connectivity issues between them since we expect every nonfailed node to respond correctly, with no regard to how many nodes may be down.

CAP conjecture is sometimes illustrated as a triangle, as if we could turn a knob and have more or less of all of the three parameters. However, while we can turn a knob and trade consistency for availability, partition tolerance is a property we cannot realistically tune or trade for anything [HALE10].

 Consistency in CAP is defined quite differently from what ACID (see Chapter 5) defines as consistency. ACID consistency describes transaction consistency: transaction brings the database from one valid state to another, maintaining all the database invariants (such as uniqueness constraints and referential integrity). In CAP, it means that operations are *atomic* (operations succeed or fail in their entirety) and *consistent* (operations never leave the data in an inconsistent state).

Availability in CAP is also different from the aforementioned *high availability* [KLEPPMANN15]. The CAP definition puts no bounds on execution latency. Additionally, availability in databases, contrary to CAP, doesn't require *every* nonfailed node to respond to *every* request.

CAP conjecture is used to explain distributed systems, reason about failure scenarios, and evaluate possible situations, but it's important to remember that there's a fine line between *giving up* consistency and serving unpredictable results.

Databases that claim to be on the availability side, when used correctly, are still able to serve consistent results from replicas, given there are enough replicas alive. Of course, there are more complicated failure scenarios and CAP conjecture is just a rule of thumb, and it doesn't necessarily tell the whole truth.[1]

Harvest and Yield

CAP conjecture discusses consistency and availability only in their strongest forms: *linearizability* and the ability of the system to eventually respond to every request.

---

1 Quorum reads and writes in the context of eventually consistent stores, which are discussed in more detail in "Eventual Consistency" on page 234.

This forces us to make a hard trade-off between the two properties. However, some applications can benefit from slightly relaxed assumptions and we can think about these properties in their weaker forms.

Instead of being *either* consistent *or* available, systems can provide relaxed guarantees. We can define two tunable metrics: *harvest* and *yield*, choosing between which still constitutes correct behavior [FOX99]:

Harvest
> Defines how complete the query is: if the query has to return 100 rows, but can fetch only 99 due to unavailability of some nodes, it still can be better than failing the query completely and returning nothing.

Yield
> Specifies the number of requests that were completed successfully, compared to the total number of attempted requests. Yield is different from the uptime, since, for example, a busy node is not down, but still can fail to respond to some of the requests.

This shifts the focus of the trade-off from the absolute to the relative terms. We can trade harvest for yield and allow some requests to return incomplete data. One of the ways to increase yield is to return query results only from the available partitions (see "Database Partitioning" on page 270). For example, if a subset of nodes storing records of some users is down, we can still continue serving requests for other users. Alternatively, we can require the critical application data to be returned only in its entirety, but allow some deviations for other requests.

Defining, measuring, and making a conscious choice between harvest and yield helps us to build systems that are more resilient to failures.

Shared Memory

For a client, the distributed system storing the data acts as if it has shared storage, similar to a single-node system. Internode communication and message passing are abstracted away and happen behind the scenes. This creates an illusion of a shared memory.

A single unit of storage, accessible by read or write operations, is usually called a *register*. We can view *shared memory* in a distributed database as an array of such registers.

We identify every operation by its *invocation* and *completion* events. We define an operation as *failed* if the process that invoked it crashes before it completes. If both invocation and completion events for one operation happen before the other operation is invoked, we say that this operation *precedes* the other one, and these two operations are *sequential*. Otherwise, we say that they are *concurrent*.

In Figure 11-1, you can see processes P_1 and P_2 executing different operations:

- a) The operation performed by process P_2 starts *after* the operation executed by P_1 has already finished, and the two operations are *sequential*.

- b) There's an overlap between the two operations, so these operations are *concurrent*.

- c) The operation executed by P_2 starts *after* and completes *before* the operation executed by P_1. These operations are *concurrent*, too.

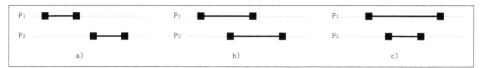

Figure 11-1. Sequential and concurrent operations

Multiple readers or writers can access the register simultaneously. Read and write operations on registers are *not immediate* and take some time. Concurrent read/write operations performed by different processes are not *serial*: depending on how registers behave when operations overlap, they might be ordered differently and may produce different results. Depending on how the register behaves in the presence of concurrent operations, we distinguish among three types of registers:

Safe
    Reads to the safe registers may return *arbitrary* values within the range of the register during a concurrent write operation (which does not sound very practical, but might describe the semantics of an asynchronous system that does not impose the order). Safe registers with binary values might appear to be *flickering* (i.e., returning results alternating between the two values) during reads concurrent to writes.

Regular
    For regular registers, we have slightly stronger guarantees: a read operation can return only the value written by the most recent *completed* write or the value written by the write operation that overlaps with the current read. In this case, the system has some notion of order, but write results are not visible to all the readers simultaneously (for example, this may happen in a replicated database, where the master accepts writes and replicates them to workers serving reads).

Atomic
    Atomic registers guarantee linearizability: every write operation has a single moment before which every read operation returns an old value and after which every read operation returns a new one. Atomicity is a fundamental property that simplifies reasoning about the system state.

Ordering

When we see a sequence of events, we have some intuition about their execution order. However, in a distributed system it's not always that easy, because it's hard to know when *exactly* something has happened and have this information available instantly across the cluster. Each participant may have its view of the state, so we have to look at every operation and define it in terms of its *invocation* and *completion* events and describe the operation bounds.

Let's define a system in which processes can execute `read(register)` and `write(register, value)` operations on shared registers. Each process executes its own set of operations sequentially (i.e., every invoked operation has to complete before it can start the next one). The combination of sequential process executions forms a global history, in which operations can be executed concurrently.

The simplest way to think about consistency models is in terms of read and write operations and ways they can overlap: read operations have no side effects, while writes change the register state. This helps to reason about when exactly data becomes readable after the write. For example, consider a history in which two processes execute the following events concurrently:

```
Process 1:     Process 2:
write(x, 1)    read(x)
               read(x)
```

When looking at these events, it's unclear what is an outcome of the `read(x)` operations in both cases. We have several possible histories:

- Write completes before both reads.
- Write and two reads can get interleaved, and can be executed between the reads.
- Both reads complete before the write.

There's no simple answer to what should happen if we have just one copy of data. In a replicated system, we have more combinations of possible states, and it can get even more complicated when we have multiple processes reading and writing the data.

If all of these operations were executed by the single process, we could enforce a strict order of events, but it's harder to do so with multiple processes. We can group the potential difficulties into two groups:

- Operations may overlap.
- Effects of the nonoverlapping calls might not be visible immediately.

To reason about the operation order and have nonambiguous descriptions of possible outcomes, we have to define consistency models. We discuss concurrency in distributed systems in terms of shared memory and concurrent systems, since most of the definitions and rules defining consistency still apply. Even though a lot of terminology between concurrent and distributed systems overlap, we can't directly apply most of the concurrent algorithms, because of differences in communication patterns, performance, and reliability.

Consistency Models

Since operations on shared memory registers are allowed to overlap, we should define clear semantics: what happens if multiple clients read or modify different copies of data simultaneously or within a short period. There's no single right answer to that question, since these semantics are different depending on the application, but they are well studied in the context of consistency models.

Consistency models provide different semantics and guarantees. You can think of a consistency model as a contract between the participants: what each replica has to do to satisfy the required semantics, and what users can expect when issuing read and write operations.

Consistency models describe what expectations clients might have in terms of possible returned values despite the existence of multiple copies of data and concurrent accesses to it. In this section, we will discuss *single-operation* consistency models.

Each model describes how far the behavior of the system is from the behavior we might expect or find natural. It helps us to distinguish between "all possible histories" of interleaving operations and "histories permissible under model X," which significantly simplifies reasoning about the visibility of state changes.

We can think about consistency from the perspective of *state*, describe which state invariants are acceptable, and establish allowable relationships between copies of the data placed onto different replicas. Alternatively, we can consider *operation* consistency, which provides an outside view on the data store, describes operations, and puts constraints on the order in which they occur [TANENBAUM06] [AGUILERA16].

Without a global clock, it is difficult to give distributed operations a precise and deterministic order. It's like a Special Relativity Theory for data: every participant has its own perspective on state and time.

Theoretically, we could grab a system-wide lock every time we want to change the system state, but it'd be highly impractical. Instead, we use a set of rules, definitions, and restrictions that limit the number of possible histories and outcomes.

Consistency models add another dimension to what we discussed in "Infamous CAP" on page 216. Now we have to juggle not only consistency and availability, but also consider consistency in terms of synchronization costs [ATTIYA94]. Synchronization costs may include latency, additional CPU cycles spent executing additional operations, disk I/O used to persist recovery information, wait time, network I/O, and everything else that can be prevented by avoiding synchronization.

First, we'll focus on visibility and propagation of operation results. Coming back to the example with concurrent reads and writes, we'll be able to limit the number of possible histories by either positioning dependent writes after one another or defining a point at which the new value is propagated.

We discuss consistency models in terms of *processes* (clients) issuing read and write operations against the database state. Since we discuss consistency in the context of replicated data, we assume that the database can have multiple replicas.

Strict Consistency

Strict consistency is the equivalent of complete replication transparency: any write by any process is instantly available for the subsequent reads by any process. It involves the concept of a global clock and, if there was a write(x, 1) at instant t_1, any read(x) will return a newly written value 1 at *any* instant $t_2 > t_1$.

Unfortunately, this is just a theoretical model, and it's impossible to implement, as the laws of physics and the way distributed systems work set limits on how fast things may happen [SINHA97].

Linearizability

Linearizability is the strongest single-object, single-operation consistency model. Under this model, effects of the write become visible to all readers exactly once at some point in time between its start and end, and no client can observe state transitions or side effects of partial (i.e., unfinished, still in-flight) or incomplete (i.e., interrupted before completion) write operations [LEE15].

Concurrent operations are represented as one of the possible sequential histories for which visibility properties hold. There is some indeterminism in linearizability, as there may exist more than one way in which the events can be ordered [HERLIHY90].

If two operations overlap, they may take effect in any order. All read operations that occur after write operation completion can observe the effects of this operation. As soon as a single read operation returns a particular value, all reads that come after it return the value *at least* as recent as the one it returns [BAILIS14a].

There is some flexibility in terms of the order in which concurrent events occur in a global history, but they cannot be reordered arbitrarily. Operation results should not become effective before the operation starts as that would require an oracle able to predict future operations. At the same time, results have to take effect before completion, since otherwise, we cannot define a linearization point.

Linearizability respects both sequential process-local operation order and the order of operations running in parallel relative to other processes, and defines a *total order* of the events.

This order should be *consistent*, which means that every read of the shared value should return the latest value written to this shared variable preceding this read, or the value of a write that overlaps with this read. Linearizable write access to a shared variable also implies mutual exclusion: between the two concurrent writes, only one can go first.

Even though operations are concurrent and have some overlap, their effects become visible in a way that makes them appear sequential. No operation happens instantaneously, but still *appears* to be atomic.

Let's consider the following history:

```
Process 1:      Process 2:      Process 3:
write(x, 1)     write(x, 2)     read(x)
                                read(x)
                                read(x)
```

In Figure 11-2, we have three processes, two of which perform write operations on the register x, which has an initial value of ∅. Read operations can observe these writes in one of the following ways:

- a) The first read operation can return 1, 2, or ∅ (the initial value, a state before both writes), since both writes are still in-flight. The first read can get ordered *before* both writes, *between* the first and second writes, and *after* both writes.

- b) The second read operation can return only 1 and 2, since the first write has completed, but the second write didn't return yet.

- c) The third read can only return 2, since the second write is ordered after the first.

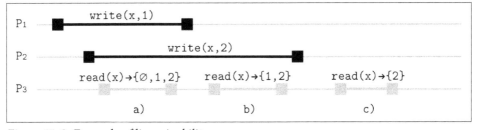

Figure 11-2. Example of linearizability

Linearization point

One of the most important traits of linearizability is visibility: once the operation is complete, everyone must see it, and the system can't "travel back in time," reverting it or making it invisible for some participants. In other words, linearization prohibits stale reads and requires reads to be monotonic.

This consistency model is best explained in terms of atomic (i.e., uninterruptible, indivisible) operations. Operations do not have to *be* instantaneous (also because there's no such thing), but their *effects* have to become visible at some point in time, making an illusion that they were instantaneous. This moment is called a *linearization point*.

Past the linearization point of the write operation (in other words, when the value becomes visible for other processes) every process has to see either the value this operation wrote or some later value, if some additional write operations are ordered after it. A visible value should remain stable until the next one becomes visible after it, and the register should not alternate between the two recent states.

 Most of the programming languages these days offer atomic primitives that allow atomic `write` and `compare-and-swap` (CAS) operations. Atomic `write` operations do not consider current register values, unlike CAS, that move from one value to the next only when the previous value is unchanged [HERLIHY94]. Reading the value, modifying it, and then writing it with CAS is more complex than simply checking and setting the value, because of the possible *ABA problem* [DECHEV10]: if CAS expects the value A to be present in the register, it will be installed even if the value B was set and then switched back to A by the other two concurrent write operations. In other words, the presence of the value A alone does not guarantee that the value hasn't been changed since the last read.

The linearization point serves as a cutoff, after which operation effects become visible. We can implement it by using locks to guard a critical section, atomic read/write, or read-modify-write primitives.

Figure 11-3 shows that linearizability assumes hard time bounds and the clock is *real time*, so the operation effects have to become visible *between* t_1, when the operation request was issued, and t_2, when the process received a response.

Figure 11-3. Time bounds of a linearizable operation

Figure 11-4 illustrates that the linearization point *cuts* the history into *before* and *after*. Before the linearization point, the old value is visible, after it, the new value is visible.

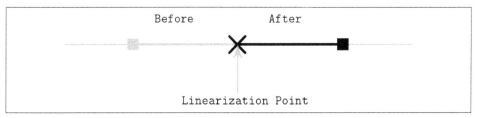

Figure 11-4. Linearization point

Cost of linearizability

Many systems avoid implementing linearizability today. Even CPUs do not offer linearizability when accessing main memory by default. This has happened because synchronization instructions are expensive, slow, and involve cross-node CPU traffic and cache invalidations. However, it is possible to implement linearizability using low-level primitives [MCKENNEY05a], [MCKENNEY05b].

In concurrent programming, you can use compare-and-swap operations to introduce linearizability. Many algorithms work by *preparing* results and then using CAS for swapping pointers and *publishing* them. For example, we can implement a concurrent queue by creating a linked list node and then atomically appending it to the tail of the list [KHANCHANDANI18].

In distributed systems, linearizability requires coordination and ordering. It can be implemented using *consensus*: clients interact with a replicated store using messages, and the consensus module is responsible for ensuring that applied operations are consistent and identical across the cluster. Each write operation will appear instantaneously, exactly once at some point between its invocation and completion events [HOWARD14].

Interestingly, linearizability in its traditional understanding is regarded as a *local* property and implies composition of independently implemented and verified elements. Combining linearizable histories produces a history that is also linearizable [HERLIHY90]. In other words, a system in which all objects are linearizable, is also linearizable. This is a very useful property, but we should remember that its scope is limited to a single object and, even though operations on two independent objects are linearizable, operations that involve both objects have to rely on additional synchronization means.

Reusable Infrastructure for Linearizability

Reusable Infrastructure for Linearizability (RIFL), is a mechanism for implementing linearizable remote procedure calls (RPCs) [LEE15]. In RIFL, messages are uniquely identified with the client ID and a client-local monotonically increasing sequence number.

To assign client IDs, RIFL uses *leases*, issued by the system-wide service: unique identifiers used to establish uniqueness and break sequence number ties. If the failed client tries to execute an operation using an expired lease, its operation will not be committed: the client has to receive a new lease and retry.

If the server crashes before it can acknowledge the write, the client may attempt to retry this operation without knowing that it has already been applied. We can even end up in a situation in which client C1 writes value V1, but doesn't receive an acknowledgment. Meanwhile, client C2 writes value V2. If C1 retries its operation and successfully writes V1, the write of C2 would be lost. To avoid this, the system needs to prevent repeated execution of retried operations. When the client retries the operation, instead of reapplying it, RIFL returns a completion object, indicating that the operation it's associated with has already been executed, and returns its result.

Completion objects are stored in a durable storage, along with the actual data records. However, their lifetimes are different: the completion object should exist until either the issuing client promises it won't retry the operation associated with it, or until the server detects a client crash, in which case all completion objects associated with it can be safely removed. Creating a completion object should be atomic with the mutation of the data record it is associated with.

Clients have to periodically renew their leases to signal their liveness. If the client fails to renew its lease, it is marked as crashed and all the data associated with its lease is garbage collected. Leases have a limited lifetime to make sure that operations that belong to the failed process won't be retained in the log forever. If the failed client tries to continue operation using an expired lease, its results will not be committed and the client will have to start from scratch.

The advantage of RIFL is that, by guaranteeing that the RPC cannot be executed more than once, an operation can be made linearizable by ensuring that its results are made visible atomically, and most of its implementation details are independent from the underlying storage system.

Sequential Consistency

Achieving linearizability might be too expensive, but it is possible to relax the model, while still providing rather strong consistency guarantees. *Sequential consistency* allows ordering operations as if they were executed in *some* sequential order, while requiring operations of each individual process to be executed in the same order they were performed by the process.

Processes can observe operations executed by other participants in the order consistent with their own history, but this view can be arbitrarily stale from the global perspective [KINGSBURY18a]. Order of execution *between* processes is undefined, as there's no shared notion of time.

Sequential consistency was initially introduced in the context of concurrency, describing it as a way to execute multiprocessor programs correctly. The original description required memory requests to the same cell to be ordered in the queue (FIFO, arrival order), did not impose global ordering on the overlapping writes to independent memory cells, and allowed reads to fetch the value from the memory cell, or the latest value from the queue if the queue was nonempty [LAMPORT79]. This example helps to understand the semantics of sequential consistency. Operations can be ordered in different ways (depending on the arrival order, or even arbitrarily in case two writes arrive simultaneously), but all processes *observe* the operations in the same order.

Each process can issue read and write requests in an order specified by its own program, which is very intuitive. Any nonconcurrent, single-threaded program executes its steps this way: one after another. All write operations propagating from the same process appear in the order they were submitted by this process. Operations propagating from different sources may be ordered *arbitrarily*, but this order will be consistent from the readers' perspective.

 Sequential consistency is often confused with linearizability since both have similar semantics. Sequential consistency, just as linearizability, requires operations to be globally ordered, but linearizability requires the local order of each process and global order to be consistent. In other words, linearizability respects a real-time operation order. Under sequential consistency, ordering holds only for the same-origin writes [VIOTTI16]. Another important distinction is composition: we can combine linearizable histories and still expect results to be linearizable, while sequentially consistent schedules are not composable [ATTIYA94].

Figure 11-5 shows how write(x,1) and write(x,2) can become visible to P$_3$ and P$_4$. Even though in wall-clock terms, 1 was written *before* 2, it can get ordered after 2. At the same time, while P$_3$ already reads the value 1, P$_4$ can still read 2. However, *both* orders, 1 → 2 and 2 → 1, are valid, as long as they're consistent for different readers. What's important here is that both P$_3$ and P$_4$ have observed values *in the same order*: first 2, and then 1 [TANENBAUM14].

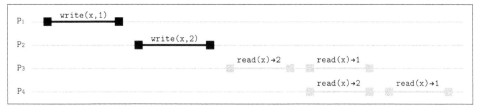

Figure 11-5. Ordering in sequential consistency

Stale reads can be explained, for example, by replica divergence: even though writes propagate to different replicas in the same order, they can arrive there at different times.

The main difference with linearizability is the absence of globally enforced time bounds. Under linearizability, an operation has to become effective within its wall-clock time bounds. By the time the write W_1 operation completes, its results have to be applied, and every reader should be able to see the value *at least* as recent as one written by W_1. Similarly, after a read operation R_1 returns, any read operation that happens after it should return the value that R_1 has seen or a later value (which, of course, has to follow the same rule).

Sequential consistency relaxes this requirement: an operation's results can become visible *after* its completion, as long as the order is consistent from the individual processors' perspective. Same-origin writes can't "jump" over each other: their program order, relative to their own executing process, has to be preserved. The other restriction is that the order in which operations have appeared must be consistent for *all* readers.

Similar to linearizability, modern CPUs do not guarantee sequential consistency by default and, since the processor can reorder instructions, we should use memory barriers (also called fences) to make sure that writes become visible to concurrently running threads in order [DREPPER07] [GEORGOPOULOS16].

Causal Consistency

> You see, there is only one constant, one universal, it is the only real truth: causality. Action. Reaction. Cause and effect.
>
> —Merovingian from *The Matrix Reloaded*

Even though having a global operation order is often unnecessary, it might be necessary to establish order between *some* operations. Under the *causal consistency* model, all processes have to see *causally related* operations in the same order. *Concurrent writes* with no causal relationship can be observed in a different order by different processors.

First, let's take a look at *why* we need causality and how writes that have no causal relationship can propagate. In Figure 11-6, processes P_1 and P_2 make writes that *aren't* causally ordered. The results of these operations can propagate to readers at different times and out of order. Process P_3 will see the value 1 before it sees 2, while P_4 will first see 2, and then 1.

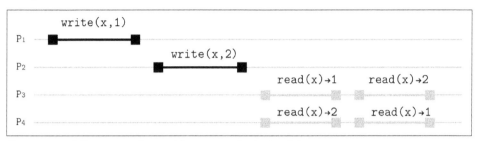

Figure 11-6. Write operations with no causal relationship

Figure 11-7 shows an example of causally related writes. In addition to a written value, we now have to specify a logical clock value that would establish a causal order between operations. P_1 starts with a write operation `write(x,∅,1)→t₁`, which starts from the initial value ∅. P_2 performs another write operation, `write(x, t₁, 2)`, and specifies that it is logically ordered *after* t_1, requiring operations to propagate *only* in the order established by the logical clock.

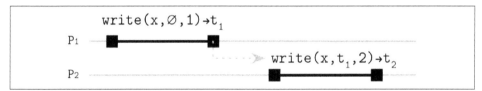

Figure 11-7. Causally related write operations

This establishes a *causal order* between these operations. Even if the latter write propagates faster than the former one, it isn't made visible until all of its dependencies arrive, and the event order is reconstructed from their logical timestamps. In other words, a happened-before relationship is established logically, without using physical clocks, and all processes agree on this order.

Figure 11-8 shows processes P_1 and P_2 making causally related writes, which propagate to P_3 and P_4 in their logical order. This prevents us from the situation shown in Figure 11-6; you can compare histories of P_3 and P_4 in both figures.

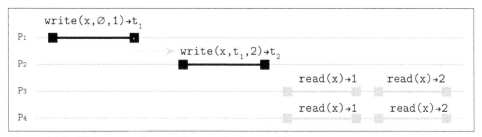

Figure 11-8. Write operations with causal relationship

You can think of this in terms of communication on some online forum: you post something online, someone sees your post and responds to it, and a third person sees this response and continues the conversation thread. It is possible for conversation threads to diverge: you can choose to respond to one of the conversations in the thread and continue the chain of events, but some threads will have only a few messages in common, so there might be no single history for all the messages.

In a causally consistent system, we get session guarantees for the application, ensuring the view of the database is consistent with its own actions, even if it executes read and write requests against different, potentially inconsistent, servers [TERRY94]. These guarantees are: monotonic reads, monotonic writes, read-your-writes, writes-follow-reads. You can find more information on these session models in "Session Models" on page 233.

Causal consistency can be implemented using logical clocks [LAMPORT78] and sending context metadata with every message, summarizing which operations logically precede the current one. When the update is received from the server, it contains the latest version of the context. Any operation can be processed only if all operations preceding it have already been applied. Messages for which contexts do not match are buffered on the server as it is too early to deliver them.

The two prominent and frequently cited projects implementing causal consistency are Clusters of Order-Preserving Servers (COPS) [LLOYD11] and Eiger [LLOYD13]. Both projects implement causality through a library (implemented as a frontend server that users connect to) and track dependencies to ensure consistency. COPS tracks dependencies through key versions, while Eiger establishes operation order instead (operations in Eiger can depend on operations executed on the other nodes; for example, in the case of multipartition transactions). Both projects do not expose out-of-order operations like eventually consistent stores might do. Instead, they detect and handle conflicts: in COPS, this is done by checking the key order and using application-specific functions, while Eiger implements the last-write-wins rule.

Vector clocks

Establishing causal order allows the system to reconstruct the sequence of events even if messages are delivered out of order, fill the gaps between the messages, and avoid publishing operation results in case some messages are still missing. For example, if messages {M1($\varnothing$, t1), M2(M1, t2), M3(M2, t3)}, each specifying their dependencies, are causally related and were propagated out of order, the process buffers them until it can collect all operation dependencies and restore their causal order [KINGSBURY18b]. Many databases, for example, Dynamo [DECANDIA07] and Riak [SHEEHY10a], use *vector clocks* [LAMPORT78] [MATTERN88] for establishing causal order.

A *vector clock* is a structure for establishing a *partial order* between the events, detecting and resolving divergence between the event chains. With vector clocks, we can simulate common time, global state, and represent asynchronous events as synchronous ones. Processes maintain vectors of *logical clocks*, with one clock per process. Every clock starts at the initial value and is incremented every time a new event arrives (for example, a write occurs). When receiving clock vectors from other processes, a process updates its local vector to the highest clock values per process from the received vectors (i.e., highest clock values the transmitting node has ever seen).

To use vector clocks for conflict resolution, whenever we make a write to the database, we first check if the value for the written key already exists locally. If the previous value already exists, we append a new version to the version vector and establish the causal relationship between the two writes. Otherwise, we start a new chain of events and initialize the value with a single version.

We were talking about consistency in terms of access to shared memory registers and wall-clock operation ordering, and first mentioned potential replica divergence when talking about sequential consistency. Since only write operations to the same memory location have to be ordered, we cannot end up in a situation where we have a write conflict if values are independent [LAMPORT79].

Since we're looking for a consistency model that would improve availability and performance, we have to allow replicas to diverge not only by serving stale reads but also by accepting potentially conflicting writes, so the system is allowed to create two independent chains of events. Figure 11-9 shows such a divergence: from the perspective of one replica, we see history as 1, 5, 7, 8 and the other one reports 1, 5, 3. Riak allows users to see and resolve divergent histories [DAILY13].

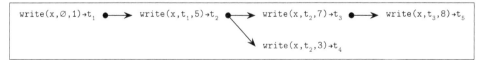

Figure 11-9. Divergent histories under causal consistency

To implement causal consistency, we have to store causal history, add garbage collection, and ask the user to reconcile divergent histories in case of a conflict. Vector clocks can tell you that the conflict has occurred, but do not propose exactly how to resolve it, since resolution semantics are often application-specific. Because of that, some eventually consistent databases, for example, Apache Cassandra, do not order operations causally and use the last-write-wins rule for conflict resolution instead [ELLIS13].

Session Models

Thinking about consistency in terms of value propagation is useful for database developers, since it helps to understand and impose required data invariants, but some things are easier understood and explained from the client point of view. We can look at our distributed system from the perspective of a single client instead of multiple clients.

Session models [VIOTTI16] (also called client-centric consistency models [TANEN-BAUM06]) help to reason about the state of the distributed system from the client perspective: how each client observes the state of the system while issuing read and write operations.

If other consistency models we discussed so far focus on explaining operation ordering in the presence of concurrent clients, client-centric consistency focuses on how a single client interacts with the system. We still assume that each client's operations are sequential: it has to finish one operation before it can start executing the next one. If the client crashes or loses connection to the server before its operation completes, we do not make any assumptions about the state of incomplete operations.

In a distributed system, clients often can connect to any available replica and, if the results of the recent write against one replica did not propagate to the other one, the client might not be able to observe the state change it has made.

One of the reasonable expectations is that every write issued by the client is visible to it. This assumption holds under the *read-own-writes* consistency model, which states that every read operation following the write on the same or the other replica has to observe the updated value. For example, read(x) that was executed immediately after write(x,V) will return the value V.

The *monotonic reads* model restricts the value visibility and states that if the read(x) has observed the value V, the following reads have to observe a value at least as recent as V or some later value.

The *monotonic writes* model assumes that values originating from the same client appear in the order this client has executed them. If, according to the client session order, write(x,V2) was made *after* write(x,V1), their effects have to become visible in the same order (i.e., V1 first, and then V2) to *all* other processes. Without this assumption, old data can be "resurrected," resulting in data loss.

Writes-follow-reads (sometimes referred as session causality) ensures that writes are ordered after writes that were observed by previous read operations. For example, if write(x,V2) is ordered after read(x) that has returned V1, write(x,V2) will be ordered *after* write(x,V1).

 Session models make *no* assumptions about operations made by *different* processes (clients) or from the different logical session [TANENBAUM14]. These models describe operation ordering from the point of view of a single process. However, the same guarantees have to hold for *every* process in the system. In other words, if P_1 can read its own writes, P_2 should be able to read *its* own writes, too.

Combining monotonic reads, monotonic writes, and read-own-writes gives Pipelined RAM (PRAM) consistency [LIPTON88] [BRZEZINSKI03], also known as FIFO consistency. PRAM guarantees that write operations originating from one process will propagate in the order they were executed by this process. Unlike under sequential consistency, writes from different processes can be observed in different order.

The properties described by client-centric consistency models are desirable and, in the majority of cases, are used by distributed systems developers to validate their systems and simplify their usage.

Eventual Consistency

Synchronization is expensive, both in multiprocessor programming and in distributed systems. As we discussed in "Consistency Models" on page 222, we can relax consistency guarantees and use models that allow some divergence between the nodes. For example, sequential consistency allows reads to be propagated at different speeds.

Under *eventual consistency*, updates propagate through the system asynchronously. Formally, it states that if there are no *additional* updates performed against the data item, *eventually* all accesses return the latest written value [VOGELS09]. In case of a conflict, the notion of *latest* value might change, as the values from diverged replicas are reconciled using a conflict resolution strategy, such as last-write-wins or using vector clocks (see "Vector clocks" on page 232).

Eventually is an interesting term to describe value propagation, since it specifies no hard time bound in which it has to happen. If the delivery service provides nothing more than an "eventually" guarantee, it doesn't sound like it can be relied upon.

However, in practice, this works well, and many databases these days are described as *eventually consistent*.

Tunable Consistency

Eventually consistent systems are sometimes described in CAP terms: you can trade availability for consistency or vice versa (see "Infamous CAP" on page 216). From the server-side perspective, eventually consistent systems usually implement tunable consistency, where data is replicated, read, and written using three variables:

Replication Factor N
> Number of nodes that will store a copy of data.

Write Consistency W
> Number of nodes that have to acknowledge a write for it to succeed.

Read Consistency R
> Number of nodes that have to respond to a read operation for it to succeed.

Choosing consistency levels where (R + W > N), the system can guarantee returning the most recent written value, because there's always an overlap between read and write sets. For example, if N = 3, W = 2, and R = 2, the system can tolerate a failure of just one node. Two nodes out of three must acknowledge the write. In the ideal scenario, the system also asynchronously replicates the write to the third node. If the third node is down, anti-entropy mechanisms (see Chapter 12) eventually propagate it.

During the read, two replicas out of three have to be available to serve the request for us to respond with consistent results. Any combination of nodes will give us at least one node that will have the most up-to-date record for a given key.

> When performing a write, the coordinator should submit it to N nodes, but can wait for only W nodes before it proceeds (or W - 1 in case the coordinator is also a replica). The rest of the write operations can complete asynchronously or fail. Similarly, when performing a read, the coordinator has to collect *at least* R responses. Some databases use speculative execution and submit extra read requests to reduce coordinator response latency. This means if one of the originally submitted read requests fails or arrives slowly, speculative requests can be counted toward R instead.

Write-heavy systems may sometimes pick W = 1 and R = N, which allows writes to be acknowledged by just one node before they succeed, but would require *all* the replicas (even potentially failed ones) to be available for reads. The same is true for the W = N,

`R = 1` combination: the latest value can be read from any node, as long as writes succeed only after being applied on *all* replicas.

Increasing read or write consistency levels increases latencies and raises requirements for node availability during requests. Decreasing them improves system availability while sacrificing consistency.

Quorums

A consistency level that consists of $\lfloor N/2 \rfloor + 1$ nodes is called a *quorum*, a majority of nodes. In the case of a network partition or node failures, in a system with `2f + 1` nodes, live nodes can continue accepting writes or reads, if up to `f` nodes are unavailable, until the rest of the cluster is available again. In other words, such systems can tolerate at most `f` node failures.

When executing read and write operations using quorums, a system cannot tolerate failures of the majority of nodes. For example, if there are three replicas in total, and two of them are down, read and write operations won't be able to achieve the number of nodes necessary for read and write consistency, since only one node out of three will be able to respond to the request.

Reading and writing using quorums does not guarantee monotonicity in cases of incomplete writes. If some write operation has failed after writing a value to one replica out of three, depending on the contacted replicas, a quorum read can return either the result of the incomplete operation, or the old value. Since subsequent same-value reads are not required to contact the same replicas, values they return can alternate. To achieve read monotonicity (at the cost of availability), we have to use blocking read-repair (see "Read Repair" on page 245).

Witness Replicas

Using quorums for read consistency helps to improve availability: even if some of the nodes are down, a database system can still accept reads and serve writes. The majority requirement guarantees that, since there's an overlap of at least one node in any majority, any quorum read will observe the most recent completed quorum write. However, using replication and majorities increases storage costs: we have to store a copy of the data on each replica. If our replication factor is five, we have to store five copies.

We can improve storage costs by using a concept called *witness replicas*. Instead of storing a copy of the record on each replica, we can split replicas into *copy* and *witness* subsets. Copy replicas still hold data records as previously. Under normal operation, witness replicas merely store the record indicating the fact that the write operation occurred. However, a situation might occur when the number of copy replicas is too low. For example, if we have three copy replicas and two witness ones, and two copy replicas go down, we end up with a quorum of one copy and two witness replicas.

In cases of write timeouts or copy replica failures, witness replicas can be *upgraded* to temporarily store the record in place of failed or timed-out copy replicas. As soon as the original copy replicas recover, upgraded replicas can revert to their previous state, or recovered replicas can become witnesses.

Let's consider a replicated system with three nodes, two of which are holding copies of data and the third serves as a witness: [1c, 2c, 3w]. We attempt to make a write, but 2c is temporarily unavailable and cannot complete the operation. In this case, we temporarily store the record on the witness replica 3w. Whenever 2c comes back up, repair mechanisms can bring it back up-to-date and remove redundant copies from witnesses.

In a different scenario, we can attempt to perform a read, and the record is present on 1c and 3w, but not on 2c. Since any two replicas are enough to constitute a quorum, if any subset of nodes of size two is available, whether it's two copy replicas [1c, 2c], or one copy replica and one witness [1c, 3w] or [2c, 3w], we can guarantee to serve consistent results. If we read from [1c, 2c], we fetch the latest record from 1c and can replicate it to 2c, since the value is missing there. In case only [2c, 3w] are available, the latest record can be fetched from 3w. To restore the original configuration and bring 2c up-to-date, the record can be replicated to it, and removed from the witness.

More generally, having n copy and m witness replicas has same availability guarantees as n + m copies, given that we follow two rules:

- Read and write operations are performed using majorities (i.e., with $N/2 + 1$ participants)
- At least one of the replicas in this quorum is *necessarily* a copy one

This works because data is guaranteed to be either on the copy or witness replicas. Copy replicas are brought up-to-date by the repair mechanism in case of a failure, and witness replicas store the data in the interim.

Using witness replicas helps to reduce storage costs while preserving consistency invariants. There are several implementations of this approach; for example, Spanner [CORBETT12] and Apache Cassandra (*https://databass.dev/links/105*).

Strong Eventual Consistency and CRDTs

We've discussed several strong consistency models, such as linearizability and serializability, and a form of weak consistency: eventual consistency. A possible middle ground between the two, offering some benefits of both models, is *strong eventual consistency*. Under this model, updates are allowed to propagate to servers late or out of order, but when all updates finally propagate to target nodes, conflicts between them can be resolved and they can be merged to produce the same valid state [GOMES17].

Under some conditions, we can relax our consistency requirements by allowing operations to preserve additional state that allows the diverged states to be reconciled (in other words, merged) after execution. One of the most prominent examples of such an approach is *Conflict-Free Replicated Data Types* (CRDTs, [SHAPIRO11a]) implemented, for example, in Redis [BIYIKOGLU13].

CRDTs are specialized data structures that preclude the existence of conflict and allow operations on these data types to be applied in any order without changing the result. This property can be extremely useful in a distributed system. For example, in a multinode system that uses conflict-free replicated counters, we can increment counter values on each node independently, even if they cannot communicate with one another due to a network partition. As soon as communication is restored, results from all nodes can be reconciled, and none of the operations applied during the partition will be lost.

This makes CRDTs useful in eventually consistent systems, since replica states in such systems are allowed to temporarily diverge. Replicas can execute operations locally, without prior synchronization with other nodes, and operations eventually propagate to all other replicas, potentially out of order. CRDTs allow us to reconstruct the complete system state from local individual states or operation sequences.

The simplest example of CRDTs is operation-based Commutative Replicated Data Types (CmRDTs). For CmRDTs to work, we need the allowed operations to be:

Side-effect free
> Their application does not change the system state.

Commutative
> Argument order does not matter: $x \bullet y = y \bullet x$. In other words, it doesn't matter whether x is merged with y, or y is merged with x.

Causally ordered
> Their successful delivery depends on the precondition, which ensures that the system has reached the state the operation can be applied to.

For example, we could implement a *grow-only counter*. Each server can hold a state vector consisting of last known counter updates from all other participants, initialized with zeros. Each server is only allowed to modify its own value in the vector. When updates are propagated, the function merge(state1, state2) merges the states from the two servers.

For example, we have three servers, with initial state vectors initialized:

```
Node 1:          Node 2:          Node 3:
[0, 0, 0]        [0, 0, 0]        [0, 0, 0]
```

If we update counters on the first and third nodes, their states change as follows:

```
Node 1:          Node 2:          Node 3:
[1, 0, 0]        [0, 0, 0]        [0, 0, 1]
```

When updates propagate, we use a merge function to combine the results by picking the maximum value for each slot:

```
Node 1 (Node 3 state vector propagated):
merge([1, 0, 0], [0, 0, 1]) = [1, 0, 1]

Node 2 (Node 1 state vector propagated):
merge([0, 0, 0], [1, 0, 0]) = [1, 0, 0]

Node 2 (Node 3 state vector propagated):
merge([1, 0, 0], [0, 0, 1]) = [1, 0, 1]

Node 3 (Node 1 state vector propagated):
merge([0, 0, 1], [1, 0, 0]) = [1, 0, 1]
```

To determine the current vector state, the sum of values in all slots is computed: sum([1, 0, 1]) = 2. The merge function is commutative. Since servers are only allowed to update their own values and these values are independent, no additional coordination is required.

It is possible to produce a *Positive-Negative-Counter* (PN-Counter) that supports both increments and decrements by using payloads consisting of two vectors: P, which nodes use for increments, and N, where they store decrements. In a larger system, to avoid propagating huge vectors, we can use *super-peers*. Super-peers replicate counter states and help to avoid constant peer-to-peer chatter [SHAPIRO11b].

To save and replicate values, we can use *registers*. The simplest version of the register is the *last-write-wins* register (LWW register), which stores a unique, globally ordered timestamp attached to each value to resolve conflicts. In case of a conflicting write, we preserve only the one with the larger timestamp. The merge operation (picking the value with the largest timestamp) here is also commutative, since it relies on the timestamp. If we cannot allow values to be discarded, we can supply application-specific merge logic and use a *multivalue* register, which stores all values that were written and allows the application to pick the right one.

Another example of CRDTs is an unordered *grow-only* set (G-Set). Each node maintains its local state and can append elements to it. Adding elements produces a valid set. Merging two sets is also a commutative operation. Similar to counters, we can use two sets to support both additions and removals. In this case, we have to preserve an invariant: only the values contained in the addition set can be added into the removal set. To reconstruct the current state of the set, all elements contained in the removal set are subtracted from the addition set [SHAPIRO11b].

An example of a conflict-free type that combines more complex structures is a conflict-free replicated JSON data type, allowing modifications such as insertions, deletions, and assignments on deeply nested JSON documents with list and map types. This algorithm performs merge operations on the client side and does not require operations to be propagated in any specific order [KLEPPMANN14].

There are quite a few possibilities CRDTs provide us with, and we can see more data stores using this concept to provide Strong Eventual Consistency (SEC). This is a powerful concept that we can add to our arsenal of tools for building fault-tolerant distributed systems.

Summary

Fault-tolerant systems use replication to improve availability: even if some processes fail or are unresponsive, the system as a whole can continue functioning correctly. However, keeping multiple copies in sync requires additional coordination.

We've discussed several single-operation consistency models, ordered from the one with the most guarantees to the one with the least:[2]

Linearizability
Operations appear to be applied instantaneously, and the real-time operation order is maintained.

Sequential consistency
Operation effects are propagated in *some* total order, and this order is consistent with the order they were executed by the individual processes.

Causal consistency
Effects of the causally related operations are visible in the same order to all processes.

---

2 These short definitions are given for recap only, the reader is advised to refer to the complete definitions for context.

PRAM/FIFO consistency
> Operation effects become visible in the same order they were executed by individual processes. Writes from different processes can be observed in different orders.

After that, we discussed multiple session models:

Read-own-writes
> Read operations reflect the previous writes. Writes propagate through the system and become available for later reads that come from the same client.

Monotonic reads
> Any read that has observed a value cannot observe a value that is older that the observed one.

Monotonic writes
> Writes coming from the same client propagate to other clients in the order they were made by this client.

Writes-follow-reads
> Write operations are ordered after the writes whose effects were observed by the previous reads executed by the same client.

Knowing and understanding these concepts can help you to understand the guarantees of the underlying systems and use them for application development. Consistency models describe rules that operations on data have to follow, but their scope is limited to a specific system. Stacking systems with weaker guarantees on top of ones with stronger guarantees or ignoring consistency implications of underlying systems may lead to unrecoverable inconsistencies and data loss.

We also discussed the concept of *eventual* and *tunable* consistency. Quorum-based systems use majorities to serve consistent data. *Witness replicas* can be used to reduce storage costs.

Further Reading

If you'd like to learn more about the concepts mentioned in this chapter, you can refer to the following sources:

Consistency models

Perrin, Matthieu. 2017. *Distributed Systems: Concurrency and Consistency* (1st Ed.). Elsevier, UK: ISTE Press.

Viotti, Paolo and Marko Vukolić. 2016. "Consistency in Non-Transactional Distributed Storage Systems." *ACM Computing Surveys* 49, no. 1 (July): Article 19. *https://doi.org/0.1145/2926965*.

Bailis, Peter, Aaron Davidson, Alan Fekete, Ali Ghodsi, Joseph M. Hellerstein, and Ion Stoica. 2013. "Highly available transactions: virtues and limitations." *Proceedings of the VLDB Endowment* 7, no. 3 (November): 181-192. *https://doi.org/10.14778/2732232.2732237*.

Aguilera, M.K., and D.B. Terry. 2016. "The Many Faces of Consistency." *Bulletin of the Technical Committee on Data Engineering* 39, no. 1 (March): 3-13.

CHAPTER 12

Anti-Entropy and Dissemination

Most of the communication patterns we've been discussing so far were either peer-to-peer or one-to-many (coordinator and replicas). To reliably propagate data records throughout the system, we need the propagating node to be available and able to reach the other nodes, but even then the throughput is limited to a single machine.

Quick and reliable propagation may be less applicable to data records and more important for the cluster-wide metadata, such as membership information (joining and leaving nodes), node states, failures, schema changes, etc. Messages containing this information are generally infrequent and small, but have to be propagated as quickly and reliably as possible.

Such updates can generally be propagated to all nodes in the cluster using one of the three broad groups of approaches [DEMERS87]; schematic depictions of these communication patterns are shown in Figure 12-1:

- a) Notification broadcast from one process to *all* others.
- b) Periodic peer-to-peer information exchange. Peers connect pairwise and exchange messages.
- c) Cooperative broadcast, where message recipients become broadcasters and help to spread the information quicker and more reliably.

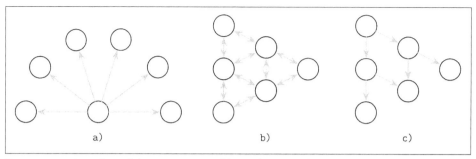

Figure 12-1. Broadcast (a), anti-entropy (b), and gossip (c)

Broadcasting the message to all other processes is the most straightforward approach that works well when the number of nodes in the cluster is small, but in large clusters it can get *expensive* because of the number of nodes, and *unreliable* because of overdependence on a single process. Individual processes may not always know about the existence of all other processes in the network. Moreover, there has to be some overlap in time during which both the broadcasting process and *each one* of its recipients are up, which might be difficult to achieve in some cases.

To relax these constraints, we can assume that *some* updates may fail to propagate. The coordinator will do its best and deliver the messages to all available participants, and then anti-entropy mechanisms will bring nodes back in sync in case there were any failures. This way, the responsibility for delivering messages is shared by all nodes in the system, and is split into two steps: primary delivery and periodic sync.

Entropy is a property that represents the measure of disorder in the system. In a distributed system, entropy represents a degree of state divergence between the nodes. Since this property is undesired and its amount should be kept to a minimum, there are many techniques that help to deal with entropy.

Anti-entropy is usually used to bring the nodes back up-to-date in case the primary delivery mechanism has failed. The system can continue functioning correctly even if the coordinator fails at some point, since the other nodes will continue spreading the information. In other words, anti-entropy is used to lower the convergence time bounds in eventually consistent systems.

To keep nodes in sync, anti-entropy triggers a background or a foreground process that compares and reconciles missing or conflicting records. Background anti-entropy processes use auxiliary structures such as Merkle trees and update logs to identify divergence. Foreground anti-entropy processes piggyback read or write requests: hinted handoff, read repairs, etc.

If replicas diverge in a replicated system, to restore consistency and bring them back in sync, we have to find and repair missing records by comparing replica states pairwise. For large datasets, this can be very costly: we have to read the whole dataset on both nodes and notify replicas about more recent state changes that weren't yet propagated. To reduce this cost, we can consider ways in which replicas can get out-of-date and patterns in which data is accessed.

Read Repair

It is easiest to detect divergence between the replicas during the read, since at that point we can contact replicas, request the queried state from each one of them, and see whether or not their responses match. Note that in this case we do not query an entire dataset stored on each replica, and we limit our goal to just the data that was requested by the client.

The coordinator performs a distributed read, optimistically assuming that replicas are in sync and have the same information available. If replicas send different responses, the coordinator sends missing updates to the replicas where they're missing.

This mechanism is called *read repair*. It is often used to detect and eliminate inconsistencies. During read repair, the coordinator node makes a request to replicas, waits for their responses, and compares them. In case some of the replicas have missed the recent updates and their responses differ, the coordinator detects inconsistencies and sends updates back to the replicas [DECANDIA07].

Some Dynamo-style databases choose to lift the requirement of contacting *all* replicas and use tunable consistency levels instead. To return consistent results, we do not have to contact and repair all the replicas, but only the number of nodes that satisfies the consistency level. If we do *quorum* reads and writes, we still get consistent results, but some of the replicas still might not contain all the writes.

Read repair can be implemented as a *blocking* or *asynchronous* operation. During blocking read repair, the original client request has to wait until the coordinator "repairs" the replicas. Asynchronous read repair simply schedules a task that can be executed after results are returned to the user.

Blocking read repair ensures read monotonicity (*https://databass.dev/links/1*) (see "Session Models" on page 233) for quorum reads: as soon as the client reads a specific value, subsequent reads return the value at least as recent as the one it has seen, since replica states were repaired. If we're not using quorums for reads, we lose this monotonicity guarantee as data might have not been propagated to the target node by the time of a subsequent read. At the same time, blocking read repair sacrifices availability, since repairs should be acknowledged by the target replicas and the read cannot return until they respond.

To detect exactly which records differ between replica responses, some databases (for example, Apache Cassandra) use specialized iterators with merge listeners (*https://databass.dev/links/2*), which reconstruct differences between the merged result and individual inputs. Its output is then used by the coordinator to notify replicas about the missing data.

Read repair assumes that replicas are *mostly* in sync and we do not expect every request to fall back to a blocking repair. Because of the read monotonicity of blocking repairs, we can also expect subsequent requests to return the same consistent results, as long as there was no write operation that has completed in the interim.

Digest Reads

Instead of issuing a full read request to each node, the coordinator can issue only one full read request and send only *digest* requests to the other replicas. A digest request reads the replica-local data and, instead of returning a full snapshot of the requested data, it computes a hash of this response. Now, the coordinator can compute a hash of the full read and compare it to digests from all other nodes. If all the digests match, it can be confident that the replicas are in sync.

In case digests do not match, the coordinator does not know which replicas are ahead, and which ones are behind. To bring lagging replicas back in sync with the rest of the nodes, the coordinator has to issue full reads to any replicas that responded with different digests, compare their responses, reconcile the data, and send updates to the lagging replicas.

 Digests are usually computed using a noncryptographic hash function, such as MD5, since it has to be computed quickly to make the "happy path" performant. Hash functions can have *collisions*, but their probability is negligible for most real-world systems. Since databases often use more than just one anti-entropy mechanism, we can expect that, even in the unlikely event of a hash collision, data will be reconciled by the different subsystem.

Hinted Handoff

Another anti-entropy approach is called *hinted handoff* [DECANDIA07], a write-side repair mechanism. If the target node fails to acknowledge the write, the write coordinator or one of the replicas stores a special record, called a *hint*, which is replayed to the target node as soon as it comes back up.

In Apache Cassandra, unless the ANY consistency level is in use [ELLIS11], hinted writes aren't counted toward the replication factor (see "Tunable Consistency" on page 235), since the data in the hint log isn't accessible for reads and is only used to help the lagging participants catch up.

Some databases, for example Riak, use *sloppy quorums* together with hinted handoff. With sloppy quorums, in case of replica failures, write operations can use additional healthy nodes from the node list, and these nodes do not have to be target replicas for the executed operations.

For example, say we have a five-node cluster with nodes {A, B, C, D, E}, where {A, B, C} are replicas for the executed write operation, and node B is down. A, being the coordinator for the query, picks node D to satisfy the sloppy quorum and maintain the desired availability and durability guarantees. Now, data is replicated to {A, D, C}. However, the record at D will have a hint in its metadata, since the write was originally intended for B. As soon as B recovers, D will attempt to forward a hint back to it. Once the hint is replayed on B, it can be safely removed without reducing the total number of replicas [DECANDIA07].

Under similar circumstances, if nodes {B, C} are briefly separated from the rest of the cluster by the network partition, and a sloppy quorum write was done against {A, D, E}, a read on {B, C}, immediately following this write, would *not* observe the latest read [DOWNEY12]. In other words, sloppy quorums improve availability at the cost of consistency.

Merkle Trees

Since read repair can only fix inconsistencies on the currently queried data, we should use different mechanisms to find and repair inconsistencies in the data that is not actively queried.

As we already discussed, finding exactly which rows have diverged between the replicas requires exchanging and comparing the data records pairwise. This is highly impractical and expensive. Many databases employ *Merkle trees* [MERKLE87] to reduce the cost of reconciliation.

Merkle trees compose a compact hashed representation of the local data, building a tree of hashes. The lowest level of this hash tree is built by scanning an entire table holding data records, and computing hashes of record ranges. Higher tree levels contain hashes of the lower-level hashes, building a hierarchical representation that allows us to quickly detect inconsistencies by comparing the hashes, following the hash tree nodes recursively to narrow down inconsistent ranges. This can be done by exchanging and comparing subtrees level-wise, or by exchanging and comparing entire trees.

Figure 12-2 shows a composition of a Merkle tree. The lowest level consists of the hashes of data record ranges. Hashes for each higher level are computed by hashing underlying level hashes, repeating this process recursively up to the tree root.

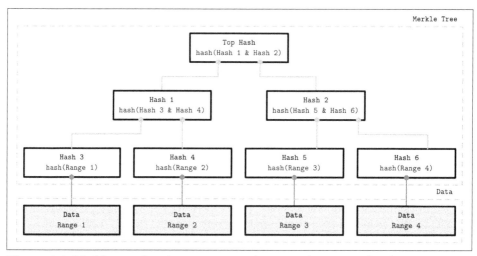

Figure 12-2. Merkle tree. Gray boxes represent data record ranges. White boxes represent a hash tree hierarchy.

To determine whether or not there's an inconsistency between the two replicas, we only need to compare the root-level hashes from their Merkle trees. By comparing hashes pairwise from top to bottom, it is possible to locate ranges holding differences between the nodes, and repair data records contained in them.

Since Merkle trees are calculated recursively from the bottom to the top, a change in data triggers recomputation of the entire subtree. There's also a trade-off between the size of a tree (consequently, sizes of exchanged messages) and its precision (how small and exact data ranges are).

Bitmap Version Vectors

More recent research on this subject introduces *bitmap version vectors* [GON-ÇALVES15], which can be used to resolve data conflicts based on *recency*: each node keeps a per-peer log of operations that have occurred locally or were replicated. During anti-entropy, logs are compared, and missing data is replicated to the target node.

Each write, coordinated by a node, is represented by a *dot* (i,n): an event with a node-local sequence number i coordinated by the node n. The sequence number i starts with 1 and is incremented each time the node executes a write operation.

To track replica states, we use node-local logical clocks. Each clock represents a set of dots, representing writes this node has seen *directly* (coordinated by the node itself), or *transitively* (coordinated by and replicated from the other nodes).

In the node logical clock, events coordinated by the node itself will have no gaps. If some writes aren't replicated from the other nodes, the clock will contain gaps. To get two nodes back in sync, they can exchange logical clocks, identify gaps represented by the missing dots, and then replicate data records associated with them. To do this, we need to reconstruct the data records each dot refers to. This information is stored in a *dotted causal container* (DCC), which maps dots to causal information for a given key. This way, conflict resolution captures causal relationships between the writes.

Figure 12-3 (adapted from [GONÇALVES15]) shows an example of the state representation of three nodes in the system, P_1, P_2 and P_3, from the perspective of P_2, tracking which values it has seen. Each time P_2 makes a write or receives a replicated value, it updates this table.

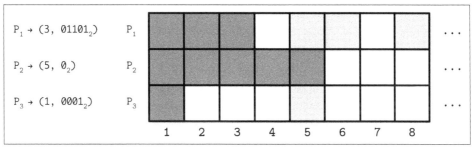

Figure 12-3. Bitmap version vector example

During replication, P_2 creates a compact representation of this state and creates a map from the node identifier to a pair of latest values, up to which it has seen consecutive writes, and a bitmap where other seen writes are encoded as 1. $(3, 01101_2)$ here means that node P_2 has seen consecutive updates up to the third value, and it has seen values on the second, third, and fifth position relative to 3 (i.e., it has seen the values with sequence numbers 5, 6, and 8).

During exchange with other nodes, it will receive the missing updates the other node has seen. As soon as all the nodes in the system have seen consecutive values up to the index i, the version vector can be truncated up to this index.

An advantage of this approach is that it captures the causal relation between the value writes and allows nodes to precisely identify the data points missing on the other nodes. A possible downside is that, if the node was down for an extended time period, peer nodes can't truncate the log, since data still has to be replicated to the lagging node once it comes back up.

Gossip Dissemination

> Masses are always breeding grounds of psychic epidemics.
>
> —Carl Jung

To involve other nodes, and propagate updates with the *reach* of a broadcast and the *reliability* of anti-entropy, we can use gossip protocols.

Gossip protocols are probabilistic communication procedures based on how rumors are spread in human society or how diseases propagate in the population. Rumors and epidemics provide rather illustrative ways to describe how these protocols work: rumors spread while the population still has an interest in hearing them; diseases propagate until there are no more susceptible members in the population.

The main objective of gossip protocols is to use cooperative propagation to disseminate information from one process to the rest of the cluster. Just as a virus spreads through the human population by being passed from one individual to another, potentially increasing in scope with each step, information is relayed through the system, getting more processes involved.

A process that holds a record that has to be spread around is said to be *infective*. Any process that hasn't received the update yet is then *susceptible*. Infective processes not willing to propagate the new state after a period of active dissemination are said to be *removed* [DEMERS87]. All processes start in a susceptible state. Whenever an update for some data record arrives, a process that received it moves to the infective state and starts disseminating the update to other *random* neighboring processes, infecting them. As soon as the infective processes become certain that the update was propagated, they move to the removed state.

To avoid explicit coordination and maintaining a global list of recipients and requiring a single coordinator to broadcast messages to each other participant in the system, this class of algorithms models completeness using the *loss of interest* function. The protocol efficiency is then determined by how quickly it can *infect* as many nodes as possible, while keeping overhead caused by redundant messages to a minimum.

Gossip can be used for asynchronous message delivery in homogeneous decentralized systems, where nodes may not have long-term membership or be organized in any topology. Since gossip protocols generally do not require explicit coordination, they can be useful in systems with flexible membership (where nodes are joining and leaving frequently) or mesh networks.

Gossip protocols are very robust and help to achieve high reliability in the presence of failures inherent to distributed systems. Since messages are relayed in a randomized manner, they still can be delivered even if some communication components between them fail, just through the different paths. It can be said that the system adapts to failures.

Gossip Mechanics

Processes periodically select f peers at random (where f is a configurable parameter, called *fanout*) and exchange currently "hot" information with them. Whenever the process learns about a new piece of information from its peers, it will attempt to pass it on further. Because peers are selected probabilistically, there will always be some overlap, and messages will get delivered repeatedly and may continue circulating for some time. *Message redundancy* is a metric that captures the overhead incurred by repeated delivery. Redundancy is an important property, and it is crucial to how gossip works.

The amount of time the system requires to reach convergence is called *latency*. There's a slight difference between reaching convergence (stopping the gossip process) and delivering the message to all peers, since there might be a short period during which all peers are notified, but gossip continues. Fanout and latency depend on the system size: in a larger system, we either have to increase the fanout to keep latency stable, or allow higher latency.

Over time, as the nodes notice they've been receiving the same information again and again, the message will start losing importance and nodes will have to eventually stop relaying it. Interest loss can be computed either *probabilistically* (the probability of propagation stop is computed for each process on every step) or using a *threshold* (the number of received duplicates is counted, and propagation is stopped when this number is too high). Both approaches have to take the cluster size and fanout into consideration. Counting duplicates to measure convergence can improve latency and reduce redundancy [DEMERS87].

In terms of consistency, gossip protocols offer *convergent* consistency [BIRMAN07]: nodes have a higher probability to have the same view of the events that occurred further in the past.

Overlay Networks

Even though gossip protocols are important and useful, they're usually applied for a narrow set of problems. Nonepidemic approaches can distribute the message with nonprobabilistic certainty, less redundancy, and generally in a more optimal way [BIRMAN07]. Gossip algorithms are often praised for their scalability and the fact it is possible to distribute a message within log N message rounds (where N is the size of the cluster) [KERMARREC07], but it's important to keep the number of *redundant* messages generated during gossip rounds in mind as well. To achieve reliability, gossip-based protocols produce *some* duplicate message deliveries.

Selecting nodes at random greatly improves system *robustness*: if there is a network partition, messages will be delivered eventually if there are links that indirectly connect two processes. The obvious downside of this approach is that it is not message-optimal: to guarantee robustness, we have to maintain redundant connections between the peers and send redundant messages.

A middle ground between the two approaches is to construct a *temporary* fixed topology in a gossip system. This can be achieved by creating an *overlay network* of peers: nodes can sample their peers and select the best contact points based on proximity (usually measured by the latency).

Nodes in the system can form *spanning trees*: unidirected, loop-free graphs with distinct edges, covering the whole network. Having such a graph, messages can be distributed in a fixed number of steps.

Figure 12-4 shows an example of a spanning tree:[1]

- a) We achieve full connectivity between the points without using all the edges.
- b) We can lose connectivity to the entire subtree if just a single link is broken.

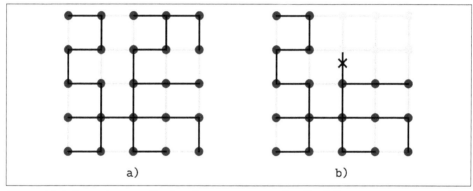

Figure 12-4. Spanning tree. Dark points represent nodes. Dark lines represent an overlay network. Gray lines represent other possible existing connections between the nodes.

One of the potential downsides of this approach is that it might lead to forming interconnected "islands" of peers having strong preferences toward each other.

To keep the number of messages low, while allowing quick recovery in case of a connectivity loss, we can mix both approaches—fixed topologies and tree-based broadcast—when the system is in a *stable* state, and fall back to gossip for *failover* and system recovery.

---

1 This example is only used for illustration: nodes in the network are generally not arranged in a grid.

Hybrid Gossip

Push/lazy-push multicast trees (Plumtrees) [LEITAO07] make a trade-off between epidemic and tree-based broadcast primitives. Plumtrees work by creating a spanning tree overlay of nodes to *actively* distribute messages with the smallest overhead. Under normal conditions, nodes send full messages to just a small subset of peers provided by the peer sampling service.

Each node sends the full message to the small subset of nodes, and for the rest of the nodes, it *lazily* forwards only the message ID. If the node receives the identifier of a message it has never seen, it can query its peers to get it. This *lazy-push* step ensures high reliability and provides a way to quickly heal the broadcast tree. In case of failures, protocol falls back to the gossip approach through lazy-push steps, broadcasting the message and repairing the overlay.

Due to the nature of distributed systems, any node or link between the nodes might fail at any time, making it impossible to traverse the tree when the segment becomes unreachable. The lazy gossip network helps to notify peers about seen messages in order to construct and repair the tree.

Figure 12-5 shows an illustration of such double connectivity: nodes are connected with an optimal spanning tree (solid lines) and the lazy gossip network (dotted lines). This illustration does not represent any particular network topology, but only *connections* between the nodes.

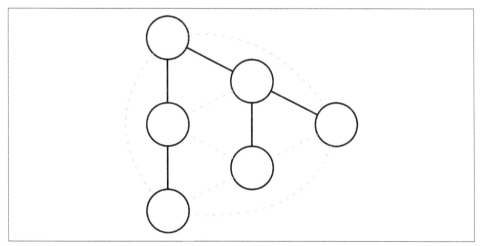

Figure 12-5. Lazy and eager push networks. Solid lines represent a broadcast tree. Dotted lines represent lazy gossip connections.

One of the advantages of using the lazy-push mechanism for tree construction and repair is that in a network with constant load, it will tend to generate a tree that also minimizes message latency, since nodes that are first to respond are added to the broadcast tree.

Partial Views

Broadcasting messages to all known peers and maintaining a full view of the cluster can get expensive and impractical, especially if the *churn* (measure of the number of joining and leaving nodes in the system) is high. To avoid this, gossip protocols often use a *peer sampling service*. This service maintains a *partial view* of the cluster, which is periodically refreshed using gossip. Partial views overlap, as some degree of redundancy is desired in gossip protocols, but too much redundancy means we're doing extra work.

For example, the Hybrid Partial View (HyParView) protocol [LEITAO07] maintains a small *active* view and a larger *passive* view of the cluster. Nodes from the active view create an overlay that can be used for dissemination. Passive view is used to maintain a list of nodes that can be used to replace the failed ones from the active view.

Periodically, nodes perform a shuffle operation, during which they exchange their active and passive views. During this exchange, nodes add the members from both passive and active views they receive from their peers to their passive views, cycling out the oldest values to cap the list size.

The active view is updated depending on the state changes of nodes in this view and requests from peers. If a process P_1 suspects that P_2, one of the peers from its active view, has failed, P_1 removes P_2 from its active view and attempts to establish a connection with a replacement process P_3 from the passive view. If the connection fails, P_3 is removed from the passive view of P_1.

Depending on the number of processes in P_1's active view, P_3 may choose to decline the connection if its active view is already full. If P_1's view is empty, P_3 *has to* replace one of its current active view peers with P_1. This helps bootstrapping or recovering nodes to quickly become effective members of the cluster at the cost of cycling some connections.

This approach helps to reduce the number of messages in the system by using only active view nodes for dissemination, while maintaining high reliability by using passive views as a recovery mechanism. One of the performance and quality measures is how quickly a peer sampling service converges to a stable overlay in cases of topology reorganization [JELASITY04]. HyParView scores rather high here, because of how the views are maintained and since it gives priority to bootstrapping processes.

HyParView and Plumtree use a *hybrid gossip* approach: using a small subset of peers for broadcasting messages and falling back to a wider network of peers in case of failures and network partitions. Both systems do not rely on a global view that includes all the peers, which can be helpful not only because of a large number of nodes in the system (which is not the case most of the time), but also because of costs associated with maintaining an up-to-date list of members on every node. Partial views allow nodes to actively communicate with only a small subset of neighboring nodes.

Summary

Eventually consistent systems allow replica state divergence. Tunable consistency allows us to trade consistency for availability and vice versa. Replica divergence can be resolved using one of the anti-entropy mechanisms:

Hinted handoff
    Temporarily store writes on neighboring nodes in case the target is down, and replay them on the target as soon as it comes back up.

Read-repair
    Reconcile requested data ranges during the read by comparing responses, detecting missing records, and sending them to lagging replicas.

Merkle trees
    Detect data ranges that require repair by computing and exchanging hierarchical trees of hashes.

Bitmap version vectors
    Detect missing replica writes by maintaining compact records containing information about the most recent writes.

These anti-entropy approaches optimize for one of the three parameters: scope reduction, recency, or completeness. We can reduce the scope of anti-entropy by only synchronizing the data that is being actively queried (read-repairs) or individual missing writes (hinted handoff). If we assume that most failures are temporary and participants recover from them as quickly as possible, we can store the log of the most recent diverged events and know exactly what to synchronize in the event of failure (bitmap version vectors). If we need to compare entire datasets on multiple nodes pairwise and efficiently locate differences between them, we can hash the data and compare hashes (Merkle trees).

To reliably distribute information in a large-scale system, gossip protocols can be used. Hybrid gossip protocols reduce the number of exchanged messages while remaining resistant to network partitions, when possible.

Many modern systems use gossip for failure detection and membership information [DECANDIA07]. HyParView is used in Partisan (*https://databass.dev/links/3*), the high-performance, high-scalability distributed computing framework. Plumtree was used in the Riak core (*https://databass.dev/links/4*) for cluster-wide information.

Further Reading

If you'd like to learn more about the concepts mentioned in this chapter, you can refer to the following sources:

Gossip protocols

Shah, Devavrat. 2009. "Gossip Algorithms." *Foundations and Trends in Networking* 3, no. 1 (January): 1-125. *https://doi.org/10.1561/1300000014*.

Jelasity, Márk. 2003. "Gossip-based Protocols for Large-scale Distributed Systems." Dissertation. *http://www.inf.u-szeged.hu/~jelasity/dr/doktori-mu.pdf*.

Demers, Alan, Dan Greene, Carl Hauser, Wes Irish, John Larson, Scott Shenker, Howard Sturgis, Dan Swinehart, and Doug Terry. 1987. "Epidemic algorithms for replicated database maintenance." In *Proceedings of the sixth annual ACM Symposium on Principles of distributed computing (PODC '87)*, 1-12. New York: Association for Computing Machinery. *https://doi.org/10.1145/41840.41841*.

CHAPTER 13
Distributed Transactions

To maintain order in a distributed system, we have to guarantee at least some consistency. In "Consistency Models" on page 222, we talked about single-object, single-operation consistency models that help us to reason about the individual operations. However, in databases we often need to execute *multiple* operations atomically.

Atomic operations are explained in terms of state transitions: the database was in state A before a particular transaction was started; by the time it finished, the state went from A to B. In operation terms, this is simple to understand, since transactions have no predetermined attached state. Instead, they apply operations to data records starting at *some* point in time. This gives us some flexibility in terms of scheduling and execution: transactions can be reordered and even retried.

The main focus of transaction processing is to determine permissible *histories*, to model and represent possible interleaving execution scenarios. History, in this case, represents a dependency graph: which transactions have been executed prior to execution of the current transaction. History is said to be *serializable* if it is equivalent (i.e., has the same dependency graph) to *some* history that executes these transactions sequentially. You can review concepts of histories, their equivalence, serializability, and other concepts in "Serializability" on page 94. Generally, this chapter is a distributed systems counterpart of Chapter 5, where we discussed node-local transaction processing.

Single-partition transactions involve the pessimistic (lock-based or tracking) or optimistic (try and validate) concurrency control schemes that we discussed in Chapter 5, but neither one of these approaches solves the problem of multipartition transactions, which require coordination between different servers, distributed commit, and rollback protocols.

Generally speaking, when transferring money from one account to another, you'd like to both credit the first account and debit the second one *simultaneously*. However, if we break down the transaction into individual steps, even debiting or crediting doesn't look atomic at first sight: we need to read the old balance, add or subtract the required amount, and save this result. Each one of these substeps involves several operations: the node receives a request, parses it, locates the data on disk, makes a write and, finally, acknowledges it. Even this is a rather high-level view: to execute a simple write, we have to perform hundreds of small steps.

This means that we have to first *execute* the transaction and only then make its results *visible*. But let's first define what transactions are. A *transaction* is a set of operations, an atomic unit of execution. Transaction atomicity implies that all its results become visible or none of them do. For example, if we modify several rows, or even tables in a single transaction, either all or none of the modifications will be applied.

To ensure atomicity, transactions should be *recoverable*. In other words, if the transaction cannot complete, is aborted, or times out, its results have to be rolled back completely. A nonrecoverable, partially executed transaction can leave the database in an inconsistent state. In summary, in case of unsuccessful transaction execution, the database state has to be reverted to its previous state, as if this transaction was never tried in the first place.

Another important aspect is network partitions and node failures: nodes in the system fail and recover independently, but their states have to remain consistent. This means that the atomicity requirement holds not only for the local operations, but also for operations executed on other nodes: changes have to be durably propagated to all of the nodes involved in the transaction or none of them [LAMPSON79].

Making Operations Appear Atomic

To make multiple operations appear atomic, especially if some of them are remote, we need to use a class of algorithms called *atomic commitment*. Atomic commitment doesn't allow disagreements between the participants: a transaction *will not* commit if even one of the participants votes against it. At the same time, this means that *failed* processes have to reach the same conclusion as the rest of the cohort. Another important implication of this fact is that atomic commitment algorithms do not work in the presence of Byzantine failures: when the process lies about its state or decides on an arbitrary value, since it contradicts unanimity [HADZILACOS05].

The problem that atomic commitment is trying to solve is reaching an agreement on whether or not to execute the proposed transaction. Cohorts cannot choose, influence, or change the proposed transaction or propose any alternative: they can only give their vote on whether or not they are willing to execute it [ROBINSON08].

Atomic commitment algorithms do not set strict requirements for the semantics of transaction *prepare*, *commit*, or *rollback* operations. Database implementers have to decide on:

- When the data is considered ready to commit, and they're just a pointer swap away from making the changes public.
- How to perform the commit itself to make transaction results visible in the shortest timeframe possible.
- How to roll back the changes made by the transaction if the algorithm decides not to commit.

We discussed node-local implementations of these processes in Chapter 5.

Many distributed systems use atomic commitment algorithms—for example, MySQL (for distributed transactions (*https://databass.dev/links/5*)) and Kafka (for producer and consumer interaction [MEHTA17]).

In databases, distributed transactions are executed by the component commonly known as a *transaction manager*. The transaction manager is a subsystem responsible for scheduling, coordinating, executing, and tracking transactions. In a distributed environment, the transaction manager is responsible for ensuring that node-local visibility guarantees are consistent with the visibility prescribed by distributed atomic operations. In other words, transactions commit in all partitions, and for all replicas.

We will discuss two atomic commitment algorithms: two-phase commit, which solves a commitment problem, but doesn't allow for failures of the coordinator process; and three-phase commit [SKEEN83], which solves a *nonblocking atomic commitment* problem,[1] and allows participants proceed even in case of coordinator failures [BABAOGLU93].

Two-Phase Commit

Let's start with the most straightforward protocol for a distributed commit that allows multipartition *atomic* updates. (For more information on partitioning, you can refer to "Database Partitioning" on page 270.) *Two-phase commit* (2PC) is usually discussed in the context of database transactions. 2PC executes in two phases. During the first phase, the decided value is distributed, and votes are collected. During the second phase, nodes just flip the switch, making the results of the first phase visible.

---

1 The fine print says "assuming a highly reliable network." In other words, a network that precludes partitions [ALHOUMAILY10]. Implications of this assumption are discussed in the paper's section about algorithm description.

2PC assumes the presence of a *leader* (or *coordinator*) that holds the state, collects votes, and is a primary point of reference for the agreement round. The rest of the nodes are called *cohorts*. Cohorts, in this case, are usually partitions that operate over disjoint datasets, against which transactions are performed. The coordinator and every cohort keep local operation logs for each executed step. Participants vote to accept or reject some *value*, proposed by the coordinator. Most often, this value is an identifier of the distributed transaction that has to be executed, but 2PC can be used in other contexts as well.

The coordinator can be a node that received a request to execute the transaction, or it can be picked at random, using a leader-election algorithm, assigned manually, or even fixed throughout the lifetime of the system. The protocol does not place restrictions on the coordinator role, and the role can be transferred to another participant for reliability or performance.

As the name suggests, a two-phase commit is executed in two steps:

Prepare

The coordinator notifies cohorts about the new transaction by sending a `Propose` message. Cohorts make a decision on whether or not they can commit the part of the transaction that applies to them. If a cohort decides that it can commit, it notifies the coordinator about the positive vote. Otherwise, it responds to the coordinator, asking it to abort the transaction. All decisions taken by cohorts are persisted in the coordinator log, and each cohort keeps a copy of its decision locally.

Commit/abort

Operations within a transaction can change state across different partitions (each represented by a cohort). If even one of the cohorts votes to abort the transaction, the coordinator sends the `Abort` message to all of them. Only if all cohorts have voted positively does the coordinator send them a final `Commit` message.

This process is shown in Figure 13-1.

During the *prepare* phase, the coordinator distributes the proposed value and collects votes from the participants on whether or not this proposed value should be committed. Cohorts may choose to reject the coordinator's proposal if, for example, another conflicting transaction has already committed a different value.

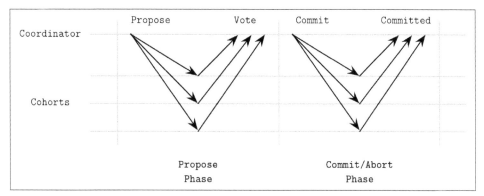

Figure 13-1. Two-phase commit protocol. During the first phase, cohorts are notified about the new transaction. During the second phase, the transaction is committed or aborted.

After the coordinator has collected the votes, it can make a decision on whether to *commit* the transaction or *abort* it. If all cohorts have voted positively, it decides to commit and notifies them by sending a Commit message. Otherwise, the coordinator sends an Abort message to all cohorts and the transaction gets rolled back. In other words, if one node rejects the proposal, the whole round is aborted.

During each step the coordinator and cohorts have to write the results of each operation to durable storage to be able to reconstruct the state and recover in case of local failures, and be able to forward and replay results for other participants.

In the context of database systems, each 2PC round is usually responsible for a single transaction. During the *prepare* phase, transaction contents (operations, identifiers, and other metadata) are transferred from the coordinator to the cohorts. The transaction is executed by the cohorts locally and is left in a *partially committed* state (sometimes called *precommitted*), making it ready for the coordinator to finalize execution during the next phase by either committing or aborting it. By the time the transaction commits, its contents are already stored durably on all other nodes [BERNSTEIN09].

Cohort Failures in 2PC

Let's consider several failure scenarios. For example, as Figure 13-2 shows, if one of the cohorts fails during the *propose* phase, the coordinator cannot proceed with a commit, since it requires all votes to be positive. If one of the cohorts is unavailable, the coordinator will abort the transaction. This requirement has a negative impact on availability: failure of a single node can prevent transactions from happening. Some systems, for example, Spanner (see "Distributed Transactions with Spanner" on page 268), perform 2PC over Paxos groups rather than individual nodes to improve protocol availability.

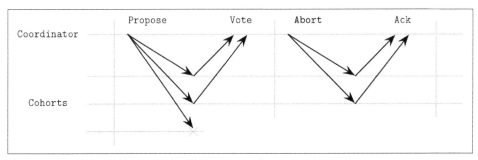

Figure 13-2. Cohort failure during the propose phase

The main idea behind 2PC is a *promise* by a cohort that, once it has positively responded to the proposal, it will not go back on its decision, so only the coordinator can abort the transaction.

If one of the cohorts has failed *after* accepting the proposal, it has to learn about the actual outcome of the vote before it can serve values correctly, since the coordinator might have aborted the commit due to the other cohorts' decisions. When a cohort node recovers, it has to get up to speed with a final coordinator decision. Usually, this is done by persisting the decision log on the coordinator side and replicating decision values to the failed participants. Until then, the cohort cannot serve requests because it is in an inconsistent state.

Since the protocol has multiple spots where processes are waiting for the other participants (when the coordinator collects votes, or when the cohort is waiting for the commit/abort phase), link failures might lead to message loss, and this wait will continue indefinitely. If the coordinator does not receive a response from the replica during the propose phase, it can trigger a timeout and abort the transaction.

Coordinator Failures in 2PC

If one of the cohorts does not receive a commit or abort command from the coordinator during the second phase, as shown in Figure 13-3, it should attempt to find out which decision was made by the coordinator. The coordinator might have decided upon the value but wasn't able to communicate it to the particular replica. In such cases, information about the decision can be replicated from the peers' transaction logs or from the backup coordinator. Replicating commit decisions is safe since it's always unanimous: the whole point of 2PC is to either commit or abort on all sites, and commit on one cohort implies that all other cohorts have to commit.

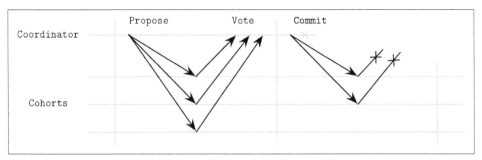

Figure 13-3. Coordinator failure after the propose phase

During the first phase, the coordinator collects votes and, subsequently, promises from cohorts, that they will wait for its explicit commit or abort command. If the coordinator fails after collecting the votes, but before broadcasting vote results, the cohorts end up in a state of uncertainty. This is shown in Figure 13-4. Cohorts do not know what precisely the coordinator has decided, and whether or not any of the participants (potentially also unreachable) might have been notified about the transaction results [BERNSTEIN87].

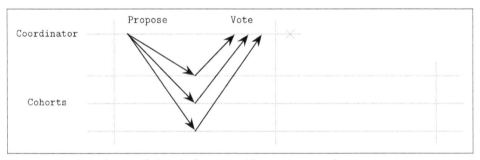

Figure 13-4. Coordinator failure before it could contact any cohorts

Inability of the coordinator to proceed with a commit or abort leaves the cluster in an undecided state. This means that cohorts will not be able to learn about the final decision in case of a permanent coordinator failure. Because of this property, we say that 2PC is a *blocking* atomic commitment algorithm. If the coordinator never recovers, its replacement has to collect votes for a given transaction again, and proceed with a final decision.

Many databases use 2PC: MySQL, PostgreSQL (*https://databass.dev/links/6*), MongoDB,[2] and others. Two-phase commit is often used to implement distributed transactions because of its simplicity (it is easy to reason about, implement, and debug)

---

2 However, the documentation says that as of v3.6, 2PC provides only transaction-*like* semantics: *https://data bass.dev/links/7*.

and low overhead (message complexity and the number of round-trips of the proto-col are low). It is important to implement proper recovery mechanisms and have backup coordinator nodes to reduce the chance of the failures just described.

Three-Phase Commit

To make an atomic commitment protocol robust against coordinator failures and avoid undecided states, the three-phase commit (3PC) protocol adds an extra step, and timeouts on *both* sides that can allow cohorts to proceed with either commit or abort in the event of coordinator failure, depending on the system state. 3PC assumes a synchronous model and that communication failures are not possible [BABAO-GLU93].

3PC adds a *prepare* phase before the commit/abort step, which communicates cohort states collected by the coordinator during the propose phase, allowing the protocol to carry on even if the coordinator fails. All other properties of 3PC and a requirement to have a coordinator for the round are similar to its two-phase sibling. Another use-ful addition to 3PC is timeouts on the cohort side. Depending on which step the pro-cess is currently executing, either a commit or abort decision is forced on timeout.

As Figure 13-5 shows, the three-phase commit round consists of three steps:

Propose
    The coordinator sends out a proposed value and collects the votes.

Prepare
    The coordinator notifies cohorts about the vote results. If the vote has passed and all cohorts have decided to commit, the coordinator sends a `Prepare` message, instructing them to prepare to commit. Otherwise, an `Abort` message is sent and the round completes.

Commit
    Cohorts are notified by the coordinator to commit the transaction.

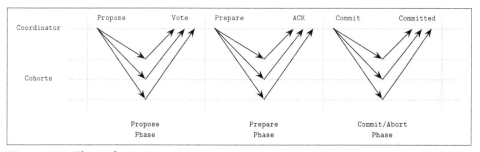

Figure 13-5. Three-phase commit

During the *propose* step, similar to 2PC, the coordinator distributes the proposed value and collects votes from cohorts, as shown in Figure 13-5. If the coordinator crashes during this phase and the operation times out, or if one of the cohorts votes negatively, the transaction will be aborted.

After collecting the votes, the coordinator makes a decision. If the coordinator decides to proceed with a transaction, it issues a `Prepare` command. It may happen that the coordinator cannot distribute prepare messages to all cohorts or it fails to receive their acknowledgments. In this case, cohorts may abort the transaction after timeout, since the algorithm hasn't moved all the way to the *prepared* state.

As soon as all the cohorts successfully move into the prepared state and the coordinator has received their prepare acknowledgments, the transaction will be committed if either side fails. This can be done since all participants at this stage have the same view of the state.

During *commit*, the coordinator communicates the results of the *prepare* phase to all the participants, resetting their timeout counters and effectively finishing the transaction.

Coordinator Failures in 3PC

All state transitions are coordinated, and cohorts can't move on to the next phase until everyone is done with the previous one: the coordinator has to wait for the replicas to continue. Cohorts can eventually abort the transaction if they do not hear from the coordinator before the timeout, if they didn't move past the prepare phase.

As we discussed previously, 2PC cannot recover from coordinator failures, and cohorts may get stuck in a nondeterministic state until the coordinator comes back. 3PC avoids blocking the processes in this case and allows cohorts to proceed with a deterministic decision.

The worst-case scenario for the 3PC is a network partition, shown in Figure 13-6. Some nodes successfully move to the prepared state, and now can proceed with commit after the timeout. Some can't communicate with the coordinator, and will abort after the timeout. This results in a split brain: some nodes proceed with a commit and some abort, all according to the protocol, leaving participants in an inconsistent and contradictory state.

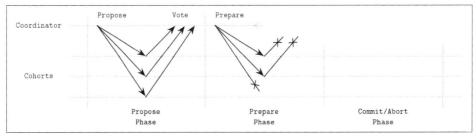

Figure 13-6. Coordinator failure during the second phase

While in theory 3PC does, to a degree, solve the problem with 2PC blocking, it has a larger message overhead, introduces potential contradictions, and does not work well in the presence of network partitions. This might be the primary reason 3PC is not widely used in practice.

Distributed Transactions with Calvin

We've already touched on the subject of synchronization costs and several ways around it. But there are other ways to reduce contention and the total amount of time during which transactions hold locks. One of the ways to do this is to let replicas agree on the execution order and transaction boundaries before acquiring locks and proceeding with execution. If we can achieve this, node failures do not cause transaction aborts, since nodes can recover state from other participants that execute the same transaction in parallel.

Traditional database systems execute transactions using two-phase locking or optimistic concurrency control and have no deterministic transaction order. This means that nodes have to be coordinated to preserve order. Deterministic transaction order removes coordination overhead during the execution phase and, since all replicas get the same inputs, they also produce equivalent outputs. This approach is commonly known as Calvin, a fast distributed transaction protocol [THOMSON12]. One of the prominent examples implementing distributed transactions using Calvin is FaunaDB (*https://databass.dev/links/8*).

To achieve deterministic order, Calvin uses a *sequencer*: an entry point for all transactions. The sequencer determines the order in which transactions are executed, and establishes a global transaction input sequence. To minimize contention and batch decisions, the timeline is split into *epochs*. The sequencer collects transactions and groups them into short time windows (the original paper mentions 10-millisecond batches), which also become replication units, so transactions do not have to be communicated separately.

As soon as a transaction batch is successfully replicated, sequencer forwards it to the *scheduler*, which orchestrates transaction execution. The scheduler uses a deterministic scheduling protocol that executes parts of transaction in parallel, while preserving the serial execution order specified by the sequencer. Since applying transaction to a specific state is guaranteed to produce only changes specified by the transaction and transaction order is predetermined, replicas do not have to further communicate with the sequencer.

Each transaction in Calvin has a *read set* (its dependencies, which is a collection of data records from the current database state required to execute it) and a *write set* (results of the transaction execution; in other words, its side effects). Calvin does not natively support transactions that rely on additional reads that would determine read and write sets.

A worker thread, managed by the scheduler, proceeds with execution in four steps:

1. It analyzes the transaction's read and write sets, determines node-local data records from the read set, and creates the list of *active* participants (i.e., ones that hold the elements of the write set, and will perform modifications on the data).

2. It collects the *local* data required to execute the transaction, in other words, the read set records that happen to reside on that node. The collected data records are forwarded to the corresponding *active* participants.

3. If this worker thread is executing on an active participant node, it receives data records forwarded from the other participants, as a counterpart of the operations executed during step 2.

4. Finally, it executes a batch of transactions, persisting results into local storage. It does not have to forward execution results to the other nodes, as they receive the same inputs for transactions and execute and persist results locally themselves.

A typical Calvin implementation colocates sequencer, scheduler, worker, and storage subsystems, as Figure 13-7 shows. To make sure that sequencers reach consensus on exactly which transactions make it into the current epoch/batch, Calvin uses the Paxos consensus algorithm (see "Paxos" on page 285) or asynchronous replication, in which a dedicated replica serves as a leader. While using a leader can improve latency, it comes with a higher cost of recovery as nodes have to reproduce the state of the failed leader in order to proceed.

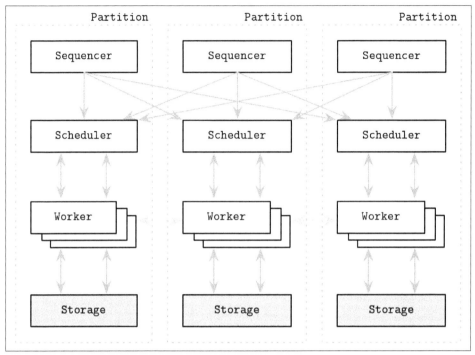

Figure 13-7. Calvin architecture

Distributed Transactions with Spanner

Calvin is often contrasted with another approach for distributed transaction management called Spanner [CORBETT12]. Its implementations (or derivatives) include several open source databases, most prominently CockroachDB (*https://databass.dev/ links/9*) and YugaByte DB (*https://databass.dev/links/10*). While Calvin establishes the global transaction execution order by reaching consensus on sequencers, Spanner uses two-phase commit over consensus groups per partition (in other words, per shard). Spanner has a rather complex setup, and we only cover high-level details in the scope of this book.

To achieve consistency and impose transaction order, Spanner uses *TrueTime*: a high-precision wall-clock API that also exposes an uncertainty bound, allowing local operations to introduce artificial slowdowns to wait for the uncertainty bound to pass.

Spanner offers three main operation types: *read-write transactions*, *read-only transactions*, and *snapshot reads*. Read-write transactions require locks, pessimistic concurrency control, and presence of the leader replica. Read-only transactions are lock-free and can be executed at any replica. A leader is required only for reads at the *latest* timestamp, which takes the latest committed value from the Paxos group. Reads at the specific timestamp are consistent, since values are versioned and snapshot contents can't be changed once written. Each data record has a timestamp assigned, which holds a value of the transaction commit time. This also implies that multiple timestamped versions of the record can be stored.

Figure 13-8 shows the Spanner architecture. Each *spanserver* (replica, a server instance that serves data to clients) holds several *tablets*, with Paxos (see "Paxos" on page 285) state machines attached to them. Replicas are grouped into replica sets called Paxos groups, a unit of data placement and replication. Each Paxos group has a long-lived leader (see "Multi-Paxos" on page 291). Leaders communicate with each other during multishard transactions.

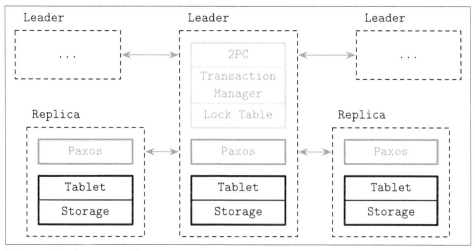

Figure 13-8. Spanner architecture

Every write has to go through the Paxos group leader, while reads can be served directly from the tablet on up-to-date replicas. The leader holds a *lock table* that is used to implement concurrency control using the two-phase locking (see "Lock-Based Concurrency Control" on page 100) mechanism and a *transaction manager* that is responsible for multishard distributed transactions. Operations that require synchronization (such as writes and reads within a transaction) have to acquire the locks from the lock table, while other operations (snapshot reads) can access the data directly.

For multishard transactions, group leaders have to coordinate and perform a two-phase commit to ensure consistency, and use two-phase locking to ensure isolation. Since the 2PC algorithm requires the presence of all participants for a successful commit, it hurts availability. Spanner solves this by using Paxos groups rather than individual nodes as cohorts. This means that 2PC can continue operating even if some of the members of the group are down. Within the Paxos group, 2PC contacts only the node that serves as a leader.

Paxos groups are used to consistently replicate transaction manager states across multiple nodes. The Paxos leader first acquires write locks, and chooses a write timestamp that is guaranteed to be larger than any previous transactions' timestamp, and records a 2PC `prepare` entry through Paxos. The transaction coordinator collects timestamps and generates a commit timestamp that is greater than any of the prepare timestamps, and logs a `commit` entry through Paxos. It then waits until *after* the timestamp it has chosen for commit, since it has to guarantee that clients will only see transaction results whose timestamps are in the past. After that, it sends this timestamp to the client and leaders, which log the `commit` record with the new timestamp in their local Paxos group and are now free to release the locks.

Single-shard transactions do not have to consult the transaction manager (and, subsequently, do not have to perform a cross-partition two-phase commit), since consulting a Paxos group and a lock table is enough to guarantee transaction order and consistency within the shard.

Spanner read-write transactions offer a serialization order called *external consistency*: transaction timestamps reflect serialization order, even in cases of distributed transactions. External consistency has real-time properties equivalent to linearizability: if transaction T_1 commits before T_2 starts, T_1's timestamp is smaller than the timestamp of T_2.

To summarize, Spanner uses Paxos for consistent transaction log replication, two-phase commit for cross-shard transactions, and TrueTime for deterministic transaction ordering. This means that multipartition transactions have a higher cost due to an additional two-phase commit round, compared to Calvin [ABADI17]. Both approaches are important to understand since they allow us to perform transactions in partitioned distributes data stores.

Database Partitioning

While discussing Spanner and Calvin, we've been using the term *partitioning* quite heavily. Let's now discuss it in more detail. Since storing all database records on a single node is rather unrealistic for the majority of modern applications, many databases use partitioning: a logical division of data into smaller manageable segments.

The most straightforward way to partition data is by splitting it into ranges and allowing *replica sets* to manage only specific ranges (partitions). When executing queries, clients (or query coordinators) have to route requests based on the *routing key* to the correct replica set for both reads and writes. This partitioning scheme is typically called *sharding*: every replica set acts as a single source for a subset of data.

To use partitions most effectively, they have to be sized, taking the load and value distribution into consideration. This means that frequently accessed, read/write heavy ranges can be split into smaller partitions to spread the load between them. At the same time, if some value ranges are more dense than other ones, it might be a good idea to split them into smaller partitions as well. For example, if we pick *zip code* as a routing key, since the country population is unevenly spread, some zip code ranges can have more data (e.g., people and orders) assigned to them.

When nodes are added to or removed from the cluster, the database has to re-partition the data to maintain the balance. To ensure consistent movements, we should relocate the data before we update the cluster metadata and start routing requests to the new targets. Some databases perform *auto-sharding* and relocate the data using placement algorithms that determine optimal partitioning. These algorithms use information about read, write loads, and amounts of data in each shard.

To find a target node from the routing key, some database systems compute a *hash* of the key, and use some form of mapping from the hash value to the node ID. One of the advantages of using the hash functions for determining replica placement is that it can help to reduce range hot-spotting, since hash values do not sort the same way as the original values. While two lexicographically close routing keys would be placed at the same replica set, using hashed values would place them on different ones.

The most straightforward way to map hash values to node IDs is by taking a remainder of the division of the hash value by the size of the cluster (modulo). If we have N nodes in the system, the target node ID is picked by computing hash(v) modulo N. The main problem with this approach is that whenever nodes are added or removed and the cluster size changes from N to N', many values returned by hash(v) modulo N' will differ from the original ones. This means that most of the data will have to be moved.

Consistent Hashing

In order to mitigate this problem, some databases, such as Apache Cassandra and Riak (among others), use a different partitioning scheme called *consistent hashing*. As previously mentioned, routing key values are hashed. Values returned by the hash function are mapped to a *ring*, so that after the largest possible value, it wraps around to its smallest value. Each node gets its own position on the ring and becomes responsible for the *range* of values, between its predecessor's and its own positions.

Using consistent hashing helps to reduce the number of relocations required for maintaining balance: a change in the ring affects only the *immediate neighbors* of the leaving or joining node, and not an entire cluster. The word *consistent* in the definition implies that, when the hash table is resized, if we have K possible hash keys and n nodes, on average we have to relocate only K/n keys. In other words, a consistent hash function output changes minimally as the function range changes [KARGER97].

Distributed Transactions with Percolator

Coming back to the subject of distributed transactions, isolation levels might be diffi-cult to reason about because of the allowed read and write anomalies. If serializability is not required by the application, one of the ways to avoid the write anomalies described in SQL-92 is to use a transactional model called *snapshot isolation* (SI).

Snapshot isolation guarantees that all reads made within the transaction are consis-tent with a snapshot of the database. The snapshot contains all values that were *com-mitted before* the transaction's start timestamp. If there's a *write-write conflict* (i.e., when two concurrently running transactions attempt to make a write to the same cell), only one of them will commit. This characteristic is usually referred to as *first committer wins*.

Snapshot isolation prevents *read skew*, an anomaly permitted under the read-committed isolation level. For example, a sum of x and y is supposed to be 100. Transaction T1 performs an operation read(x), and reads the value 70. T2 updates two values write(x, 50) and write(y, 50), and commits. If T1 attempts to run read(y), and proceeds with transaction execution based on the value of y (50), newly committed by T2, it will lead to an inconsistency. The value of x that T1 has read *before* T2 committed and the new value of y aren't consistent with each other. Since snapshot isolation only makes values up to a specific timestamp visible for transac-tions, the new value of y, 50, won't be visible to T1 [BERENSON95].

Snapshot isolation has several convenient properties:

- It allows *only* repeatable reads of committed data.
- Values are consistent, as they're read from the snapshot at a specific timestamp.
- Conflicting writes are aborted and retried to prevent inconsistencies.

Despite that, histories under snapshot isolation are *not* serializable. Since only con-flicting writes to the *same cells* are aborted, we can still end up with a *write skew* (see "Read and Write Anomalies" on page 95). Write skew occurs when two transactions modify disjoint sets of values, each preserving invariants for the data it writes. Both transactions are allowed to commit, but a combination of writes performed by these transactions may violate these invariants.

Snapshot isolation provides semantics that can be useful for many applications and has the major advantage of efficient reads, because no locks have to be acquired since snapshot data cannot be changed.

Percolator is a library that implements a transactional API on top of the distributed database *Bigtable* (see "Wide Column Stores" on page 15). This is a great example of building a transaction API on top of the existing system. Percolator stores data records, committed data point locations (write metadata), and locks in different columns. To avoid race conditions and reliably lock tables in a single RPC call, it uses a conditional mutation Bigtable API that allows it to perform read-modify-write operations with a single remote call.

Each transaction has to consult the *timestamp oracle* (a source of clusterwide-consistent monotonically increasing timestamps) twice: for a transaction start timestamp, and during commit. Writes are buffered and committed using a client-driven two-phase commit (see "Two-Phase Commit" on page 259).

Figure 13-9 shows how the contents of the table change during execution of the transaction steps:

- a) Initial state. After the execution of the previous transaction, TS1 is the latest timestamp for both accounts. No locks are held.
- b) The first phase, called *prewrite*. The transaction attempts to acquire locks for all cells written during the transaction. One of the locks is marked as *primary* and is used for client recovery. The transaction checks for the possible conflicts: if any other transaction has already written any data with a later timestamp or there are unreleased locks at any timestamp. If any conflict is detected, the transaction aborts.
- c) If all locks were successfully acquired and the possibility of conflict is ruled out, the transaction can continue. During the second phase, the client releases its locks, starting with the primary one. It publishes its write by replacing the lock with a write record, updating write metadata with the timestamp of the latest data point.

Since the client may fail while trying to commit the transaction, we need to make sure that partial transactions are finalized or rolled back. If a later transaction encounters an incomplete state, it should attempt to release the primary lock and commit the transaction. If the primary lock is already released, transaction contents *have to be* committed. Only one transaction can hold a lock at a time and all state transitions are atomic, so situations in which two transactions attempt to perform operations on the contents are not possible.

		Data	Locks	Write Metadata
Account1	TS2	-	-	TS1 is latest
	TS1	$100	-	-
Account2	TS2	-	-	TS1 is latest
	TS1	$200	-	-

a) Initial State before moving $150 from Account2 to Account1

		Data	Locks	Write Metadata
Account1	TS3	$250	Primary	-
	TS2	-	-	TS1 is latest
	TS1	$100	-	-
Account2	TS3	$50	Primary at Account1	-
	TS2	-	-	TS1 is latest
	TS1	$200	-	-

b) State after taking locks and updating accounts

		Data	Locks	Write Metadata
Account1	TS4	-	-	TS3 is latest
	TS3	$250	-	-
	TS2	-	-	TS1 is latest
	TS1	$100	-	-
Account2	TS4	-	-	TS3 is latest
	TS3	$50	-	-
	TS2	-	-	TS1 is latest
	TS1	$200	-	-

c) Transaction commit releases locks and updates metadata with latest timestamp

Figure 13-9. Percolator transaction execution steps. Transaction credits $150 from Account2 and debits it to Account1.

Snapshot isolation is an important and useful abstraction, commonly used in transaction processing. Since it simplifies semantics, precludes some of the anomalies, and opens up an opportunity to improve concurrency and performance, many MVCC systems offer this isolation level.

One of the examples of databases based on the Percolator model is TiDB (*https://data bass.dev/links/11*) ("Ti" stands for Titatium). TiDB is a strongly consistent, highly available, and horizontally scalable open source database, compatible with MySQL.

Coordination Avoidance

One more example, discussing costs of serializability and attempting to reduce the amount of coordination while still providing strong consistency guarantees, is coordination avoidance [BAILIS14b]. Coordination can be avoided, while preserving data integrity constraints, if operations are invariant confluent. Invariant Confluence (*I*-Confluence) is defined as a property that ensures that two invariant-valid but diverged database states can be merged into a single valid, final state. Invariants in this case preserve consistency in ACID terms.

Because any two valid states can be merged into a valid state, *I*-Confluent operations can be executed without additional coordination, which significantly improves performance characteristics and scalability potential.

To preserve this invariant, in addition to defining an operation that brings our database to the new state, we have to define a *merge* function that accepts two states. This function is used in case states were updated independently and bring diverged states back to convergence.

Transactions are executed against the local database versions (snapshots). If a transaction requires any state from other partitions for execution, this state is made available for it locally. If a transaction commits, resulting changes made to the local snapshot are migrated and merged with the snapshots on the other nodes. A system model that allows coordination avoidance has to guarantee the following properties:

Global validity
> Required invariants are always satisfied, for both merged and divergent committed database states, and transactions cannot observe invalid states.

Availability
> If all nodes holding states are reachable by the client, the transaction has to reach a commit decision, or abort, if committing it would violate one of the transaction invariants.

Convergence
> Nodes can maintain their local states independently, but in the absence of further transactions and indefinite network partitions, they have to be able to reach the same state.

Coordination freedom
> Local transaction execution is independent from the operations against the local states performed on behalf of the other nodes.

One of the examples of implementing coordination avoidance is Read-Atomic Multi Partition (RAMP) transactions [BAILIS14c]. RAMP uses multiversion concurrency control and metadata of current in-flight operations to fetch any missing state updates from other nodes, allowing read and write operations to be executed concurrently. For example, readers that overlap with some writer modifying the same entry can be detected and, if necessary, *repaired* by retrieving required information from the in-flight write metadata in an additional round of communication.

Using lock-based approaches in a distributed environment might be not the best idea, and instead of doing that, RAMP provides two properties:

Synchronization independence
> One client's transactions won't stall, abort, or force the other client's transactions to wait.

Partition independence
> Clients do not have to contact partitions whose values aren't involved in their transactions.

RAMP introduces the *read atomic* isolation level: transactions cannot observe any in-process state changes from in-flight, uncommitted, and aborted transactions. In other words, all (or none) transaction updates are visible to concurrent transactions. By that definition, the read atomic isolation level also precludes *fractured reads*: when a transaction observes only a subset of writes executed by some other transaction.

RAMP offers atomic write visibility without requiring mutual exclusion, which other solutions, such as distributed locks, often couple together. This means that transactions can proceed without stalling each other.

RAMP distributes transaction metadata that allows reads to detect concurrent in-flight writes. By using this metadata, transactions can detect the presence of newer record versions, find and fetch the latest ones, and operate on them. To avoid coordination, all local commit decisions must also be valid globally. In RAMP, this is solved by requiring that, by the time a write becomes visible in one partition, writes from the same transaction in all other involved partitions are also visible for readers in those partitions.

To allow readers and writers to proceed without blocking other concurrent readers and writers, while maintaining the read atomic isolation level both locally and system-wide (in all other partitions modified by the committing transaction), writes in RAMP are installed and made visible using two-phase commit:

Prepare
> The first phase prepares and places writes to their respective target partitions without making them visible.

Commit/abort
> The second phase publishes the state changes made by the write operation of the committing transaction, making them available atomically across all partitions, or rolls back the changes.

RAMP allows multiple versions of the same record to be present at any given moment: latest value, in-flight uncommitted changes, and stale versions, overwritten by later transactions. Stale versions have to be kept around only for in-progress read requests. As soon as all concurrent readers complete, stale values can be discarded.

Making distributed transactions performant and scalable is difficult because of the coordination overhead associated with preventing, detecting, and avoiding conflicts for the concurrent operations. The larger the system, or the more transactions it attempts to serve, the more overhead it incurs. The approaches described in this section attempt to reduce the amount of coordination by using invariants to determine where coordination can be avoided, and only paying the full price if it's absolutely necessary.

Summary

In this chapter, we discussed several ways of implementing distributed transactions. First, we discussed two atomic commitment algorithms: two- and three-phase commits. The big advantage of these algorithms is that they're easy to understand and implement, but have several shortcomings. In 2PC, a coordinator (or at least its substitute) has to be alive for the length of the commitment process, which significantly reduces availability. 3PC lifts this requirement for some cases, but is prone to split brain in case of network partition.

Distributed transactions in modern database systems are often implemented using consensus algorithms, which we're going to discuss in the next chapter. For example, both Calvin and Spanner, discussed in this chapter, use Paxos.

Consensus algorithms are more involved than atomic commit ones, but have much better fault-tolerance properties, and decouple decisions from their initiators and allow participants to decide on *a value* rather than on whether or not to accept *the value* [GRAY04].

Further Reading

If you'd like to learn more about the concepts mentioned in this chapter, you can refer to the following sources:

Atomic commitment integration with local transaction processing and recovery subsystems

> Silberschatz, Abraham, Henry F. Korth, and S. Sudarshan. 2010. *Database Systems Concepts* (6th Ed.). New York: McGraw-Hill.

> Garcia-Molina, Hector, Jeffrey D. Ullman, and Jennifer Widom. 2008. *Database Systems: The Complete Book* (2nd Ed.). Boston: Pearson.

Recent progress in the area of distributed transactions (ordered chronologically; this list is not intended to be exhaustive)

> Cowling, James and Barbara Liskov. 2012. "Granola: low-overhead distributed transaction coordination." In *Proceedings of the 2012 USENIX conference on Annual Technical Conference (USENIX ATC '12)*: 21-21. USENIX.

> Balakrishnan, Mahesh, Dahlia Malkhi, Ted Wobber, Ming Wu, Vijayan Prabhakaran, Michael Wei, John D. Davis, Sriram Rao, Tao Zou, and Aviad Zuck. 2013. "Tango: distributed data structures over a shared log." In *Proceedings of the Twenty-Fourth ACM Symposium on Operating Systems Principles (SOSP '13)*: 324-340.

> Ding, Bailu, Lucja Kot, Alan Demers, and Johannes Gehrke. 2015. "Centiman: elastic, high performance optimistic concurrency control by watermarking." In *Proceedings of the Sixth ACM Symposium on Cloud Computing (SoCC '15)*: 262-275.

> Dragojević, Aleksandar, Dushyanth Narayanan, Edmund B. Nightingale, Matthew Renzelmann, Alex Shamis, Anirudh Badam, and Miguel Castro. 2015. "No compromises: distributed transactions with consistency, availability, and performance." In *Proceedings of the 25th Symposium on Operating Systems Principles (SOSP '15)*: 54-70.

> Zhang, Irene, Naveen Kr. Sharma, Adriana Szekeres, Arvind Krishnamurthy, and Dan R. K. Ports. 2015. "Building consistent transactions with inconsistent replication." In *Proceedings of the 25th Symposium on Operating Systems Principles (SOSP '15)*: 263-278.

CHAPTER 14

Consensus

We've discussed quite a few concepts in distributed systems, starting with basics, such as links and processes, problems with distributed computing; then going through failure models, failure detectors, and leader election; discussed consistency models; and we're finally ready to put it all together for a pinnacle of distributed systems research: distributed consensus.

Consensus algorithms in distributed systems allow multiple processes to reach an agreement on a value. FLP impossibility (see "FLP Impossibility" on page 189) shows that it is impossible to guarantee consensus in a completely asynchronous system in a bounded time. Even if message delivery is guaranteed, it is impossible for one process to know whether the other one has crashed or is running slowly.

In Chapter 9, we discussed that there's a trade-off between failure-detection accuracy and how quickly the failure can be detected. Consensus algorithms assume an asynchronous model and guarantee safety, while an external failure detector can provide information about other processes, guaranteeing liveness [CHANDRA96]. Since failure detection is not always fully accurate, there will be situations when a consensus algorithm waits for a process failure to be detected, or when the algorithm is restarted because some process is incorrectly suspected to be faulty.

Processes have to agree on some value proposed by one of the participants, even if some of them happen to crash. A process is said to be *correct* if hasn't crashed and continues executing algorithm steps. Consensus is extremely useful for putting events in a particular order, and ensuring consistency among the participants. Using consensus, we can have a system where processes move from one value to the next one without losing certainty about which values the clients observe.

From a theoretical perspective, consensus algorithms have three properties:

Agreement
: The decision value is the same for all *correct* processes.

Validity
: The decided value was proposed by one of the processes.

Termination
: All *correct* processes eventually reach the decision.

Each one of these properties is extremely important. The agreement is embedded in the human understanding of consensus. The dictionary definition of consensus (*https://databass.dev/links/66*) has the word "unanimity" in it. This means that upon the agreement, no process is allowed to have a different opinion about the outcome. Think of it as an agreement to meet at a particular time and place with your friends: all of you would like to meet, and only the specifics of the event are being agreed upon.

Validity is essential, because without it consensus can be trivial. Consensus algorithms require all processes to agree on some value. If processes use some predetermined, arbitrary default value as a decision output regardless of the proposed values, they will reach unanimity, but the output of such an algorithm will not be valid and it wouldn't be useful in reality.

Without termination, our algorithm will continue forever without reaching any conclusion or will wait indefinitely for a crashed process to come back, which is not very useful, either. Processes have to agree eventually and, for a consensus algorithm to be practical, this has to happen rather quickly.

Broadcast

A *broadcast* is a communication abstraction often used in distributed systems. Broadcast algorithms are used to disseminate information among a set of processes. There exist many broadcast algorithms, making different assumptions and providing different guarantees. Broadcast is an important primitive and is used in many places, including consensus algorithms. We've discussed one of the forms of broadcast—gossip dissemination—already (see "Gossip Dissemination" on page 250).

Broadcasts are often used for database replication when a single coordinator node has to distribute the data to all other participants. However, making this process reliable is not a trivial matter: if the coordinator crashes after distributing the message to some nodes but not the other ones, it leaves the system in an inconsistent state: some of the nodes observe a new message and some do not.

The simplest and the most straightforward way to broadcast messages is through a *best effort broadcast* [CACHIN11]. In this case, the sender is responsible for ensuring message delivery to all the targets. If it fails, the other participants do not try to rebroadcast the message, and in the case of coordinator crash, this type of broadcast will fail silently.

For a broadcast to be *reliable*, it needs to guarantee that all correct processes receive the same messages, even if the sender crashes during transmission.

To implement a naive version of a reliable broadcast, we can use a failure detector and a fallback mechanism. The most straightforward fallback mechanism is to allow every process that received the message to forward it to every other process it's aware of. When the source process fails, other processes detect the failure and continue broadcasting the message, effectively *flooding* the network with N^2 messages (as shown in Figure 14-1). Even if the sender has crashed, messages still are picked up and delivered by the rest of the system, improving its reliability, and allowing all receivers to see the same messages [CACHIN11].

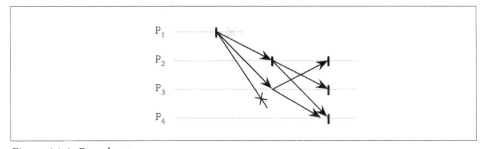

Figure 14-1. Broadcast

One of the downsides of this approach is the fact that it uses N^2 messages, where N is the number of *remaining* recipients (since every broadcasting process excludes the original process and itself). Ideally, we'd want to reduce the number of messages required for a reliable broadcast.

Atomic Broadcast

Even though the flooding algorithm just described can ensure message delivery, it does not guarantee delivery in any particular order. Messages reach their destination eventually, at an unknown time. If we need to deliver messages in order, we have to use the *atomic broadcast* (also called the *total order multicast*), which guarantees both reliable delivery and total order.

While a reliable broadcast ensures that the processes agree on the set of messages delivered, an atomic broadcast also ensures they agree on the same sequence of messages (i.e., message delivery order is the same for every target).

In summary, an atomic broadcast has to ensure two essential properties:

Atomicity
    Processes have to agree on the set of received messages. Either all nonfailed processes deliver the message, or none do.

Order
    All nonfailed processes deliver the messages in the same order.

Messages here are delivered *atomically*: every message is either delivered to all processes or none of them and, if the message is delivered, every other message is ordered before or after this message.

Virtual Synchrony

One of the frameworks for group communication using broadcast is called *virtual synchrony*. An atomic broadcast helps to deliver totally ordered messages to a *static* group of processes, and virtual synchrony delivers totally ordered messages to a *dynamic* group of peers.

Virtual synchrony organizes processes into groups. As long as the group exists, messages are delivered to all of its members in the same order. In this case, the order is not specified by the model, and some implementations can take this to their advantage for performance gains, as long as the order they provide is consistent across all members [BIRMAN10].

Processes have the same view of the group, and messages are associated with the group identity: processes can see the identical messages only as long as they belong to the same group.

As soon as one of the participants joins, leaves the group, or fails and is forced out of it, the group view changes. This happens by announcing the group change to all its members. Each message is uniquely associated with the group it has originated from.

Virtual synchrony distinguishes between the message *receipt* (when a group member receives the message) and its *delivery* (which happens when all the group members receive the message). If the message was *sent* in one view, it can be *delivered* only in the same view, which can be determined by comparing the current group with the group the message is associated with. Received messages remain pending in the queue until the process is notified about successful delivery.

Since every message belongs to a specific group, unless all processes in the group have *received* it before the view change, no group member can consider this message *delivered*. This implies that all messages are sent and delivered *between* the view changes, which gives us atomic delivery guarantees. In this case, group views serve as a barrier that message broadcasts cannot pass.

Some total broadcast algorithms order messages by using a single process (sequencer) that is responsible for determining it. Such algorithms can be easier to implement, but rely on detecting the leader failures for liveness. Using a sequencer can improve performance, since we do not need to establish consensus between processes for every message, and can use a sequencer-local view instead. This approach can still scale by partitioning the requests.

Despite its technical soundness, virtual synchrony has not received broad adoption and isn't commonly used in end-user commercial systems [BIRMAN06].

Zookeeper Atomic Broadcast (ZAB)

One of the most popular and widely known implementations of the atomic broadcast is ZAB used by Apache Zookeeper (*https://databass.dev/links/67*) [HUNT10] [JUN-QUEIRA11], a hierarchical distributed key-value store, where it's used to ensure the total order of events and atomic delivery necessary to maintain consistency between the replica states.

Processes in ZAB can take on one of two roles: *leader* and *follower*. Leader is a temporary role. It drives the process by executing algorithm steps, broadcasts messages to followers, and establishes the event order. To write new records and execute reads that observe the most recent values, clients connect to one of the nodes in the cluster. If the node happens to be a leader, it will handle the request. Otherwise, it forwards the request to the leader.

To guarantee leader uniqueness, the protocol timeline is split into *epochs*, identified with a unique monotonically- and incrementally-sequenced number. During any epoch, there can be only one leader. The process starts from finding a *prospective leader* using any election algorithm, as long as it chooses a process that is up with a high probability. Since safety is guaranteed by the further algorithm steps, determining a prospective leader is more of a performance optimization. A prospective leader can also emerge as a consequence of the previous leader's failure.

As soon as a prospective leader is established, it executes a protocol in three phases:

Discovery
> The prospective leader learns about the latest epoch known by every other process, and proposes a new epoch that is *greater* than the current epoch of any follower. Followers respond to the epoch proposal with the identifier of the latest transaction seen in the previous epoch. After this step, no process will accept broadcast proposals for the earlier epochs.

Synchronization
> This phase is used to recover from the previous leader's failure and bring lagging followers up to speed. The prospective leader sends a message to the followers proposing itself as a leader for the new epoch and collects their acknowledg-

ments. As soon as acknowledgments are received, the leader is established. After this step, followers will not accept attempts to become the epoch leader from any other processes. During synchronization, the new leader ensures that followers have the same history and delivers committed proposals from the established leaders of earlier epochs. These proposals are delivered *before* any proposal from the new epoch is delivered.

Broadcast

As soon as the followers are back in sync, active messaging starts. During this phase, the leader receives client messages, establishes their order, and broadcasts them to the followers: it sends a new proposal, waits for a quorum of followers to respond with acknowledgments and, finally, commits it. This process is similar to a two-phase commit without aborts: votes are just acknowledgments, and the client cannot vote against a valid leader's proposal. However, proposals from the leaders from incorrect epochs should *not* be acknowledged. The broadcast phase continues until the leader crashes, is partitioned from the followers, or is suspected to be crashed due to the message delay.

Figure 14-2 shows the three phases of the ZAB algorithm, and messages exchanged during each step.

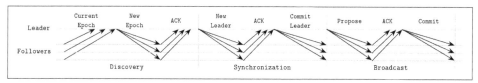

Figure 14-2. ZAB protocol summary

The safety of this protocol is guaranteed if followers ensure they accept proposals only from the leader of the established epoch. Two processes may *attempt* to get elected, but only one of them can win and establish itself as an epoch leader. It is also assumed that processes perform the prescribed steps in good faith and follow the protocol.

Both the leader and followers rely on heartbeats to determine the liveness of the remote processes. If the leader does not receive heartbeats from the quorum of followers, it steps down as a leader, and restarts the election process. Similarly, if one of the followers has determined the leader crashed, it starts a new election process.

Messages are totally ordered, and the leader will not attempt to send the next message until the message that preceded it was acknowledged. Even if some messages are received by a follower more than once, their repeated application do not produce additional side effects, as long as delivery order is followed. ZAB is able to handle multiple outstanding concurrent state changes from clients, since a unique leader will receive write requests, establish the event order, and broadcast the changes.

Total message order also allows ZAB to improve recovery efficiency. During the synchronization phase, followers respond with a highest committed proposal. The leader can simply choose the node with the highest proposal for recovery, and this can be the only node messages have to be copied from.

One of the advantages of ZAB is its efficiency: the broadcast process requires only two rounds of messages, and leader failures can be recovered from by streaming the missing messages from a single up-to-date process. Having a long-lived leader can have a positive impact on performance: we do not require additional consensus rounds to establish a history of events, since the leader can sequence them based on its local view.

Paxos

An atomic broadcast is a problem equivalent to consensus in an asynchronous system with crash failures [CHANDRA96], since participants have to *agree* on the message order and must be able to learn about it. You will see many similarities in both motivation and implementation between atomic broadcast and consensus algorithms.

Probably the most widely known consensus algorithm is *Paxos*. It was first introduced by Leslie Lamport in "The Part-Time Parliament" paper [LAMPORT98]. In this paper, consensus is described in terms of terminology inspired by the legislative and voting process on the Aegian island of Paxos. In 2001, the author released a follow-up paper titled "Paxos Made Simple" [LAMPORT01] that introduced simpler terms, which are now commonly used to explain this algorithm.

Participants in Paxos can take one of three roles: *proposers*, *acceptors*, or *learners*:

Proposers
Receive values from clients, create proposals to accept these values, and attempt to collect votes from acceptors.

Acceptors
Vote to accept or reject the values proposed by the proposer. For fault tolerance, the algorithm requires the presence of multiple acceptors, but for liveness, only a quorum (majority) of acceptor votes is required to accept the proposal.

Learners
Take the role of replicas, storing the outcomes of the accepted proposals.

Any participant can take any role, and most implementations colocate them: a single process can simultaneously be a proposer, an acceptor, and a learner.

Every proposal consists of a *value*, proposed by the client, and a unique monotonically increasing proposal number. This number is then used to ensure a total order of executed operations and establish happened-before/after relationships among them.

Proposal numbers are often implemented using an (`id`, `timestamp`) pair, where node IDs are also comparable and can be used to break ties for timestamps.

Paxos Algorithm

The Paxos algorithm can be generally split into two phases: *voting* (or *propose* phase) and *replication*. During the voting phase, proposers compete to establish their leadership. During replication, the proposer distributes the value to the acceptors.

The proposer is an initial point of contact for the client. It receives a value that should be decided upon, and attempts to collect votes from the quorum of acceptors. When this is done, acceptors distribute the information about the agreed value to the learners, ratifying the result. Learners increase the replication factor of the value that's been agreed on.

Only one proposer can collect the majority of votes. Under some circumstances, votes may get split evenly between the proposers, and neither one of them will be able to collect a majority during this round, forcing them to restart. We discuss this and other scenarios of competing proposers in "Failure Scenarios" on page 288.

During the propose phase, the *proposer* sends a `Prepare(n)` message (where n is a proposal number) to a majority of acceptors and attempts to collect their votes.

When the *acceptor* receives the prepare request, it has to respond, preserving the following invariants [LAMPORT01]:

- If this acceptor hasn't responded to a prepare request with a higher sequence number yet, it *promises* that it will not accept any proposal with a lower sequence number.

- If this acceptor has already accepted (received an `Accept!(m,`$v_{accepted}$`)` message) any other proposal earlier, it responds with a `Promise(m, `$v_{accepted}$`)` message, notifying the proposer that it has already accepted the proposal with a sequence number m.

- If this acceptor has already responded to a prepare request with a higher sequence number, it notifies the proposer about the existence of a higher-numbered proposal.

- Acceptor can respond to more than one prepare request, as long as the later one has a higher sequence number .

During the replication phase, after collecting a majority of votes, the *proposer* can start the replication, where it commits the proposal by sending acceptors an `Accept! (n, v)` message with value v and proposal number n. v is the value associated with the highest-numbered proposal among the responses it received from acceptors, or any value of its own if their responses did not contain old accepted proposals.

The *acceptor* accepts the proposal with a number n, unless during the propose phase it has already responded to `Prepare(m)`, where m is greater than n. If the acceptor rejects the proposal, it notifies the proposer about it by sending the highest sequence number it has seen along with the request to help the proposer catch up [LAMP-ORT01].

You can see a generalized depiction of a Paxos round in Figure 14-3.

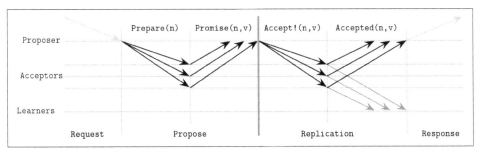

Figure 14-3. Paxos algorithm: normal execution

Once a consensus was reached on the value (in other words, it was accepted by at least one acceptor), future proposers have to decide on the same value to guarantee the agreement. This is why acceptors respond with the latest value they've accepted. If no acceptor has seen a previous value, the proposer is free to choose its own value.

A learner has to find out the value that has been decided, which it can know after receiving notification from the majority of acceptors. To let the learner know about the new value as soon as possible, acceptors can notify it about the value as soon as they accept it. If there's more than one learner, each acceptor will have to notify each learner. One or more learners can be *distinguished*, in which case it will notify other learners about accepted values.

In summary, the goal of the first algorithm phase is to establish a leader for the round and understand which value is going to be accepted, allowing the leader to proceed with the second phase: broadcasting the value. For the purpose of the base algorithm, we assume that we have to perform both phases every time we'd like to decide on a value. In practice, we'd like to reduce the number of steps in the algorithm, so we allow the proposer to propose more than one value. We discuss this in more detail later in "Multi-Paxos" on page 291.

Quorums in Paxos

Quorums are used to make sure that *some* of the participants can fail, but we still can proceed as long as we can collect votes from the alive ones. A *quorum* is the *minimum* number of votes required for the operation to be performed. This number usually constitutes a *majority* of participants. The main idea behind quorums is that even if participants fail or happen to be separated by the network partition, there's at least one participant that acts as an arbiter, ensuring protocol correctness.

Once a sufficient number of participants accept the proposal, the value is guaranteed to be accepted by the protocol, since any two majorities have at least one participant in common.

Paxos guarantees safety in the presence of any number of failures. There's no configuration that can produce incorrect or inconsistent states since this would contradict the definition of consensus.

Liveness is guaranteed in the presence of f failed processes. For that, the protocol requires 2f + 1 processes in total so that, if f processes happen to fail, there are still f + 1 processes able to proceed. By using quorums, rather than requiring the presence of all processes, Paxos (and other consensus algorithms) guarantee results even when f process failures occur. In "Flexible Paxos" on page 296, we talk about quorums in slightly different terms and describe how to build protocols requiring quorum intersection between algorithm *steps* only.

 It is important to remember that quorums only describe the blocking properties of the system. To guarantee safety, for each step we have to wait for responses from *at least* a quorum of nodes. We can send proposals and accept commands to more nodes; we just do not have to wait for their responses to proceed. We may send messages to more nodes (some systems use *speculative execution*: issuing redundant queries that help to achieve the required response count in case of node failures), but to guarantee liveness, we can proceed as soon as we hear from the quorum.

Failure Scenarios

Discussing distributed algorithms gets particularly interesting when failures are discussed. One of the failure scenarios, demonstrating fault tolerance, is when the proposer fails during the second phase, before it is able to broadcast the value to all the acceptors (a similar situation can happen if the proposer is alive but is slow or cannot communicate with some acceptors). In this case, the new proposer may pick up and commit the value, distributing it to the other participants.

Figure 14-4 shows this situation:

- Proposer P_1 goes through the election phase with a proposal number 1, but fails after sending the value V1 to just one acceptor A_1.

- Another proposer P_2 starts a new round with a higher proposal number 2, collects a quorum of acceptor responses (A_1 and A_2 in this case), and proceeds by committing the *old* value V1, proposed by P_1.

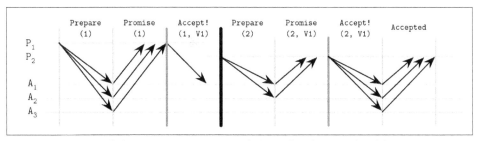

Figure 14-4. Paxos failure scenario: proposer failure, deciding on the old value

Since the algorithm state is replicated to multiple nodes, proposer failure does not result in failure to reach a consensus. If the current proposer fails after even a single acceptor A_1 has accepted the value, its proposal *can* be picked by the next proposer. This also implies that all of it may happen without the original proposer knowing about it.

In a client/server application, where the client is connected only to the original proposer, this might lead to situations where the client doesn't know about the result of the Paxos round execution.[1]

However, other scenarios are possible, too, as Figure 14-5 shows. For example:

- P_1 has failed just like in the previous example, after sending the value V1 only to A_1.

- The next proposer, P_2, starts a new round with a higher proposal number 2, and collects a quorum of acceptor responses, but this time A_2 and A_3 are first to respond. After collecting a quorum, P_2 commits *its own value* despite the fact that theoretically there's a different committed value on A_1.

---

1 For example, such a situation was described in *https://databass.dev/links/68*.

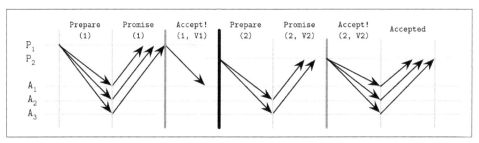

Figure 14-5. Paxos failure scenario: proposer failure, deciding on the new value

There's one more possibility here, shown in Figure 14-6:

- Proposer P_1 fails after only one acceptor A_1 accepts the value V1. A_1 fails shortly after accepting the proposal, before it can notify the next proposer about its value.

- Proposer P_2, which started the round after P_1 failed, does not overlap with A_1 and proceeds to commit its value instead.

- Any proposer that comes *after* this round that will overlap with A_1, will ignore A_1's value and choose a more recent accepted proposal instead.

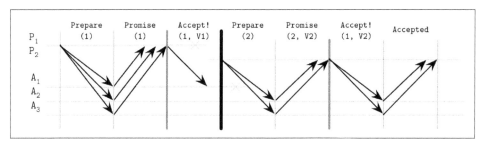

Figure 14-6. Paxos failure scenario: proposer failure, followed by the acceptor failure

Another failure scenario is when two or more proposers start competing, each trying to get through the propose phase, but keep failing to collect a majority because the other one beat them to it.

While acceptors promise not to accept any proposals with a lower number, they still may respond to multiple prepare requests, as long as the later one has a higher sequence number. When a proposer tries to commit the value, it might find that acceptors have already responded to a prepare request with a higher sequence number. This may lead to multiple proposers constantly retrying and preventing each other from further progress. This problem is usually solved by incorporating a random backoff, which eventually lets one of the proposers proceed while the other one sleeps.

The Paxos algorithm can tolerate acceptor failures, but only if there are still enough acceptors alive to form a majority.

Multi-Paxos

So far we discussed the classic Paxos algorithm, where we pick an arbitrary proposer and attempt to start a Paxos round. One of the problems with this approach is that a propose round is required for each replication round that occurs in the system. Only after the proposer is established for the round, which happens after a majority of acceptors respond with a `Promise` to the proposer's `Prepare`, can it start the replication. To avoid repeating the propose phase and let the proposer reuse its recognized position, we can use Multi-Paxos, which introduces the concept of a *leader*: a *distinguished proposer* [LAMPORT01]. This is a crucial addition, significantly improving algorithm efficiency.

Having an established leader, we can skip the propose phase and proceed straight to replication: distributing a value and collecting acceptor acknowledgments.

In the classic Paxos algorithm, reads can be implemented by running a Paxos round that would collect any values from incomplete rounds if they're present. This has to be done because the last known proposer is not guaranteed to hold the most recent data, since there might have been a different proposer that has modified state without the proposer knowing about it.

A similar situation may occur in Multi-Paxos: we're trying to perform a read from the known leader *after* the other leader is already elected, returning stale data, which contradicts the linearizability guarantees of consensus. To avoid that and guarantee that no other process can successfully submit values, some Multi-Paxos implementations use *leases*. The leader periodically contacts the participants, notifying them that it is still alive, effectively prolonging its lease. Participants have to respond and allow the leader to continue operation, promising that they will not accept proposals from other leaders for the period of the lease [CHANDRA07].

Leases are not a correctness guarantee, but a performance optimization that allows reads from the active leader without collecting a quorum. To guarantee safety, leases rely on the bounded clock synchrony between the participants. If their clocks drift too much and the leader assumes its lease is still valid while other participants think its lease has expired, linearizability *cannot* be guaranteed.

Multi-Paxos is sometimes described as a *replicated log* of operations applied to some structure. The algorithm is oblivious to the semantics of this structure and is only concerned with consistently replicating values that will be appended to this log. To preserve the state in case of process crashes, participants keep a durable log of received messages.

To prevent a log from growing indefinitely large, its contents should be applied to the aforementioned structure. After the log contents are synchronized with a primary structure, creating a snapshot, the log can be truncated. Log and state snapshots should be mutually consistent, and snapshot changes should be applied atomically with truncation of the log segment [CHANDRA07].

We can think of single-decree Paxos as a *write-once register*: we have a slot where we can put a value, and as soon as we've written the value there, no subsequent modifications are possible. During the first step, proposers compete for ownership of the register, and during the second phase, one of them writes the value. At the same time, Multi-Paxos can be thought of as an append-only log, consisting of a sequence of such values: we can write one value at a time, all values are strictly ordered, and we cannot modify already written values [RYSTSOV16]. There are examples of consensus algorithms that offer collections of read-modify-write registers and use state sharing rather than replicated state machines, such as Active Disk Paxos [CHOCKLER15] and CASPaxos [RYSTSOV18].

Fast Paxos

We can reduce the number of round-trips by one, compared to the classic Paxos algorithm, by letting *any* proposer contact acceptors directly rather than going through the leader. For this, we need to increase the quorum size to 2f + 1 (where f is the number of processes allowed to fail), compared to f + 1 in classic Paxos, and a total number of acceptors to 3f + 1 [JUNQUEIRA07]. This optimization is called *Fast Paxos* [LAMPORT06].

The classic Paxos algorithm has a condition, where during the replication phase, the proposer can pick any value it has collected during the propose phase. Fast Paxos has two types of rounds: *classic*, where the algorithm proceeds the same way as the classic version, and *fast*, where it allows acceptors to accept other values.

While describing this algorithm, we will refer to the proposer that has collected a sufficient number of responses during the propose phase as a *coordinator*, and reserve term *proposer* for all other proposers. Some Fast Paxos descriptions say that *clients* can contact acceptors directly [ZHAO15].

In a fast round, if the coordinator is permitted to pick its own value during the replication phase, it can instead issue a special Any message to acceptors. Acceptors, in this case, are allowed to treat *any* proposer's value as if it is a classic round and they received a message with this value from the coordinator. In other words, acceptors independently decide on values they receive from different proposers.

Figure 14-7 shows an example of classic and fast rounds in Fast Paxos. From the image it might look like the fast round has more execution steps, but keep in mind that in a classic round, in order to submit its value, the proposer would need to go through the coordinator to get its value committed.

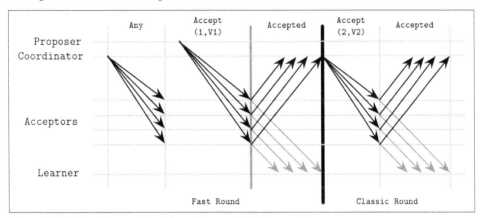

Figure 14-7. Fast Paxos algorithm: fast and classic rounds

This algorithm is prone to *collisions*, which occur if two or more proposers attempt to use the *fast* step and reduce the number of round-trips, and acceptors receive different values. The coordinator has to intervene and start recovery by initiating a new round.

This means that acceptors, after receiving values from different proposers, may decide on conflicting values. When the coordinator detects a conflict (value collision), it has to reinitiate a Propose phase to let acceptors converge to a single value.

One of the disadvantages of Fast Paxos is the increased number of round-trips and request latency on collisions if the request rate is high. [JUNQUEIRA07] shows that, due to the increased number of replicas and, subsequently, *messages* exchanged between the participants, despite a reduced number of steps, Fast Paxos can have higher latencies than its classic counterpart.

Egalitarian Paxos

Using a distinguished proposer as a leader makes a system prone to failures: as soon as the leader fails, the system has to elect a new one before it can proceed with further steps. Another problem is that having a leader can put a disproportionate load on it, impairing system performance.

One of the ways to avoid putting an entire system load on the leader is *partitioning*. Many systems split the range of possible values into smaller segments and allow a part of the system to be responsible for a specific range without having to worry about the other parts. This helps with availability (by isolating failures to a single partition and preventing propagation to other parts of the system), performance (since segments serving different values are nonoverlapping), and scalability (since we can scale the system by increasing the number of partitions). It is important to keep in mind that performing an operation against *multiple* partitions will require an atomic commitment.

Instead of using a leader and proposal numbers for sequencing commands, we can use a leader responsible for the commit of the *specific* command, and establish the order by looking up and setting dependencies. This approach is commonly called Egalitarian Paxos, or EPaxos [MORARU11]. The idea of allowing nonconflicting writes to be committed to the replicated state machine independently was first introduced in [LAMPORT05] and called Generalized Paxos. EPaxos is a first implementation of Generalized Paxos.

EPaxos attempts to offer benefits of both the classic Paxos algorithm and Multi-Paxos. Classic Paxos offers high availability, since a leader is established during each round, but has a higher message complexity. Multi-Paxos offers high throughput and requires fewer messages, but a leader may become a bottleneck.

EPaxos starts with a *Pre-Accept* phase, during which a process becomes a leader for the specific proposal. Every proposal has to include:

Dependencies
> All commands that potentially interfere with a current proposal, but are not necessarily already committed.

A sequence number
> This breaks cycles between the dependencies. Set it with a value larger than any sequence number of the known dependencies.

After collecting this information, it forwards a `Pre-Accept` message to a *fast quorum* of replicas. A fast quorum is $\lceil 3f/4 \rceil$ replicas, where f is the number of tolerated failures.

Replicas check their local command logs, update the proposal dependencies based on their view of potentially conflicting proposals, and send this information back to the leader. If the leader receives responses from a fast quorum of replicas, and their dependency lists are in agreement with each other and the leader itself, it can commit the command.

If the leader does not receive enough responses or if the command lists received from the replicas differ and contain interfering commands, it updates its proposal with a new dependency list and a sequence number. The new dependency list is based on previous replica responses and combines *all* collected dependencies. The new sequence number has to be larger than the highest sequence number seen by the replicas. After that, the leader sends the new, updated command to $\lfloor f/2 \rfloor + 1$ replicas. After this is done, the leader can finally commit the proposal.

Effectively, we have two possible scenarios:

Fast path

    When dependencies match and the leader can safely proceed with the commit phase with only a *fast quorum* of replicas.

Slow path

    When there's a disagreement between the replicas, and their command lists have to be updated before the leader can proceed with a commit.

Figure 14-8 shows these scenarios—P_1 initiating a fast path run, and P_5 initiating a slow path run:

- P_1 starts with proposal number 1 and no dependencies, and sends a `PreAc cept(1, ∅)` message. Since the command logs of P_2 and P_3 are empty, P_1 can proceed with a commit.

- P_5 creates a proposal with sequence number 2. Since its command log is empty by that point, it also declares no dependencies and sends a `PreAccept(2, ∅)` message. P_4 is not aware of the committed proposal 1, but P_3 notifies P_5 about the conflict and sends its command log: {1}.

- P_5 updates its local dependency list and sends a message to make sure replicas have the same dependencies: `Accept(2,{1})`. As soon as the replicas respond, it can commit the value.

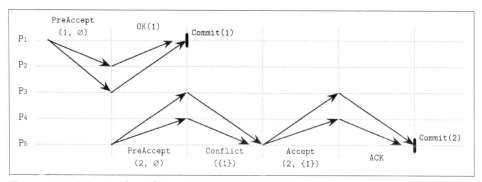

Figure 14-8. EPaxos algorithm run

Two commands, A and B, interfere only if their execution order matters; in other words, if executing A before B and executing B before A produce different results.

Commit is done by responding to the client and asynchronously notifying replicas with a Commit message. Commands are executed *after* they're committed.

Since dependencies are collected during the Pre-Accept phase, by the time requests are executed, the command order is already established and no command can suddenly appear somewhere in-between: it can only get appended *after* the command with the largest sequence number.

To execute a command, replicas build a dependency graph and execute all commands in a reverse dependency order. In other words, before a command can be executed, all its dependencies (and, subsequently, all their dependencies) have to be executed. Since only interfering commands have to depend on each other, this situation should be relatively rare for most workloads [MORARU13].

Similar to Paxos, EPaxos uses proposal numbers, which prevent stale messages from being propagated. Sequence numbers consist of an *epoch* (identifier of the current cluster configuration that changes when nodes leave and join the cluster), a monotonically incremented node-local counter, and a replica ID. If a replica receives a proposal with a sequence number lower than one it has already seen, it negatively acknowledges the proposal, and sends the highest sequence number and an updated command list known to it in response.

Flexible Paxos

A quorum is usually defined as a majority of processes. By definition, we have an *intersection* between two quorums no matter how we pick nodes: there's always at least one node that can break ties.

We have to answer two important questions:

- Is it necessary to contact the *majority* of servers during *every* execution step?
- Do *all* quorums have to intersect? In other words, does a quorum we use to pick a distinguished proposer (first phase), a quorum we use to decide on a value (second phase), and every execution instance (for example, if multiple instances of the second step are executed concurrently), have to have nodes in common?

Since we're still talking about consensus, we cannot change any safety definitions: the algorithm has to guarantee the agreement.

In Multi-Paxos, the leader election phase is infrequent, and the distinguished proposer is allowed to commit several values without rerunning the election phase, potentially staying in the lead for a longer period. In "Tunable Consistency" on page 235, we discussed formulae that help us to find configurations where we have intersections between the node sets. One of the examples was to wait for just one node to acknowledge the write (and let the requests to the rest of nodes finish asynchronously), and read from *all* the nodes. In other words, as long as we keep R + W > N, there's at least one node in common between read and write sets.

Can we use a similar logic for consensus? It turns out that we can, and in Paxos we only require the group of nodes from the first phase (that elects a leader) to overlap with the group from the second phase (that participates in accepting proposals).

In other words, a quorum doesn't have to be defined as a majority, but only as a nonempty group of nodes. If we define a total number of participants as N, the number of nodes required for a propose phase to succeed as Q_1, and the number of nodes required for the accept phase to succeed as Q_2, we only need to ensure that $Q_1 + Q_2 > N$. Since the second phase is usually more common than the first one, Q_2 can contain only N/2 acceptors, as long as Q_1 is adjusted to be correspondingly larger ($Q_1 = N - Q_2 + 1$). This finding is an important observation crucial for understanding consensus. The algorithm that uses this approach is called *Flexible Paxos* [HOWARD16].

For example, if we have five acceptors, as long as we require collecting votes from four of them to win the election round, we can allow the leader to wait for responses from two nodes during the replication stage. Moreover, since there's an overlap between *any* subset consisting of two acceptors with the leader election quorum, we can submit proposals to disjoint sets of acceptors. Intuitively, this works because whenever a new leader is elected without the current one being aware of it, there will always be at least one acceptor that knows about the existence of the new leader.

Flexible Paxos allows trading availability for latency: we reduce the number of nodes participating in the second phase but have to collect more votes, requiring more participants to be available during the leader election phase. The good news is that this configuration can continue the replication phase and tolerate failures of up to N - Q_2 nodes, as long as the current leader is stable and a new election round is not required.

Another Paxos variant using the idea of intersecting quorums is Vertical Paxos. Vertical Paxos distinguishes between read and write quorums. These quorums must intersect. A leader has to collect a smaller read quorum for one or more lower-numbered proposals, and a larger write quorum for its own proposal [LAMPORT09]. [LAMPSON01] also distinguishes between the *out* and *decision* quorums, which translate to prepare and accept phases, and gives a quorum definition similar to Flexible Paxos.

Generalized Solution to Consensus

Paxos might sometimes be a bit difficult to reason about: multiple roles, steps, and all the possible variations are hard to keep track of. But we can think of it in simpler terms. Instead of splitting roles between the participants and having decision rounds, we can use a simple set of concepts and rules to achieve guarantees of a single-decree

Paxos. We discuss this approach only briefly as this is a relatively new development [HOWARD19]—it's important to know, but we've yet to see its implementations and practical applications.

We have a client and a set of servers. Each server has multiple *registers*. A register has an index identifying it, can be written only once, and it can be in one of three states: unwritten, containing a *value*, and containing *nil* (a special empty value).

Registers with the same index located on different servers form a *register set*. Each register set can have one or more quorums. Depending on the state of the registers in it, a quorum can be in one of the *undecided* (`Any` and `Maybe v`), or *decided* (`None` and `Decided v`) states:

`Any`
> Depending on future operations, this quorum set can decide on any value.

`Maybe v`
> If this quorum reaches a decision, its decision can only be v.

`None`
> This quorum cannot decide on the value.

`Decided v`
> This quorum has decided on the value v.

The client exchanges messages with the servers and maintains a state table, where it keeps track of values and registers, and can infer decisions made by the quorums.

To maintain correctness, we have to limit how clients can interact with servers and which values they may write and which they may not. In terms of reading values, the client can output the decided value only if it has read it from the quorum of servers in the same register set.

The writing rules are slightly more involved because to guarantee algorithm safety, we have to preserve several invariants. First, we have to make sure that the client doesn't just come up with new values: it is allowed to write a specific value to the register only if it has received it as input or has read it from a register. Clients cannot write values that allow different quorums in the same register to decide on different values. Lastly, clients cannot write values that override previous decisions made in the previous register sets (decisions made in register sets up to `r - 1` have to be `None`, `Maybe v`, or `Decided v`).

Generalized Paxos algorithm

Putting all these rules together, we can implement a generalized Paxos algorithm that achieves consensus over a single value using write-once registers [HOWARD19]. Let's say we have three servers [`S0`, `S1`, `S2`], registers [`R0`, `R1`, …], and clients

[C0, C1, ...], where the client can only write to the assigned subset of registers. We use simple majority quorums for all registers ({S0, S1}, {S0, S2}, {S1, S2}).

The decision process here consists of two phases. The first phase ensures that it is safe to write a value to the register, and the second phase writes the value to the register:

During phase 1

The client checks if the register it is about to write is unwritten by sending a P1ₐ(register) command to the server. If the register is unwritten, all registers up to register - 1 are set to nil, which prevents clients from writing to previous registers. The server responds with a set of registers written so far. If it receives responses from the majority of servers, the client chooses either the non-empty value from the register with the largest index or its own value in case no value is present. Otherwise, it restarts the first phase.

During phase 2

The client notifies all servers about the value it has picked during the first phase by sending them P2ₐ(register, value). If the majority of servers respond to this message, it can output the decision value. Otherwise, it starts again from phase 1.

Figure 14-9 shows this generalization of Paxos (adapted from [HOWARD19]). Client C0 tries to commit value V. During the first step, its state table is empty, and servers S0 and S1 respond with the empty register set, indicating that no registers were written so far. During the second step, it can submit its value V, since no other value was written.

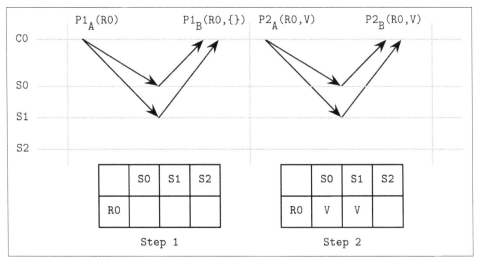

Figure 14-9. Generalization of Paxos

At that point, any other client can query servers to find out the current state. Quorum {S0, S1} has reached Decided A state, and quorums {S0, S2} and {S1, S2} have reached the Maybe V state for R0, so C1 chooses the value V. At that point, no client can decide on a value other than V.

This approach helps to understand the semantics of Paxos. Instead of thinking about the state from the perspective of interactions of remote actors (e.g., a proposer finding out whether or not an acceptor has already accepted a different proposal), we can think in terms of the last known state, making our decision process simple and removing possible ambiguities. Immutable state and message passing can also be easier to implement correctly.

We can also draw parallels with original Paxos. For example, in a scenario in which the client finds that one of the previous register sets has the Maybe V decision, it picks up V and attempts to commit it again, which is similar to how a proposer in Paxos can propose the value after the failure of the previous proposer that was able to commit the value to at least one acceptor. Similarly, if in Paxos leader conflicts are resolved by restarting the vote with a higher proposal number, in the generalized algorithm any unwritten lower-ranked registers are set to nil.

Raft

Paxos was *the* consensus algorithm for over a decade, but in the distributed systems community it's been known as difficult to reason about. In 2013, a new algorithm called Raft appeared. The researchers who developed it wanted to create an algorithm that's easy to understand and implement. It was first presented in a paper titled "In Search of an Understandable Consensus Algorithm" [ONGARO14].

There's enough inherent complexity in distributed systems, and having simpler algorithms is very desirable. Along with a paper, the authors have released a reference implementation called LogCabin (*https://databass.dev/links/69*) to resolve possible ambiguities and help future implementors to gain a better understanding.

Locally, participants store a log containing the sequence of commands executed by the state machine. Since inputs that processes receive are identical and logs contain the same commands in the same order, applying these commands to the state machine guarantees the same output. Raft simplifies consensus by making the concept of leader a first-class citizen. A leader is used to coordinate state machine manipulation and replication. There are many similarities between Raft and atomic broadcast algorithms, as well as Multi-Paxos: a single leader emerges from replicas, makes atomic decisions, and establishes the message order.

Each participant in Raft can take one of three roles:

Candidate
> Leadership is a temporary condition, and any participant can take this role. To become a leader, the node first has to transition into a candidate state, and attempt to collect a majority of votes. If a candidate neither wins nor loses the election (the vote is split between multiple candidates and none of them has a majority of votes), the new term is slated and election restarts.

Leader
> A current, temporary cluster leader that handles client requests and interacts with a replicated state machine. The leader is elected for a period called a *term*. Each term is identified by a monotonically increasing number and may continue for an arbitrary time period. A new leader is elected if the current one crashes, becomes unresponsive, or is suspected by other processes to have failed, which can happen because of network partitions and message delays.

Follower
> A passive participant that persists log entries and responds to requests from the leader and candidates. Follower in Raft is a role similar to acceptor *and* learner from Paxos. Every process begins as a follower.

To guarantee global partial ordering without relying on clock synchronization, time is divided into *terms* (also called epoch), during which the leader is unique and stable. Terms are monotonically numbered, and each command is uniquely identified by the term number and the message number within the term [HOWARD14].

It may happen that different participants disagree on which term is *current*, since they can find out about the new term at different times, or could have missed the leader election for one or multiple terms. Since each message contains a term identifier, if one of the participants discovers that its term is out-of-date, it updates the term to the higher-numbered one [ONGARO14]. This means that there *may be* several terms in flight at any given point in time, but the higher-numbered one wins in case of a conflict. A node updates the term only if it starts a new election process or finds out that its term is out-of-date.

On startup, or whenever a follower doesn't receive messages from the leader and suspects that it has crashed, it starts the leader election process. A participant attempts to become a leader by transitioning into the candidate state and collecting votes from the majority of nodes.

Figure 14-10 shows a sequence diagram representing the main components of the Raft algorithm:

Leader election

Candidate `P1` sends a `RequestVote` message to the other processes. This message includes the candidate's term, the last term known by it, and the ID of the last log entry it has observed. After collecting a majority of votes, the candidate is successfully elected as a leader for the term. Each process can give its vote to at most one candidate.

Periodic heartbeats

The protocol uses a heartbeat mechanism to ensure the liveness of participants. The leader periodically sends heartbeats to all followers to maintain its term. If a follower doesn't receive new heartbeats for a period called an *election timeout*, it assumes that the leader has failed and starts a new election.

Log replication / broadcast

The leader can repeatedly append new values to the replicated log by sending `AppendEntries` messages. The message includes the leader's term, index, and term of the log entry that immediately precedes the ones it's currently sending, and *one or more* entries to store.

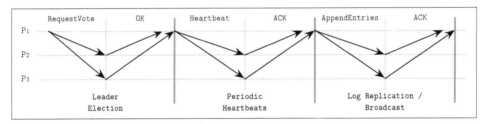

Figure 14-10. Raft consensus algorithm summary

Leader Role in Raft

A leader can be elected only from the nodes holding all committed entries: if during the election, the follower's log information is more up-to-date (in other words, has a higher term ID, or a longer log entry sequence, if terms are equal) than the candidate's, its vote is denied.

To win the vote, a candidate has to collect a majority of votes. Entries are always replicated in order, so it is always enough to compare IDs of the latest entries to understand whether or not one of the participants is up-to-date.

Once elected, the leader has to accept client requests (which can also be forwarded to it from other nodes) and replicate them to the followers. This is done by appending the entry to its log and sending it to all the followers in parallel.

When a follower receives an `AppendEntries` message, it appends the entries from the message to the local log, and acknowledges the message, letting the leader know that it was persisted. As soon as enough replicas send their acknowledgments, the entry is considered committed and is marked correspondingly in the leader log.

Since only the most up-to-date candidates can become a leader, followers never have to bring the leader up-to-date, and log entries are only flowing from leader to follower and not vice versa.

Figure 14-11 shows this process:

- a) A new command x = 8 is appended to the leader's log.
- b) Before the value can be committed, it has to be replicated to the majority of participants.
- c) As soon as the leader is done with replication, it commits the value locally.
- d) The commit decision is replicated to the followers.

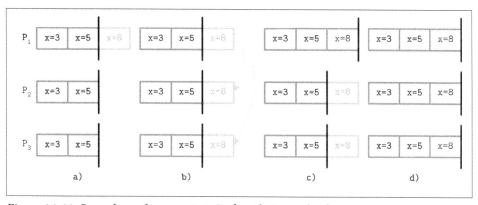

Figure 14-11. Procedure of a commit in Raft with P_1 as a leader

Figure 14-12 shows an example of a consensus round where P₁ is a leader, which has the most recent view of the events. The leader proceeds by replicating the entries to the followers, and committing them after collecting acknowledgments. Committing an entry also commits all entries preceding it in the log. Only the leader can make a decision on whether or not the entry can be committed. Each log entry is marked with a term ID (a number in the top-right corner of each log entry box) and a log index, identifying its position in the log. Committed entries are guaranteed to be replicated to the quorum of participants and are safe to be applied to the state machine in the order they appear in the log.

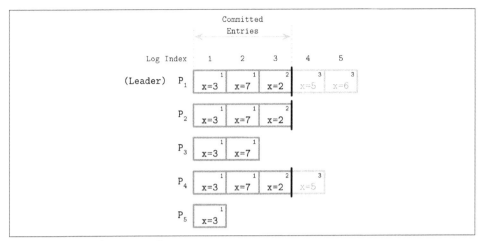

Figure 14-12. Raft state machine

Failure Scenarios

When multiple followers decide to become candidates, and no candidate can collect a majority of votes, the situation is called a *split vote*. Raft uses randomized timers to reduce the probability of multiple subsequent elections ending up in a split vote. One of the candidates can start the next election round earlier and collect enough votes, while the others sleep and give way to it. This approach speeds up the election without requiring any additional coordination between candidates.

Followers may be down or slow to respond, and the leader has to make the best effort to ensure message delivery. It can try sending messages again if it doesn't receive an acknowledgment within the expected time bounds. As a performance optimization, it can send multiple messages in parallel.

Since entries replicated by the leader are uniquely identified, repeated message delivery is guaranteed not to break the log order. Followers deduplicate messages using their sequence IDs, ensuring that double delivery has no undesired side effects.

Sequence IDs are also used to ensure the log ordering. A follower rejects a higher-numbered entry if the ID and term of the entry that immediately precedes it, sent by the leader, do not match the highest entry according to its own records. If entries in two logs on different replicas have the same term and the same index, they store the same command and all entries that precede them are the same.

Raft guarantees to never show an uncommitted message as a committed one, but, due to network or replica slowness, already committed messages can still be seen as *in progress*, which is a rather harmless property and can be worked around by retrying a client command until it is finally committed [HOWARD14].

For failure detection, the leader has to send heartbeats to the followers. This way, the leader maintains its term. When one of the nodes notices that the current leader is down, it attempts to initiate the election. The newly elected leader has to restore the state of the cluster to the last known up-to-date log entry. It does so by finding a *common ground* (the highest log entry on which both the leader and follower agree), and ordering followers to *discard* all (uncommitted) entries appended after this point. It then sends the most recent entries from its log, overwriting the followers' history. The leader's own log records are never removed or overwritten: it can only append entries to its own log.

Summing up, the Raft algorithm provides the following guarantees:

- Only one leader can be elected at a time for a given term; no two leaders can be active during the same term.

- The leader does not remove or reorder its log contents; it only appends new messages to it.

- Committed log entries are guaranteed to be present in logs for subsequent leaders and cannot get reverted, since before the entry is committed it is known to be replicated by the leader.

- All messages are identified uniquely by the message and term IDs; neither current nor subsequent leaders can reuse the same identifier for the different entry.

Since its appearance, Raft has become very popular and is currently used in many databases and other distributed systems, including CockroachDB (*https://data bass.dev/links/70*), Etcd (*https://databass.dev/links/71*), and Consul (*https://data bass.dev/links/72*). This can be attributed to its simplicity, but also may mean that Raft lives up to the promise of being a reliable consensus algorithm.

Byzantine Consensus

All the consensus algorithms we have been discussing so far assume non-Byzantine failures (see "Arbitrary Faults" on page 193). In other words, nodes execute the algorithm in "good faith" and do not try to exploit it or forge the results.

As we will see, this assumption allows achieving consensus with a smaller number of available participants and with fewer round-trips required for a commit. However, distributed systems are sometimes deployed in potentially adversarial environments, where the nodes are not controlled by the same entity, and we need algorithms that can ensure a system can function correctly even if some nodes behave erratically or even maliciously. Besides ill intentions, Byzantine failures can also be caused by bugs, misconfiguration, hardware issues, or data corruption.

Most Byzantine consensus algorithms require N^2 messages to complete an algorithm step, where N is the size of the quorum, since each node in the quorum has to communicate with each other. This is required to cross-validate each step against other nodes, since nodes cannot rely on each other or on the leader and have to verify other nodes' behaviors by comparing returned results with the majority responses.

We'll only discuss one Byzantine consensus algorithm here, Practical Byzantine Fault Tolerance (PBFT) [CASTRO99]. PBFT assumes independent node failures (i.e., failures can be coordinated, but the entire system cannot be taken over at once, or at least with the same exploit method). The system makes weak synchrony assumptions, like how you would expect a network to behave normally: failures may occur, but they are not indefinite and are eventually recovered from.

All communication between the nodes is encrypted, which serves to prevent message forging and network attacks. Replicas know one another's public keys to verify identities and encrypt messages. Faulty nodes may leak information from inside the system, since, even though encryption is used, every node needs to interpret message contents to react upon them. This doesn't undermine the algorithm, since it serves a different purpose.

PBFT Algorithm

For PBFT to guarantee both safety and liveness, no more than $(n - 1)/3$ replicas can be faulty (where n is the total number of participants). For a system to sustain f compromised nodes, it is required to have at least $n = 3f + 1$ nodes. This is the case because a majority of nodes have to agree on the value: f replicas might be faulty, and there might be f replicas that are not responding but may not be faulty (for example, due to a network partition, power failure, or maintenance). The algorithm has to be able to collect enough responses from nonfaulty replicas to *still* outnumber those from the faulty ones.

Consensus properties for PBFT are similar to those of other consensus algorithms: all nonfaulty replicas have to agree both on the set of received values and their order, despite the possible failures.

To distinguish between cluster configurations, PBFT uses *views*. In each view, one of the replicas is a *primary* and the rest of them are considered *backups*. All nodes are numbered consecutively, and the index of the primary node is $v \bmod N$, where v is the view ID, and N is the number of nodes in the current configuration. The view can change in cases when the primary fails. Clients execute their operations against the primary. The primary broadcasts the requests to the backups, which execute the requests and send a response back to the client. The client waits for $f + 1$ replicas to respond with *the same result* for any operation to succeed.

After the primary receives a client request, protocol execution proceeds in three phases:

Pre-prepare

The primary broadcasts a message containing a view ID, a unique monotonically increasing identifier, a payload (client request), and a payload digest. Digests are computed using a strong collision-resistant hash function, and are signed by the sender. The backup accepts the message if its view matches with the primary view and the client request hasn't been tampered with: the calculated payload digest matches the received one.

Prepare

If the backup accepts the pre-prepare message, it enters the prepare phase and starts broadcasting `Prepare` messages, containing a view ID, message ID, and a payload digest, but without the payload itself, to all other replicas (including the primary). Replicas can move past the prepare state only if they receive 2f prepares from *different* backups that match the message received during pre-prepare: they have to have the same view, same ID, and a digest.

Commit

After that, the backup moves to the commit phase, where it broadcasts `Commit` messages to all other replicas and waits to collect 2f + 1 matching `Commit` messages (possibly including its own) from the other participants.

A *digest* in this case is used to reduce the message size during the prepare phase, since it's not necessary to rebroadcast an entire payload for verification, as the digest serves as a payload summary. Cryptographic hash functions are resistant to collisions: it is difficult to produce two values that have the same digest, let alone two messages with matching digests that *make sense* in the context of the system. In addition, digests are *signed* to make sure that the digest itself is coming from a trusted source.

The number 2f is important, since the algorithm has to make sure that at least f + 1 nonfaulty replicas respond to the client.

Figure 14-13 shows a sequence diagram of a normal-case PBFT algorithm round: the client sends a request to P_1, and nodes move between phases by collecting a sufficient number of matching responses from *properly behaving* peers. P_4 may have failed or could've responded with unmatching messages, so its responses wouldn't have been counted.

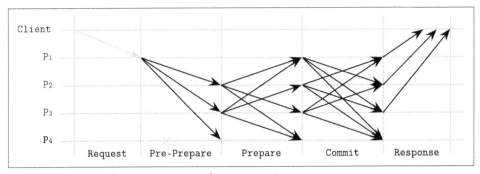

Figure 14-13. PBFT consensus, normal-case operation

During the prepare and commit phases, nodes communicate by sending messages to each other node and waiting for the messages from the corresponding number of other nodes, to check if they match and make sure that incorrect messages are not broadcasted. Peers cross-validate all messages so that only nonfaulty nodes can successfully commit messages. If a sufficient number of matching messages cannot be collected, the node doesn't move to the next step.

When replicas collect enough commit messages, they notify the client, finishing the round. The client cannot be certain about whether or not execution was fulfilled correctly until it receives f + 1 matching responses.

View changes occur when replicas notice that the primary is inactive, and suspect that it might have failed. Nodes that detect a primary failure stop responding to further messages (apart from checkpoint and view-change related ones), broadcast a view change notification, and wait for confirmations. When the primary of the new view receives 2f view change events, it initiates a new view.

To reduce the number of messages in the protocol, clients can collect 2f + 1 matching responses from nodes that *tentatively* execute a request (e.g., after they've collected a sufficient number of matching Prepared messages). If the client cannot collect enough matching tentative responses, it retries and waits for f + 1 nontentative responses as described previously.

Read-only operations in PBFT can be done in just one round-trip. The client sends a read request to all replicas. Replicas execute the request in their tentative states, after all ongoing state changes to the read value are committed, and respond to the client. After collecting 2f + 1 responses with the same value from different replicas, the operation completes.

Recovery and Checkpointing

Replicas save accepted messages in a stable log. Every message has to be kept until it has been executed by at least f + 1 nodes. This log can be used to get other replicas up to speed in case of a network partition, but recovering replicas need some means of verifying that the state they receive is correct, since otherwise recovery can be used as an attack vector.

To show that the state is correct, nodes compute a digest of the state for messages up to a given sequence number. Nodes can compare digests, verify state integrity, and make sure that messages they received during recovery add up to a correct final state. This process is too expensive to perform on every request.

After every N requests, where N is a configurable constant, the primary makes a *stable checkpoint*, where it broadcasts the latest sequence number of the latest request whose execution is reflected in the state, and the digest of this state. It then waits for 2f + 1 replicas to respond. These responses constitute a proof for this checkpoint, and a guarantee that replicas can safely discard state for all pre-prepare, prepare, commit, and checkpoint messages up to the given sequence number.

Byzantine fault tolerance is essential to understand and is used in storage systems deployed in potentially adversarial networks. Most of the time, it is enough to authenticate and encrypt internode communication, but when there's no trust between the parts of the system, algorithms similar to PBFT have to be employed.

Since algorithms resistant to Byzantine faults impose significant overhead in terms of the number of exchanged messages, it is important to understand their use cases. Other protocols, such as the ones described in [BAUDET19] and [BUCHMAN18], attempt to optimize the PBFT algorithm for systems with a large number of participants.

Summary

Consensus algorithms are one of the most interesting yet most complex subjects in distributed systems. Over the last few years, new algorithms and many implementations of the existing algorithms have emerged, which proves the rising importance and popularity of the subject.

In this chapter, we discussed the classic Paxos algorithm, and several variants of Paxos, each one improving its different properties:

Multi-Paxos
    Allows a proposer to retain its role and replicate multiple values instead of just one.

Fast Paxos
> Allows us to reduce a number of messages by using *fast* rounds, when acceptors can proceed with messages from proposers other than the established leader.

EPaxos
> Establishes event order by resolving dependencies between submitted messages.

Flexible Paxos
> Relaxes quorum requirements and only requires a quorum for the first phase (voting) to intersect with a quorum for the second phase (replication).

Raft simplifies the terms in which consensus is described, and makes leadership a first-class citizen in the algorithm. Raft separates log replication, leader election, and safety.

To guarantee consensus safety in adversarial environments, Byzantine fault-tolerant algorithms should be used; for example, PBFT. In PBFT, participants cross-validate one another's responses and only proceed with execution steps when there's enough nodes that obey the prescribed algorithm rules.

Further Reading

If you'd like to learn more about the concepts mentioned in this chapter, you can refer to the following sources:

Atomic broadcast
> Junqueira, Flavio P., Benjamin C. Reed, and Marco Serafini. "Zab: High-performance broadcast for primary-backup systems." 2011. In *Proceedings of the 2011 IEEE/IFIP 41st International Conference on Dependable Systems & Networks (DSN '11)*: 245-256.
>
> Hunt, Patrick, Mahadev Konar, Flavio P. Junqueira, and Benjamin Reed. 2010. "ZooKeeper: wait-free coordination for internet-scale systems." In *Proceedings of the 2010 USENIX conference on USENIX annual technical conference (USENIX-ATC'10)*: 11.
>
> Oki, Brian M., and Barbara H. Liskov. 1988. "Viewstamped Replication: A New Primary Copy Method to Support Highly-Available Distributed Systems." In *Proceedings of the seventh annual ACM Symposium on Principles of distributed computing (PODC '88)*: 8-17.
>
> Van Renesse, Robbert, Nicolas Schiper, and Fred B. Schneider. 2014. "Vive la Différence: Paxos vs. Viewstamped Replication vs. Zab."

Classic Paxos
> Lamport, Leslie. 1998. "The part-time parliament." *ACM Transactions on Computer Systems* 16, no. 2 (May): 133-169.

Lamport, Leslie. 2001. "Paxos made simple." ACM SIGACT News 32, no. 4: 51-58.

Lamport, Leslie. 2005. "Generalized Consensus and Paxos." Technical Report MSR-TR-2005-33. Microsoft Research, Mountain View, CA.

Primi, Marco. 2009. "Paxos made code: Implementing a high throughput Atomic Broadcast." (Libpaxos code: *https://bitbucket.org/sciascid/libpaxos/src/master/*.

Fast Paxos

Lamport, Leslie. 2005. "Fast Paxos." 14 July 2005. Microsoft Research.

Multi-Paxos

Chandra, Tushar D., Robert Griesemer, and Joshua Redstone. 2007. "Paxos made live: an engineering perspective." In *Proceedings of the twenty-sixth annual ACM symposium on Principles of distributed computing (PODC '07)*: 398-407.

Van Renesse, Robbert and Deniz Altinbuken. 2015. "Paxos Made Moderately Complex." *ACM Computing Surveys* 47, no. 3 (February): Article 42. *https://doi.org/10.1145/2673577*.

EPaxos

Moraru, Iulian, David G. Andersen, and Michael Kaminsky. 2013. "There is more consensus in Egalitarian parliaments." In *Proceedings of the Twenty-Fourth ACM Symposium on Operating Systems Principles (SOSP '13)*: 358-372.

Moraru, I., D. G. Andersen, and M. Kaminsky. 2013. "A proof of correctness for Egalitarian Paxos." Technical report, Parallel Data Laboratory, Carnegie Mellon University, Aug. 2013.

Raft

Ongaro, Diego, and John Ousterhout. 2014. "In search of an understandable consensus algorithm." In *Proceedings of the 2014 USENIX conference on USENIX Annual Technical Conference (USENIX ATC'14)*, Garth Gibson and Nickolai Zeldovich (Eds.): 305-320.

Howard, H. 2014. "ARC: Analysis of Raft Consensus." Technical Report UCAM-CL-TR-857, University of Cambridge, Computer Laboratory, July 2014.

Howard, Heidi, Malte Schwarzkopf, Anil Madhavapeddy, and Jon Crowcroft. 2015. "Raft Refloated: Do We Have Consensus?" *SIGOPS Operating Systems Review* 49, no. 1 (January): 12-21. *https://doi.org/10.1145/2723872.2723876*.

Recent developments

Howard, Heidi and Richard Mortier. 2019. "A Generalised Solution to Distributed Consensus." 18 Feb 2019.

Part II Conclusion

Performance and scalability are important properties of any database system. The storage engine and node-local read-write path can have a larger impact on *performance* of the system: how quickly it can process requests locally. At the same time, a subsystem responsible for communication in the cluster often has a larger impact on the *scalability* of the database system: maximum cluster size and capacity. However, the storage engine can only be used for a limited number of use cases if it's not scalable and its performance degrades as the dataset grows. At the same time, putting a slow atomic commit protocol on top of the fastest storage engine will not yield good results.

Distributed, cluster-wide, and node-local processes are interconnected, and have to be considered holistically. When designing a database system, you have to consider how different subsystems fit and work together.

Part II began with a discussion of how distributed systems are different from single-node applications, and which difficulties are to be expected in such environments.

We discussed the basic distributed system building blocks, different consistency models, and several important classes of distributed algorithms, some of which can be used to implement these consistency models:

Failure detection
Identify remote process failures accurately and efficiently.

Leader election
Quickly and reliably choose a single process to temporarily serve as a coordinator.

Dissemination
Reliably distribute information using peer-to-peer communication.

Anti-entropy
Identify and repair state divergence between the nodes.

Distributed transactions
   Execute series of operations against multiple partitions atomically.

Consensus
   Reach an agreement between remote participants while tolerating process
   failures.

These algorithms are used in many database systems, message queues, schedulers,
and other important infrastructure software. Using the knowledge from this book,
you'll be able to better understand how they work, which, in turn, will help to make
better decisions about which software to use, and identify potential problems.

Further Reading

At the end of each chapter, you can find resources related to the material presented in
the chapter. Here, you'll find books you can address for further study, covering both
concepts mentioned in this book and other concepts. This list is not meant to be
complete, but these sources contain a lot of important and useful information relevant for database systems enthusiasts, some of which is not covered in this book:

Database systems
   Bernstein, Philip A., Vassco Hadzilacos, and Nathan Goodman. 1987. *Concurrency Control and Recovery in Database Systems*. Boston: Addison-Wesley Longman.

   Korth, Henry F. and Abraham Silberschatz. 1986. *Database System Concepts*. New
   York: McGraw-Hill.

   Gray, Jim and Andreas Reuter. 1992. *Transaction Processing: Concepts and Techniques* (1st Ed.). San Francisco: Morgan Kaufmann.

   Stonebraker, Michael and Joseph M. Hellerstein (Eds.). 1998. *Readings in Database Systems* (3rd Ed.). San Francisco: Morgan Kaufmann.

   Weikum, Gerhard and Gottfried Vossen. 2001. *Transactional Information Systems: Theory, Algorithms, and the Practice of Concurrency Control and Recovery*.
   San Francisco: Morgan Kaufmann.

   Ramakrishnan, Raghu and Johannes Gehrke. 2002. *Database Management Systems* (3 Ed.). New York: McGraw-Hill.

   Garcia-Molina, Hector, Jeffrey D. Ullman, and Jennifer Widom. 2008. *Database
   Systems: The Complete Book* (2 Ed.). Upper Saddle River, NJ: Prentice Hall.

   Bernstein, Philip A. and Eric Newcomer. 2009. *Principles of Transaction Processing* (2nd Ed.). San Francisco: Morgan Kaufmann.

Elmasri, Ramez and Shamkant Navathe. 2010. *Fundamentals of Database Systems* (6th Ed.). Boston: Addison-Wesley.

Lake, Peter and Paul Crowther. 2013. *Concise Guide to Databases: A Practical Introduction*. New York: Springer.

Härder, Theo, Caetano Sauer, Goetz Graefe, and Wey Guy. 2015. *Instant recovery with write-ahead logging*. Datenbank-Spektrum.

Distributed systems

Lynch, Nancy A. *Distributed Algorithms*. 1996. San Francisco: Morgan Kaufmann.

Attiya, Hagit, and Jennifer Welch. 2004. *Distributed Computing: Fundamentals, Simulations and Advanced Topics*. Hoboken, NJ: John Wiley & Sons.

Birman, Kenneth P. 2005. *Reliable Distributed Systems: Technologies, Web Services, and Applications*. Berlin: Springer-Verlag.

Cachin, Christian, Rachid Guerraoui, and Lus Rodrigues. 2011. *Introduction to Reliable and Secure Distributed Programming* (2nd Ed.). New York: Springer.

Fokkink, Wan. 2013. *Distributed Algorithms: An Intuitive Approach*. The MIT Press.

Ghosh, Sukumar. *Distributed Systems: An Algorithmic Approach* (2nd Ed.). Chapman & Hall/CRC.

Tanenbaum Andrew S. and Maarten van Steen. 2017. *Distributed Systems: Principles and Paradigms* (3rd Ed.). Boston: Pearson.

Operating databases

Beyer, Betsy, Chris Jones, Jennifer Petoff, and Niall Richard Murphy. 2016 *Site Reliability Engineering: How Google Runs Production Systems* (1st Ed.). Boston: O'Reilly Media.

Blank-Edelman, David N. 2018. *Seeking SRE*. Boston: O'Reilly Media.

Campbell, Laine and Charity Majors. 2017. *Database Reliability Engineering: Designing and Operating Resilient Database Systems* (1st Ed.). Boston: O'Reilly Media. +Sridharan, Cindy. 2018. *Distributed Systems Observability: A Guide to Building Robust Systems*. Boston: O'Reilly Media.

Bibliography

1. [ABADI12] Abadi, Daniel. 2012. "Consistency Tradeoffs in Modern Distributed Database System Design: CAP is Only Part of the Story." *Computer* 45, no. 2 (February): 37-42. *https://doi.org/10.1109/MC.2012.33.*

2. [ABADI17] Abadi, Daniel. 2017. "Distributed consistency at scale: Spanner vs. Calvin." *Fauna* (blog). April 6, 2017. *https://fauna.com/blog/distributed-consistency-at-scale-spanner-vs-calvin.*

3. [ABADI13] Abadi, Daniel, Peter Boncz, Stavros Harizopoulos, Stratos Idreaos, and Samuel Madden. 2013. *The Design and Implementation of Modern Column-Oriented Database Systems.* Hanover, MA: Now Publishers Inc.

4. [ABRAHAM13] Abraham, Ittai, Danny Dolev, and Joseph Y. Halpern. 2013. "Distributed Protocols for Leader Election: A Game-TheoreticPerspective." In *Distributed Computing*, edited by Yehuda Afek, 61-75. Berlin: Springer, Berlin, Heidelberg.

5. [AGGARWAL88] Aggarwal, Alok, and Jeffrey S. Vitter. 1988. "The input/output complexity of sorting and related problems." *Communications of the ACM* 31, no. 9 (September): 1116-1127. *https://doi.org/10.1145/48529.48535.*

6. [AGRAWAL09] Agrawal, Devesh, Deepak Ganesan, Ramesh Sitaraman, Yanlei Diao, Shashi Singh. 2009. "Lazy-Adaptive Tree: an optimized index structure for flash devices." *Proceedings of the VLDB Endowment* 2, no. 1 (January): 361-372.

7. [AGRAWAL08] Agrawal, Nitin, Vijayan Prabhakaran, Ted Wobber, John D. Davis, Mark Manasse, and Rina Panigrahy. 2008. "Design tradeoffs for SSD performance." *USENIX 2008 Annual Technical Conference (ATC '08)*, 57-70. USENIX.

8. [AGUILERA97] Aguilera, Marcos K., Wei Chen, and Sam Toueg. 1997. "Heartbeat: a Timeout-Free Failure Detector for Quiescent Reliable Communication."

In *Distributed Algorithms*, edited by M. Mavronicolas and P. Tsigas, 126-140. Berlin: Springer, Berlin, Heidelberg.

9. [AGUILERA01] Aguilera, Marcos Kawazoe, Carole Delporte-Gallet, Hugues Fauconnier, and Sam Toueg. 2001. "Stable Leader Election." In *Proceedings of the 15th International Conference on Distributed Computing (DISC '01)*, edited by Jennifer L. Welch, 108-122. London: Springer-Verlag.

10. [AGUILERA16] Aguilera, M. K., and D. B. Terry. 2016. "The Many Faces of Consistency." *Bulletin of the Technical Committee on Data Engineering* 39, no. 1 (March): 3-13.

11. [ALHOUMAILY10] Al-Houmaily, Yousef J. 2010. "Atomic commit protocols, their integration, and their optimisations in distributed database systems." *International Journal of Intelligent Information and Database Systems* 4, no. 4 (September): 373–412. *https://doi.org/10.1504/IJIIDS.2010.035582.*

12. [ARJOMANDI83] Arjomandi, Eshrat, Michael J. Fischer, and Nancy A. Lynch. 1983. "Efficiency of Synchronous Versus Asynchronous Distributed Systems." *Journal of the ACM* 30, no. 3 (July): 449-456. *https://doi.org/10.1145/2402.322387.*

13. [ARULRAJ17] Arulraj, J. and A. Pavlo. 2017. "How to Build a Non-Volatile Memory Database Management System." In *Proceedings of the 2017 ACM International Conference on Management of Data*: 1753-1758. *https://doi.org/10.1145/3035918.3054780.*

14. [ATHANASSOULIS16] Athanassoulis, Manos, Michael S. Kester, Lukas M. Maas, Radu Stoica, Stratos Idreos, Anastasia Ailamaki, and Mark Callaghan. 2016. "Designing Access Methods: The RUM Conjecture." In *International Conference on Extending Database Technology (EDBT)*. *https://stratos.seas.harvard.edu/files/stratos/files/rum.pdf.*

15. [ATTIYA94] Attiyaand, Hagit and Jennifer L. Welch. 1994. "Sequential consistency versus linearizability." *ACM Transactions on Computer Systems* 12, no. 2 (May): 91-122. *https://doi.org/10.1145/176575.176576.*

16. [BABAOGLU93] Babaoglu, Ozalp and Sam Toueg. 1993. "Understanding Non-Blocking Atomic Commitment." Technical Report. University of Bologna.

17. [BAILIS14a] Bailis, Peter. 2014. "Linearizability versus Serializability." *Highly Available, Seldom Consistent* (blog). September 24, 2014. *https://www.bailis.org/blog/linearizability-versus-serializability.*

18. [BAILIS14b] Bailis, Peter, Alan Fekete, Michael J. Franklin, Ali Ghodsi, Joseph M. Hellerstein, and Ion Stoica. 2014. "Coordination Avoidance in Database Systems." *Proceedings of the VLDB Endowment* 8, no. 3 (November): 185-196. *https://doi.org/10.14778/2735508.2735509.*

19. [BAILIS14c] Bailis, Peter, Alan Fekete, Ali Ghodsi, Joseph M. Hellerstein, and Ion Stoica. 2014. "Scalable Atomic Visibility with RAMP Transactions." *ACM Transactions on Database Systems* 41, no. 3 (July). *https://doi.org/10.1145/2909870.*

20. [BARTLETT16] Bartlett, Robert P. III, and Justin McCrary. 2016. "How Rigged Are Stock Markets?: Evidence From Microsecond Timestamps." UC Berkeley Public Law Research Paper. *https://doi.org/10.2139/ssrn.2812123.*

21. [BAUDET19] Baudet, Mathieu, Avery Ching, Andrey Chursin, George Danezis, François Garillot, Zekun Li, Dahlia Malkhi, Oded Naor, Dmitri Perelman, and Alberto Sonnino. 2019. "State Machine Replication in the Libra Blockchain." *https://developers.libra.org/docs/assets/papers/libra-consensus-state-machine-replication-in-the-libra-blockchain.pdf.*

22. [BAYER72] Bayer, R., and E. M. McCreight. 1972. "Organization and maintenance of large ordered indices." *Acta Informatica* 1, no. 3 (September): 173-189. *https://doi.org/10.1007/BF00288683.*

23. [BEDALY69] Belady, L. A., R. A. Nelson, and G. S. Shedler. 1969. "An anomaly in space-time characteristics of certain programs running in a paging machine." *Communications of the ACM* 12, no. 6 (June): 349-353. *https://doi.org/10.1145/363011.363155.*

24. [BENDER05] Bender, Michael A., Erik D. Demaine, and Martin Farach-Colton. 2005. "Cache-Oblivious B-Trees." *SIAM Journal on Computing* 35, no. 2 (August): 341-358. *https://doi.org/10.1137/S0097539701389956.*

25. [BERENSON95] Berenson, Hal, Phil Bernstein, Jim Gray, Jim Melton, Elizabeth O'Neil, and Patrick O'Neil. 1995. "A critique of ANSI SQL isolation levels." *ACM SIGMOD Record* 24, no. 2 (May): 1-10. *https://doi.org/10.1145/568271.223785.*

26. [BERNSTEIN87] Bernstein, Philip A., Vassco Hadzilacos, and Nathan Goodman. 1987. *Concurrency Control and Recovery in Database Systems.* Boston: Addison-Wesley Longman.

27. [BERNSTEIN09] Bernstein, Philip A. and Eric Newcomer. 2009. *Principles of Transaction Processing.* San Francisco: Morgan Kaufmann.

28. [BHATTACHARJEE17] Bhattacharjee, Abhishek, Daniel Lustig, and Margaret Martonosi. 2017. *Architectural and Operating System Support for Virtual Memory.* San Rafael, CA: Morgan & Claypool Publishers.

29. [BIRMAN07] Birman, Ken. 2007. "The promise, and limitations, of gossip protocols." *ACM SIGOPS Operating Systems Review* 41, no. 5 (October): 8-13. *https://doi.org/10.1145/1317379.1317382.*

30. [BIRMAN10] Birman, Ken. 2010. "A History of the Virtual Synchrony Replication Model" In *Replication*, edited by Bernadette Charron-Bost, Fernando Pedone, and André Schiper, 91-120. Berlin: Springer-Verlag, Berlin, Heidelberg.

31. [BIRMAN06] Birman, Ken, Coimbatore Chandersekaran, Danny Dolev, Robbert vanRenesse. 2006. "How the Hidden Hand Shapes the Market for Software Reliability." In *First Workshop on Applied Software Reliability (WASR 2006)*. IEEE.

32. [BIYIKOGLU13] Biyikoglu, Cihan. 2013. "Under the Hood: Redis CRDTs (Conflict-free Replicated Data Types)." http://lp.redislabs.com/rs/915-NFD-128/images/WP-RedisLabs-Redis-Conflict-free-Replicated-Data-Types.pdf.

33. [BJØRLING17] Bjørling, Matias, Javier González, and Philippe Bonnet. 2017. "LightNVM: the Linux open-channel SSD subsystem." In *Proceedings of the 15th Usenix Conference on File and Storage Technologies (FAST'17)*, 359-373. USENIX.

34. [BLOOM70] Bloom, Burton H. 1970. "Space/time trade-offs in hash coding with allowable errors." *Communications of the ACM* 13, no. 7 (July): 422-426. *https://doi.org/10.1145/362686.362692.*

35. [BREWER00] Brewer, Eric. 2000. "Towards robust distributed systems." *Proceedings of the nineteenth annual ACM symposium on Principles of distributed computing (PODC '00).* New York: Association for Computing Machinery. *https://doi.org/10.1145/343477.343502.*

36. [BRZEZINSKI03] Brzezinski, Jerzy, Cezary Sobaniec, and Dariusz Wawrzyniak. 2003. "Session Guarantees to Achieve PRAM Consistency of Replicated Shared Objects." In *Parallel Processing and Applied Mathematics*, 1–8. Berlin: Springer, Berlin, Heidelberg.

37. [BUCHMAN18] Buchman, Ethan, Jae Kwon, and Zarko Milosevic. 2018. "The latest gossip on BFT consensus." *https://arxiv.org/pdf/1807.04938.pdf.*

38. [CACHIN11] Cachin, Christian, Rachid Guerraoui, and Luis Rodrigues. 2011. *Introduction to Reliable and Secure Distributed Programming (2nd Ed.).* New York: Springer.

39. [CASTRO99] Castro, Miguel. and Barbara Liskov. 1999. "Practical Byzantine Fault Tolerance." In *OSDI '99 Proceedings of the third symposium on Operating systems design and implementation*, 173-186.

40. [CESATI05] Cesati, Marco, and Daniel P. Bovet. 2005. *Understanding the Linux Kernel.* Third Edition. Sebastopol: O'Reilly Media, Inc.

41. [CHAMBERLIN81] Chamberlin, Donald D., Morton M. Astrahan, Michael W. Blasgen, James N. Gray, W. Frank King, Bruce G. Lindsay, Raymond Lorie, James W. Mehl, Thomas G. Price, Franco Putzolu, Patricia Griffiths Selinger, Mario Schkolnick, Donald R. Slutz, Irving L. Traiger, Bradford W. Wade, and Robert A. Yost. 1981. "A history and evaluation of System R." *Communications of the ACM* 24, no. 10 (October): 632–646. *https://doi.org/10.1145/358769.358784.*

42. [CHANDRA07] Chandra, Tushar D., Robert Griesemer, and Joshua Redstone. 2007. "Paxos made live: an engineering perspective." In *Proceedings of the twenty-sixth annual ACM symposium on Principles of distributed computing (PODC '07),*

398-407. New York: Association for Computing Machinery. *https://doi.org/10.1145/1281100.1281103.*

43. [CHANDRA96] Chandra, Tushar Deepak, and Sam Toueg. 1996. "Unreliable failure detectors for reliable distributed systems." *Journal of the ACM* 43, no. 2 (March): 225-267. *https://doi.org/10.1145/226643.226647.*

44. [CHANG79] Chang, Ernest, and Rosemary Roberts. 1979. "An improved algorithm for decentralized extrema-finding in circular configurations of processes." *Communications of the ACM* 22, no. 5 (May): 281–283. *https://doi.org/10.1145/359104.359108.*

45. [CHANG06] Chang, Fay, Jeffrey Dean, Sanjay Ghemawat, Wilson C. Hsieh, Deborah A.Wallach, Mike Burrows, Tushar Chandra, Andrew Fikes, and Robert E. Gruber. 2006. "Bigtable: A Distributed Storage System for Structured Data." In *7th USENIX Symposium on Operating Systems Design and Implementation (OSDI '06).* USENIX.

46. [CHAZELLE86] Chazelle, Bernard, and Leonidas J. Guibas. 1986. "Fractional Cascading, A Data Structuring Technique." *Algorithmica* 1: 133-162. *https://doi.org/10.1007/BF01840440.*

47. [CHOCKLER15] Chockler, Gregory, and Dahlia Malkhi. 2015. "Active disk paxos with infinitely many processes." In *Proceedings of the twenty-first annual symposium on Principles of distributed computing (PODC '02)*, 78-87. New York: Association for Computing Machinery. *https://doi.org/10.1145/571825.571837.*

48. [COMER79] Comer, Douglas. 1979. "Ubiquitous B-Tree." *ACM Computing Survey* 11, no. 2 (June): 121-137. *https://doi.org/10.1145/356770.356776.*

49. [CORBET18] Corbet, Jonathan. 2018. "PostgreSQL's fsync() surprise." *https://lwn.net/Articles/752063.*

50. [CORBETT12] Corbett, James C., Jeffrey Dean, Andrew Fikes, Christopher Frost, JJ Furman, Sanjay Ghemawat, Andrey Gubarev, Christopher Heiser, Peter Hochschild, Wilson Hsieh, Sebastian Kanthak, Eugene Kogan, Hongyi Li, Alexander Lloyd, Sergey Melnik, David Mwaura, David Nagle, Sean Quinlan, Rajesh Rao, Lindsay Rolig, Yasushi Saito, Michal Szymaniak, Christopher Taylor, Ruth Wang, and Dale Woodford. 2012. "Spanner: Google's Globally-Distributed Database." In *10th USENIX Symposium on Operating Systems Design and Implementation (OSDI '12)*, 261-264. USENIX.

51. [CORMODE04] Cormode, G. and S. Muthukrishnan. 2004. "An improved data stream summary: The count-min sketch and its applications." *Journal of Algorithms* 55, No. 1 (April): 58-75. *https://doi.org/10.1016/j.jalgor.2003.12.001.*

52. [CORMODE11] Cormode, Graham, and S. Muthukrishnan. 2011. "Approximating Data with the Count-Min Data Structure." *http://dimacs.rutgers.edu/~graham/pubs/papers/cmsoft.pdf.*

53. [CORMODE12] Cormode, Graham and Senthilmurugan Muthukrishnan. 2012. "Approximating Data with the Count-Min Data Structure."

54. [CHRISTIAN91] Cristian, Flavin. 1991. "Understanding fault-tolerant distributed systems." *Communications of the ACM* 34, no. 2 (February): 56-78. *https://doi.org/10.1145/102792.102801.*

55. [DAILY13] Daily, John. 2013. "Clocks Are Bad, Or, Welcome to the Wonderful World of Distributed Systems." *Riak* (blog). November 12, 2013. *https://riak.com/clocks-are-bad-or-welcome-to-distributed-systems.*

56. [DECANDIA07] DeCandia, Giuseppe, Deniz Hastorun, Madan Jampani, Gunavardhan Kakulapati, Avinash Lakshman, Alex Pilchin, Swaminathan Sivasubramanian, Peter Vosshall, and Werner Vogels. 2007. "Dynamo: amazon's highly available key-value store." *SIGOPS Operating Systems Review* 41, no. 6 (October): 205-220. *https://doi.org/10.1145/1323293.1294281.*

57. [DECHEV10] Dechev, Damian, Peter Pirkelbauer, and Bjarne Stroustrup. 2010. "Understanding and Effectively Preventing the ABA Problem in Descriptor-Based Lock-Free Designs." *Proceedings of the 2010 13th IEEE International Symposium on Object/Component/Service-Oriented Real-Time Distributed Computing (ISORC '10)*: 185–192. *https://doi.org/10.1109/ISORC.2010.10.*

58. [DEMAINE02] Demaine, Erik D. 2002. "Cache-Oblivious Algorithms and Data Structures." In *Lecture Notes from the EEF Summer School on Massive Data Sets.* Denmark: University of Aarhus.

59. [DEMERS87] Demers, Alan, Dan Greene, Carl Hauser, Wes Irish, John Larson, Scott Shenker, Howard Sturgis, Dan Swinehart, and Doug Terry. 1987. "Epidemic algorithms for replicated database maintenance." In *Proceedings of the sixth annual ACM Symposium on Principles of distributed computing (PODC '87)*, 1-12. New York: Association for Computing Machinery. *https://doi.org/10.1145/41840.41841.*

60. [DENNING68] Denning, Peter J. 1968. "The working set model for program behavior". *Communications of the ACM* 11, no. 5 (May): 323-333. *https://doi.org/10.1145/363095.363141.*

61. [DIACONU13] Diaconu, Cristian, Craig Freedman, Erik Ismert, Per-Åke Larson, Pravin Mittal, Ryan Stonecipher, Nitin Verma, and Mike Zwilling. 2013. "Hekaton: SQL Server's Memory-Optimized OLTP Engine." In *Proceedings of the 2013 ACM SIGMOD International Conference on Management of Data (SIGMOD '13)*, 1243-1254. New York: Association for Computing Machinery. *https://doi.org/10.1145/2463676.2463710.*

62. [DOWNEY12] Downey, Jim. 2012. "Be Careful with Sloppy Quorums." *Jim Downey* (blog). March 5, 2012. *https://jimdowney.net/2012/03/05/be-careful-with-sloppy-quorums.*

63. [DREPPER07] Drepper, Ulrich. 2007. *What Every Programmer Should Know About Memory*. Boston: Red Hat, Inc.

64. [DUNAGAN04] Dunagan, John, Nicholas J. A. Harvey, Michael B. Jones, Dejan Kostić, MarvinTheimer, and Alec Wolman. 2004. "FUSE: lightweight guaranteed distributed failure notification." In *Proceedings of the 6th conference on Symposium on Operating Systems Design & Implementation - Volume 6 (OSDI'04)*, 11-11. USENIX.

65. [DWORK88] Dwork, Cynthia, Nancy Lynch, and Larry Stockmeyer. 1988. "Consensus in the presence of partial synchrony." *Journal of the ACM* 35, no. 2 (April): 288-323. *https://doi.org/10.1145/42282.42283*.

66. [EINZIGER15] Einziger, Gil and Roy Friedman. 2015. "A formal analysis of conservative update based approximate counting." In *2015 International Conference on Computing, Networking and Communications (ICNC)*, 260-264. IEEE.

67. [EINZIGER17] Einziger, Gil, Roy Friedman, and Ben Manes. 2017. "TinyLFU: A Highly Efficient Cache Admission Policy." In *2014 22nd Euromicro International Conference on Parallel, Distributed, and Network-Based Processing*, 146-153. IEEE.

68. [ELLIS11] Ellis, Jonathan. 2011. "Understanding Hinted Handoff." *Datastax* (blog). May 31, 2011. *https://www.datastax.com/dev/blog/understanding-hinted-handoff*.

69. [ELLIS13] Ellis, Jonathan. 2013. "Why Cassandra doesn't need vector clocks." *Datastax* (blog). September 3, 2013. *https://www.datastax.com/dev/blog/why-cassandra-doesnt-need-vector-clocks*.

70. [ELMASRI11] Elmasri, Ramez and Shamkant Navathe. 2011. *Fundamentals of Database Systems (6th Ed.)*. Boston: Pearson.

71. [FEKETE04] Fekete, Alan, Elizabeth O'Neil, and Patrick O'Neil. 2004. "A read-only transaction anomaly under snapshot isolation." *ACM SIGMOD Record* 33, no. 3 (September): 12-14. *https://doi.org/10.1145/1031570.1031573*.

72. [FISCHER85] Fischer, Michael J., Nancy A. Lynch, and Michael S. Paterson. 1985. "Impossibility of distributed consensus with one faulty process." *Journal of the ACM* 32, 2 (April): 374-382. *https://doi.org/10.1145/3149.214121*.

73. [FLAJOLET12] Flajolet, Philippe, Eric Fusy, Olivier Gandouet, and Frédéric Meunier. 2012. "HyperLogLog: The analysis of a near-optimal cardinality estimation algorithm." In *AOFA '07: Proceedings of the 2007 International Conference on Analysis of Algorithms*.

74. [FOWLER11] Fowler, Martin. 2011. "The LMAX Architecture." *Martin Fowler*. July 12, 2011. *https://martinfowler.com/articles/lmax.html*.

75. [FOX99] Fox, Armando and Eric A. Brewer. 1999. "Harvest, Yield, and Scalable Tolerant Systems." In *Proceedings of the Seventh Workshop on Hot Topics in Operating Systems*, 174-178.

76. [FREILING11] Freiling, Felix C., Rachid Guerraoui, and Petr Kuznetsov. 2011. "The failure detector abstraction." *ACM Computing Surveys* 43, no. 2 (January): Article 9. *https://doi.org/10.1145/1883612.1883616*.

77. [GARCIAMOLINA82] Garcia-Molina, H. 1982. "Elections in a Distributed Computing System." *IEEE Transactions on Computers* 31, no. 1 (January): 48-59. *https://dx.doi.org/10.1109/TC.1982.1675885*.

78. [GARCIAMOLINA92] Garcia-Molina, H. and K. Salem. 1992. "Main Memory Database Systems: An Overview." *IEEE Transactions on Knowledge and Data Engineering* 4, no. 6 (December): 509-516. *https://doi.org/10.1109/69.180602*.

79. [GARCIAMOLINA08] Garcia-Molina, Hector, Jeffrey D. Ullman, and Jennifer Widom. 2008. *Database Systems: The Complete Book* (2nd Ed.). Boston: Pearson.

80. [GEORGOPOULOS16] Georgopoulos, Georgios. 2016. "Memory Consistency Models of Modern CPUs." *https://es.cs.uni-kl.de/publications/datarsg/Geor16.pdf*.

81. [GHOLIPOUR09] Gholipour, Majid, M. S. Kordafshari, Mohsen Jahanshahi, and Amir Masoud Rahmani. 2009. "A New Approach For Election Algorithm in Distributed Systems." In *2009 Second International Conference on Communication Theory, Reliability, and Quality of Service*, 70-74. IEEE. *https://doi.org/10.1109/CTRQ.2009.32*.

82. [GIAMPAOLO98] Giampaolo, Dominic. 1998. *Practical File System Design with the be File System*. San Francisco: Morgan Kaufmann.

83. [GILAD17] Gilad, Yossi, Rotem Hemo, Silvio Micali, Georgios Vlachos, and Nickolai Zeldovich. 2017. "Algorand: Scaling Byzantine Agreements for Cryptocurrencies." *Proceedings of the 26th Symposium on Operating Systems Principles* (October): 51–68. *https://doi.org/10.1145/3132747.3132757*.

84. [GILBERT02] Gilbert, Seth and Nancy Lynch. 2002. "Brewer's conjecture and the feasibility of consistent, available, partition-tolerant web services." *ACM SIGACT News* 33, no. 2 (June): 51-59. *https://doi.org/10.1145/564585.564601*.

85. [GILBERT12] Gilbert, Seth and Nancy Lynch. 2012. "Perspectives on the CAP Theorem." *Computer* 45, no. 2 (February): 30-36. *https://doi.org/10.1109/MC.2011.389*.

86. [GOMES17] Gomes, Victor B. F., Martin Kleppmann, Dominic P. Mulligan, and Alastair R. Beresford. 2017. "Verifying strong eventual consistency in distributed systems." *Proceedings of the ACM on Programming Languages* 1 (October). *https://doi.org/10.1145/3133933*.

87. [GONÇALVES15] Gonçalves, Ricardo, Paulo Sérgio Almeida, Carlos Baquero, and Victor Fonte. 2015. "Concise Server-Wide Causality Management for Eventually Consistent Data Stores." In *Distributed Applications and Interoperable Systems*, 66-79. Berlin: Springer.

88. [GOOSSAERT14] Goossaert, Emmanuel. 2014. "Coding For SSDs." *CodeCapsule* (blog). February 12, 2014. *http://codecapsule.com/2014/02/12/coding-for-ssds-part-1-introduction-and-table-of-contents.*

89. [GRAEFE04] Graefe, Goetz. 2004. "Write-Optimized B-Trees." In *Proceedings of the Thirtieth international conference on Very large data bases - Volume 30 (VLDB '04)*, 672-683. VLDB Endowment.

90. [GRAEFE07] Graefe, Goetz. 2007. "Hierarchical locking in B-tree indexes." *https://www.semanticscholar.org/paper/Hierarchical-locking-in-B-tree-indexes-Graefe/270669b1eb0d31a99fe99bec67e47e9b11b4553f.*

91. [GRAEFE10] Graefe, Goetz. 2010. "A survey of B-tree locking techniques." *ACM Transactions on Database Systems* 35, no. 3, (July). *https://doi.org/10.1145/1806907.1806908.*

92. [GRAEFE11] Graefe, Goetz. 2011. "Modern B-Tree Techniques." *Foundations and Trends in Databases* 3, no. 4 (April): 203-402. *https://doi.org/10.1561/1900000028.*

93. [GRAY05] Gray, Jim, and Catharine van Ingen. 2005. "Empirical Measurements of Disk Failure Rates and Error Rates." Accessed March 4, 2013. *https://arxiv.org/pdf/cs/0701166.pdf.*

94. [GRAY04] Gray, Jim, and Leslie Lamport. 2004. "Consensus on Transaction Commit." *ACM Transactions on Database Systems* 31, no. 1 (March): 133-160. *https://doi.org/10.1145/1132863.1132867.*

95. [GUERRAOUI07] Guerraoui, Rachid. 2007. "Revisiting the relationship between non-blocking atomiccommitment and consensus." In *Distributed Algorithms*, 87-100. Berlin: Springer, Berlin, Heidelberg. *https://doi.org/10.1007/BFb0022140.*

96. [GUERRAOUI97] Guerraoui, Rachid, and André Schiper. 1997. "Consensus: The Big Misunderstanding." In *Proceedings of the Sixth IEEE Computer Society Workshop on Future Trends of Distributed Computing Systems*, 183-188. IEEE.

97. [GUPTA01] Gupta, Indranil, Tushar D. Chandra, and Germán S. Goldszmidt. 2001. "On scalable and efficient distributed failure detectors." In *Proceedings of the twentieth annual ACM symposium on Principles of distributed computing (PODC '01)* New York: Association for Computing Machinery. *https://doi.org/10.1145/383962.384010.*

98. [HADZILACOS05] Hadzilacos, Vassos. 2005. "On the relationship between the atomic commitment and consensus problems." In *Fault-Tolerant Distributed Computing*, 201-208. London: Springer-Verlag.

99. [HAERDER83] Haerder, Theo, and Andreas Reuter. 1983. "Principles of transaction-oriented database recovery." *ACM Computing Surveys* 15 no. 4 (December):287–317. *https://doi.org/10.1145/289.291.*

100. [HALE10] Hale, Coda. 2010. "You Can't Sacrifice Partition Tolerance." *Coda Hale* (blog). *https://codahale.com/you-cant-sacrifice-partition-tolerance.*

101. [HALPERN90] Halpern, Joseph Y., and Yoram Moses. 1990. "Knowledge and common knowledge in a distributed environment." *Journal of the ACM* 37, no. 3 (July): 549-587. *https://doi.org/10.1145/79147.79161.*

102. [HARDING17] Harding, Rachael, Dana Van Aken, Andrew Pavlo, and Michael Stonebraker. 2017. "An Evaluation of Distributed Concurrency Control." *Proceedings of the VLDB Endowment* 10, no. 5 (January): 553-564. *https://doi.org/10.14778/3055540.3055548.*

103. [HAYASHIBARA04] Hayashibara, N., X. Defago, R.Yared, and T. Katayama. 2004. "The Φ Accrual Failure Detector." In *IEEE Symposium on Reliable Distributed Systems*, 66-78. *https://doi.org/10.1109/RELDIS.2004.1353004.*

104. [HELLAND15] Helland, Pat. 2015. "Immutability Changes Everything." *Queue* 13, no. 9 (November). *https://doi.org/10.1145/2857274.2884038.*

105. [HELLERSTEIN07] Hellerstein, Joseph M., Michael Stonebraker, and James Hamilton. 2007. "Architecture of a Database System." *Foundations and Trends in Databases* 1, no. 2 (February): 141-259. *https://doi.org/10.1561/1900000002.*

106. [HERLIHY94] Herlihy, Maurice. 1994. "Wait-Free Synchronization." *ACM Transactions on Programming Languages and Systems* 13, no. 1 (January): 124-149. *http://dx.doi.org/10.1145/114005.102808.*

107. [HERLIHY10] Herlihy, Maurice, Yossi Lev, Victor Luchangco, and Nir Shavit. 2010. "A Provably Correct Scalable Concurrent Skip List." *https://www.cs.tau.ac.il/~shanir/nir-pubs-web/Papers/OPODIS2006-BA.pdf.*

108. [HERLIHY90] Herlihy, Maurice P., and Jeannette M. Wing. 1990. "Linearizability: a correctness condition for concurrent object." *ACM Transactions on Programming Languages and Systems* 12, no. 3 (July): 463-492. *https://doi.org/10.1145/78969.78972.*

109. [HOWARD14] Howard, Heidi. 2014. "ARC: Analysis of Raft Consensus." Technical Report UCAM-CL-TR-857. Cambridge: University of Cambridge

110. [HOWARD16] Howard, Heidi, Dahlia Malkhi, and Alexander Spiegelman. 2016. "Flexible Paxos: Quorum intersection revisited." *https://arxiv.org/abs/1608.06696.*

111. [HOWARD19] Howard, Heidi, and Richard Mortier. 2019. "A Generalised Solution to Distributed Consensus." *https://arxiv.org/abs/1902.06776.*

112. [HUNT10] Hunt, Patrick, Mahadev Konar, Flavio P. Junqueira, and Benjamin Reed. 2010. "ZooKeeper: wait-free coordination for internet-scale systems." In

Proceedings of the 2010 USENIX conference on USENIX annual technical confer-
ence (USENIXATC'10), 11. USENIX.

113. [INTEL14] Intel Corporation. 2014. "Partition Alignment of Intel® SSDs for Achieving Maximum Performance and Endurance." (February). *https://*
www.intel.com/content/dam/www/public/us/en/documents/technology-briefs/ssd-
partition-alignment-tech-brief.pdf.

114. [JELASITY04] Jelasity, Márk, Rachid Guerraoui, Anne-Marie Kermarrec, and
Maarten van Steen. 2004. "The Peer Sampling Service: Experimental Evaluation
of Unstructured Gossip-Based Implementations." In *Middleware '04 Proceedings*
of the 5th ACM/IFIP/USENIX international conference on Middleware, 79-98.
Berlin: Springer-Verlag, Berlin, Heidelberg.

115. [JELASITY07] Jelasity, Márk, Spyros Voulgaris, Rachid Guerraoui, Anne-Marie
Kermarrec, and Maarten van Steen. 2007. "Gossip-based Peer Sampling." *ACM*
Transactions on Computer Systems 25, no. 3 (August). *http://doi.org/*
10.1145/1275517.1275520.

116. [JONSON94] Johnson, Theodore, and Dennis Shasha. 1994. "2Q: A Low Over-
head High Performance Buffer Management Replacement Algorithm. " In
VLDB '94 Proceedings of the 20th International Conference on Very Large Data
Bases, 439-450. San Francisco: Morgan Kaufmann.

117. [JUNQUEIRA07] Junqueira, Flavio, Yanhua Mao, and Keith Marzullo. 2007.
"Classic Paxos vs. fast Paxos: caveat emptor." In *Proceedings of the 3rd workshop*
on on Hot Topics in System Dependability (HotDep'07). USENIX.

118. [JUNQUEIRA11] Junqueira, Flavio P., Benjamin C. Reed, and Marco Serafini.
2011. "Zab: High-performance broadcast for primary-backup systems." *2011*
IEEE/IFIP 41st International Conference on Dependable Systems & Networks
(DSN) (June): 245–256. *https://doi.org/10.1109/DSN.2011.5958223.*

119. [KANNAN18] Kannan, Sudarsun, Nitish Bhat, Ada Gavrilovska, Andrea Arpaci-
Dusseau, and Remzi Arpaci-Dusseau. 2018. "Redesigning LSMs for Nonvolatile
Memory with NoveLSM." In *USENIX ATC '18 Proceedings of the 2018 USENIX*
Conference on Usenix Annual Technical Conference, 993-1005. USENIX.

120. [KARGER97] Karger, D., E. Lehman, T. Leighton, R. Panigrahy, M. Levine, and
D. Lewin. 1997. "Consistent hashing and random trees: distributed caching protocols for relieving hot spots on the World Wide Web." In *STOC '97 Proceedings*
of the twenty-ninth annual ACM symposium on Theory of computing , 654-663.
New York: Association for Computing Machinery.

121. [KEARNEY17] Kearney, Joe. 2017. "Two Phase Commit an old friend." *Joe's Mots*
(blog). January 6, 2017. *https://www.joekearney.co.uk/posts/two-phase-commit.*

122. [KEND94] Kendall, Samuel C., Jim Waldo, Ann Wollrath, and Geoff Wyant. 1994. "A Note on Distributed Computing." Technical Report. Mountain View, CA: Sun Microsystems, Inc.

123. [KERMARREC07] Kermarrec, Anne-Marie, and Maarten van Steen. 2007. "Gossiping in distributed systems." *SIGOPS Operating Systems Review* 41, no. 5 (October): 2-7. *https://doi.org/10.1145/1317379.1317381.*

124. [KERRISK10] Kerrisk, Michael. 2010. *The Linux Programming Interface.* San Francisco: No Starch Press.

125. [KHANCHANDANI18] Khanchandani, Pankaj, and Roger Wattenhofer. 2018. "Reducing Compare-and-Swap to Consensus Number One Primitives." *https://arxiv.org/abs/1802.03844.*

126. [KIM12] Kim, Jaehong, Sangwon Seo, Dawoon Jung, Jin-Soo Kim, and Jaehyuk Huh. 2012. "Parameter-Aware I/O Management for Solid State Disks (SSDs)." *IEEE Transactions on Computers* 61, no. 5 (May): 636-649. *https://doi.org/10.1109/TC.2011.76.*

127. [KINGSBURY18a] Kingsbury, Kyle. 2018. "Sequential Consistency." *https://jepsen.io/consistency/models/sequential. 2018. (https://jepsen.io/consistency/models/sequential)*

128. [KINGSBURY18b] Kingsbury, Kyle. 2018. "Strong consistency models." *Aphyr* (blog). August 8, 2018. *https://aphyr.com/posts/313-strong-consistency-models.*

129. [KLEPPMANN15] Kleppmann, Martin. 2015. "Please stop calling databases CP or AP." *Martin Kleppmann* (blog). May 11, 2015. *https://martin.kleppmann.com/2015/05/11/please-stop-calling-databases-cp-or-ap.html.*

130. [KLEPPMANN14] Kleppmann, Martin, and Alastair R. Beresford. 2014. "A Conflict-Free Replicated JSON Datatype." *https://arxiv.org/abs/1608.03960.*

131. [KNUTH97] Knuth, Donald E. 1997. *The Art of Computer Programming, Volume 1 (3rd Ed.): Fundamental Algorithms.* Boston: Addison-Wesley Longman.

132. [KNUTH98] Knuth, Donald E. 1998. *The Art of Computer Programming, Volume 3: (2nd Ed.): Sorting and Searching.* Boston: Addison-Wesley Longman.

133. [KOOPMAN15] Koopman, Philip, Kevin R. Driscoll, and Brendan Hall. 2015. "Selection of Cyclic Redundancy Code and Checksum Algorithms to Ensure Critical Data Integrity." *U.S. Department of Transportation Federal Aviation Administration. https://www.faa.gov/aircraft/air_cert/design_approvals/air_software/media/TC-14–49.pdf.*

134. [KORDAFSHARI05] Kordafshari, M. S., M. Gholipour, M. Mosakhani, A. T. Haghighat, and M. Dehghan. 2005. "Modified bully election algorithm in distributed systems." *Proceedings of the 9th WSEAS International Conference on*

Computers (ICCOMP'05), edited by Nikos E. Mastorakis, Article 10. Stevens Point: World Scientific and Engineering Academy and Society.

135. [KRASKA18] Kraska, Time, Alex Beutel, Ed H. Chi, Jeffrey Dean, and Neoklis Polyzotis. 2018. "The Case for Learned Index Structures." In *SIGMOD '18 Proceedings of the 2018 International Conference on Management of Data*, 489-504. New York: Association for Computing Machinery.

136. [LAMPORT77] Lamport, Leslie. 1977. "Proving the Correctness of Multiprocess Programs." *IEEE Transactions on Software Engineering* 3, no. 2 (March): 125-143. *https://doi.org/10.1109/TSE.1977.229904.*

137. [LAMPORT78] Lamport, Leslie. 1978. "Time, Clocks, and the Ordering of Events in a Distributed System." *Communications of the ACM* 21, no. 7 (July): 558-565

138. [LAMPORT79] Lamport, Leslie. 1979. "How to Make a Multiprocessor Computer That Correctly Executes Multiprocess Programs." *IEEE Transactions on Computers* 28, no. 9 (September): 690-691. *https://doi.org/10.1109/TC.1979.1675439.*

139. [LAMPORT98] Lamport, Leslie. 1998. "The part-time parliament." *ACM Transactions on Computer Systems* 16, no. 2 (May): 133-169. *https://doi.org/10.1145/279227.279229.*

140. [LAMPORT01] Lamport, Leslie. 2001. "Paxos Made Simple." *ACM SIGACT News (Distributed Computing Column)* 32, no. 4 (December): 51-58. *https://www.microsoft.com/en-us/research/publication/paxos-made-simple.*

141. [LAMPORT05] Lamport, Leslie. 2005. "Generalized Consensus and Paxos." *https://www.microsoft.com/en-us/research/publication/generalized-consensus-and-paxos.*

142. [LAMPORT06] Lamport, Leslie. 2006. "Fast Paxos." *Distributed Computing* 19, no. 2 (July): 79-103. *https://doi.org/10.1007/s00446-006-0005-x.*

143. [LAMPORT09] Lamport, Leslie, Dahlia Malkhi, and Lidong Zhou. 2009. "Vertical Paxos and Primary-Backup Replication." In *PODC '09 Proceedings of the 28th ACM symposium on Principles of distributed computing*, 312-313. *https://doi.org/10.1145/1582716.1582783.*

144. [LAMPSON01] Lampson, Butler. 2001. "The ABCD's of Paxos." In *PODC '01 Proceedings of the twentieth annual ACM symposium on Principles of distributed computing*, 13. *https://doi.org/10.1145/383962.383969.*

145. [LAMPSON79] Lampson, Butler W., and Howard E. 1979. "Crash Recovery in a Distributed Data Storage System." *https://www.microsoft.com/en-us/research/publication/crash-recovery-in-a-distributed-data-storage-system'* (*https://www.microsoft.com/en-us/research/publication/crash-recovery-in-a-distributed-data-storage-system*).

146. [LARRIVEE15] Larrivee, Steve. 2015. "Solid State Drive Primer." *Cactus Technologies* (blog). February 9th, 2015. *https://www.cactus-tech.com/resources/blog/details/solid-state-drive-primer-1-the-basic-nand-flash-cell*.

147. [LARSON81] Larson, Per-Åke, and Åbo Akedemi. 1981. "Analysis of index-sequential files with overflow chaining". *ACM Transactions on Database Systems.* 6, no. 4 (December): 671-680. *https://doi.org/10.1145/319628.319665*.

148. [LEE15] Lee, Collin, Seo Jin Park, Ankita Kejriwal, Satoshi Matsushita, and John Ousterhout. 2015. "Implementing linearizability at large scale and low latency." In *SOSP '15 Proceedings of the 25th Symposium on Operating Systems Principles*, 71-86. *https://doi.org/10.1145/2815400.2815416*.

149. [LEHMAN81] Lehman, Philip L., and s. Bing Yao. 1981. "Efficient locking for concurrent operations on B-trees." *ACM Transactions on Database Systems* 6, no. 4 (December): 650-670. *https://doi.org/10.1145/319628.319663*.

150. [LEITAO07] Leitao, Joao, Jose Pereira, and Luis Rodrigues. 2007. "Epidemic Broadcast Trees." In *SRDS '07 Proceedings of the 26th IEEE International Symposium on Reliable Distributed Systems*, 301-310. IEEE.

151. [LEVANDOSKI14] Levandoski, Justin J., David B. Lomet, and Sudipta Sengupta. 2013. "The Bw-Tree: A B-tree for new hardware platforms." In *Proceedings of the 2013 IEEE International Conference on Data Engineering (ICDE '13)*, 302-313. IEEE. *https://doi.org/10.1109/ICDE.2013.6544834*.

152. [LI10] Li, Yinan, Bingsheng He, Robin Jun Yang, Qiong Luo, and Ke Yi. 2010. "Tree Indexing on Solid State Drives." *Proceedings of the VLDB Endowment* 3, no. 1-2 (September): 1195-1206. *https://doi.org/10.14778/1920841.1920990*.

153. [LIPTON88] Lipton, Richard J., and Jonathan S. Sandberg. 1988. "PRAM: A scalable shared memory." Technical Report, Princeton University. *https://www.cs.princeton.edu/research/techreps/TR-180-88*.

154. [LLOYD11] Lloyd, W., M. J. Freedman, M. Kaminsky, and D. G. Andersen. 2011. "Don't settle for eventual: scalable causal consistency for wide-area storage with COPS." In *Proceedings of the Twenty-Third ACM Symposium on Operating Systems Principles (SOSP '11)*, 401-416. New York: Association for Computing Machinery. *https://doi.org/10.1145/2043556.2043593*.

155. [LLOYD13] Lloyd, W., M. J. Freedman, M. Kaminsky, and D. G. Andersen. 2013. "Stronger semantics for low-latency geo-replicated storage." In *10th USENIX Symposium on Networked Systems Design and Implementation (NSDI '13)*, 313-328. USENIX.

156. [LU16] Lu, Lanyue, Thanumalayan Sankaranarayana Pillai, Hariharan Gopalakrishnan, Andrea C. Arpaci-Dusseau, and Remzi H. Arpaci-Dusseau. 2017. "WiscKey: Separating Keys from Values in SSD-Conscious Storage." *ACM Trans-*

actions on Storage (TOS) 13, no. 1 (March): Article 5. *https://doi.org/ 10.1145/3033273*.

157. [MATTERN88] Mattern, Friedemann. 1988. "Virtual Time and Global States of Distributed Systems." *http://courses.csail.mit.edu/6.852/01/papers/VirtTime_Glob-State.pdf*.

158. [MCKENNEY05a] McKenney, Paul E. 2005. "Memory Ordering in Modern Microprocessors, Part I." *Linux Journal* no. 136 (August): 2.

159. [MCKENNEY05b] McKenney, Paul E. 2005. "Memory Ordering in Modern Microprocessors, Part II." *Linux Journal* no. 137 (September): 5.

160. [MEHTA17] Mehta, Apurva, and Jason Gustafson. 2017. "Transactions in Apache Kafka." *Confluent* (blog). November 17, 2017. *https://www.confluent.io/ blog/transactions-apache-kafka*.

161. [MELLORCRUMMEY91] Mellor-Crummey, John M., and Michael L. Scott. 1991. "Algorithms for scalable synchronization on shared-memory multiprocessors." *ACM Transactions on Computer Systems* 9, no. 1 (February): 21-65. *https:// doi.org/10.1145/103727.103729*.

162. [MELTON06] Melton, Jim. 2006. "Database Language SQL." In *International Organization for Standardization (ISO)*, 105–132. Berlin: Springer. *https://doi.org/ 10.1007/b137905*.

163. [MERKLE87] Merkle, Ralph C. 1987. "A Digital Signature Based on a Conventional Encryption Function." *A Conference on the Theory and Applications of Cryptographic Techniques on Advances in Cryptology (CRYPTO '87)*, edited by Carl Pomerance. London: Springer-Verlag, 369–378. *https://dl.acm.org/cita-tion.cfm?id=704751*.

164. [MILLER78] Miller, R., and L. Snyder. 1978. "Multiple access to B-trees." *Proceedings of the Conference on Information Sciences and Systems*, Baltimore: Johns Hopkins University (March).

165. [MILOSEVIC11] Milosevic, Z., M. Hutle, and A. Schiper. 2011. "On the Reduction of Atomic Broadcast to Consensus with Byzantine Faults." In *Proceedings of the 2011 IEEE 30th International Symposium on Reliable Distributed Systems (SRDS '11)*, 235-244. IEEE. *https://doi.org/10.1109/SRDS.2011.36*.

166. [MOHAN92] Mohan, C., Don Haderle, Bruce Lindsay, Hamid Pirahesh, and Peter Schwarz. 1992. "ARIES: a transaction recovery method supporting fine-granularity locking and partial rollbacks using write-ahead logging." *Transactions on Database Systems* 17, no. 1 (March): 94-162. *https://doi.org/ 10.1145/128765.128770*.

167. [MORARU11] Moraru, Iulian, David G. Andersen, and Michael Kaminsky. 2013. "A Proof of Correctness for Egalitarian Paxos." *https://www.pdl.cmu.edu/PDL-FTP/associated/CMU-PDL-13-111.pdf*.

168. [MORARU13] Moraru, Iulian, David G. Andersen, and Michael Kaminsky. 2013. "There Is More Consensus in Egalitarian Parliaments." In *Proceedings of the Twenty-Fourth ACM Symposium on Operating Systems Principles (SOSP '13)*, 358-372. *https://doi.org/10.1145/2517349.2517350*.

169. [MURSHED12] Murshed, Md. Golam, and Alastair R. Allen. 2012. "Enhanced Bully Algorithm for Leader Node Election in Synchronous Distributed Systems." *Computers* 1, no. 1: 3-23. *https://doi.org/10.3390/computers1010003*.

170. [NICHOLS66] Nichols, Ann Eljenholm. 1966. "The Past Participle of 'Overflow:' 'Overflowed' or 'Overflown.'" *American Speech* 41, no. 1 (February): 52–55. *https://doi.org/10.2307/453244*.

171. [NIEVERGELT74] Nievergelt, J. 1974. "Binary search trees and file organization." In *Proceedings of 1972 ACM-SIGFIDET workshop on Data description, access and control (SIGFIDET '72)*, 165-187. *https://doi.org/10.1145/800295.811490*.

172. [NORVIG01] Norvig, Peter. 2001. "Teach Yourself Programming in Ten Years." *https://norvig.com/21-days.html*.

173. [ONEIL93] O'Neil, Elizabeth J., Patrick E. O'Neil, and Gerhard Weikum. 1993. "The LRU-K page replacement algorithm for database disk buffering." In *Proceedings of the 1993 ACM SIGMOD international conference on Management of data (SIGMOD '93)*, 297-306. *https://doi.org/10.1145/170035.170081*.

174. [ONEIL96] O'Neil, Patrick, Edward Cheng, Dieter Gawlick, and Elizabeth O'Neil. 1996. "The log-structured merge-tree (LSM-tree)." *Acta Informatica* 33, no. 4: 351-385. *https://doi.org/10.1007/s002360050048*.

175. [ONGARO14] Ongaro, Diego and John Ousterhout. 2014. "In Search of an Understandable Consensus Algorithm." In *Proceedings of the 2014 USENIX conference on USENIX Annual Technical Conference (USENIX ATC'14)*, 305-320. USENIX.

176. [OUYANG14] Ouyang, Jian, Shiding Lin, Song Jiang, Zhenyu Hou, Yong Wang, and Yuanzheng Wang. 2014. "SDF: software-defined flash for web-scale internet storage systems." *ACM SIGARCH Computer Architecture News* 42, no. 1 (February): 471-484. *https://doi.org/10.1145/2654822.2541959*.

177. [PAPADAKIS93] Papadakis, Thomas. 1993. "Skip lists and probabilistic analysis of algorithms." Doctoral Dissertation, University of Waterloo. *https://cs.uwaterloo.ca/research/tr/1993/28/root2side.pdf*.

178. [PUGH90a] Pugh, William. 1990. "Concurrent Maintenance of Skip Lists." Technical Report, University of Maryland. *https://drum.lib.umd.edu/handle/1903/542*.

179. [PUGH90b] Pugh, William. 1990. "Skip lists: a probabilistic alternative to balanced trees." *Communications of the ACM* 33, no. 6 (June): 668-676. *https://doi.org/10.1145/78973.78977*.

180. [RAMAKRISHNAN03] Ramakrishnan, Raghu, and Johannes Gehrke. 2002. *Database Management Systems (3rd Ed.).* New York: McGraw-Hill.

181. [RAY95] Ray, Gautam, Jayant Haritsa, and S. Seshadri. 1995. "Database Compression: A Performance Enhancement Tool." In *Proceedings of 7th International Conference on Management of Data (COMAD).* New York: McGraw Hill.

182. [RAYNAL99] Raynal, M., and F. Tronel. 1999. "Group membership failure detection: a simple protocol and its probabilistic analysis." *Distributed Systems Engineering* 6, no. 3 (September): 95-102. *https://doi.org/10.1088/0967-1846/6/3/301.*

183. [REED78] Reed, D. P. 1978. "Naming and synchronization in a decentralized computer system." Technical Report, MIT. *https://dspace.mit.edu/handle/1721.1/16279.*

184. [REN16] Ren, Kun, Jose M. Faleiro, and Daniel J. Abadi. 2016. "Design Principles for Scaling Multi-core OLTP Under High Contention." In *Proceedings of the 2016 International Conference on Management of Data (SIGMOD '16),* 1583-1598. *https://doi.org/10.1145/2882903.2882958.*

185. [ROBINSON08] Robinson, Henry. 2008. "Consensus Protocols: Two-Phase Commit." *The Paper Trail* (blog). November 27, 2008. *https://www.the-paper-trail.org/post/2008-11-27-consensus-protocols-two-phase-commit.*

186. [ROSENBLUM92] Rosenblum, Mendel, and John K. Ousterhout. 1992. "The Design and Implementation of a Log Structured File System." *ACM Transactions on Computer Systems* 10, no. 1 (February): 26-52. *https://doi.org/10.1145/146941.146943.*

187. [ROY12] Roy, Arjun G., Mohammad K. Hossain, Arijit Chatterjee, and William Perrizo. 2012. "Column-oriented Database Systems: A Comparison Study." In *Proceedings of the ISCA 27th International Conference on Computers and Their Applications,* 264-269.

188. [RUSSEL12] Russell, Sears. 2012. "A concurrent skiplist with hazard pointers." *http://rsea.rs/skiplist.*

189. [RYSTSOV16] Rystsov, Denis. 2016. "Best of both worlds: Raft's joint consensus + Single Decree Paxos." *Rystsov.info* (blog). January 5, 2016. *http://rystsov.info/2016/01/05/raft-paxos.html.*

190. [RYSTSOV18] Rystsov, Denis. 2018. "Replicated State Machines without logs." *https://arxiv.org/abs/1802.07000.*

191. [SATZGER07] Satzger, Benjamin, Andreas Pietzowski, Wolfgang Trumler, and Theo Ungerer. 2007. "A new adaptive accrual failure detector for dependable distributed systems." In *Proceedings of the 2007 ACM symposium on Applied computing (SAC '07),* 551-555. *https://doi.org/10.1145/1244002.1244129.*

192. [SAVARD05] Savard, John. 2005. "Floating-Point Formats." *http://www.quadibloc.com/comp/cp0201.htm*.

193. [SCHWARZ86] Schwarz, P., W. Chang, J. C. Freytag, G. Lohman, J. McPherson, C. Mohan, and H. Pirahesh. 1986. "Extensibility in the Starburst database system." In *OODS '86 Proceedings on the 1986 international workshop on Object-oriented database systems*, 85–92. IEEE.

194. [SEDGEWICK11] Sedgewick, Robert, and Kevin Wayne. 2011. *Algorithms (4th Ed.)*. Boston: Pearson.

195. [SHAPIRO11a] Shapiro, Marc, Nuno Preguiça, Carlos Baquero, and Marek Zawirski. 2011. "Conflict-free Replicated Data Types." In *Stabilization, Safety, and Security of Distributed Systems*, 386-400. Berlin: Springer, Berlin, Heidelberg.

196. [SHAPIRO11b] Shapiro, Marc, Nuno Preguiça, Carlos Baquero, and Marek Zawirski. 2011. "A comprehensive study of Convergent and Commutative Replicated Data Types." *https://hal.inria.fr/inria-00555588/document*.

197. [SHEEHY10a] Sheehy, Justin. 2010. "Why Vector Clocks Are Hard." *Riak* (blog). April 5, 2010. *https://riak.com/posts/technical/why-vector-clocks-are-hard*.

198. [SHEEHY10b] Sheehy, Justin, and David Smith. 2010. "Bitcask, A Log-Structured Hash Table for Fast Key/Value Data."

199. [SILBERSCHATZ10] Silberschatz, Abraham, Henry F. Korth, and S. Sudarshan. 2010. *Database Systems Concepts (6th Ed.)*. New York: McGraw-Hill.

200. [SINHA97] Sinha, Pradeep K. 1997. *Distributed Operating Systems: Concepts and Design*. Hoboken, NJ: Wiley.

201. [SKEEN82] Skeen, Dale. 1982. "A Quorum-Based Commit Protocol." Technical Report, Cornell University.

202. [SKEEN83] Skeen, Dale, and M. Stonebraker. 1983. "A Formal Model of Crash Recovery in a Distributed System." *IEEE Transactions on Software Engineering* 9, no. 3 (May): 219-228. *https://doi.org/10.1109/TSE.1983.236608*.

203. [SOUNDARARARJAN06] Soundararajan, Gokul. 2006. "Implementing a Better Cache Replacement Algorithm in Apache Derby Progress Report." *https://pdfs.semanticscholar.org/220b/2fe62f13478f1ec75cf17ad085874689c604.pdf*.

204. [STONE98] Stone, J., M. Greenwald, C. Partridge and J. Hughes. 1998. "Performance of checksums and CRCs over real data." *IEEE/ACM Transactions on Networking* 6, no. 5 (October): 529-543. *https://doi.org/10.1109/90.731187*.

205. [TANENBAUM14] Tanenbaum, Andrew S., and Herbert Bos. 2014. *Modern Operating Systems (4th Ed.)*. Upper Saddle River: Prentice Hall Press.

206. [TANENBAUM06] Tanenbaum, Andrew S., and Maarten van Steen. 2006. *Distributed Systems: Principles and Paradigms*. Boston: Pearson.

207. [TARIQ11] Tariq, Ovais. 2011. "Understanding InnoDB clustered indexes." *Ovais Tariq* (blog). January 20, 2011. *http://www.ovaistariq.net/521/understanding-innodb-clustered-indexes/#.XTtaUpNKj5Y.*

208. [TERRY94] Terry, Douglas B., Alan J. Demers, Karin Petersen, Mike J. Spreitzer, Marvin M. Theimer, and Brent B. Welch. 1994. "Session Guarantees for Weakly Consistent Replicated Data." In *PDIS '94 Proceedings of the Third International Conference on Parallel and Distributed Information Systems*, 140–149. IEEE.

209. [THOMAS79] Thomas, Robert H. 1979. "A majority consensus approach to concurrency control for multiple copy databases." *ACM Transactions on Database Systems* 4, no. 2 (June): 180–209. *https://doi.org/10.1145/320071.320076.*

210. [THOMSON12] Thomson, Alexander, Thaddeus Diamond, Shu-Chun Weng, Kun Ren, Philip Shao, and Daniel J. Abadi. 2012. "Calvin: Fast distributed transactions for partitioned database systems." In *Proceedings of the ACM SIGMOD International Conference on Management of Data (SIGMOD '12)*. New York: Association for Computing Machinery. *https://doi.org/10.1145/2213836.2213838.*

211. [VANRENESSE98] van Renesse, Robbert, Yaron Minsky, and Mark Hayden. 1998. "A Gossip-Style Failure Detection Service." In *Middleware '98 Proceedings of the IFIP International Conference on Distributed Systems Platforms and Open Distributed Processing*, 55–70. London: Springer-Verlag.

212. [VENKATARAMAN11] Venkataraman, Shivaram, Niraj Tolia, Parthasarathy Ranganathan, and Roy H. Campbell. 2011. "Consistent and Durable Data Structures for Non-Volatile Byte-Addressable Memory." In *Proceedings of the 9th USENIX conference on File and stroage technologies (FAST'11)*, 5. USENIX.

213. [VINOSKI08] Vinoski, Steve. 2008. "Convenience Over Correctness." *IEEE Internet Computing* 12, no. 4 (August): 89–92. *https://doi.org/10.1109/MIC.2008.75.*

214. [VIOTTI16] Viotti, Paolo, and Marko Vukolić. 2016. "Consistency in Non-Transactional Distributed Storage Systems." *ACM Computing Surveys* 49, no. 1 (July): Article 19. *https://doi.org/0.1145/2926965.*

215. [VOGELS09] Vogels, Werner. 2009. "Eventually consistent." *Communications of the ACM* 52, no. 1 (January): 40–44. *https://doi.org/10.1145/1435417.1435432.*

216. [WALDO96] Waldo, Jim, Geoff Wyant, Ann Wollrath, and Samuel C. Kendall. 1996. "A Note on Distributed Computing." *Selected Presentations and Invited Papers SecondInternational Workshop on Mobile Object Systems—Towards the Programmable Internet* (July): 49–64. *https://dl.acm.org/citation.cfm?id=747342.*

217. [WANG13] Wang, Peng, Guangyu Sun, Song Jiang, Jian Ouyang, Shiding Lin, Chen Zhang, and Jason Cong. 2014. "An Efficient Design and Implementation of LSM-tree based Key-Value Store on Open-Channel SSD." *EuroSys '14 Proceedings of the Ninth European Conference on Computer Systems* (April): Article 16. *https://doi.org/10.1145/2592798.2592804.*

218. [WANG18] Wang, Ziqi, Andrew Pavlo, Hyeontaek Lim, Viktor Leis, Huanchen Zhang, Michael Kaminsky, and David G. Andersen. 2018. "Building a Bw-Tree Takes More Than Just Buzz Words." *Proceedings of the 2018 International Conference on Management of Data (SIGMOD '18)*, 473–488. *https://doi.org/10.1145/3183713.3196895.*

219. [WEIKUM01] Weikum, Gerhard, and Gottfried Vossen. 2001. *Transactional Information Systems: Theory, Algorithms, and the Practice of Concurrency Control and Recovery*. San Francisco: Morgan Kaufmann Publishers Inc.

220. [XIA17] Xia, Fei, Dejun Jiang, Jin Xiong, and Ninghui Sun. 2017. "HiKV: A Hybrid Index Key-Value Store for DRAM-NVM Memory Systems." *Proceedings of the 2017 USENIX Annual Technical Conference (USENIX ATC '17)*, 349–362. USENIX.

221. [YANG14] Yang, Jingpei, Ned Plasson, Greg Gillis, Nisha Talagala, and Swaminathan Sundararaman. 2014. "Don't stack your Log on my Log." *INFLOW* (October). *https://www.usenix.org/system/files/conference/inflow14/inflow14-yang.pdf.*

222. [ZHAO15] Zhao, Wenbing. 2015. "Fast Paxos Made Easy: Theory and Implementation." *International Journal of Distributed Systems and Technologies* 6, no. 1 (January): 15-33. *https://doi.org/10.4018/ijdst.2015010102.*

Index

P

root nodes, 26, 35
routing keys, 270
row keys, 16
row locators, 18
row-oriented data layout, 12-15
rows, 12
RUM Conjecture, 144

S

safe registers, 220
safety guarantees, 195, 205
sanity checks, 62
scaling horizontally (scaling out), xiii, 167
scaling vertically (scaling up), xiii, 167
schedulers, 267
schedules, 94
search keys, 17
secondary indexes, 19
sectors, 30
seeks, 30
separator keys, 36, 38, 63
sequence numbers, 183
sequencers, 266
sequential consistency, 227
sequential I/O, 30
sequential operations, 219
serial operations, 220
serial schedules, 94
serializability, 94, 96, 257
serialization, 48
session causality, 234
session models, 233
shadow paging, 91
shadowing, 18
sharding, 270
shared memory, 172, 219
shared state, 173
short-time bursts, 176
shrinking phase, 100
sibling links, 62, 107
sign, 48
single-operation consistency models, 222
single-partition transactions, 257
size-tiered compaction, 143
skiplists, 115, 149
sloppy quorums, 246
slot directory, 53
slotted pages, 18, 52, 56, 74
snapshot isolation (SI), 97, 272

snapshot reads, 268
snapshots, 12
Software Defined Flash (SDF), 162
software errors, 181
solid state drives (SSDs), 30, 157, 161
Sophia, 2
Sorted String Tables (SSTables), 145
space amplification, 144-145
Spanner, 268
spanning trees, 252
spanservers, 269
speculative execution, 288
spinning disks, 30
split brain, 205, 208
split delta nodes, 122
split point, 39
split SMOs, 122
split vote, 304
splits, 35, 39, 68, 122
SQLite
    overflow pages, 65
    page header content, 61
    quickbalance, 72
    rightmost pointers, 63
    unoccupied segments (freeblocks), 57
SSTable-Attached Secondary Indexes (SASI),
    146
stable checkpoints, 309
stable leader election, 213
state, 168, 168, 222
state consistency, 177
steal/no-steal policy, 91
steps, 168
storage engines
    responsibilities of, 1, 10
    understanding trade-offs, 5
strategy, 57
strict consistency, 223
strings, 30, 49, 53
strong eventual consistency, 238
structural modification operations (SMOs), 122
stubborn links, 184
subtrees, 26, 36
super-peers, 239
susceptible processes, 250
suspected processes, 195
suspicion level, 199
sync checkpoint, 90
synchrony, 173, 190

About the Author

Alex Petrov is a data infrastructure engineer, database and storage systems enthusiast, Apache Cassandra committer, and PMC member interested in storage, distributed systems, and algorithms.

Colophon

The animal on the cover of *Database Internals* is the peacock flounder, a name given to both *Bothus lunatus* and *Bothus mancus*, inhabitants of the shallow coastal waters of the mid-Atlantic and Indo-Pacific ocean, respectively.

While the blue floral-patterned skin gives the peacock flounder its moniker, these flounders have the ability to change their appearance based on their immediate surroundings. This camouflage ability may be related to the fish's vision, because it is unable to change its appearance if one of its eyes is covered.

Adult flatfishes swim in a horizontal attitude rather than in a vertical, back-up/belly-down, orientation as most other fishes do. When they swim, flatfishes tend to glide only an inch (2.54 cm) or so off the bottom while closely following the contour of the sea floor. One of this flat fish's eyes migrates during maturation to join the other on a single side, allowing the fish to look both forward and backward at once. Understandably, rather than swim vertically, the peacock flounder tends to glide an inch or so off the sea floor, closely following the contour of the terrain with its patterned side always facing up.

While the peacock flounder's current conservation status is designated as of Least Concern, many of the animals on O'Reilly covers are endangered; all of them are important to the world.

The cover illustration is by Karen Montgomery, based on a black and white engraving from Lowry's *The Museum of Natural History*. The cover fonts are Gilroy Semibold and Guardian Sans. The text font is Adobe Minion Pro; the heading font is Adobe Myriad Condensed; and the code font is Dalton Maag's Ubuntu Mono.

O'REILLY®

There's much more where this came from.

Experience books, videos, live online training courses, and more from O'Reilly and our 200+ partners—all in one place.

Learn more at oreilly.com/online-learning

9 781492 040347